Understanding and Evaluating
QUALITATIVE EDUCATIONAL RESEARCH

EDITOR
Marilyn Lichtman
Virginia Tech

SAGE

Los Angeles | London | New Delhi
Singapore | Washington DC

For information:

SAGE Publications, Inc.
2455 Teller Road
Thousand Oaks, California 91320
E-mail: order@sagepub.com

SAGE Publications India Pvt. Ltd.
B 1/I 1 Mohan Cooperative Industrial Area
Mathura Road, New Delhi 110 044
India

SAGE Publications Ltd.
1 Oliver's Yard
55 City Road
London, EC1Y 1SP
United Kingdom

SAGE Publications Asia-Pacific Pte. Ltd.
33 Pekin Street #02-01
Far East Square
Singapore 048763

Printed in the United States of America

Library of Congress Cataloging-in-Publication Data
Understanding and evaluating qualitative educational research / Marilyn Lichtman, editor.
      p. cm.
Includes index.
ISBN 978-1-4129-7526-1 (pbk.)
   1. Education—Research—Methodology. 2. Qualitative research. 3. Research methods. I. Lichtman, Marilyn.

LB1028.U41 2011
370.7'21—dc22   2009043898

Printed on acid-free paper

10   11   12   13   14   10   9   8   7   6   5   4   3   2   1

Acquiring Editor:	Diane McDaniel
Associate Editor:	Deya Saoud
Editorial Assistant:	Ashley Conlon
Production Editor:	Brittany Bauhaus
Copy Editor:	Alison Hope
Proofreader:	Christina West
Indexer:	Diggs Publication Services, Inc.
Typesetter:	C&M Digitals (P) Ltd.
Cover Designer:	Janet Kiesel
Marketing Manager:	Carmel Schrire

BRIEF CONTENTS

DETAILED CONTENTS

PREFACE

I have written this book to introduce you to the writing *of* and *about* qualitative research. In Part I, I provide examples of journal articles that illustrate a variety of research approaches. In Part II, I present writing about current issues in the field of qualitative research. I assume you have some familiarity with what qualitative research is, what various research approaches are, and how you as a researcher should conduct your own research.

THE STRUCTURE

Part I considers seven different research approaches. I selected articles that illustrate how different researchers do research related to each approach. Some of the writers are new to the field while others have been writing for some time. To the extent possible, the articles relate to education. The approaches covered are ethnography, grounded theory, phenomenology, case study, action research, narrative, and mixed methods. I provide embedded comments, along with commentary before and after each article, that should help you understand and evaluate each approach and each article.

In Chapter 1, I provide you with two examples of ethnography. Ethnography is the study of cultures, and the methods derive from the field of anthropology. Ethnographers used to be quite clear on what they meant when they talked about studying culture. Ethnographers usually include thick and rich descriptions of those they study. Postmodernism has led to questioning our boundaries of cultures. Some issues facing ethnographers today are the same as those in the past: how to define the boundaries of time and space of what is studied. Other issues arise that are more pertinent to today's world: Can ethnography be a virtual rather than actual ethnography? Are there or should there be political overtones for the ethnographer? You might enjoy reading Sarah Henderson Lee's educational ethnographic blog online at http://sarahhendersonlee.blogspot.com/. At the time of my writing, her most recent posting was June 27, 2009.

In Chapter 2, I offer you two examples of articles on the topic of grounded theory. Grounded theory developed from the writings of Glaser and Strauss in 1967. Some would say it is not a research approach at all, but rather a way of generating theory; however, I choose to call it a research approach in this book. Of all the research approaches, grounded theory is the most "objective" and scientific. (It is important to understand that Glaser and Strauss came to a parting of the ways, and that Strauss wrote many of the later texts with Corbin.) The key elements to consider are type of coding and theoretical saturation. You might find the blog by the Lonely Dissertator interesting. It includes at least 12 entries on grounded theory, especially from the viewpoint of Glaser. You can read it at http://lonelydissertator.blogspot.com. At the time of my writing, the most recent posting was October 17, 2009.

Chapter 3 introduces you to research using phenomenology. Phenomenology has its basis in philosophy, especially existentialism. Widely used in nursing research, phenomenology also has been used to study the lived experiences of those in education. Vicky Teinaki in January 2009 provides a good discussion in the Johnny Holland blog at http://johnnyholland.org/2009/01/19/phenomenology-invisible-interfaces-are-a-myth/.

The case study approach to research is covered in Chapter 4. Many disciplines make use of case studies. In qualitative research, you can think of a case study of a program, a class, a school, or of an individual. Helena Bukvova provides links to excellent references in her November 2009 blog at http://bukvova.wordpress.com/2009/11/16/case-study/.

Action research is the subject of Chapter 5. Closely related to case study, action research also focuses on a program, class, or school. You can read an excellent pamphlet about the topic by Eileen Ferrance, published by the Northeast and Islands Regional Laboratory at Brown University in 2000. These labs are supported with federal funds from the Office of Educational Research and Improvement, U.S. Department of Education: http://www.alliance.brown.edu/pubs/themes_ed/act_research.pdf.

A teacher whose primary purpose is to make changes in the classroom often designs action research studies. Bendriss offers some interesting discussions in his blog on teaching English. You can read it at http://www.teachingenglish.org.uk/blogs/bendriss/action-research. At the time of my writing, the most recent posting was February 13, 2009.

Chapter 6 includes articles illustrating a narrative approach to qualitative research. In essence, narratives represent the stories of our lives and their meaning. It is closely aligned with life history and biography. In addition to the articles you should find Bud Goodall's book *Writing Qualitative Inquiry: Self, Stories, and Academic life* (2008) on creative nonfiction stimulating.

The final chapter of Part I, Chapter 7, presents studies that use a mixed method approach to conducting research. These studies are said to combine elements of both quantitative and qualitative research approaches. You might find a review of the workshop offered by Riesmann especially helpful. You can see it at http://www.narrativenetworkaustralia.org.au/NarRes08/NarResrchCourse08.pdf.

You can read Christina Pikas's commentary on using mixed methods at http://scienceblogs.com/christinaslisrant/2009/06/in_search_of_pragmatism_and_mi.php?utm_source=sbhomepage&utm_medium=link&utm_content=channellink. Finally, you can view slides on the topic at http://www.slideboom.com/presentations/72121/CH19-Mixed-Methods.

Part II deals with important issues related to the theory and practice of conducting qualitative research. Due to space considerations, I have included only brief extracts of the actual articles in this text.

It may seem strange to you since you have just finished reading articles selected to illustrate different research approaches, but the first issue I deal with is a consideration of clarifying and distinguishing among approaches. Perhaps when you finished reading Part I, you found yourself thinking that some of the approaches seemed remarkably similar to each other. In Chapter 8, I address clarifying research approaches and examine various research approaches, especially looking outside the field of education.

Another issue that has gained interest recently relates to quality and accountability in the new millenium. I offer some comments from recent writings in Chapter 9. Chapter 10 discusses standards for evaluating qualitative research. I caution that there is no single set of standards that apply to all types of qualitative research. Chapter 11 is devoted to academic freedom, research ethics, and institutional review boards. It is closely tied to the topic I discuss in Chapter 10. In Chapter 12, I offer readings on writing and presenting qualitative research. In keeping with my philosophy about the value of self-reflection, I offer you some readings about reflexivity in Chapter 13. Chapter 14 concludes Part II with some writings about negotiating through graduate school. The epilogue addresses my thoughts on reading, writing, and thinking about qualitative research.

Complete citations for all articles appear in the reference list at the back of the book. Links to journal articles are included in Part I. In addition, specific references appear at the end of each chapter in Part II.

Selection of Individual Articles

When I began thinking about this book in 2008, I had to consider a process for selection of journal articles. What research approaches should I include? What journals would I use? What time frame would I include? How could I select content that would be interesting and meaningful to my readers? I knew that I wanted a range of authors—those new to the field as well as those who had published previously. These are the steps that I followed:

- *I decided on the research approaches.* I identified research approaches that many writers in the qualitative research field consider important. My reviewers were helpful in this regard. I recognize that I did not include all possible research approaches. For instance, I did not include articles that illustrate feminist research, nor did I include articles on autoethnography. Also, I did not select articles that illustrate biography. This does not mean I do not consider these important: I do. Rather, it was a matter of space. It is quite interesting that within several approaches there are differences in how the approach might be addressed. One view might be classic or basic while an alternative to the same research approach might be considered more avant garde. To the extent possible, I tried to choose articles that illustrate a variety of ways people are doing and writing about qualitative research.

- *I decided on the journals.* My preference was to select journals that specifically publish articles that are qualitative in nature. I began with these journals: *Qualitative Inquiry* (first issue 1995; first interdisciplinary international journal providing a forum for qualitative methodology; U.S. based); *Qualitative Research* (first issue 2001; U.K. based); the *Qualitative Report* (first issue 1990; online; U.S. based); *International Journal of Qualitative Studies in Education* (QSE; first issue 1988; U.K. based); *Forum: Qualitative Social Research* (first issue 1999; online; Berlin based; multilingual). I reviewed all issues of these journals for the years 2006, 2007, 2008, and 2009 (through May). I also reviewed other journals that I knew published relevant articles. I had complete access to all these journals, as well as all others that participate in either SAGE's Journals Online or Virginia Tech's library system.

- *I decided on the time period.* I had decided in the early conception of this volume to concentrate on recent articles. I wanted to offer you what is available and current as you read this book. Since the field has gone through many changes, I did not want you to read articles that were written following principles that many no longer consider important. The 14 journal articles I present cover the following dates: 2006 (three articles), 2007 (two articles), 2008 (six articles), and 2009 (three articles).

- *I decided on the content.* One criterion I used was that the articles should be interesting to students in education. I also selected articles that represented a range of writing styles. I do not include any dissertations, because they tend to be too long, although I include some dissertations rewritten as journal articles. I do not include any reviews of research.

- *I decided on the authors.* I did not want to be influenced by the background or experience of the authors. I discovered after the fact that some of the articles were based on the dissertation of the author. Although I had hoped to cover authors from a broad base of expertise, for the most part authors were connected with universities or academic settings.

I read many articles before I selected the ones that appear in this book. Some were too technical. Some did not really illustrate the research approach as well as I initially expected from the abstract. Some included content that was not related to education.

It is important to understand that these 14 articles are a small sampling of articles from thousands. Another author might have chosen a completely different group. I was not familiar with any of the articles before I chose them, nor did I know any of the authors. Nevertheless, I believe they represent a set from which you can learn and gain insight into how others do and write about qualitative research.

SELECTION OF ISSUES

In addition to locating articles for this book, I also came across a number of issues that were written about repeatedly. Many are not usually addressed in textbooks. Many affect how we do research, how we make our needs known to the larger academy, and how we see ourselves operating within a larger group of educational researchers. I selected seven issues of particular interest that I think are very important for you to read.

EVALUATING QUALITATIVE RESEARCH

Qualitative research approaches take many forms. Grounded theory approaches tend to be closer in style and form to quantitative research approaches. Action research tends to be practical and applicable to immediate problem solving. Even within a particular approach, the way a researcher might handle particular aspects may differ. Because of this, we cannot develop one specific set of criteria that can be applied to all situations. Consequently, there are not concrete rules or expectations that you can use as a guideline when deciding to what extent a published article represents "good" research or a "good" example of a particular research approach.

If you read articles about how to evaluate a research study, you will not find agreement as to what makes a "good" study. Journal editors struggle with the problem. Government funding agencies are conflicted. Institutional review boards are challenged. How can you as a student new to the field deal with this complex issue?

Here are some general guidelines you might find helpful:

- *The writing.* Although a researcher might have planned and conducted a piece of research in an appropriate and interesting manner, it is ultimately the way in which it is communicated that is the key to whether the study succeeds. I would like you to begin with how the research is communicated.[1] Here are some questions you might consider: Are you drawn into the research? Can you understand what is written? Does it make sense in terms of what you know? Are complex issues explained clearly? Does the writer engage you so you will feel compelled to continue to read? Does the writing avoid remoteness and obtuseness? I think you get the idea.

- *The research approach.* Does the writer help you understand the approach he or she took in conducting the research? Does the research approach appear suitable for the research questions that the author is trying to answer? Does the author explain elements of the research approach? Does the author apply those elements appropriately?

- *The meaningfulness and value.* It is the researcher's responsibility to help you see why the study is important. While you may not personally find a study of interest, you can still determine whether it is of importance to others by reading what the researcher has to say about it.

Whatever research approach was taken, I look for some very basic elements.

Things I really like to find in a study

- A way to engage the audience
- Interconnection of all the parts
- Clear explanations
- Writing that draws me in
- The voice of the researcher and of the participants
- The writer's interpretation of how the study contributes to the field

Things that annoy me about a qualitative study

- Unfounded claims and interpretations
- A literature review that is just there, that is not connected to the remainder of the study in any meaningful way
- Use of jargon
- Forcing a study to be more quantitative by constructing tables and using statistics that do not fit the data

I believe you will find the content of the articles to come especially interesting. Many deal with students, parents, schools, and education. I also expect that you will be able to gain a better understanding of the similarities and differences between and among various qualitative research approaches.

For comments or questions, please contact me at MarilynLichtman09@gmail.com or mlichtma @vt.edu.

NOTE

1. In this book, I only consider written communication. Researchers might also choose to communicate via video, live performance, or other means.

ACKNOWLEDGMENTS

Recently, I extensively revised *Qualitative Research in Education: A User's Guide.* That book, which was published in April 2009, is aimed at students taking coursework in qualitative research.

One thing was missing from that book: there were no examples of different kinds of qualitative research approaches for students to read. While I provided links to articles in the field through the student study site, I still felt something was lacking. *Understanding and Evaluating Qualitative Educational Research* addresses that missing piece.

It was Diane McDaniel's vision that led to this book. She worked with me extensively in designing a proposal and in developing the vision for the book. Her insight and encouragement drove me to move ahead with the project. SAGE is fortunate to have her.

On a day-to-day basis, Deya Saoud kept me going. She answered my questions with grace and alacrity. She figured out ways to solve the myriad technological difficulties I encountered as I tried to interact with the research articles I wanted to include. I owe her a personal debt of gratitude for making the details happen. Again, SAGE knows how to identify staff that keeps its authors happy.

Alison Hope has worked closely with me on every detail: checking facts, making sure that dates and references were accurate, rewriting my sometimes obtuse text.

Sarah K. Quesenberry and Brittany Bauhaus worked with me on production.

Any omissions, misstatements or other errors are mine.

Thanks to the staff of the library at Virginia Tech for providing me support and computer access and for answering the many questions I posed from the comfort of my home.

I would also like to thank the reviewers of this text:

Nataliya Ivankova, *University of Alabama-Birmingham*

Trina Paulus, *University of Tennessee*

LeAnn Putney, *University of Nevada-Las Vegas*

Katrina Rodriguez, *University of Northern Colorado*

James Valadez, *Cal Lutheran University*

For the past two years, I have been extensively involved as assistant chairman and chairman of the Corcoran Gallery of Art's Docent Council. Located one block from the White House in Washington, DC, the Corcoran Gallery opened its doors in 1897. It is one of the oldest private museums in the United States. For its time, it was on the forefront of recognizing American art. In my leadership positions, my mind often turned toward the art world. I always connected art and research, and still do. I want to thank the staff at the Corcoran—especially Linda Powell and Joanna Anderson—for making my chairmanship run smoothly. I also want to thank my docent council members who generously gave of their time and talents. I would never have had time for this book without all those other pieces of my life working so well.

Since leaving active teaching at Virginia Tech in 2004, I no longer have immediate contact with faculty and students. This writing task turned out to be a solitary activity. I thank my many friends who are probably tired of hearing me say I am working on my book and not available for other things. To Shirley Cohen, Phyllis Leonard, Louise Appell, Judy Barokas, Beverly Flowers, Dorothy Sargeant, Ruth Bell, Irene Schulkin, and Rita Girshman—I can finally stop telling you I am not available. To all my other fellow exercise friends and bridge buddies, I thank you for being my friends.

And without the ongoing love and support I receive from all my family members none of this would be worth doing. To my children Ellen, David, and Judy, you are my rock. To my brother Lee and my sister-in-law Claire, how lucky I am to be related to you. To my other family members—Margaret, Jim, Anath, Michael, and Lilah—you are a great bunch of people.

And always on my mind and in my heart is my late husband and best friend, Marty Gerstein. I only wish you were here to share my accomplishment.

PART I

QUALITATIVE RESEARCH APPROACHES

As of this writing in 2009, there is an abundance of published studies that make use of various qualitative research approaches. There are a number of journals devoted exclusively to articles of a qualitative nature. In addition, many other journals accept articles written from a qualitative research perspective.

This was not always the case, however. In the 1980s, some in the field of education—dissatisfied with the paucity of research about the culture of classrooms and schools—began to apply ethnographic methods to address questions about schooling, teaching, and learning. One of the first works specifically devoted to qualitative research methods in education, Robert Bogdan and Sari Biklen's textbook *Qualitative Research for Education* (first edition 1982, second edition 1992), emphasized ethnographic methods. Throughout the decade of the 1980s and into the early 1990s, other qualitative research approaches found their way into education. Yvonna Lincoln and Egon Guba introduced the provocative work *Naturalistic Inquiry* (1985), which challenged us to think about the very assumptions on which traditional quantitative research was based. The educational research field was undergoing tremendous change.

Throughout this period, qualitative researchers began to look for outlets to publish their research. Qualitative researchers were also finding their way. Many of the traditional journals and editors struggled with these new approaches to conducting research. Traditional journals and editors were in somewhat of a quandary: What was qualitative research? Was there more than one type? Was there a "right" way to do it? Could it be more than ethnography? What made for "good" qualitative research? How could they judge something that was dynamic and emerging? Who would set the criteria? The traditional way of doing research was being turned on its head—often by those whose voices had not been heard previously. Beginning in 1988, the U.K.-based *International Journal of Qualitative Studies in Education (QSE)* became a specific source for publication of qualitative educational studies. Although not limited to the educational field, other journals became more open to publishing qualitative studies in education (e.g., *The Qualitative Report, Educational Researcher, Qualitative Inquiry, and Qualitative Research,* among others).

In 1998, John Creswell published *Qualitative Inquiry and Research Design: Choosing Among Five Traditions.* For the first time, qualitative researchers had available to them a text that presented ways of doing qualitative research that were different from ethnography. Qualitative research had arrived. The second edition of Creswell's book (2007) saw a subtle change in the title: *Qualitative Inquiry and Research Design: Choosing Among Five Approaches.* This 2007 edition included five approaches (i.e., narrative, phenomenological, grounded theory, ethnographic, and case study). Narrative had replaced biography in this edition, and the term "approaches" had replaced "traditions." Creswell's text was not specific to education, but it was quite applicable to the field.

By the late 1990s, there was an explosion of journals, some online, that were more accepting of publishing articles that did not follow a traditional, quantitative approach. Most of these journals were targeted to a general readership in the social sciences rather than specifically to education. As we approach the end of the first decade of the 21st century, we continue to see many new avenues for researchers to have their work available to larger audiences. In addition to online journals, communication using the Internet has resulted in work becoming immediately available. Although much of this writing does not go through the usual peer review process, it is available for the worldwide community. I believe this global community of scholars may bring about new ways and new criteria for evaluating and judging.

In 2006, I published *Qualitative Research in Education,* which was revised in 2010. That textbook targeted the educational community, and the book you are about to read builds on it. It provides many examples drawn from a wide variety of sources to illustrate the ways in which qualitative educational researchers try to answer questions and conduct research. It owes a strong debt to Creswell's work.

I have selected seven different research approaches for you to consider. I struggled with terms for some time. Should I call these research designs, research methods, or research approaches? Which ones should I choose? During the early planning of this volume, several reviewers made suggestions about which approaches should be illustrated. In addition to the five identified by Creswell, I added action research and mixed methods research. Obviously, I did not include all approaches. I would have liked to include examples of feminist approaches, autoethnography, biography, teacher research, and combined qualitative approaches, but space was a limiting factor.

I recall one of the first times I taught a course in qualitative research methods, in the late 1980s. I combed numerous journals (online searches were not yet available) looking for examples of published work and ways of thinking about research. I sought permissions and prepared packets of material for students. I strained to find good examples. It was difficult to locate enough pertinent material.

Close to 30 years later, I faced a different set of problems. So much is out there—almost too much to absorb. All is available to me through search engines and a computerized system available through Virginia Tech. I could do all my exploring from the comfort of my own home. Rather than not having sufficient material, I had too much.

I hope you will enjoy reading these different research studies. I did. Some are by those new to the field, and others are by those whose names you will recognize. I hope my comments that accompany each article will help you better understand the research approach.

I chose to begin with articles that represent ethnography. Chapter 1 contains two articles. As I said earlier, that is the qualitative research approach that has been most closely associated with education. In fact, many ethnographies are published in book form. The two ethnographies I chose for you represent different perspectives. Nukaga uses a traditional ethnographic model. Jackson explores ethnography from a post-structural viewpoint.

In contrast to ethnographic research, which has few details about how to analyze data, I introduce you to grounded theory in Chapter 2. Grounded theory is the most structured and objective of the qualitative research approaches, especially with respect to data analysis. Although based on work from the 1960s, it actually was much more popular in the nursing field than in education. Eich's work is an example applied to the field of higher education. Coyne and Cowley (from the nursing field) provide an example of data analysis using grounded theory methods.

In Chapter 3, I provide you with examples of phenomenological studies. Phenomenology attempts to determine the essence of lived experiences. I think educational qualitative researchers are still learning about how to do this. Perhaps the philosophical underpinnings of the approach present some practical problems. Hines and his colleagues study technology use among high school administrators. I don't think they quite get to the lived experience or its essence, but you should still find the study interesting. Bambara and her colleagues explore the lived experiences of those involved in online courses.

In Chapter 4, I offer you an example of a case study conducted by Bouck in a rural high school. The second article I offer you in the chapter is somewhat challenging. Watts reacts to the writings of Stake, one of the leading writers in the field of case study. Although not a research study, I believe it has much to offer. A word of caution, however. The format of the article is somewhat confusing. We were not able to reproduce the unusual spacing found in the original published article. If you are interested, you should look at the original.

Action research approaches are presented in Chapter 5. These are close to those of you in education. Miskovic and Hoop present a comprehensive example of participatory action research. Such an approach usually leads to a call to action and often is political in nature. Fisher and Phelps use a play format to present information about action research.

In Chapter 6, I introduce narrative approaches. Creswell chose to replace the tradition of biography with that of the narrative. I also chose to use narrative approaches since it is much broader than just biography. Seaton's account of a communal narrative is very moving. In his essay, Barone suggests that the movement toward a return to the "gold standard" may challenge the very nature of using narrative as a qualitative research approach.

I conclude Part 1 with Chapter 7, in which I introduce you to studies using a combination of quantitative and qualitative methods. Actually, the first article by Creswell in this chapter is not a study per se, but an explanation of the role of mixed methods in today's world. I was surprised to learn that Creswell was a proponent of this viewpoint; I did not know that when I began to use his text in the late 1990s. The chapter concludes with Scott and Sutton's study of professional development of teachers.

REFERENCES

Bogdan, R., & Biklen, S. (1982, 1992). Qualitative research for education: An introduction to theory and methods. Boston: Allyn & Bacon.

Creswell, J. (1998). *Qualitative inquiry and research design: Choosing among five traditions.* Thousand Oaks, CA: Sage.

Creswell, J. (2007). *Qualitative inquiry and research design: Choosing among five approaches.* Thousand Oaks, CA: Sage.

Lincoln, Y., & Guba, E. (1985). *Naturalistic Inquiry.* Thousand Oaks CA: Sage.

Lichtman, M. (2006, 2010). *Qualitative research in education: A user's guide.* Thousand Oaks, CA: Sage.

Chapter 1

READING ETHNOGRAPHY

I t is now time to look closely at published ethnographies. I have selected two ethnographies for you to read. Both use high school students as the central figures, are written by women students, use writing styles that are direct and personal, and are written in the first person.

In the early days of ethnography, researchers typically studied cultures that were dramatically different from their own. In those cases, researchers were always in a dominant position with relation to those they studied, and power rested with the researchers. Those researchers traveled to the far reaches of the world. Today's ethnographers tend to stay closer to home—but some travel around the world via the Internet. Although the relationship between the researcher and those studied is not always as one-sided as it once was, we still see power differences. Some researchers have tried to reduce the power discrepancy by identifying those studied as co-researchers. In my view, however, this still does not solve the problem.

KEY ELEMENTS OF ETHNOGRAPHY

- Ethnography consists of an in-depth look at a culture or subculture;
- often limits the study to a specific aspect of culture;
- relies on the field of anthropology for its theoretical base;
- addresses issues of gaining access, role of observer, power issues; and
- often uses words of participants in written presentations.
- Much of the research in ethnography comes out of the field of education.

The first article is by Misako Nukaga. It is a study of Korean-American students in Los Angeles. Specifically, it targets how children use food as a symbolic resource to negotiate group boundaries in peer interaction. Nukaga doesn't travel to another country to study a culture different from her own. Instead, she selects Korean-American students who attend school in a large urban area. Because she is of Japanese descent, Nukaga says it is easy for her to study other Asian students. Nukaga's study of

Korean-American children during their school lunchtime presents a slice of culture that will be unfamiliar to many of you. Because she is an adult and working in the school, power discrepancies occur. Nukaga does try to minimize them by sitting with the kids and "becoming one of them." Nukaga was a student when this article was published, and received a fellowship to support her dissertation.

The study follows a traditional approach to ethnography. It includes a detailed review of the literature that focuses on issues related to food and ethnicity. As a fairly traditional ethnography, she writes in a somewhat remote and objective style, and not in the personal style that you will encounter in the second study in this chapter. Unlike a contemporary ethnography, which might explore issues of feminism, power, and reflexivity, this study is more traditional in its look and in its format. In addition, it includes detailed quotes.

In contrast to Nukaga's study, Alecia Jackson's study presents an ethnography that is less traditional. She calls it "post-structural." On first glance, it appears that Jackson's ethnography is a study of high school girls in a small town. As you read in greater depth, however, you will discover the article is really about Jackson's role and how she negotiates and comes to understand being an ethnographer in a personal setting. In fact, it goes far afield from what you might expect. It fits quite well into a post-structural model because she relies on the philosophical contributions of Michel Foucault, a French philosopher who wrote about power and knowledge.

In her study, which she conducted in the same high school she had attended years before, Jackson turns the idea of looking at diverse cultures on its head. She does not want to place herself in a position of power, and in fact struggles at times with trying to move away from the power role. Jackson does a good job of explaining some of the philosophical underpinnings of Foucault's philosophy.

There were several reasons I selected this article for you to read: first, because it is written in a very engaging manner; second, because it is about students. A third reason I chose this work is because Jackson wrote it while she was still a doctoral student. You should be able to identify with her more readily than if she had been a professor for many years.

Conducting ethnographies in school settings is challenging. You will see my comments interspersed in both studies related to some of the issues. You should anticipate that issues might include gaining access, keeping confidences, negotiating boundaries, getting appropriate permissions with minors, and allowing sufficient time for observations.

You will find that both writers use some basic techniques as they study aspects of the culture of a particular group. They directly observe the students over some time. And they reveal information about themselves.

ADVANCE PREPARATIONS

Begin by reading the title and the abstract, then flipping through the article and reading the major headings and subheadings. Once you have an idea of the article's structure, go back and read through the article carefully. When you finish reading, you will need to decide the extent to which the article is successful. To do so, ask yourself four questions:

- Does it provide new information and insights related to the topic?
- Is it engaging and written in a clear manner?
- Does it illustrate elements you would expect to find in an ethnography?
- Do the positive aspects of the article outweigh the potential drawbacks?

Article 1.1. The Underlife of Kids' School Lunchtime: Negotiating Ethnic Boundaries and Identity in Food Exchange (2008)

Misako Nukaga

My Expectations

I am now ready to look at the article in depth. I anticipate it will follow a fairly traditional approach to conducting ethnography. I expect to see a fairly detailed review of the literature that would focus on the issues related to food exchange and ethnicity. The author of a traditional ethnography would probably write in a somewhat remote and objective style, as opposed to a personal style. Unlike a contemporary ethnography that would get into issues of feminism, power, and reflexivity, I anticipate that this study will avoid those topics. I expect to see detailed quotes from the field, also.

The title is appealing to me, but I wonder what the author means by "underlife." She seems to be studying a topic I know something about. I know that various cultural groups connect their identity with food, and that many important exchanges occur when people come together in a common activity. Although my experience with Koreans is limited, I live in a diverse area of the country, and I believe my experiences with other ethnic groups might help me understand this study.

From the abstract, I discover the direction the study will take. I focus on key descriptions in the abstract: food serves as a symbolic resource; group boundaries will be negotiated somehow through food; there are two kinds of food (dry and wet); and food is exchanged in one of three different ways (as a gift, as a shared resource, or as a traded commodity). Nukaga's last sentence in the abstract is not clear to me. I will have to read further to understand what is meant by "layered and situated ethnic identity." Given the issues in various societies regarding race, I find this topic particularly relevant.

As I move through the headings, I note that there is no heading for several pages. I know that it is common for writers to omit a heading such as *Introduction*, so I know that this first part will be some kind of introduction to the problem and the issues that surround it. I encounter the

ABSTRACT

While the literature on ethnic identity takes traditional "adult-centered" socialization theory for granted, this study breaks away from such a perspective, and instead uses ethnographic data on children's food exchange during lunchtime in two predominantly Korean (-American) elementary schools to explore how children use food as a symbolic resource to negotiate group boundaries in peer interaction. Following a discussion of lunchtime seating patterns, this article presents children practicing exchange of "dry food (mass-consumed)" and "wet food (homemade)" that takes three different forms—gift-giving, sharing, and trading—each of which have different relevance for marking, maintaining, and muting ethnic boundaries and other social differences. Taking a child-centered perspective, the study finds that children's ethnic identity development is by no means a universal linear process. Instead, preadolescent children, although constrained by external forces, learn to do layered and situated ethnic identity through using cultural resources in peer interaction.

In her insightful fieldwork at a racially and ethnically mixed high school in urban California, Olsen (1997) reveals a striking racial divide and conflict among American adolescents and a pressure against immigrant adolescents to conform to this racialization process at school. A white girl in her study talked about the changing relationship with her best friend in elementary school, who was African American. As the racial divide became increasingly intensified through middle school to high school, she lost contact with her African American friend who continued to go to the same school with heading *Children's Racial and Ethnic Identity*. I expect to find some kind of literature review in this section, although I am not sure how broad it will be. I see that the review is quite long. *Children's Participation in Gift Economy* seems to include another body of literature about gifting. I remember the abstract suggested that children exchange food in one of three ways: as a gift, as a shared resource, and as a traded commodity. I do not know whether the author read the literature before she embarked on her study. I know that different researchers choose different strategies to look at the related research. If you have skimmed the headings, you will notice that *Setting and Method* follows these two reviews of the literature. I anticipate learning in that section where the study was done, how schools were selected, how the researcher gained entry, how she negotiated joining kids during lunch, how long she spent in the field, and other issues related to doing ethnography. I see that this section on method is also quite long, so I anticipate learning much of the detail regarding the "how" of her study.

I am surprised the author tells us so quickly about the gist of her study. Do you find it helpful for her to have done so?

Marking, maintaining, and muting boundaries—I wish she had said more about these topics.

her. While cross-racial ethnic friendship may be much more salient during preadolescence, previous studies at elementary schools show that preadolescent children also tend to segregate according to their race and ethnicity under some circumstances (Ausdale and Feagin 2001; Lewis 2005; Thorne forthcoming). Fine and Sandstrom (1988) argue that "preadolescents, perhaps more than any other age group, are concerned about the nature of proper relationship with others" (p. 55). Since learning to affiliate with a "proper" racial and ethnic group is one of the crucial tasks for preadolescents, racial and ethnic divides at school start to crystallize at a very young age. To promote cooperative relationships among children from different racial and ethnic backgrounds, we first need to understand how preadolescent children construct racial and ethnic boundaries and come to develop ethnic identity at an elementary school setting.

The constructionist view of race and ethnicity, which has gained popularity in the last several decades, suggests that racial and ethnic identities are created, elaborated, and reconstructed in the interaction between internal identification and external categorization (Barth 1969; Cornell and Hartmann 1998; Nagel 1994). This view rejects a conceptualization of ethnic and racial identity as static entities, and instead assumes that they vary across space and change across time (Cornell and Hartman 1998, 101). While an increasing number of case studies focus on ethnic identity formation of adults and adolescents, there are few studies that have paid full attention to how small children construct ethnic boundaries and identity. The traditional socialization framework is still prevalent in this genre of study, which consequentially neglects children as learners of the norms and values of the established adult society. Children's experience is not understood on its own terms, but interpreted as molding children into members of a presumed ethnic group in society. Such an "adult-centered framework" (Thorne 1987) relegates children to passive recipients of adult culture, and dismisses processes of how children, with limited autonomy, actively negotiate their ethnic differences and identities.

Conducting participant observations of children's peer interaction during lunchtime in two predominantly Korean (-American) elementary schools in Los Angeles, this study reveals how the fourth-grade children negotiated ethnic boundaries through using food as a symbolic resource in an intricate system of distribution, which they cooperatively constructed without teachers noticing. Adopting the sociology of childhood perspective (see Corsaro 1997), this study demonstrates children as "active economic agents" (Zelizer 2002), who skillfully selected the use of two types of food, "dry food (mass-consumed)" and "wet food (homemade)" in three forms of exchange—gift-giving, sharing, and trading—to control their relationships with peers as well as to mark, maintain, and mute ethnic boundaries. As I will show, such ethnic boundary negotiation usually accompanied children's marking of differences based on gender, age, classroom, and to some extent, social class. Simultaneously, I find that construction of these various boundaries are confined by a larger social context, such as school demography and social class inequality. These findings suggest the pitfalls of previous racial and ethnic studies that have neglected children's active construction of ethnic boundaries and identity. A child-centered perspective allows us to understand that children's ethnic identity development is not a universal linear process that is automatically triggered as children go through a series of distinct stages of intellectual ability (see Piaget 1965). Rather, preadolescent children, although constrained by external forces, learn to do emergent, layered, and situated ethnicity through creating and using cultural resources in peer interaction.

The author has presented a brief summary of her findings and conclusions. Most authors do not do this at the beginning of a journal article.

CHILDREN'S RACIAL AND ETHNIC IDENTITY

This author has included a very detailed and comprehensive review of the literature. Some authors omit writing a review at this point. One thing you should look for later in the article is the extent to which she ties her own findings to the literature that she reviews here.

Although a growing number of studies examine construction of race and ethnicity among adolescents and adults, little attention has been devoted to how small children "do" race and ethnicity (West and Fenstermaker 1995) in everyday settings.

. . .

Instead, preadolescent children's race and ethnicity have often been studied by the use of sociometric tests, which have become a popular quantitative method to examine children's friendship bonds (Hallinan and Teixeira 1987). One of the important contributions that these studies have made is the revelation that race and gender are both crucial determinants of children's friendship choices, with gender producing a much stronger effect than race (Sagar, Schofield, and Sneyder 1983; Schofield and Whitley 1983; Singleton and Asher 1977). Still, these studies perceive children's ethnic differentiation as fixed and stable patterns that are replicated across different social contexts. Conducting both sociometric tests and observation in elementary school classrooms, Denscombe et al. (1993) point to a dissonance between the results obtained from the two methods and maintain that sociometric research fails to capture the complexity of children's friendship choice and ethnic differentiation. In studies that rely on sociometric tests, race and ethnicity are considered independent variables that affect children's social relationships, and not dependent variables to be explored. These studies conceptualize children's social identities as "fixed and often essentialized categories rather than as multifaceted, situated, and socially constructed processes" (Orellana and Bowman 2003, 26). Consequently, they do not tell us how children construct ethnic identities in interactional contexts, let alone how such processes are

The following develops an argument for her perspective on how to study the topic.

related to the construction of gender identity which is presumably more salient than race and ethnicity. These gaps can only be addressed by conducting direct observation of children's interaction.

To illuminate children's construction of ethnic identity, I rely on an emerging perspective provided by a "new sociology of childhood," which attempts to break away from a Piagetian socialization model and individualistic biases concerning children (see Corsaro 1997; Fine 1987; Goodwin 1991; Thorne 1993). Corsaro (1997) argues that a new sociology of childhood conceptualizes children as innovative agents who constantly engage in a process of appropriation, reinvention, and reproduction of their social world. This approach to children's socialization highlights children's collective creation and the reproduction of peer culture in interactional contexts, and looks at how children participate in such culture with others. It questions the universal linear model of children's development assumed in the Piagetian model, and calls attention to more flexible ways in which children present and form a sense of self and identities.

The author assumes the reader is familiar with Piaget, and "the Piagetian model."

. . .

While there are increasing numbers of ethnographic studies that have focused on preadolescent children's construction of gender identity using sociology of childhood as well as symbolic interactionist perspectives (see Adler and Adler 1998; Adler, Kless, and Adler 1992; Best 1983; Eder and Parker 1987; Eder 1985; Thorne 1993), few have studied racial and ethnic identity using these frameworks since most studies have been conducted at predominantly white schools. As Ausdale and Feagin (2001) suggest, Corsaro's overview of recent sociology of childhood literature says little about children's understandings and practice of race and ethnicity. Yet, Thorne's pioneering study of children's gender identity formation (1993) is suggestive in studying children's race and ethnicity. Observing fourth- and fifth-grade children's behavior on a school playground, Thorne argues that girls and boys engaged in a range of "borderwork," which evoked a sense of boys and girls as opposite groups and exaggerated gender separation and stereotypes. Simultaneously, she cautions not to take gender dualism for granted, suggesting that

This is part of the build-up and argument for doing this study. I am happy to see this here since it adds to my belief about the importance of the interconnection of various pieces of an article.

> Gender boundaries are episodic and ambiguous, and the notion of "borderwork" should be coupled with a parallel term—such as "neutralization"—for processes though which girls and boys (and adults who enter into their social relations) neutralize or undermine a sense of gender as division and opposition." (Thorne 1993, 84)

To capture children's dynamic construction of gender, Thorne stresses the need to examine how gender is played out *in contex.*

We can surmise the author chose this group because of her own racial background. Perhaps it was easier for her to gain access to these students than to other students, or perhaps she felt she could identify with them more closely than with other minority groups. In the next study you will read, the author, Jackson, actually goes to her own high school in a small town where she had broad access. Researchers often deal with problems of access and "fitting in" when they select a group to study.

As Thorne (1993) argues, race and ethnicity are usually less visible and more ambiguous than gender, which is "clearly marked by dress and by language." The few existing ethnographic studies in this field mostly focus on race rather than ethnicity, which requires actors' continuous affirmation and recreation of ethnic boundaries (Ferguson 2000; Lewis 2005; Moore 2001; Schofield 1982). Between race and ethnicity, the latter conveys more changing and constructed quality since it has emphasis on "self-consciousness, the participation of groups themselves in the construction, reproduction, and transformation of their own identities" (Cornell and Hartmann 1998, 37), whereas racial identity is usually based on perceived physical differences. In this study, I strategically chose a racially and ethnically diverse site where Koreans are the largest ethnic group, to expand and deepen the understanding of "the fluid, situational, volitional, and dynamic character of ethnic identification" (Nagel 1994, 152). Furthermore, while African American children are given the most attention in previous studies, little attention has been devoted to Asian American children (Howes and Wu 1990). The selection of the site and the subject will also give voice to these minority children who have often been neglected in previous studies on children's social development.

Culture plays a crucial role in constructing ethnic boundaries and identity (Nagel 1994; Cornell and Hartmann 1998). To understand how children do ethnicity in everyday settings, Swidler's conceptualization of culture is particularly useful. According to Swidler, culture is "a 'tool kit' from which actors select differing pieces for constructing lines of actions" (Swidler 1986, 277). From a sociology of childhood perspective, children, like adults, *appropriate, produce,* and *use* culture in their peer interactions to negotiate group boundaries, and in that process, come to see themselves as members of a certain ethnic group. Previous studies have shown that children use various cultural objects (e.g., dress and possession) as well as language to mark gender, racial, and ethnic boundaries (Ausdale and Feagin 2000; Ferguson 2000). Play and games are also important rituals that children produce and use to negotiate their relationships and identities (Evaldesson 1993, 2003; Goodwin 1991 and 2001; Levinson 2005; Thorne 1993). Adding to the literature, this study finds that *children's use of food and collaborative production of food exchange during lunchtime plays a crucial role in children's formation of ethnic boundaries and identity.* In this sense, this study also adds to previous research that has studied gift economy, but in which children's activities are mostly invisible. Brief reviews of these areas of literature are provided in the following section.

. . .

A small number of ethnographic studies have shown that preadolescent children actively construct a gift economy with peers in classrooms, lunchrooms, playgrounds, and on the streets (Chin 2001; Ferguson 2000; Katriel 1987; Thorne 1993 and 2005). Katriel (1987) conducted an ethnographic study of the Israeli sharing routine "xibùdim," and found that children carefully assessed and negotiated a "normal bite" size of the food for each person so that "everybody can get a share, leaving about half of it for the giver" (p. 315). She maintains that this ritualized sharing serves an important socializing function by providing a context where "a symbolic sacrifice in which one's self interest and primordial greed are controlled and subordinated to an idea of sociality shaped by particular cultural values, such as equality and generalized reciprocity" (p. 318). Her study shows that children actively create and maintain social solidarity by participating in such gift economy.

Other studies show that gift exchange marked a degree of friendship and also emphasized social differences. Chin (2001) found that children carefully selected to whom they would give gifts of money, food, and objects. In her observation, children gave gifts to their best friends first and then to less intimate classmates. In observing "underground economy of food and objects" which children practiced behind teachers' scrutinizing eyes in classrooms, Thorne (1993) observed that the pattern of exchange strongly marked the separation between boys' and girls' friendship groups (pp. 20–23). Objects that were exchanged also marked gender differences. She found that boys brought in "toy cars and trucks, magnets, and compasses" while girls possessed "tubes of lip gross, nail polish, barrettes, necklaces, little stuffed animals, and doll furniture" (p. 21). In her recent study of lunchtime at a mixed-income ethnically diverse elementary school in California, Thorne (2005) briefly discusses how children used valued food to mark lines of friendship, gender, social class, and race differences.

> I find it surprising the author tells us the outcome of the study at this point.

Building on this literature, this study shows how children construct, participate, and use food economy during lunchtime to organize peer relationships and group boundaries, and in that process come to develop ethnic identity. Extending Thorne's observation of lunchtime, I focus not only on "valued food" that encouraged the flow of the economy, but also "ethnic food" that mostly Korean children brought from home and exchanged with their peers. It will be shown that Korean children understood their "ethnic" food as a symbol of their Korean self and negotiated its meanings and value in interacting with their peers. Furthermore, looking closely at different forms of food exchange, I reveal that each form had different relevance for marking, maintaining, and muting ethnic boundaries.

> In a sense, the author integrates the literature and her findings even before we know what she did and how she did it. Although it is unusual, it is appealing to me.

I find it interesting the author makes a serious case for studying children during their lunchtime. If we think about it, we can see so many advantages. It is a time when children interact without any academic activities and without any direct supervision. We see them at their most natural situation during lunchtime.

SETTING AND METHOD

School lunchtime is an ideal site to dig into children's friendship, group boundary construction, and identity formation. It is the time when children associate freely with their peers under minimal adult surveillance and form a strong sense of solidarity through sitting and eating together. Such experience is what Durkheim (1968 [1915]) called "collective effervescence," which creates emotional foundations of moral bonds. Simultaneously, it is the time when children negotiate their differences through interacting with others and develop identification with a certain social group. In introducing theoretical frameworks for exploring contexts, differences, and trajectories of children's development, Thorne (2005) argues for the advantages of studying school lunchtime as follows:

> Like the Balinese cockfight analyzed by Clifford Geertz (1973), school lunchtime is a public and collective "text" with many, sometimes contradictory, layers of meaning. The lunchtime scene, especially in a school where students come from strikingly divergent backgrounds, is a fruitful site for uncovering practices to mark, mute, and negotiate social differences. When these practices involve labeling or group formation, they may become especially consequential for trajectories of personal change. (p.14)

Now that she begins to tell you about the study, she shifts into a more personal style, relying heavily on the use of the first person pronoun.

Several studies on children's friendship and social differentiation have studied seating arrangements during lunchtime both qualitatively (Eder 1985; Zisman and Wilson 1992) and quantitatively (Clack, Dixon, and Tredoux 2005; McCauley, Plummer, and Moskalenko 2001). By contrast, this study provides new insights into school lunchtime by mainly focusing on children's ritualized food exchange.

My ethnographic research of school lunchtime was conducted at two elementary schools in Los Angeles, which I call "Hamilton" School and "Claremont" School. These two schools were mixed-income ethnically diverse public elementary schools located just two miles apart in an affluent community. I chose these two schools as my fieldsites because of the similarity in racial and ethnic diversity of the children, with Korean as the most prevalent ethnic group. According to the Los Angeles Unified School District 2005 statistics, at Hamilton, about 50 percent of the students were classified as "Asian," 25 percent were "White," 12 percent were "Hispanic," and 13 percent were "African American." At Claremont, 61 percent of the students were "Asian," 19 percent were "White," 12 percent were Hispanic, and 8 percent were "African American." Most of the children who fell into "Asian" category were Korean. For both schools, about one-third of the students were English learners, most of whom were Koreans. The fourth grade children (ages nine and ten) whom I observed were aware of racial and ethnic differences to some extent, and used the following categories to describe themselves and others: "Korean," "Chinese," "Jewish," "Black," "White," and "Latino or Latina." White and Latino children who were not born in the United States also associated themselves with the country where they were born (e.g., Australia, Guatemala, Mexico, Honduras, etc.). These racial and ethnic labels will be used to describe children's racial and ethnic identity throughout this article.

With regard to children's social class backgrounds, most of the children came from upper- or middle-class families, although there were also quite a number of children who qualified for free/reduced lunch program (14 percent at Hamilton and 25 percent at Claremont). When looking at the children who frequently ate cafeteria food, they tended to be Latino/a and Black, rather than White and Korean. However, since most of the children possessed a meal card, which did not indicate a child's reduced or free lunch status in any way, I was not able to tell clearly who qualified for these programs. The social class differences among these children were not very visible because of the schools' rather successful efforts to obscure class differences. When I asked a principal at Hamilton if she thought that children knew about their social class differences, she answered as follows:

> No. We try not to let children become aware of such differences. . . . I can tell you the percentage of the students who are in reduced or free lunch program, but I can't give you the names of the children who are in these programs. Same for the children and parents. We try to be very careful. We don't want children to humiliate one another.

Hence, at two schools, I found that talk about class differences was much less common among kids compared to other social differences. Nevertheless, class differences entered into kids' interaction during lunchtime in a very subtle way. As will be shown later, White and Korean kids brought more food from home to school than Latino/a and Black kids, and thus they were at the center of the food economy as the main distributors.

From February through June 2004, I visited Hamilton School on different days of the week, ranging from one to three times a week. I visited Ms. Gill's fourth-grade class and observed kids' interaction in the class, during lunchtime, and at recess, and sat and participated in their activities through eating and playing with them. Hamilton had two cafeterias: outside picnic tables for kids who brought a lunch from home and a much smaller indoor space for those who ate cafeteria food. In the outside cafeteria, kids could freely choose their eating companions and sit at any of the twenty-two tables in the area, while the indoor cafeteria was much more

---

Notice how she weaves information that she gained during the study into the description of how she did her study.

We don't know how she obtained this information. Would it be helpful for her to give the source or sources of her data?

Again, we find an interweaving of data she collected and a description of the process. Authors choose various techniques to keep reader interest high. Nakuga may have chosen her method to maintain interest and connect the process and the findings.

She writes about entering the school as if it were easy to do so, but I know that is not true. Large school districts such as Los Angeles would normally have a process of requests and approvals to follow. It would be helpful for the author to describe how she gained access to the school. Do you think the author's racial background facilitated her gaining access? Do you think the fact she was a student at UCLA helped her?

Here the author talks about her extensive fieldnotes. Later, she says she did not take notes in front of the children, but rather wrote them up later. Ethnographers often write up notes upon leaving the site. Also, we don't learn anything about whether she gained parental permission to study the students. Did she get parental approval? Since the children were in the lunchroom—in a public space in the school—this might have been seen as tacit approval. However, in today's world of sensitivity to privacy issues, most researchers would assure that they have received appropriate approvals.

I wonder what she wrote in her e-mail. Do you think she told the principal she was a volunteer? If so, do you think it was appropriate for her to have done so?

controlled by a lunch aide. Food exchange occurred mostly in the outdoor cafeteria where kids brought various kinds of food from home. Kids who ate cafeteria food often participated in this food exchange after they finished eating lunch and left the indoor cafeteria. I ended up collecting sixteen sets of fieldnotes that described kids' interaction in the outdoor cafeteria and three sets of fieldnotes from the indoor cafeteria. I also have ten sets of fieldnotes for kids' activities inside Ms. Gill's classroom and during recess. I also conducted focus group interviews (twenty minutes each) with twenty-three kids in Ms. Gill's fourth-grade class, and informal interviews with Ms. Gill, the school principal, a lunch duty aide, and three Korean mothers.

From the end of October 2004 to February 2005, and again in September 2005, I visited nearby Claremont School. Like Hamilton, access to the school was made possible by a principal responding to my e-mail. Introduced by a vice principal, I entered Ms. Wood's fourth-grade classroom as "a volunteer," and sometimes helped kids do their activities in the classroom. During lunchtime, I sat at one of the three lunch tables that were assigned to Ms. Wood's class and ate lunch I had brought from home with kids in the class. Unlike Hamilton, which had two separate cafeterias, there was only one cafeteria at Claremont. Each classroom was assigned three tables, and kids in the same class had to sit at one of these tables. From these participant observations, I collected twenty-three sets of fieldnotes of lunchtime. I also have twenty sets of fieldnotes describing children's interaction in Ms. Wood's class and during recess.

At both schools during lunchtime, I tried to immerse myself into the site. I brought my own lunch that I packed at home, and ate with different kids at different tables on different days. Ethnographers who studied kids and their activities devised various ways of dealing with the age and power barriers that lie between adult-ethnographer and kids (Corsaro 2003; Fine and Sandstrom 1988; Mandell 1988; Thorne 1993). Like Thorne (1993), I refrained from adult roles of authority, and instead related to the kids as their friend willing to learn from them and understand their experiences. My Japanese background seemed to have appealed to kids' interests in schools where the majority of the kids spoke more than one language. Kids asked me how to say certain words in Japanese and we ended up telling and chanting words in different languages in a friendly manner. While my ethnic background contributed to building friendly relationships with the kids, my gender often interfered with my access to boys' friendship groups. As I will discuss in the next section, girls and boys usually sat at different cafeteria tables, creating what they called "girls' tables" and "boys' tables." Even though I am a female, boys did not mind me sitting with them because in their eyes my adult status overrode my gender. However, whenever

The issue she raises here is interesting. Are you surprised she believes gaining access to boys was hampered by her own gender?

Ethnographers struggle continuously to define themselves with relation to those they study. Should they be friends, thus removing themselves from the presumed power relationship? If so, can they "make friends" successfully? You will see what happened to Jackson in the next study. Both authors you read here are female, and both were students when they did their research. Do you think this makes a difference in how they defined themselves?

The author was clearly not a teacher, and was introduced as a volunteer. We don't know whether it was common for volunteers to just "appear" at the school. In many schools, volunteers are regularly welcomed to assist teachers; we do not know whether that is true at this school.

girls found me at the boys' table, they would ask, "What are you doing at boys' table? You'll get cooties!" and forcefully invited me to come over to their table. Sometimes, girls would come to sit next to me at the boys' table, consequently outnumbering the boys and driving them away to another table. I tried to stop the boys from leaving, but was not always successful. Such dilemmas in the field made me highly aware of the gender separation among preadolescent kids (see Adler and Adler 1998).

It was not long after I started to sit and eat with the kids as their "friend" that they started to give me various kinds of food even without my asking and invited me to participate in their communal food exchange. They also asked if they could have some of my food, especially when I brought a bag of chips or crackers. Through my attempt to immerse myself into the kids' world, I discovered that food exchange was an important ritual that children made use of to create and strengthen friendships with others.

It needs to be emphasized that although food exchange was a prime ritual during lunchtime that involved almost all the kids in school, it was not apparent or accessible to the teachers. Classroom teachers hardly knew anything about children's interaction in the school cafeteria, because they usually went straight to the teachers' lounge to have their lunch. Besides, food exchange was a hidden activity especially at Hamilton, where the principal prohibited children from sharing food because of health concerns. At this school, teachers sent a notification home to parents stating that children were not to share food at school because some children are allergic to certain types of food. During lunchtime, lunch aides warned children to stop sharing whenever they found such activities. However, behind the eyes of the adult surveillance, children's food exchange ritual continued to flourish. They skillfully gave and received food under the table or behind their lunch bags and carefully watched out for the lunch aides, prepared to hide the activity whenever they came close. The giving and receiving of food, which involved minor resistance and challenge to school rules, constituted the *underlife* of school lunchtime. The idea of an underlife is important for her study. According to Goffman (1961), underlives develop in any kind of social establishment; they become an arena where individuals practice secondary adjustments which "represent ways in which the individual stands apart from the role and the self that were taken for granted for him by the institution" (p. 189). Corsaro (2003) and Thorne (1993) observe similar activities among children who defy school rules by bringing in and exchanging snacks and small objects in the classroom. She does an excellent job of interweaving the literature that she reviewed into her own study.

Like Thorne (1993) who participated in children's secret exchange and felt pulled between her loyalty to children and her

Do you think the author behaved appropriately in continuing to break a school rule?

It is interesting that the author writes about her struggle here. I wonder if this conflict will preclude her from continuing her study in the schools.

This point is very important: she didn't know precisely where her study of kids and lunchtime was going to take her.

The author does not clarify what is meant by "retroduction." Do you think she should have done so?

In my opinion, the author should discuss in much greater detail how she went about her coding. As I mentioned in the introduction, this study represents a traditional approach to ethnography. As such, it is not surprising that she chose a traditional approach to data analysis.

The following discussion of her findings is very long and somewhat complicated. Seve ral paragraphs have been omitted due to space considerations. You can see the structure of this next section from the main headings. I suggest you look at them before you continue reading. The main heading—Age, Classroom, Gender, and Ethnicity in Seating Patterns— helps me anticipate what will follow. I have read in the popular literature that kids tend to sit with others of their ethnic

identification with and dependence on the teacher (p. 22), I also could not stop feeling a slight sense of guilt at Hamilton where food exchange was prohibited. It was only after a month of fieldwork that I discovered this school rule, but even after that, I continued to take a laissez-fairest position. I believed that the fourth graders were well aware of the types of food that they were allergic to, and hence there was little concern for children getting sick through sharing food. However, my affiliation with kids and participation in their rule-breaking, which was one of the strategies to gain access to their world (Fine 1987), continued to collide with my loyalty to the principal who kindly invited me to her school.

While sitting, eating, and sharing food with the kids, I focused on the moments when the kids' various lines of differences became visible in their interaction (Thorne 2005, forthcoming). Although I entered the field with an initial interest in kids' negotiation of ethnic differences, I took an open-minded approach and attempted to gain a holistic understanding of kids' various activities during lunchtime. Seeking immersion in kids' lunchtime, I refrained from taking any notes while I was sitting at the cafeteria table with the kids. Only after I left the school, did I jot down the things I saw and heard during lunchtime. I later used these memos to write up detailed fieldnotes. Analysis of the fieldnotes involved retroduction, moving "constantly from observation and analysis to conceptual refining and reframing and then back to seek new forms of data relevant to their emerging theoretical concerns and categories" (Emerson 2001, 284; see Bulmer 1979; Katz 1983). Using a grounded theory approach (Glaser and Strauss 1967), I started from open-coding of the fieldnotes and developed them into more integrative memos as I continuously honed theoretical ideas.

AGE, CLASSROOM, GENDER, AND ETHNICITY IN SEATING PATTERNS

Choosing a place to sit and with whom to sit marks the beginning of school lunchtime. Within certain institutional limits, kids can freely choose their eating companions, and thus the seating arrangements tell much about kids' friendship patterns (Eder 1985; Thorne 1993; Zisman and Wilson 1992). In this section, I provide a general portrait of the friendship pattern in two schools from their seating arrangements during lunchtime. This gives an important backdrop of the hidden food exchange that took place after kids were seated at the cafeteria tables. From the seating pattern, I show that age/grade, classroom, gender, and ethnicity helped shape kids' friendship patterns.

group in the lunchroom, and I suspect they also sit with their friends. Two subheadings will no doubt go into detail about the choices kids make. I need to remind myself that I am just getting the structure of the article now so I push on with the remaining headings. According to the next heading, the author will address two kinds of food—dry and wet. I am sure she will explain the difference between these types of food. Next she gets into three forms of exchange: giving, sharing, and trading. I remember that she mentioned them in the abstract, and I see that these will be dealt with in detail here. The author includes quite a long conclusion that I hope will integrate what she did with the related literature. Several figures in the appendix at the end of the paper provide a visual representation of the food exchanges. Note that we have omitted the appendix with its figures from this discussion due to space considerations. She makes the presentation of her results seem quite easy. If you think about it, though, she had to organize her data to come up with the three strategies for students to position themselves to be with friends.

This author skillfully weaves her findings with the related literature, and discusses physical proximity as a signifier for development of friendship and intimacy. Have you ever thought of using data from seemingly unplanned events in this way?

Kids' Strategies to Sit With Friends

Seating arrangements are shaped through kids' continuous negotiations. Although kids had a choice to choose their seats within certain institutional limits, they were never sure that they could sit with their friends in the same spot every day. From her ethnographic study of lunchtime seating, Eder (1985) found that seating patterns started to stabilize after the seventh grade. Sixth graders in her study had a flexible seating pattern, and they sat with different groups on a daily basis. My observation of the fourth graders also suggests this flexible seating pattern and a lack of stable hierarchical cliques, although I found kids making a considerable effort to sit with a small number of "best" friends (usually one to three) as they entered the cafeteria each day. They used three types of strategies to sit with their friends: choosing seats and/or getting in the cafeteria line with their friends, saving seats, and making space on the bench.

At the two schools, kids usually entered the cafeteria in two lines led by the classroom teacher. When they approached the cafeteria and the lines were dismissed, kids started to rush toward either the cafeteria line or the tables if they brought lunch from home. In this process, kids would break up into small friendship groups, and two or three friends would start walking hastily side by side. For those who bought the cafeteria lunch, kids would get in line with their friends. At Hamilton, those who brought their lunch from home strolled together in the cafeteria area in a small group searching for a clean empty table. Once they found a table, kids usually sat next to each other, and not face to face. Even when the group was big, they often chose to sit on the same side of the table in a long line, instead of separating themselves into different sides. This was also a common practice among friends at Claremont. As many studies have shown, physical proximity is an important marker of kids' friendship and an expression of intimacy (see Epstein and Karweit 1983; Rizzo 1989).

Kids who wanted to sit together did not always arrive at the cafeteria at the same time for various reasons. In these cases, saving seats for friends was an effective strategy that kids used to make sure that they could sit with their friends. Brandon (White) at Hamilton said, "Usually my friends take seats for me. When I go first, I take seats for them." At two schools, I observed various ways kids tried to save seats for their friends: spreading out their property on the table, stretching their legs on the bench, spreading their arms widely on the table, etc. When someone approached these seats and attempted to sit there, they would say, "This seat is taken," or "I'm saving these seats," and try to make others leave. As they saw their friends coming to the cafeteria, they stood up, waved and called out

The unplanned events in this study have to do with where the students choose to sit at the lunch table. I don't think she expected this to be important.

Many ethnographers include a detailed and vivid description of the setting and those they studied. By doing so, they follow a technique called "thick description." If you want to learn more about this idea, you should read Clifford Geertz's work.

their friends' names to make sure that their friends found them in the crowded and noisy cafeteria.

Kids often faced the problem that there was not enough space to sit next to their friends. Even when kids attempted to save seats for their friends, as other kids started to fill the table, they were not always able to save enough room for all their friends to sit. In these cases, kids managed to sit together by scooting over and making space, so that their friends could squeeze in next to them. Consequently, physical proximity among friends became intensified. Sitting next to each other in a small space, they touch each other's shoulders, arms, buttocks, and legs, which seems to generate an intimate basis for eating together as well as the food exchange that is about to begin.

Social Differences and Friendship Patterns

Through the processes that I have just described, all the kids are finally seated at the table and they start eating lunch. At Claremont, where kids were assigned tables according to their classroom, I took note of the seating patterns among thirty-one kids in Ms. Wood's class each time I visited the school. There was a great deal of variation of seating on different days, although some general patterns were found. These patterns were shaped by kids' differences in age, classroom, gender, and ethnicity. Figure 1 in the appendix shows seating arrangements on one typical day at Claremont. Kids who are circled showed strong sense of friendship to one another by walking together toward the table, saving seats, making space, and sitting closely next to each other.

. . .

In this next section, she breaks her analysis down by age and classroom, by gender, and by ethnicity. Since the pri mary emphasis in this study is on ethnicity, I only have included details about her findings on that topic.

Differentiation by ethnicity. Friendship grouping along ethnic lines, which is the focus of this study, was less salient among the fourth graders at the two schools compared to separation by age/grade, classroom, and gender. . . . Even at Hamilton where kids could freely associate with peers from other classrooms, kids rarely created a "Korean-only" table, despite the fact that there were enough Korean kids at the school to create one. While kids talked openly about "girls' tables" and "boys' tables," as well as tables differentiated by grade and classroom, racial or ethnic group labels were less verbalized during lunchtime.

Much has been written about how children separate themselves by ethnicity. This study of Korean children adds to the literature.

However, this does not mean that ethnic difference was not an important identity element in peer interactions among the fourth graders. A close look at the formation of seating reveals that Korean kids and other "minority" kids at both schools tended to generate separate groups.

. . .

At Hamilton, the separation between Koreans and non-Koreans in Ms. Gill's class sometimes became more visible than at Claremont, because kids did not have to sit with their classmates. Among boys, I sometimes saw five to seven Koreans eating at the same table, while three Latino boys were sitting next to each other, and also a White and a Black boy sitting together, each group at a different table. Among girls in Ms. Gill's class, Korean and Chinese girls were frequently seen eating together, while a pair of a Latina and a Black girl and another pair of two White girls (one Jewish and the other Australian) usually sat together, separating themselves from these Asian girls.

In general, perhaps because Koreans were the majority group at both schools, there were more interracial and interethnic mixing among non-Korean kids, which consequentially highlighted the separation between Korean and non-Korean kids. However, it should be emphasized that such patterns of ethnic separation were neither static nor strong. Kids from different ethnic backgrounds chose to sit together at the same table on different days. Although ethnographic studies of middle schools and high schools report that adolescents have a strong tendency to segregate themselves according to race and ethnicity (Institute for the Study of Social Change 1992; Olsen 1997), it appears that preadolescent kids are only starting to strengthen their ethnic identity in peer interaction.

In the following sections, I argue that food exchange during lunchtime provided the kids with opportunities to negotiate ethnic and gender boundaries and their meanings. Through the use of food that they bring from home, kids maintained and strengthened ethnic and gender boundaries that were to some extent already visible in seating patterns. Simultaneously, it will be shown that kids also used food to renegotiate, cross, and mute these boundaries.

FOOD IN KIDS' FOOD EXCHANGE: "DRY FOOD" AND "WET FOOD"

In kids' hidden social exchanges, there were two types of food that were frequently given and received: one was store-bought, mass-consumed food products and the other was food that kids brought from home, including Korean "ethnic" food.

Dry Food

The dry food included snacks like cookies (e.g., Chips-Ahoy), chocolates (e.g., M&Ms, Twix, Milky Way), gummies, chips (e.g., Doritos, Cheetos, Fritos), as well as "Lunchables," a prepackaged meal, usually containing meat, cheese, and crackers. Some kids

Here we see an interweaving of related literature and the author's own study.

This paragraph provides a segue for what is to come.

I have never thought of separating food into these types of categories. Have you?

described these fun sharable food items as "dry food." These are nonsticky food items that are easy to share as well as to play with. These fun dry foods were the central items that moved the flow of kid's hidden social exchange. Kids who brought these items caught much attention from other kids in the cafeteria, and often became the target of begging and coercing. As many have argued, commercial brand-named food has turned into "the lingua franca of the twenty-first century" (Thorne 2005) for kids who have become active consumers in global capitalism (Langer 2005; Zelizer 2002). Regardless of their racial and ethnic backgrounds, kids that I observed all had access to these dry foods and brought them to school from time to time for sharing and exchange.

It sounds like the term "dry food" comes from the kids and not from the author. Often ethnographers and other qualitative researchers use words used by participants in their write-ups.

Wet Food

On the contrary, many kids showed unease toward exchanging "wet food" that was made and packed at home. When I asked kids what kinds of food they liked to share at school, Chris (White) at Claremont said, "I only share dry food. I don't like to share sandwich and stuff 'cause that's gross." Erica (Australian) said, "I share chips. Only dry foods. I don't ask my friends to give me other kinds of stuff, because I don't really know what they are and I haven't eaten them before."

There were practical and symbolic differences between exchanging dry food and wet food. In contrast to dry food, which a receiver can pick up without a giver touching it, wet food is hard to share without the other person "contaminating" it with his or her mouth, hand, or with eating utensils (fork or chopsticks) with his or her saliva attached. In my observation, kids often showed disgust for food that another person had touched with his or her hands. Because a physical substance of a giver is attached, the exchange of these foods seemed to engender the notion of pollution in kids' minds, and threaten bodily and self-integrity. By preadolescent age, kids have developed the notion of *homo clausus* (Elias 1978), the sense of self that is encapsulated in one's body and is clearly cut off from others. Violation to this bodily boundary would arouse in them fear and disgust.

This is an interesting interpretation of why students exchange dry food but not wet food.

However, it should be emphasized that kids who regarded themselves as best friends did not seem to care much about sharing wet food and eating food that other person's eating utensils had touched. For instance, I often watched kids giving their food to their closest friends with chopsticks and forks that they had been using. Sometimes, even having wet food that another person's mouth had touched was acceptable among close friends. I frequently saw kids sipping a drink from the same can. It appears then that close friends shared strong bonds that allowed them to breach the bodily boundary that generally separates individuals. Indeed, the sharing of wet food marked and reinforced their affection for one another.

In general, Korean and White children were more likely to possess and share wet food with others than Latino and Black children, many of whom appeared to qualify for a reduced/free lunch. Several Latino and Black kids told me that their parents leave early in the morning for work and they do not have time to fix their lunch. On the contrary, White and Korean parents in general seemed to come from economically advantaged backgrounds and had time to prepare lunch for their kids. Several White and Korean kids told me that they did not like cafeteria food and they always asked their parents to fix lunch for them. Judy (Jewish) told me she could not eat in the cafeteria "because I'm Jewish, and we are supposed to eat only what's called Kosher. And the cafeteria food is not Kosher."

What was interesting was the fact that Korean kids frequently brought Korean food from home. In interviewing Anna's mother (Korean), she told me that Anna resisted eating cafeteria food and insisted on bringing Korean food and rice to school because they were her favorites. During lunchtime, some Korean kids often commented on their homemade food as "Korean" and showed their pride in it. For instance, at Claremont, Cindy (Korean girl) usually expressed joy and excitement when she opened her lunchbox:

> Cindy opened the lid of her thermal lunchbox. Inside, she found pieces of meat that looked like Burgogi (Korean BBQ meat) and cooked bean sprouts on top of steamed rice. She exclaimed with joy, "Oh, I love this!" When I asked what they were, Cindy replied, "I don't know what it's called, but it's Korean."

In sum, wet food strongly reflected and represented the self of kids who owned it. However, Korean kids, who frequently brought "Korean" food from home, had more of an advantage than other kids to attach ethnic meanings to their wet food and use it as a token of their ethnic identity. Non-Korean kids brought in sandwiches, spaghetti, pizza, and hotdogs from home, but these foods were never attached to ethnic meanings. Even what is usually considered "Mexican" food such as burritos, tacos, and taquitos became everyday food and had little ethnic meanings for the kids since these foods appeared frequently on the school lunch menu and everyone had access to them. Korean food, on the other hand, only belonged to Korean kids and they were usually exchanged and shared among Koreans, who would appreciate the value of the food. By consciously selecting the receiver of their wet food, Korean kids identified who is "Korean" and who is not. Equipped with a symbolic resource, Korean kids had more opportunities than other kids to build ethnic boundaries and identity in food exchange.

The author enhanced her observations and interviews with the children by talking to their parents. Here is an example of how she used information gleaned from talking to one of the mothers. Ethnographers often rely on multiple sources of data as they try to gain an understanding of the culture of a group.

Here the author begins to explore the idea of identity.

THREE FORMS OF HIDDEN SOCIAL EXCHANGE AND ETHNIC BOUNDARY NEGOTIATION

. . .

I have trouble with the interpretation offered by the author with respect to differences among the three different kinds of exchange. Do you think she could have explained the concept more clearly?

While gift-giving had a closed structure that only incorporated a few number of selected kids, sharing had an open structure that enabled any kids nearby to participate or at least to try participating. Thus, it had the power to expand the group boundary and form a larger group, although it generally marked weaker friendship bonds. Unlike gift-giving, which started with the giver's voluntary offer, sharing was initiated by the receiver sending cues that indicated his or her interest in the giver's food, such as "staring at food" or giving comments like "Oh, I love that" or "That looks so good." It was also triggered by the receiver's more straightforward asking, "Can I have some?"

What made sharing a ritual that incorporated a large number of kids was that whenever others asked the giver for his or her food, the giver was obliged to give. It was often the case that when one kid received food from the giver, others who witnessed this event approached the giver and started to beg one after another, "Can I have some too?" The giver, sometimes unwillingly, offered food to everyone and the sharing developed like a chain reaction until everyone got some share. What was striking was that the giver would give food to someone whom she or he did not even know. Kids said they did this because people came and begged for their food. They said they did not care about the immediate return.

However, kids became upset when the receiver refused to give some of his or her food in the future, breaking the norms that underlie sharing. Andrew (Black) said to me as follows: "One thing I don't like is that when someone asks me for food, people I never seen, people I don't know at school, I give it to them, but then, when I ask the same person to give me food, they act like they don't remember me, and don't give them to me." His friend, Tim (White) echoes: "Yeah, and if they don't give it to him, he just stops giving it to them forever. He remembers them."

Similar to what Katriel (1987) found in Israeli children's sharing ritual, the underlying norm of sharing at the schools that I observed was that both the giver and the receiver needed to control their self-interest and show respect toward one another. When asked, the giver usually kept control over the amount of food they gave, and the receiver politely accepted whatever amount they were offered. Sometimes, the giver would hand a bag of snacks to the receiver, but even then, the receiver would take only "a piece" from the bag in the first round of sharing. If she wanted more, she would ask the giver "Can I have some more?"

Because of the large number at school and their possession of various foods, Korean kids frequently engaged in sharing wet food while non-Korean kids did not attempt to participate in such sharing. When Korean kids shared miso soup and noodle soup (udon and ryanmen) from the same cup or bowl, the ethnic boundary became especially visible because of the physical proximity among these kids (see Figure 3 in the appendix):

> Toward the end of lunchtime, Jonathan (Korean) started to drink an instant noodle soup directly from the plastic bowl. On the side of the bowl, several Korean letters were printed. Donald, a Korean boy sitting facing Jonathan, pointed at the bowl and asked, "Can I have some?" Jonathan lifted his face from the bowl and nodded. Donald stood up and walked over besides Jonathan. Jonathan also stood up, and now two boys stood face to face. Jonathan handed out the cup to Donald, who received it and started drinking directly from the cup. After a few seconds, Donald removed his lip from the edge of the cup, and returned it to Jonathan. Jonathan started to drink some soup. Then, Michael, another Korean boy who sat next to Donald, stood up and approached the two boys. He stood next to Jonathan and asked him, "Can I have some too?" Lifting his face from the cup, Jonathan passed the cup to Michael keeping its position the way he got it back from Donald. Michael received the cup and stepped forward. Now three boys were standing in a triangle. After Michael removed his lip from the cup, he pointed at the place where his lip touched with his forefinger. Then, he passed it to Jonathan, also keeping the cup in the same position so that each of them would not drink from where others' mouth had touched. The cup was passed on to Jonathan, Donald, and Michael for several times. While three kids stood up beside the table in a triangle, two Latino boys and an African American boy were left at the table sitting next to each other. Joseph (Black) glimpsed these boys several times, but did not join the sharing.

Donald and Michael were not necessarily Jonathan's best friends, as the two usually did not sit next to him at the table. Still, Jonathan offered his soup when the two politely asked him for some share. This sharing ritual made visible an ethnic boundary that was not apparent from the seating pattern. The non-Korean boys were excluded from the sharing, when the two Korean boys approached Jonathan and turned their back on them standing in a triangle facing each other. The Korean boys built a kind of fort with their bodies that outsiders could not easily enter. Drinking soup from the same bowl further highlighted and strengthened their group solidarity. Simultaneously, the way they circulated the bowl in the same position and refrained from drinking from the same spot indicates their less intimate relationship. Still, in the eyes of other kids, this wet food sharing expressed a strong bond among Korean kids.

　. . .

Conclusion

If you have been reading this article carefully, you might have gotten bogged down in details. Here the author brings us back to the central purpose and finding of her study. Her statement here is cogent: children create peer cultures connected to food, a culture essentially hidden from adults.

Here, the author successfully brings into play the literature that she presented earlier.

Notice her choice of words here: children learn to "do ethnicity." This study makes an important contribution to our understanding of socialization in children.

Corsaro (1997) argues that preadolescence "is a time when children struggle to gain stable identities, and their peer cultures provide both a sense of autonomy from adults and an arena for dealing with uncertainties of an increasingly complex world" (p. 188). Looking closely at children's interaction during lunchtime, fourth graders in this study collaboratively created peer cultures that emanate from establishing and participating in food economy, which was hidden from adults' eyes and thus operated largely on its own. While previous studies have focused on game, play, and disputes as an arena for children's friendship and identity construction (see Corsaro 2003, Evaldesson 1993, 2003; Goodwin 1991 and 2001; Levinson 2005; Thorne 1993), this study has shown that food economy is another sphere where children organize peer relationships and negotiate various social identities. As Zelizer (2002) forcefully argues, children are "active economic agents" (p. 377) who possess an ability to create and participate in economic activity, including distribution. As shown by their use of dry/wet food as well as three forms of food exchange, children created an intricate system and culture of food economy, through which they negotiated various ties with others while marking, maintaining, strengthening, and muting social differences. In this process, ethnic boundaries and identities were marked and developed. The study shows that children do not become ethnic by passively "internalizing" ethnic culture in the adult world, as the traditional socialization model would assume; rather, children learn to do ethnicity by making use of cultural objects (food) in the exchange system that they collaboratively create.

Looking closely at *how* children negotiate ethnic boundaries in food exchange, I have shown "the fluid, situational, volitional, and dynamic character of ethnic identification" (Nagel 1994, 152), which preadolescent children become increasingly adept in negotiating. Children frequently marked and strengthened ethnic boundaries using dry and wet food in gift-giving, sharing, and trading, but as demonstrated in children's sharing of dry food, these boundaries were often muted to incorporate children from different ethnic backgrounds. Like Thorne's (1993) conceptualization of borderwork, which not only worked to emphasize gender separation but also created a space where girls and boys could come together and "cross" the gender divide, children's participation in food economy also created the dynamics of both marking and muting ethnic boundaries. When muting occurred, other identities based on classroom, age, and/or gender came to the fore instead.

This finding also suggests that children's construction of ethnic boundaries usually accompany a creation and negotiation of other boundaries related to gender, age, classroom, and social class.

Here, again, she refers to children "doing ethnicity." Do you think she should have explained the term?

Gift-giving and sharing among children from the same ethnic background normally occurred within the same gender group. This observation confirms the results gained from previous sociometric studies, which indicate that children's friendship is affected first by their gender and then by race/ethnicity (see Sagar et al., 1983). It appears that children learn to do ethnicity at the same time they position themselves in either of the gender category. Identities based on age and classroom were also implicated in children's construction of ethnic boundaries, since children usually engaged in food exchange with peers from the same grade and classroom. These identities were highlighted when children muted ethnic boundaries through sharing of dry food. Even social class differences, which were mostly obscured by school efforts, sometimes surfaced in the process of food exchange. White and Korean children in this study saw African American children who always "begged" for food as "poor." Here, children's understandings of the ethnic differences appear to accompany their emergent sense of social class positioning. These findings suggest that children's ethnic identity formation is a flexible ongoing process that should be understood in conjunction with the formation of other local categories such as gender, classroom, age, and social class. Different identities are activated at different moments and thus, this process is by no means linear or universal.

While children skillfully negotiated ethnic boundaries and identity in food exchange, this process also depended on larger social contexts which infused the dynamics of children's interaction. As the constructionist view suggests, ethnic identity is not simply a personal choice but, in fact, a product of a dialect between internal identification and external categorization; in other words, between agency and structure (Barth 1969, Brubaker, Loveman, and Stamatv 2004; Nagel 1994). This study has shown that school demography and social class inequality constrain which differences are marked and which ethnic group has the most cultural resources and opportunities to negotiate and construct ethnic boundaries and identity. Studying Black immigrant adolescents in New York City, Waters (1999) finds that the Black immigrant ratio of the students has a strong influence on whether Black immigrant adolescents would identify themselves as "Americans," "Ethnic," or "Immigrants." Similarly, Thorne (forthcoming) argues that "the availability of differences that may be successfully deployed in the naming of identities and the organization of groups" partly depends on "local demography and knowledge." At predominantly Korean schools in this study, Korean children were in a much better position to mark their difference and assert their ethnic identity in a positive way. Because of the large number of Korean children, various Korean foods moved the flow of food economy, making more opportunities for Korean children than for non-Koreans to engage in exchange and thereby to negotiate ethnic boundaries and create ethnic solidarity. Some Korean foods such as seaweed became a popular dry food among children at school, and therefore Korean children, who had access to these foods, were more active as givers. They could use these foods to enhance egalitarian friendship that cross ethnic boundaries, but in several occasions, they also used them in trading to practice power against African American children. Furthermore, Korean children's middle-class background enabled them to bring various kinds of homemade wet food that contributed to their active engagement in food exchange. Latino and African American children, many of whom qualified for free/reduced cafeteria lunches, had fewer cultural resources to construct boundaries in ethnic terms.

Breaking away from the traditional socialization model and demonstrating the situated, multilayered nature of children's ethnic identity which children cooperatively construct in their everyday life, this study suggests the need for more ethnographic case studies that take serious consideration of children's meaning-making process in interaction. As this study has shown, preadolescent children learn to negotiate ethnic boundaries and develop ethnic identity by participating in peer culture. Thus, the question of *how* and *when* children construct ethnic boundaries as well as *who* has the resources to do so should be answered by adopting a child-centered perspective and carefully observing children's peer interaction. Since children's ethnic identification differs according to contexts that they are in, as more case studies at schools of varied racial/ethnic composition accumulate, we will be in a better position to understand the dynamics of the ethnic boundary construction and its relevance to the construction of other social differences.

Finally, the findings gained from this study have some specific practical implications for schools and teachers to create culturally inclusive environments. Although studies of playgrounds have reported that boys are in a much stronger position to invade girls' activities and control more space on the playground (Grant 1984; Oswald et al. 1987; Thorne 1993), I observed that lunchtime provides much space for cross-gender and cross-ethnic friendship. Among the three forms of social exchange, sharing of dry food provided a tool for children to interact with one another harmoniously without any shameful teasing or power enforcement. Regardless of their social backgrounds, they engaged in sharing as "kids" in the same classroom, while maintaining and fostering the mutual respect and trust that underlies any sharing ritual.

The major barrier that prevented cross-gender and cross-ethnic sharing was kids' physical distance during lunchtime: namely, they

---

The author might be making a political and social statement here.

These suggestions relate her study to more practical aspects. Sometimes researchers get bogged down in theory and basic ideas; however, this author applies some of her findings to real situations.

usually chose to sit at different tables. On the other hand, whenever they had a chance to sit together, they started to practice sharing which often led to "food talk" and "food play," which further fostered emotional ties across gender and ethnic lines. How is it possible to encourage relaxed cross-ethnic and cross-gender interactions during lunchtime? Perhaps teachers can assign the table to children and intentionally make mixed-gender and mixed-ethnic tables in cafeteria. Also, studies suggest that an adult presence can ameliorate gender divides (Adler and Adler 1998; Moore 2001; Thorne 1993). I also found that my presence at the table encouraged boys and girls to sit together and engage in sharing. If classroom teachers sit and eat with children even once in a while, they can play an important role in fostering cross-gender and cross-ethnic friendship by naturally creating mixed-gender and mixed-ethnic tables. They can also caution against some practices that may cause negative results in peer relationships: teasing food, excessive begging, unfair trading, and so forth. In the United States, eating with teachers is given to children as a "privilege" or a reward for their good behavior. In my fieldwork, children very much appreciated this privilege and looked forward to eating lunch with their teachers. Teachers can perhaps find a way to organize their busy schedules, and sit and eat with the whole class once in a while. Lunchtime is a rich opportunity not only for children to maintain and cultivate friendships with their classmates, but also for the teachers to deepen their understanding about children and their worlds which are full of surprising creativity.

Source: Nukaga, M. (2008). The underlife of kids' school lunchtime: Negotiating ethnic boundaries and identity in food exchange. *Journal of Contemporary Ethnography, 37*(3), 342–380. Reprinted with permission of SAGE Publications.

Summary and Review

One reason I selected this article is that it is about kids in school. Although it does not specifically deal with kids in classes, it does occur in school settings. I want you to see how researchers have to deal with issues related to doing research in schools. It was only after I had selected and read the article that I learned the author was a graduate student, which places it very close to your own level of experience. It is a bonus that you begin reading a journal article written by a fairly new researcher. Finally, I wanted you to start by reading an article from the *Journal of Contemporary Ethnography.* As its name suggests, the articles published in it are related to ethnography.

Nukaga immediately lets you know her position with regard to race and ethnicity. She mentions the constructionist view that identity varies across space and changes over time. Have you ever heard of that view? Does it fit with your own personal view? Do you think she presents sufficient evidence that this view can be supported? Is it the only viewpoint? She puts forth the reason she wants to do this study. She argues that people have not studied children of this age as people, but rather tend to see children as "passive recipients of adult culture." She immediately captures our attention by making these statements in her introduction. Remember, the purpose of the introduction is to draw the reader into the study, convincing the reader of the study's value.

I am somewhat puzzled why she chose to tell you her findings in the second paragraph of her research. I prefer to read about the study before I read what was found. In a way, this second paragraph is like the opening remarks made by a lawyer in a court trial. "The evidence will show that . . .," and so forth. This is a stylistic issue. At what point do you think an author should tell the reader of findings and what they mean? She chose to do it right at the beginning. Perhaps that is a vehicle for making the reader want to read more.

I believe you found her review of literature especially enlightening. I shortened the review and omitted references and the appendix due to space limitations, but you will be able to access many of her references quite easily.

Many of us work with children each day. Even though our focus is on teaching and learning, it is critical for us to gain insight into how children perceive themselves and negotiate their own identities as we try to understand the whole child. I doubt that many of us face the question of how children "do and learn" race and ethnicity in everyday social interaction. Nukaga makes an argument for doing ethnographic research rather than relying on sociometric studies. She also addresses what she refers to as a new model of the construction of ethnic identity, and argues that the ethnographic studies that have been conducted have concentrated on gender identity. Even though you may not be familiar with the literature she cites, she puts forth her argument extremely well. You would do well to use her literature review as an example of how to do one. By now, you understand that Nukaga belongs to the same racial group as the Koreans she studies, but does not belong to the same ethnic group.

She provides a somewhat shorter review on the topic of gift-giving. Nukaga's strategy of weaving the results of her own study into the narrative of the literature review is somewhat off-putting to me. If we think of doing a qualitative study in a dynamic fashion, though, we can imagine she wrote the text of this article after she completed the study and not before. It seems clear that the writer has a good understanding of the related research. She writes about it as though it is not new to her.

You will do well to examine the section *Setting and Method* to learn the details of how she did the study. She follows the usual practice of adopting pseudonyms for the two schools in which her study was done, but provides sufficient detail about their location and racial composition. I am not familiar with the Los Angeles school system and so do not know if the actual schools could be identified. To what extent this might compromise the study is unknown. She provides details about the characteristics of the student body. As I mentioned at the outset, ethnography that follows a fairly traditional style would normally include this kind of information. Some might say that ethnography includes this information to make it more "scientific" or to fit the expectations of a quantitative study. Some like the details, and others think they are not important. It is clear from the quote given by one principal that the school is very protective of its ethnographic information.

She provides details about her visits to the two schools. She used e-mail to communicate with the school. She says she ate and played with the students. I do not know her age, but I presume she is fairly young. In addition to observation and extensive fieldnotes, she conducted some interviews and focus groups. I am surprised she does not mention whether or how she obtained parental permission to study the students. She addresses potential issues regarding power between adult and student, and seemed to pass herself off as a friend rather than as an authority figure. Her age and her own ethnicity (Japanese), which is similar to the students' (Korean), obviously made this easier. She acknowledges that being female sometimes presented problems with her access to boys. The details she provides help the reader to get a clear picture of how her study was done.

This study provides an example of an inductive method. An inductive study moves from the particular to the general, unlike experimental research studies that begin with a general idea (or hypothesis) and then gather data to test the hypothesis. Often, when you do an ethnographic study, you really don't know what you are looking for. Nukaga knew she wanted to study this age group and this ethnic group. Being torn between information she learned and her own ethical standards, she brings up an issue regarding the illegality of food exchange in one of the schools. She readily acknowledges the position she took. Her recognition that teachers don't really know what is going on at lunch might be correct. Teachers relish this all-too-short break from the kids and an opportunity to engage in adult conversation—but look at how much Nukaga learned during this time. Perhaps the teachers themselves could gain similar information about the children.

Almost nothing is said about how she analyzed her data. For instance, I don't know what she means by "retroduction." And what a surprise: she now moves into what she calls a "grounded theory approach," using open coding of fieldnotes. I believe she chose to use a grounded theory approach because she was trying to make her study more "acceptable" to those who were overseeing it. I give some examples of grounded theory approaches in a later chapter. Remember, an ethnographic approach does not offer a clear pathway for data analysis. She collected an enormous amount of data, according to her own account, yet she tells us almost nothing about the analysis. What she did with interview data, focus group data, and other information from adults is left unstated.

Much of this article is taken up with detailed descriptions. For instance, she discusses seating patterns, and, when appropriate, she includes references that support her own position or interpretation of the meaning of what she found. For example, she talks about physical proximity as a marker of friendship.

You may recall that a classic ethnography is supposed to provide a rich and detailed description of the setting. Nukaga does this and enhances her description with the seating arrangement figures provided at the end of the article.

Were you surprised about the differences she observed between sharing what she calls "dry food" and "wet food"? I don't think I ever really thought about it. Apparently the kids she studied were reluctant to share food they brought from home. Were they embarrassed, or did they value it too much? She argues they were concerned about touching it, although there were exceptions. For instance, best friends could share wet food. Her interpretation appears to come from what the kids said.

It is in the section about hidden forms of social exchange that Nukaga makes her best case. She suggests that the different forms relate to marking, strengthening, or muting ethnic boundaries and their relationship to friendship. These ideas may be new to you unless you have studied some of the sociological issues and interpretations. She relates Goffman's work, demonstrating her knowledge of the related research.

The paper concludes with a fairly lengthy discussion of the meaning and interpretation of the findings. The writer weaves the relevant literature together with her own data to support her results.

If you return to the four questions I posed at the beginning of this chapter, you can see the extent to which this article was successful. In my opinion, you can answer yes to each of these questions.

- Does it provide new information and insights related to the topic?

- Is it engaging and written in a clear manner?

- Does it illustrate aspects of the Korean sub-culture that you expect to find in an ethnography?

- Do the positive aspects of the article outweigh the potential drawbacks?

I hope you enjoyed reading the article about Korean students and food exchange. The next article is also about students, but this time is about high school girls from a small town where the researcher–author grew up.

━━━━━━━━━━━━━━━━

Article 1.2. Power and Pleasure in Ethnographic Home-Work: Producing a Recognizable Ethics (2008)

Alecia Jackson

My Expectations

Before I read an article, I find it helpful to connect my own learning with what I am about to read. I ask myself a series of questions based on my own knowledge. For instance, I recognize that Jackson's 2008 study will probably fit into a category of being a postmodern or post-structural ethnography rather than a traditional ethnography. I think some initial clues are the style in which she writes and the personal tone of the writing. As such, I will look for issues associated with that type of ethnography. Does she address power? If so, how does she do so? In what ways does she deal with reflexivity?

I will also look for other important areas. Does she provide a clear explanation of the theory on which her study is based? Michel Foucault is an important French philosopher who wrote about power and knowledge. When I finish reading the section on Foucault in this article I hope I will understand his theories better. Does she write in an engaging manner to draw me in and help me to see what she sees? Does she acknowledge my own experiences—what I see? Are her conclusions justified or supported with what she writes? Do I connect with this study? What can I take away from the study that will be useful to me in my own work? What techniques or strategies do I find engaging? What parts do I want to change? Overall, how successful is she at accomplishing her goals?

At first glance, it appears that Jackson's ethnography will be a study of high school girls in a small town. As you read the study, however, you will discover that it is really about her role and how she negotiates and comes to understand what it means to be an ethnographer in a personal setting. In fact, the article takes a different path from what you might expect. It fits quite well into a post-structural model in that she relies on Foucault's philosophical contributions.

In her study, which was conducted in the high school she herself attended, Jackson turns the idea of looking at diverse cultures on its head. She does not want to place herself in a position of power, yet she struggles at times with trying to move away from the power role. I will talk about these issues in my comments. In this article, Jackson does a good job of explaining some of the philosophical underpinnings of Foucault's philosophy.

I have to admit I'm not sure I know what the title means. I am intrigued with the terms "power" and "pleasure" in it, though. I know the two terms separately, but when joined I am not sure what they mean. Does the author mean that power can be pleasurable, or that pleasure leads to power? What is ethnographic "home-work"? That is an unusual spelling. By hyphenating the two parts of the word is she implying that we should focus on both terms? Finally, I see the phrase "recognizable ethics." Again, I am somewhat stumped. I know I need to continue reading. So, in this study I find that the title is challenging. If the title is so complex that I am discouraged, I will not read further. If the title simply challenges me, I will read on.

This very brief abstract is quite a bit easier to understand than was the title. While I might not actually remember quite what Foucault says, I know he is a postmodern writer and philosopher. So now I see that the power–pleasure concept mentioned in the title comes from Foucault. I need to try to refresh my mind about some details of Foucault, but for now I just make a note to do it later. I am drawn in to the article by the second sentence in the abstract. "Through two data stories, the author recounts her own pleasurable acts while carrying out an ethnographic study in her hometown high school." This is right up my alley: a study in one's own school that brought pleasure. I am not sure that I ever thought that doing research could bring pleasure. And now I have a glimmer of an idea about what she means by "home-work." Perhaps it means doing work in one's own home setting. The last part of the abstract is another important clue to the purpose of her study: she is going to explore the ethics of the experience of the self. This makes me think about reflexivity.

In the introduction, Jackson provides a brief explanation about her study. She immediately explains her connection to the place she studied—her home town. She quickly explains and acknowledges her own subjectivity. She provides an explanation of the term "home-work": it is ethnographic work at home. I wonder if that is a little too cute. She suggests that the pleasure of power in qualitative research is

ABSTRACT

The author uses Michel Foucault's power/knowledge/pleasure combination to analyze the production of ethical practices in qualitative research. Through two data stories, the author recounts her own pleasurable acts while carrying out an ethnographic study in her hometown high school. The pleasures of conducting such home-work are analyzed to point out the ethics of constituting the experience of the self in qualitative research.

INTRODUCTION

I was called home, after a 16-year absence, to conduct qualitative research. I could loosely use the words, "I returned home" or "I chose to study" to introduce this work. But in reality, home seduced me and produced my desire to see what life was like there, in the school system, 16 years later. I was called home to conduct a post-structural ethnography of small-town schooling, yet I too am a product of the same cultural structures and institutions that I sought to study. I was persuaded by my own, already-inscribed subjectivity to critically examine the culture of schooling in my hometown of Garner.

In this article, I describe power and pleasure in conducting such ethnographic work at home, or home-work. I use power and pleasure as it has been recently reinvented in post-structuralism through the works of Michel Foucault. Foucault's concept of power has been aptly utilized in post-structural qualitative research in recent years (e.g., see Collins, 2000; Ferguson, 2001; Finders, 1997; Lesko, 2000; Toll and Crumpler, 2004; Vadeboncoeur, 2005). Power as producing pleasure is noticeably absent in qualitative inquiry, though Erica McWilliam's studies of the teaching profession (1999, 2004) and of women's academic work (2000) have explored "proper pleasure" and desire as an effect of disciplinary power.

To argue for more attention to pleasure as an ethical, productive practice in qualitative research, and to offer a framework for critiquing pleasurable moments in such work, I first describe the methodology I used to do home-work. Next, I provide an overview of Foucault's power and pleasure and explain how he linked the two concepts to his idea of an ethical subject. I then move into two data stories to elucidate my practices of Foucault's ethics through the "use of pleasure" in my home-work at Garner. I use Foucault's power/knowledge/pleasure combination to make meaning of the ethics of my subjectivity as I negotiated the field.

lacking. Furthermore, she suggests that pursuing pleasure in doing research should be seen as an ethical practice. It is interesting that she puts forth her viewpoint and takes a stand here. All too often researchers place themselves in a position of being objective and neutral. However, those ethnographers who adopt a postmodern or post-structural stance would probably agree with Jackson's taking a position, even if they have not actually thought of the position she takes. In the third paragraph, she briefly outlines the remainder of the article. Again, using this style helps you as a reader know what is to come and to set a framework.

This first paragraph works very well as a lure, or hook—something to draw the reader in. It is direct and engaging and immediate. Although I might be intimidated by what is to follow, for now I am willing to continue reading.

Now I know you probably have a tendency to avoid the literature reviews. Perhaps you just want to get on with the stories. For Jackson, though, the theory of power and pleasure that is discussed in the literature is the fulcrum on which her research rests. You should really forge ahead and read about Foucault. I hope that somewhere along the way you have read some of his work or at least heard his name. If you want to read more, Jackson's references include seven works by Foucault.

Let's try to make sense of Jackson's explanation of Foucault. Put yourself in the situation of entering a high school to study

METHODOLOGY

There is a sense of nostalgia when thinking of small-town schools in the United States. Images of safety, family, autonomy, and community emerge when picturing small schools. According to some research, small schools have "better" everything: attendance, test scores, relationships, curriculum, student achievement, teacher satisfaction, safety, democratic and equitable structures, graduation rates, and college-going rates (e.g., see Ayers et al., 2000; Darling-Hammond et al., 2002; Meier, 2002, 2003; Toch, 2003; Wasley and Lear, 2001).

In the years leading up to my ethnographic home-work, I had been captivated by the rhetorical allure of "less is more" when it comes to small schools. As a product of a small school, I questioned the appeal of such places and desired to engage in a post-structural critique of the culture of my own small-town schooling. I was uninterested in the "truth" of the romanticization and idealization of small schools and drawn to how those ideals get constructed, deployed, and circulated in discourse in specific places. In particular, I was interested in how community members who are invested in the schools produce their vision of schooling through their material, political, and cultural practices.

To conduct my home-work of small-town schooling, I engaged in one year of fieldwork in which I used the following ethnographic methods: I interviewed former classmates and community members, I reviewed historical documents of the school system, and I functioned as a participant–observer at Garner High, shadowing seniors who had attended the school system since kindergarten. These fieldwork experiences produced multiple subject positions for me as a researcher, a southern woman, a product of the small-school system, a PhD student, and a feminist. As I talked with former teachers and classmates and spent time with children of former teachers, I felt my own subjectivity slipping and protesting in response to an intricate network of cultural practices and power relations. These relations and practices intersected and produced competing ways of constructing myself (and of my being constructed) in particular, contextualized situations. The ongoing construction of my researcher subjectivity, then, became a heavy task of taking up certain subject positions that were available at the time, haunted by excesses of my other more recent selves. It became obvious to me that "identity is not a fixed "thing," it is negotiated, open, shifting, ambiguous—the result of culturally available meanings and the open-ended, power-laden enactments of those meanings" (Kondo, 1990: 24). Therefore, my subjectivity remained neither stable nor coherent during my fieldwork. Rather the culture. You are an adult, so you have more status than the students have. Jackson's situation is somewhat different from the typical adult in a high school, though. This was *her* high school, in *her* hometown. People might remember her. Some of her family members might be in the school. She certainly seems to have an entrée into the system. If you or I were to try to study this same small town, we would probably be viewed quite differently by the community. I know my accent would be different from the accents in that town, for instance. How would my accent affect my ability to be welcomed into the school? Jackson suggests that Foucault's position vis-à-vis a power relationship is actually unstable and can shift because it is characterized by freedom, but this explanation works only if the individuals in the relationship are free.

I have chosen to place these comments here, but I want you to look ahead at all the headings before you read further. Writers use headings to structure their writing. If you read the headings, you should be able to understand the structure imposed by the author. In writing ethnographies, there are not agreed upon, or required, headings. The author is free to organize the written work in any manner. Look at what Jackson decided to include:

- Introduction (very brief, only three paragraphs in length)

than being a "fixed point of departure or arrival" (de Lauretis, 1984, p. 159) to which I could safely return, my subjectivity in the field emerged as an excessive *effect* of the interrelationships among social practices, power relations, and my specific experiences as a researcher.

This post-structural view of the self has been theorized in field-work at home. Hoodfar (1994) likens the construction of the self in fieldwork at home to a "schizophrenic experience," and Caputo (2000) referred to her ethnographic identity at home as always partial in response to the shifting and oftentimes stressful instability of the ground. Caputo (2000: 28) aptly refers to the field at home as a "swirl of sites" and recounts the difficulty of sustaining her positionality while being at once "at home" and "away." Hastrup (1987: 105) claims the field is "everywhere"—a "third culture" of sorts— and thus the ethnographer "lives and works in the third person." Hastrup's "third person" is not an omniscient observer who is detached and objectively knows everything, but one who is the combined effect of memory, history, place, and culture. It is one who is a contradictory, splintered self—a rupturing and hybridization of meaning systems, consciousness, and identity (Chaudhry, 1997).

A turn toward home, the present, and the familiar in Western social anthropology has produced a methodological awareness that is unique to studying home, including greater personal insight and keener reflexivity (Amit-Talai, 1994; Caputo, 2000; Hastrup, 1987; Jackson, 1987; Strathern, 1987). Yet problematic for the self in studying home is realizing the limits of memory, negotiating the insider/outsider binary, and experiencing the stress and anxiety of constant self-monitoring (Caputo, 2000; Chaudhry, 1997; Coffey, 1999; Hastrup, 1987, 1992; Jackson, 1987; Kondo, 1990; Stack, 1996; Strathern, 1987; Visweswaran, 1994). While I certainly experienced all of these problems of subjectivity while conducting home-work, I am attempting to theorize them differently by reconceptualizing the ethnographic self as an ethical construct produced by power and pleasure.

In order to interrogate and disrupt certainties about the self in home-work—even those certainties regarding fractured subjectivities— I attend to issues of power and pleasure in novel ways. I remember preparing myself for fieldwork at home by anticipating that I would in many ways become a split subject and would encounter many moments of collapsed subjectivity while at home. Yet as I experienced my self in the field, I came to understand that my split subjectivity, while in constant tension, was something that I looked forward to, that offered pleasant insights, and that actually delighted me in surprising ways. Interrogating power in this way offered a different sort of negotiation of the self that produced

- Methodology (several pages long)
- Theories of Power and Pleasure (I guess this will explain what Foucault meant and provide some kind of a literature review.)
- Data Story 1 (Now I remember that she said she was going to include two data stories. This first one takes place in the teachers' lounge. That should be fun.)
- Data Story 2 (This is intriguing, since it is about pleasure.)
- Conclusion (We return to recognizable ethics. Again, I am not sure what this will be about.)

Why do you think she chooses to place the word truth in quotation marks? Could it be because she does not believe that there is a single truth? If so, that is the position taken by Foucault.

Here she reveals so much about herself, displaying the self-reflexivity that is seen in post-structural writing.

If you take some time to think about what she says here, you will see her struggling with issues of role, power, and subjectivity. Do you think she will resolve the issues in this article? Do you think it is important to acknowledge them? I do.

I suspect she was drawn to look at the research she writes

pleasures while in the field. This negotiation of the self is unlike other theories of subjectivity in ethnography at home. That is, the work cited above recounts the anxieties and difficulties of subjectivity; of course, my own experiences of my self were often rife with tumult. However, I contend that constructs of a hybrid self may enable possibilities for transformation that produce certain freedoms in the research process. To reconceptualize the self in homework is to interpret ethical practices as not only constrained and disciplined, but also engendering freedom and agency. Furthermore, an ethical construction of the ethnographic self can produce certain pleasures that enable a particular type of knowing in the research process. I turn to Foucault's theories of power and pleasure, and their connection to the ethical construction of the self, to explicate how researchers might confront the plays of power in the making of their ethnographic selves.

THEORIES OF POWER AND PLEASURE

In a 1976 lecture, Foucault (1980) critiqued conventional notions of power by arguing that a structural, repressive view of power is limited and limiting because it ignores the fluid and relational characteristics of power and the subtle ways in which power operates. Foucault was interested in thinking about power as more than simply prohibitive or repressive and explained that power becomes possible through the mutability of unequal and unstable local relations. To put it simply, there is a power relationship between two people when one is attempting to "control the conduct of the other" (Foucault, 1994a: 292). Foucault believed that power relations are unstable and can shift within conflict because they are characterized by freedom. Foucault (1994a: 292) believed

> power relations are possible only insofar as the subjects are free. If one were completely at the other's disposal and became his thing, an object on which he could wreak boundless and limitless violence, there wouldn't be any relations of power. Thus, in order for power relations to come into play, there must be at least a certain degree of freedom on both sides.

Plays of power, then, occur among free subjects who are caught up in complex webs of control and conflict. Power relations exist only when the field of possibilities is open and people may react to each other in various ways. Furthermore, power relations are endowed "with processes which are more or less adjusted to the about after she realized her own struggle. This is an example of how a researcher weaves her own story and the larger body of research around a relevant topic.

Do you like this term she introduces—"fractured subjectivities"? Jackson uses the terms "fractured subjectivity," "collapsed subjectivity," and "split subjectivity." What do you think these terms mean? Initially, I thought she saw this as a problem, but here she says that she takes pleasure in her split subjectivity.

I particularly like the lead-in to the literature review on Foucault. It places the review as a direct part of her research rather than as a requirement that just needs to be done and never thought about again. She clearly is thinking about power and pleasure.

This section is somewhat technical, but Jackson does an excellent job of providing an explanation to some complex material. If you have time, you should read it.

Jackson provides a nice connection between the literature review and her research. This is a sign of a review that is "connected" and not just "stuck" in an article. Try to create a similar segue in your own writing.

situation" (Foucault, 2000: 224). That is, power relations are specific and local to subjects who are in mutual relations with one another. Power, then, "is everywhere; not because it embraces everything, but because it comes from everywhere"; it is a repetitious and self-producing effect of mobile, strategical practices and relations within particular social networks (Foucault, 1978: 93). As a network of relations, power is "constantly in tension, in activity," and power relations are made of various points of instability that *produce* multiple sites and modes of activity, including both compliance and resistance (Foucault, 1977: 26).

Because Foucault thought that power is embedded in relationships rather than existing merely as a possession that is wielded over others, his work focused on studying the functions and effects of power, not its origin. Foucault investigated *the strategical and productive effects of power as it circulates through the practices of people in their daily lives.* To explain productive power, Foucault said, "What makes power hold good, what makes it accepted, is simply the fact that it doesn't only weigh on us as a force that says no, but that it traverses and produces things, it induces *pleasure*" (1980: 119, emphasis added).

Productive power that "induces pleasure" is of particular use to me as I think about my undertaking of home-work in Garner. In this analysis, I am interested in examining those pleasurable moments as a product of power within the available discourses of small-town schooling in Garner. It is important to distinguish the French *jouissance* from *plaisir,* the form that Foucault used in his work on pleasure. *Jouissance* often refers to sensual pleasures, or to signal an intensity of pleasure, while *plaisir* translates into joy, delight, enjoyment, or fun. *Plaisir* can also be conjugated to indicate the phrase "to please someone," as in being a people-pleaser, which is of most relevance to my work here. Barthes (1975) used *jouissance* and *plaisir* in a similar vein, which is also helpful in my thinking about forms of pleasure. Barthes's (1975: 14) *plaisir* signifies "comfort" and "fulfillment." To think of pleasure this way—as joy, contentment, or comfort produced by power and organized through discourse—is to situate pleasure within Foucault's work on sexuality, particularly in his work *The Use of Pleasure.*

Similar to his analysis of power, Foucault's (1985) interest was not in the origins, essential nature, or meanings of pleasure but in "the ontology of force that linked together acts, pleasures, and desires" (1985: 43). That is, Foucault investigated the dynamic interplay of rules and conditions that enabled individuals (i.e., the ancient Greeks) to manage and conduct their own acts in order to achieve the "proper use of pleasure" (1985: 63). Freedom and power produce "proper pleasure" through the use of moderation; that is, to form oneself as a free, ethical subject is to "rule" pleasure, bring pleasure "under authority," and "dominate" pleasure within the conditions of knowledge that govern acts and desires (1985: 86). Such pleasure emphasizes reason over desire; pleasure's use must be "adaptable to the needs, times and circumstances" of the situation (1985: 87). In other words, people use their knowledge of what they "ought" to do to guide their acts. Only the knowledgeable, only the "self-controlled have power" to moderate themselves, subduing their desires and regulating their behavior (1985: 87). "Stylized" freedom is produced by this power/knowledge; this ability to govern, rule, and control one's self is in response to a particular condition. The power/knowledge/ freedom combination, then, produces the correct or acceptable feelings of proper pleasure, of harmony, of contentment within contextualized situations.

Power-induced pleasure came to be recognizable through the discourses that regulated and elaborated the cultural practices and relations during my fieldwork, or home-work, in Garner. It is now that I turn to stories from the field to consider how I came to shape myself as a desiring researcher and a "subject of ethical conduct" (Foucault, 1985: 251), or how I governed my own behavior as I was taught to do as a young girl.

DATA STORY ONE: THE/MY TEACHERS' LOUNGE

"Oh, we're going to have a PhD!" My former ninth grade typing teacher, Mrs. Anderson, clapped in approval. She sat across from me in the teachers' lounge, my former ninth-grade English teacher sat to my right, and my former eleventh- and twelfth-grade English teacher, Mrs. Hill, was on my left. Mrs. Hill was also my "informant" for the time that I would spend at my former high school, Garner High, as part of an ethnographic study I was conducting on small-town schooling. The teachers sipped coffee at 7:15 A.M. before their school day began; I abstained, not needing any extra stimulant on my first day of fieldwork. They wanted to know what I had been doing since my 1986 graduation. As I glossed over the highlights, I repeatedly glanced at a half-sheet of paper on the table in front of Mrs. Hill, a list I knew contained the names of several senior girls she recommended that I observe for my ethnography—girls who had been students in this small school system since kindergarten and who would be willing to share their experiences of small-town schooling with me (I was particularly interested in girls' perspectives because of my own history). We adults reminisced, my former teachers

If you have given yourself the challenge of reading Jackson's explanation of power and pleasure, then you are ready to read her stories. It is here that you learn that Foucault spoke of the subject of ethical conduct; this is not Jackson's construct.

In the first story, you will find yourself in just the kind of setting that is so attractive to ethnographers. Here, Jackson presents a detailed description of the teachers' lounge. While she doesn't specifically say it, you should be able to surmise that the story is probably an amalgam of several stories and events that Jackson weaves together to make key points. After you take some time to read the story, try to see what points she makes. Although she is introduced by her former teacher as a PhD, this research is part of her dissertation work leading to her degree. Imagine all that this must mean in the context of this small town— what it means both to the staff and students. She refers to Mrs. Hill as her informant, but she does not provide an explanation of what she means by that term. Many ethnographers use the term "informant". In fact, qualitative researchers tend to use terms such as "respondent," "informant," or "co-researcher" when they refer to those from whom they gather data. They specifically avoid the term "sample," because that is often associated with quantitative research studies, After you have read the story, come back and think about these questions: Were you surprised when you finished the first story? Did you think you were going to learn about schooling in a small town? Did you anticipate Jackson's interpretation of what happened to her and her anticipated way of doing business? Why do you think she wrote this story?

Here Jackson writes in an engaging manner, drawing you immediately into the setting.

It might be helpful to know what year she did this fieldwork. How much time had gone by? She weaves information into the story in a seamless manner.

Although Jackson might want to keep identities hidden, it would be a simple matter to determine her hometown and the name and identity of the school and teachers. Other researchers have commented on problems of keeping things anonymous. Since Jackson reveals that this indeed is her high school, it is not possible to maintain anonymity. In this research, it does not appear to be an issue, but it could be in other studies.

Do you agree that Jackson should have selected Abbey as a participant in the study? It is difficult to turn your mind around alternative ways of doing things. In this case, there are so many connections

attempting to specifically place me by asking, "Now, who else was in your class?" and "What teachers did you have?" My responses were met with exclamations of "Oh yes! I remember that!" or "Mrs. Booker is still here! You'll have to stop by her room and say hello!" The three teachers who welcomed me back that first day had begun their teaching careers at Garner as many as 28 years before. One had missed teaching my own mother by just a few years, each of them had taught my younger sister, and the next year they would begin teaching the children of several of my high school classmates.

Just after the 7:30 A.M. bell rang, Mrs. Hill and I emerged from the teachers' lounge. I followed her down the hallway to her classroom; walking side by side was impossible given the congestion of students who were going to their lockers and socializing with their friends. Mrs. Hill stopped behind one girl who had her back to us, and Mrs. Hill stroked the girl's long, naturally curly dark hair. "She's mine," Mrs. Hill said to me, over her shoulder. "She's one you're going to follow." The girl turned around, her brown eyes bright, and flashed a smile at us.

"Is that Abbey?" I asked, as I continued to trail behind Mrs. Hill. She nodded yes. Mrs. Hill was pregnant with Abbey when I was a sophomore, and I was astonished that her now 18-year-old daughter would be one of the many participants in my study.

We took a left down an adjoining hallway, and Mrs. Hill's room was the first door on the left. This was the "Humanities" wing: four English classrooms, four History classrooms, one Spanish and one French classroom, and the Art Studio. Mrs. Hill unlocked the door to her room, and we walked in. Though the high school was a new building and therefore hers was a different physical room from the one I occupied as her student for two years, the inside was uncannily similar to its late 1980s look that I remembered: the same Shakespeare posters, the podium that all of her students sign as seniors (yes, I found my name), the desks arranged in five rows of five. Even the notes written on the dry-erase board rang familiar. The seniors were reading *The Hollow Hills,* just as my class had 16 years before.

Mrs. Hill crossed the front of the room to her desk, which was situated in the back right corner. We sat at her desk, and she handed me the list I had been coveting since my arrival a half-hour earlier. She explained that when she received the e-mail from Regina about my project, she knew immediately who would "be perfect" for me to shadow. "I tried to come up with a wide variety of girls," Mrs. Hill told me. She took me through the list while students were trickling into her classroom. I would rather have had the conversation in private, but she did not seem concerned. She said,

Destiny is in first period, my lowest level class. She used to be on the college track, but she dropped down. She's perfectly capable of doing college between teachers, participants, and the researcher that it is clear that "fractured subjectivity" might become an issue. What is important is that Jackson acknowledges and makes the issue explicit. Later, she actually turns it into a positive aspect of doing the study.

Including considerable detail is typical of ethnographic studies. Clifford Geertz talks about "thick description," and I think this qualifies. His work is considered seminal in the field.

Do you think she was surprised or comforted that so much had remained the same?

Jackson intersperses a private thought here, but doesn't really address how she could have changed the situation. Do you think she should have said something to Mrs. Hill about the lack of privacy? Do you think she behaves in a professional way here?

Do you wonder how Jackson obtained this long quote? She has not told us that she is taping her interviews. Do you think she used "artistic license"?

What about issues of informed consent? Do you think the girls really had a "choice" whether to participate?

This is a very significant observation on Jackson's part. Do you think her dual role compromised the data she was able to get? Or, alternatively, did it facilitate her entry and access to the school?

work; she's just lazy. Marin is in my Advanced Placement class. She's Mrs. Cleary's daughter and is just brilliant. One of the best writers I have. Yesterday when I announced to my classes that you would be here today, Marin was the first to volunteer. Then in third period is my Abbey, who wants to be an aerospace engineer, whatever that is. She built a model of the Endeavor space shuttle using a computer program. I don't know where she gets it! Alexis is in fifth period, college prep. She's really active in the band as captain of the color guard. Quenisha is in that class too. She is just the nicest young lady, always has a smile on her face. I taught her daddy. And in my last class is Justice. She's a new mother. She told me, "Mrs. Hill, it was my first time. I was a virgin." And she got pregnant.

Mrs. Hill beamed. She had carefully selected the participants for my study based on the criteria I had provided in the proposal I sent to Regina, who forwarded them to Mrs. Hill. Mrs. Hill understood that I wanted to study small-town schooling and that I was especially interested in girls' perspectives on their schooling. These girls should be seniors in high school, should have attended Garner City Schools since kindergarten, and that among the girls there should be diversity in race, class, academic ability, and extracurricular interests and activities. The day before, Mrs. Hill had spoken to each girl whom she thought would be suitable to ensure their participation and to prepare them for my arrival. She described, in broad strokes, this group of six senior girls: four White, two Black; college- or vocational-bound; singers, dancers, writers, musicians, actresses, athletes, tutors, volunteers, class officers, mathematicians, Christians; a teenage mother. All would represent Garner well, and all were social enough to "keep me busy," Mrs. Hill told me.

In designing my research, I had hardly expected to show up on the first day of fieldwork with my participants selected, somewhat informed, and ready for me to begin shadowing them. In my research design, I had planned to spend a couple of days in Mrs. Hill's room observing all of her senior classes so that I could watch everyone and talk to her about certain seniors, especially girls, who might offer unique perspectives on small-town schooling. In the moment that she showed me the list, I was a bit annoyed that she was controlling such a vital part of the research process. But I came to recognize myself as her student again, wanting to please my favorite teacher. I thanked her for the list of girls, for thinking so carefully about her choices and preparing them for my arrival, and, rather disappointed that one of the most important steps in my research design was thwarted, I settled into my researcher space to observe. I knew my place and not to question it.

My desire to acquiesce was produced by the historically laden power relationship between Mrs. Hill and me, a desire that made visible the institutional discourses of small-town schooling in Garner. As my former teacher, she knew best, and perhaps she intended her

Are we into power issues here? Does Jackson shift roles as she returns to her personal environment? How does this affect her issues about pleasure that she discusses?

Reframing seems quite a novel way to address what many might perceive as a problem as her role became so controlled by the teachers at her former school. I wonder if she had anticipated any of these issues.

Do you think this section provides insight into the teachers' lounge? How much is Jackson sticking to her intended objectives? Actually, are you clear what her intended research objectives are? Sometimes researchers make them explicit, and in other cases researchers allow them to emerge gradually. This study does not have any section that specifically addresses research objectives or purpose. In an ethnographic study, usually the researcher's main goal is to study the culture of a particular group. Actually it turns out that the purpose of this article is not to report on the culture of a small town high school. It seems the purpose might be about the researcher's understanding of her role as a researcher and the pleasure principle. If you return to the article's title, you can see this more clearly.

I'm not sure what the term "discursive practice" means. Can you guess at its meaning from the context?

Approval by authorities within a setting is an interesting way to gain entrée into a setting. On one level, you can see this is helpful. In contrast, however, those in the

actions to be that of "southern hospitality," of helpfulness—not of control, as it felt on my receiving end. Yet, to act as Foucault's ethical subject—to moderate my own desires in the face of conflict— left me with a surprising feeling of pleasure in reinhabiting a space that I had long since left: that of a nice, quiet, people-pleaser. I slipped rather quickly—though not easily—back into the comfortable discourses of my childhood and schooling that subjected me as a working-class, southern girl. I became acutely aware of how control is actually characterized by freedom, and I shaped my ethnographic self through the range of choices available to me at the time. As an ethical subject, I moderated my competing desires to comply, to argue, to flat-out resist and made a choice to enact what Foucault names "stylized freedom." Within the power relations and discursive practices of being back in Garner, I knew what I "ought" to do as a former student who was now a guest in the school system: to do what I was told and not make trouble. Admittedly, and most importantly, I took pleasure in the fact that I could return to Garner, go back to the school, and not embarrass my family.

I also realized, during my first day of fieldwork, that my memories and my past selves were functioning to enable sense-making of my experience. Coffey (1999) emphasizes the importance of the relationship between fieldwork and memory, and she asserts that memory helps to contextualize the self in relation to the field. Indeed, memories of my former selves as a southern girl in a small-town school helped me to understand how I should respond to certain contextual situations while doing home-work. Memory-work, in the context of home-work, actually led to my experiencing and conceptualizing my ethnographic self as pleasurable. That is, the tension and negotiation of memory and the present, in regard to my subjectivity, heightened my awareness of how to behave in the moment—what Foucault would regard as an ethical practice of the (ethnographic) self.

DATA STORY TWO: PLEASURES OF SOUTHERN GIRLHOOD

Even though Mrs. Hill selected senior girls to host me while I was a participant–observer at Garner High, leaving me at the start of my project with a feeling of loss, her discursive practice enabled a particular relationship between me and my participants. Because Mrs. Hill seemingly sanctioned my project via her historical relationship with me, the girls received my project with enthusiasm, even a sense of superiority to others. By the end of the school day on that first day of fieldwork, I had met all six girls. In Mrs. Hill's classes, they seemed well-liked, polite, respectful, and helpful to others. I began to glean Mrs. Hill's rationale for choosing these girls; they were truly hospitable, and they seemed excited about being in a "book." Throughout the day, just before the beginning of each English class, Mrs. Hill setting might feel that they do not really have a choice to refuse to participate. I have seen this problem when studying work environments—the managers might give approval and the workers have to "go along" with the approval. In some cases, the consequences of refusing to participate are quite serious for workers or for students.

Notice how she introduces this important component almost as an afterthought. You can be sure that Jackson had planned to gain consent from each girl. She may not have been clear under what circumstances, but she knew of the importance of such consent. Parental consent is usually needed for minors.

introduced me to Destiny, Marin, Abbey, Alexis, Justice, and Quenisha. My spiel to each of them was, "I am writing a book about small-town schooling. I'd like to follow you to all of your classes and extracurricular activities to see what your day is like and casually talk to you about going to school in a small town." I also handed each a letter of informed consent to read and sign. Each girl smiled and said something like, "Yes ma'am. That will be fine" before returning to her seat (I almost always expected a polite, southern curtsey to follow). As Mrs. Hill began each class, she introduced me to all of the students in the senior class and allowed me to explain what I was doing there. I recited my spiel again, and Mrs. Hill was always certain to add, with pride, "And she was one of my former students." (I noticed that, without fail, each of the girls said to the person sitting closest to her, "I'm going to be in her book!") Marin actually took ownership of *me;* as I talked with other seniors about their experiences, she jokingly said, "Don't talk to my shadow!" or "I'm in her book; you can't be!" All of the girls eventually became protective of me and my work, and they produced me as a marker of their privilege.

Other seniors asked questions of me: What are you doing here? Who were your teachers when you were at Garner? Are you married? Do you have children? Do you want to shadow me? Are you going to the prom/awards ceremony/spring play/band concert? When can we read the book you are writing? Can I be in the book? Seniors welcomed me into their school culture, collected data about me, and offered information when I did not ask for it—data about living in Garner, going to school there, and liking and disliking certain teachers and rules of the school. Often, when I was having a conversation with one or two students, surrounding seniors would join in and offer their perceptions of the topic, especially in casual situations such as lunch and break. My field notebook continued to be a source of intrigue; seniors constantly asked me what I was writing "in there" and would often make statements for the sole purpose of my recording them (e.g., "This school is all about football. If you don't play football, you're nobody"). I was constructed by the seniors as someone who "got out": I had attended Garner High; I "knew" what it was like; I was a model for escape. Students even asked me, "Was it as awful then as it is now?"

As a working-class girl at Garner High in the 1980s, I had hardly experienced such immediate acceptance and sensations of importance—of "fitting in"—as I did upon my return to Garner. My ethical decision to become "recognizable" (Butler, 2004) was a significant act in the discourse of southern girlhood at Garner High. To be popular, there needed to be a seemingly seamless connection between my past self and my present self. I needed to look and act the part—not necessarily that of an adolescent girl, but that of a southern woman to whom the seniors could partially relate and identify. Each morning I carefully considered how I would present

What do you think she means here by the term "intelligibility"? I am not really sure. A cautionary word—it is good to avoid jargon or unfamiliar terms in your writing.

myself by shaping my physical appearance in a way that would meet the approval of the girls and their peers. I ate the "right" lunches, knew just enough pop culture to converse intelligibly with the Garner seniors, and wore enviable shoes. During the day, I knew how to be polite and accommodating to adults in the building (and as a former public school teacher, I carried a bit of intelligibility in that regard). And with the seniors, I did not participate in critiques of the school, did not get caught up in love triangles, offered advice only when asked, and certainly did not condone some of the more deviant behaviors I learned about. My knowledge of southern girlhood made possible my practices of being an educated southern woman, and somewhat of an "authority" figure, but most of all, one who knew how to exhibit proper pleasure in her work.

The freedom I felt—at once constrained and produced by discourse—to construct a particular version of myself offered me power-induced pleasurable moments of living parts of my past that I missed, or even missed out on. Fitting in, being popular, feeling important—all were the result of my careful self-control to abstain from speaking out against injustices I saw in the school, critiquing the administration for illegal decisions (e.g., Title IX violations), or stepping in the way of some of the students' destructive behaviors that I learned about. I had ample opportunities to do each of these, yet my desire to moderate myself was made possible by the discursive power/knowledge relations embedded in the social networks at Garner High. I prioritized my efforts to exert power over other parts of my self that would have made data collection quite problematic. To the point, I did not want to disappoint my former teachers by not fitting into the community or even not fitting the image they had of me. Though I had long left my hometown high school, my renewed contact with those from my past sharpened the disjuncture between my self working-class girl who was schooled to be a competent secretary and my more recent self as a PhD. I was returning (parading?) home as a different (better?) woman, proving to others that I had "made something of myself," as one teacher introduced me. It felt good to have surrounding adults proud of me, and those were proper pleasures to have within the discourse of small-town schooling and southern girlhood. Indeed, part of being a southern girl was conducting one's self within the knowledge of how to please others.

The freedom and power to refuse to "break with culture" (Barthes, 1975: 14) and to choose to present myself as someone "recognizable" (Butler, 2004) to my historical others was comfortable and comforting. As Judith Butler (2004: 2) writes, "The Hegelian tradition links desire with recognition, claiming that desire is always a desire for recognition and that it is only through the experience of recognition that any of us becomes constituted as socially viable beings." Butler goes on to elaborate this idea, arguing that recognition is in actuality a site of power where who gets to be recognized, and by whom, is governed by social norms. Furthermore, Butler maintains, the choice to be recognized (or not) within the constraints of normativity is a condition of agency in the doing, and undoing, of gender.

This section provides clues to what this study is really about.

This idea of "recognition" and its connection to pleasure and power in qualitative fieldwork—or in my case, home-work—became significantly apparent to me. There were all sorts of ways that I could have been recognized in my ethnographic home-work, whether I knew it or not. The point is not to emphasize the extent to which anyone was aware of this but to accentuate what this recognizability *produced*. The social norms that constituted my practices produced a range of options for me that I described in the data stories above. I realized that I flickered between *being* "recognizable" to myself and *becoming* "recognizable" to others involved in my research. This, of course, meant living in paradox: to embrace the conditions of existence that I normally refused in order to make myself possible. As I have narrated here, such paradoxical pleasures can become rich sources of data that require ethical critique. Rajchman (1986: 166) wrote that such an ethical critique considers "who we are said to be, and what, therefore, it is possible for us to become." The implications of this ethical consideration of subjectivity, of reinventing experience to analyze how it constitutes possibilities for becoming and knowing, are elaborated by Foucault, who reminds me that my enacting "stylized freedom" was more than simply doing my work well as a qualitative researcher. For example, my ethical choices to achieve recognizability—as disciplined as they were—enabled situated ways of knowing in my home-work. Eating lunch with the seniors in the high school cafeteria and parking my car in the student lot did not provide more true or real data for my ethnography, but my ethical practices certainly made possible the students' choices to reveal (or not) particular views of small-town schooling.

Were you surprised by the second story? It did not really seem to be a story in the usual sense of the word. In this story, Jackson gets into freedom and power. She has even incorporated a few comments from the literature.

Conclusion: A Recognizable Ethics

The last section of the paper should take her on the journey that she set out on in the beginning. I want you to read this and think about the extent to which she convinces you of her argument.

To critique my pleasurable acts as those of ethics is not to look to my experiences in the field in order to rationalize them or to compare them against a moral good to justify my choices and decisions. Pleasure emerged within power and discourse as an ethical substance to render me recognizable, to comfort me, to push me beyond my current and historical borders. Though I came to relive spaces (and even places) that I had historically refused, my iterations of identity were not ones based on my essential nature—or even on whom I used to be. This moves the source of my self from my history, my experiences, my *a priori* knowledge of myself to the constitution of my self through the material and discursive intersections of power, knowledge, pleasure, and freedom. This is the ethical work of subject construction in Foucault's oeuvre. Certain pleasures became available to me through my home-work, pleasures that had never been free for my taking before. Performing pleasure—or enacting "stylized freedom"—is Foucault's ethical practice: *one that asked me to transform myself in order to make myself viable within social norms.*

Though I described, in the data stories, my ethical obligations as fitting in to avoid shame and failure, Foucault would claim that these practices were, rather, incitements to enter into the "game of truth" and form myself as a knowing, "proper," and "right" kind of person, within relations of power (Foucault, 1994b). Foucault (1985: 28) describes the very deliberate, practical work of ethical subject formation as this process:

> The individual delimits that part of himself that will form the object of his moral practice, define his position relative to the precept he will follow, and decides on a certain mode of being that will serve as his moral goal. And this requires him to act on himself, to monitor, test, improve, and transform himself.

Such delimiting, positioning, and transforming myself in relation to others was to make myself active, rather than passive, in moderating my pleasures—or keeping them in their proper place. These ethical practices involved a constant reinvention of myself—neither as the high school girl I was nor as the woman I had become—but someone else (much like Hastrup's "third person"). I transgressed neither identity (as Foucault would have it) but crafted, even fictionalized, a discontinuous self that called into question the truth of my being.

Achieving what I am calling a "recognizable ethics" in my research through the authoring of my subjectivity was a practice of determining the kind of person I could be, or the kinds of actions I could perform, in a certain time and place (Rajchman, 1986). The possibilities for recognition came not only from conflicting discourses but also from my choices to live out the ethical practices that were conditioned by those freedoms. Those ethical, pleasurable efforts of self-control, of mastery, of moderation, of seeming consistency emerged as "decisive events in [my] ethical tradition"; deciding what to wear, what and where to eat, how to speak to others, what to do with my self (and their unforeseen consequences) were not only discursive but also practical, material issues that made me who I was, that constituted my experience of my self (Rajchman, 1986: 169).

As I have illustrated above, analyses of power-induced pleasures reveal the different ways in which the self is performed that might otherwise go unnoticed. While these ethics have particular meaning for research at home, they also have implications for constructing an ethical self in fieldwork. Performing pleasure, becoming recognized, practicing ethics—all point to Foucault's imperative that we turn our attention to how we make ourselves, critique those formations or truths of the self, and constantly engage in freeing ourselves from ourselves in order to transform who we can become in relation to the ethnographic field.

Source: Jackson, A. (2008). Power and pleasure in ethnographic home-work: producing a recognizable ethics. *Qualitative Research, 8*(1), 37–51. Reprinted with permission of SAGE Publications and the author.

Summary and Review

Jackson raises some interesting points in the *Methodology* section. In a sense, you could say she acknowledges her own agenda. Rather than to be looked down upon, this way of doing research fits the conceptual understanding of doing this type of post-structural ethnography. You might want her to tell you more about the data she collected. She is a little vague, although she provides some detail in a footnote. She also suggests that this study is her dissertation, since she says she was a PhD student at the time. I don't know what she means when she says she "felt her own subjectivity slipping and protesting in response to an intricate network of cultural practices and power relations." Here you might ask: is this study about her or about the small town school, or perhaps about the intertwining of the two? She deals a lot with her subjectivity, which is an issue that ethnographers writing from a particular position often address. Why she raises the issue in the section on methodology is unclear to me. You should notice how she weaves available literature here. It is important to recognize that Jackson has thought about these issues quite a bit and read the literature. She takes you on a new dimension when she talks about reconceptualizing the ethnographic self. I suspect that at this point you might find the positions Jackson takes to be unfamiliar. You might feel as though you are treading on untrammeled ground. Perhaps you can take away the idea that she is thinking very hard about the self and studying what was once her home territory. Yet, at the same time, she is quite removed from the location—some sixteen years removed, according to her own account.

I get a little lost when trying to follow her pathway. She seems to be making new claims about the "negotiation of the self" that are not addressed in the literature on subjectivity. Whether and to what extent you "buy in" to these claims is your choice. All of this leads to what she calls the ethical construction of the self. Remember, you learned earlier that this is the thesis of her research. One thing we do not know: did she begin with this premise or did she come to it after being in the field? I suspect the latter, although she does not say for sure.

Finally, if you return to the four questions I posed at the beginning of this chapter, you can see the extent to which this article was successful. In my opinion, you can answer yes to each of these questions.

- Does it provide new information and insights related to the topic?
- Is it engaging and written in a clear manner?
- Does it illustrate aspects you expect to find in a post-structural ethnography (e.g. power, the self, negotiating)?
- Do the positive aspects of the article outweigh the potential drawbacks?

FINAL COMMENTS

At this point, you have read two very different ethnographies. Each represents an example of a way that ethnographies are written today. Nukaga's article takes a fairly traditional approach. In contrast, Jackson's article introduces ideas that are more contemporary.

You can access the complete articles at www.sagepub.com/lichtmanreadings.

Chapter 2

READING GROUNDED THEORY

This chapter introduces you to two articles using grounded theory. In contrast to writers using an ethnographic approach who tend to be less structured, especially those writing from a post-structural stance, many writers using a grounded theory approach tend to be very systematic and traditional.

You will recall that grounded theory is an approach that involves the generation of theory based on the data. In other words, the theory is grounded in the data. It is the qualitative research approach most closely associated with quantitative research. Researchers who conduct this type of research tend to write in a more remote style.

The grounded theory approach is also one of the few research approaches that rely on more or less prescribed methods of data analysis. Although originally developed in 1967 by Glaser and Strauss, by the 1980s these two authors had broken away from each other. Strauss published two works explaining his interpretations of the theory; in 1992 Glaser published his amplifications. Many students report that it is difficult to learn how to conduct the analysis. Most researchers do not provide detailed descriptions of how they analyzed the data. In fact, many researchers using a variety of research approaches do not explain their analysis procedures. Some might consider it more important that a grounded theory study explain the steps in data analysis. Some writers refer to the data analysis process as the constant comparative method. At times, I find that articles use the right words but do not necessarily follow the tenets of a particular approach. That is especially true when I read grounded theory.

There are several key elements that you expect to find in a grounded theory study. One, of course, is the use of a specific method of data analysis. In addition, many use the idea of theoretical saturation and theoretical sampling. Theoretical saturation is the idea that additional data continue to be gathered until the researcher believes no new ideas or information can be gained from additional information gathering. Theoretical sampling is a closely associated idea. Remember that in traditional sampling researchers plan in advance both the sample size and the sample source. In quantitative approaches to conducting research, a researcher strives to gather some type of a random sample. In most qualitative approaches to research, a researcher does not aim to draw a sample at random, although he or she usually has a predetermined idea of how many participants will be studied. Grounded theory is different from these approaches, however. The grounded theory researcher conducts an analysis as part of the overall research design, rather than waiting until all data have been gathered. Additional data are collected when the data analysis is informed by new ideas.

In my experience, many who actually conduct grounded theory only pay lip service to the concept of theoretical saturation. I suspect that the data analysis does not usually occur until most or all of the data are collected. As you read these articles, you will see if any clues are offered with regard to such sampling techniques.

KEY ELEMENTS OF GROUNDED THEORY

- Grounded theory uses an inductive approach to generate theory from data;
- uses the constant comparative coding scheme;
- relies on theoretical sampling and saturation; and
- may omit a literature review prior to collecting data.
- Much of the research in grounded theory comes out of the field of nursing.

To help you in your understanding, I have selected two articles that are different from each other. Darin Eich's study of leadership programs is conducted across four programs and involves a large number of interviews. This is in contrast to much of qualitative research, which relies on data from fewer sources. After you read Eich's study, you can begin to think about how and why he did it this way. Note that Eich's study is published in the *Journal of Leadership & Organizational Studies*, which is not a journal that specifically publishes qualitative research. Also, his training and background are more geared toward consulting and action than to scholarly writing.

The second article does not actually include examples of grounded theory per se. Instead, it uses data drawn from grounded theory research to illustrate and explain principles of the theory. It comes from the nursing field. In fact, nurses have conducted much of the research in grounded theory. Imelda Coyne and Sarah Cowley draw on data from their study of parent participation to illustrate components of grounded theory.

Although grounded theory approaches are popular, it is rare to find actual studies done in school settings. Teachers and administrators are more likely to look for specific answers to problems than to select an approach that will lead to theory building. Another reason grounded theory studies are not done in schools is that the techniques for data analysis are difficult to learn.

As with the other articles you have read, I would like you for to begin with the title, the abstract, and the headings. I also think it is important for you to anticipate what you will find in the article.

I do not have space here to include a very interesting article by Helen Heath. It is titled "Exploring the influences and use of the literature during a grounded theory study," and was published in the *Journal of Research in Nursing* (2006, 11, 6, 519–528).

ADVANCE PREPARATIONS

Begin by reading the title and the abstract, then flipping through the article and reading the major headings and subheadings. Once you have an idea of the article's structure, go back and read through the article carefully. When you finish reading, you will need to decide the extent to which the article is successful. To do so, ask yourself four questions:

- Does it provide new information and insights related to the topic?

- Is it engaging and written in a clear manner?

- Does it illustrate elements you would expect to find in grounded theory?

- Do the positive aspects of the article outweigh the potential drawbacks?

Article 2.1. A Grounded Theory of High-Quality Leadership Programs: Perspectives from Student Leadership Development Programs in Higher Education (2008)

Darin Eich

My Expectations

As I begin to read this article, I anticipate that the author will employ traditional methods of conducting a grounded theory. I am especially interested in the ways the data are analyzed. Ultimately, the results should center on theories that emerge from the data. I know how important student leadership programs are and I anticipate that I will gain new insights into leadership programs.

The brief literature review includes two topics related to attributes—higher education and leadership programs. The section on method includes grounded theory research design with a very brief section on the constant comparative method, the sample, and data collection. The paper ends with *Findings, Discussion, and Implications*. The writing style is objective and distant. I have omitted the brief reference list since I am not going to discuss it.

ABSTRACT

Drawing on the experiences and perspectives of multiple stakeholders closely associated with diverse types of successful student leadership programs, the purpose of this study was to identify the attributes of leadership programs—including the specific actions associated with these attributes—that contribute significantly to undergraduate student leadership development. A total of 62 interviews was conducted with individuals across the four programs in the sample. The researcher employed the constant comparative method to construct a grounded theory model. The theory of high-quality leadership programs developed in this study is grounded in those programmatic attributes that, when enacted, contribute significantly to enhancing student learning and leadership development. The data analysis revealed 16 attributes of high-quality leadership programs organized into three clusters: (a) participants engaged in building and sustaining a learning community; (b) student-centered experiential learning experiences; and (c) research-grounded continuous program development.

The abstract gives us the highlights of the study. The author wanted to identify the attributes of leadership programs that contribute to undergraduate student leadership development. You can

Many prominent leadership scholars (Burns, 1978; Gardner, 1990; Greenleaf, 1977; Wren, 1995) argue that our nation is in a "leadership crisis," one that requires more and better leadership in all areas of our society. Within the field of higher education, Astin, Astin, and associates (2000) declare that it is difficult to overstate the importance of the role that higher education plays in shaping the see almost immediately that the style of writing and the choice of words make this type of research as close to quantitative research as it is possible to be. A large number of interviews were conducted. The writer talks about programs in the sample. He refers to using the constant– comparative method. (Presumably, he will explain that method later.) Results are described in an objective, almost scientific manner. Since grounded theory is a conservative approach to doing research, you should not be surprised at the style of writing and the content you find in the abstract.

The first section (without a heading) provides an introduction. If you look at the *American Psychological Association* (APA) *Manual of Style,* you will find many suggestions as to structure and format for headings. Here is a link to an excellent online resource you can use to learn about APA headings: http://owl.english.purdue .edu/owl/resource/560/16/

quality of leadership in modern American society. Leadership development is undoubtedly an important outcome of an undergraduate education. University mission statements reflect the value placed on educating citizens who can engage successfully in the leadership process and contribute to the growth of our society (Council for the Advancement of Standards, 2003; Cress, Astin, Zimmerman-Oster, & Burkhardt, 2001; Roberts, 2003).

Teaching leadership to students through programs is a recent trend in higher education as both co-curricular and academic leadership development programs have proliferated on many college campuses (Riggio, Ciulla, & Sorenson, 2003; Schwartz, Axtman, & Freeman, 1998). Notably, there has been little empirical research on student leadership program quality and program activities that contribute significantly to leadership development and learning.

Definitional differences aside, books used to teach leadership to college students (Higher Education Research Institute, 1996; Hughes, Ginnett, & Curphy 2001; Komives, Lucas, & McMahon, 2006; Kouzes & Posner, 2002; Northouse, 2001; Wren, 1995) conceptualize leadership in common terms as a process in which all individuals have the capability of developing and engaging in whether they hold a formal position or not. In the postindustrial leadership paradigm (Rost, 1993; Rost & Barker, 2000), leadership can be developed in students and in organizations. As opposed to older notions of leadership as positional or as an inherent characteristic, all students who involve themselves in leadership education have the potential to increase their skills and knowledge (Higher Education Research Institute, 1996; Komives et al., 2006; Wren, 1995). Leadership in the Making, a Kellogg Foundation project that studied 31 Kellogg-funded leadership development endeavors, concluded that leadership potential exists in every student, and colleges and universities can develop this potential through leadership programs and activities (Zimmerman-Oster & Burkhardt, 1999).

LITERATURE REVIEW

Attributes Associated With High-Quality Higher Education Programs

Higher education scholars (Astin, 1993; Haworth & Conrad, 1997; Pascarella & Terenzini, 2005) recommend an examination into the "black box" of the educational experience to identify the attributes of high-quality programs rather than relying on assumptions of quality. Scholars point to research-based attributes and practices that are important for programs seeking to enhance student learning and development. Major themes of both engagement- and learning-focused teaching appear repeatedly in the literature on education quality. In their extensive study of academic programs, Haworth and Conrad (1997) found that high-quality programs that contribute to student learning and development feature attributes of diverse and engaged participants, participatory cultures, interactive teaching and learning, connected program requirements, and adequate resources.

Research from George Kuh and colleagues shows that the level of academic challenge, active and collaborative learning, student–faculty interaction, enriching educational experience, and a supportive campus environment are five cluster areas linked to desired college student learning and development outcomes (National Survey of Student Engagement [NSSE], 2004). Similar to the NSSE findings, Chickering and Gamson (1991) identified key practices of student–faculty contact, student cooperation, active learning, prompt feedback, time on task, high expectations, and respect for diverse talents and ways of learning as those that matter most for learning and development in undergraduate education. These researchers have identified multiple attributes and practices that are valuable for programs to positively affect students.

This review is cursory, without any evaluation or interpretation on the part of the author. In fact, you will see when you complete the article that Eich does not really integrate this review into his own findings. The article would be improved if Eich had connected the research to his own work.

Attributes Associated With Leadership Programs

First, to bring in general leadership development intervention research, the Center for Creative Leadership (Van Velsor & McCauley, 2004) explains elements of an effective leadership development experience in general organizations (not focused on college students) including assessment, challenge, and support. Day's (2001) review of leadership development research finds that the practices of 360-degree feedback, executive coaching, mentoring, networking, job assignment, and action learning have all been lauded as beneficial for leadership development in one application or another but that little hard evaluation data support the claims.

Publications on developing college student leadership education experiences (Eich, 2003, 2005; Komives, Lucas, & McMahon, 1998) highlight the salience of service and experiential learning (Kolb, 1981) in leadership education and, especially, through group experience. Kolb's (1984) experiential learning model is a practical pedagogy for teaching students how to engage in the leadership process through constructing meaning and making connections between their own experiences and reflection.

This literature review is superficial. It seems to be placed here because the writer thought he had to include it rather than to help the reader understand why the study is being done or what its place is in the larger body of research.

Although the individual element effect is unknown, leadership programs in higher education offer a variety of elements or activities designed for the purpose of enhancing student leadership development and learning. Program elements used by more than 80% of Kellogg-funded programs include seminars and workshops, mentors, and guest speakers (Zimmerman-Oster & Burkhardt, 1999).

METHOD

Grounded Theory Research Design

I do not find this explanation to be clear. It is more a brief statement. Based on what Eich writes here, can you really tell what is meant by "grounded theory"? This lack of clarity is one of the shortcomings of this article.

Within this multicase study design, grounded theory (Conrad, 1982; Glaser & Strauss, 1967; Strauss & Corbin, 1990) was used to construct a theory or model of what it is about the leadership programs (described by attributes and actions) that contributes to significant student learning and development. This method was selected because it is a qualitative way of inductively developing theory from the ground up through a systematic process.

The constant comparative method—comparing incidents applicable to each category, integrating categories and their properties, delimiting the theory, and writing the theory—is a four-stage process that was used to make meaning of the data (Glaser & Strauss, 1967). Glaser and Strauss point out that

Again, this seems like just so many words and is really not clear. It does not acknowledge the divergence between the two authors and how the model evolved since the time it was first written almost 50 years ago.

Eich uses words that appear to have been taken from Conrad, but he does not explain the reference so that the reader can understand how the different concepts are interrelated. The article would be improved if Eich had chosen to incorporate his own explanations.

When you read this section on Sample you will think you are reading about a quantitative study. He implies that he draws his sample from all the undergraduate leadership programs in the United States, but later in his article he explains that he is using a theoretical sampling strategy. You might remember that the theoretical sampling strategy is one of the key elements of grounded theory, yet he does not mention it in his discussion of

> joint collection, coding, and analysis of data is the underlying operation. The generation of theory, coupled with the notion of theory as process, requires that all three operations be done together as much as possible. They should blur and intertwine continually, from the beginning of an investigation to its end (p. 43).

This multifaceted and flexible method combines systematic data collection, coding, and analysis with theoretical sampling to generate theory that is integrated, close to the data, and expressed in a form clear enough for further testing (Conrad, 1982).

Sample

The population under investigation included undergraduate leadership programs in the United States. What represented a leadership program varied at different schools. These programs included a single leadership course, a week-long leadership retreat, a co-curricular program, and a service leadership program. Individual case studies at diverse sites were also included in this study to provide insight for a wide variety of leadership programs.

Purposeful sampling decisions were made at the onset of the study to select both case sites and participants. These decisions were made to include alternative delivery methods of leadership programs as well as multiple stakeholder perspectives at the individual programs.

Selection and Access

The leadership programs and their stakeholders included in the sample were chosen through a theoretical sampling strategy. The grounded theory directly above. He explains the sampling procedure in great detail. I wish he had explained the analysis procedure in such detail. Later in the article, you will learn that he studied both students and teachers or administrators.

Perhaps he should have made clear what he means by schools: were they universities, colleges, or some other educational institution?

It would be helpful if he explained clearly what he did, rather than using vague terms such as "purposeful sampling." This is another example of how he attempts to place this article in a "traditional" and objective format.

But immediately above he said he used purposeful sampling techniques. These two ideas are not synonymous. Now he needs to explain what is meant by "theoretical sampling strategy."

goal was not to scientifically identify the highest-quality programs in existence but rather to create a pool of different quality leadership programs. Selection was made from this pool to begin discovering what it is about each program that is contributing most to learning and development. Criteria used to select programs include the following:

1. The program was identified as being effective in contributing significantly to student learning and leadership development. The program's own assessment and evaluation data assisted in identifying quality programs.

2. The program had at least a 5-year history of operation. This length allowed for an improvement process of the program to make it more effective, serve more students, and acquire more experience.

3. The program had a sufficient number of stakeholders including students, teachers, staff, and alumni to interview to achieve saturation of at least 15 interviewees. This breadth is important, as the research is grounded in diverse stakeholder perspectives and experiences.

4. The program was prominent. Successful programs were identified through articles, national conferences, and leadership education leaders in the field. Through the National Clearinghouse for Leadership Programs and the International Leadership Association, contact was made with the administrators who could give access to successful programs at six sites.

5. The program teaches leadership as a collaborative process in which anyone can engage. This conceptualization is connected to the relational leadership definition presented earlier by Komives et al. (2006).

6. The program dedicated significant time to educating the student. A minimum of roughly the equivalent of a single semester-long course was required to qualify as a leadership program for this study. This time minimum allows for both substantial participant experience and a substantive intervention for meaningful development to occur.

7. The programs had different formats as well as differences in program goals and in methods of teaching leadership.

The author seems to confuse theoretical sampling (a tenet of grounded theory) with purposeful sampling. He also seems to be using sampling strategies that researchers use when conducting case studies.

Through the theoretical sampling procedure, different types of leadership programs in the United States that share comparable desired student outcomes and leadership philosophies were accessed. The researcher began by purposefully sampling four common alternative methods of delivering student leadership education. The programs in the sample included an academic interdisciplinary course at a large public Midwest university, a week-long retreat program for college students offered by a nonprofit organization at a large public

Midwest university, a 4-year comprehensive co-curricular program at a large public Western university, and a 4-year service leadership program funded by a national foundation at a small private Southeast college.

Data Collection

The data collection was guided initially by the major research question and later by the requirements of theoretical sampling, the process of collecting data for comparative analysis to facilitate the generation of grounded theory. Accordingly, data were organized into the following:

1. Attributes of the programs that significantly enhance student learning and leadership development. Properties of these attributes will describe the themes in more detail.

2. Actions that enact each of the attributes. This includes examples of how programs put the attributes into practice.

3. Student outcomes. How and in what ways was the students' learning and leadership development enhanced as a result of the program attributes and specific actions?

Interview Process and Protocols

Interviews were the primary source of data used to develop the grounded theory of this study. The researcher conducted and recorded approximately 1-hour interviews with volunteer study participants who are deeply involved with the program and who have already completed the primary leadership education experience. I wonder if he also transcribed the recordings. If so, this would be an enormous amount of data to process. The constant–comparative method involves the almost simultaneous tasks of data collection and data analysis, until such time that the researcher believes that theoretical saturation has been reached. The process explained here does not seem to take that into account. Stakeholders including students, administrators, teachers, alumni, and student staff were interviewed to shed light on the program attributes that contribute significantly to student learning and leadership development. Interviews were also used to test the developing theory, which was being continually constructed from multiple stakeholders' perspectives.

Coordinators of the four observed leadership programs identified a pool of study participants; a total of 62 (36 female and 26 male) were interviewed. Of the 62 stakeholders, 47 were White and 15 were people of color. A total of 45 of the 62 were students and

What are the requirements of theoretical sampling? He writes as though they are somehow written in stone. I wish he had provided a reference here.

That seems like an awkward phrase.

Interviews are a common method of collecting data in all qualitative research approaches.

Eich states that he interviewed a variety of stakeholders. I think it is good to get various viewpoints.

17 were practitioners, meaning teachers and/or administrators. The following are three key interview questions posed to generate data:

1. In thinking about the program, what about the program had the most effect on your (students') learning and leadership development?

2. Tell me more about what happened, some examples, or what was done in the program that helped you (students) learn and develop?

3. How did that enhance your (students') leadership development and learning?

Trustworthiness of the Research Findings

To address the standard that this qualitative study is believable, accurate, and represents the stakeholder voices, multiple techniques were used. The researcher collected and triangulated data between different documents and interviews, between individual interviewees, between students and administrators, and between different programs. Member checks were conducted with individual interviewees and program coordinators. Data management and analysis was done with the grounding of a research assistant, and NVIVO qualitative research software was used. All data and constructs ranging from interview audio and transcripts to memos and to codes and developing theory categories are stored in the software for the purposes of a confirmability audit to show that the findings and constructed theory are aligned with the data.

FINDINGS

For the purposes of this study, high-quality leadership programs are defined as those programs that have a significant positive effect on student learning and leadership development. Quality is defined in terms of student learning and leadership development for two primary reasons. First, student learning is the primary goal of educational programs and of the higher education mission. Second, leadership development of the student is the primary desired outcome of leadership programs; it is learning and development of the individual in the context of the subject matter of the program. In this study, it was the participants who spoke directly to what had a significant positive effect on their learning and development.

When referring to the leadership development outcome for students, leadership is defined as a "relational and ethical process of people together attempting to accomplish positive change" (Komives et al., 2006, p. 11). Komives and colleagues' relational model of leadership includes dimensions of being inclusive, empowering,

In what follows, he seems to say the right words, but I cannot tell precisely what he did. He talks about triangulation and member checks. He says he used NVIVO, but I do not find any references to it. If you are familiar with this qualitative software program, you will know it is very complicated. I wonder what kind of support Eich had in conducting the study. Did he do his own transcriptions? How much data were actually generated? How long were the interviews? These are questions you might ask yourself as you read his explanations. He seems to be silent on the matter.

Again, the concepts he has just discussed are very traditional, and even though the publication date for the article is 2008, they are not necessarily supported in the current literature on grounded theory.

Eich includes a lengthy section on Findings. He seems to have developed a format and then follows it throughout his presentation. I have omitted some of it from the article.

purposeful, ethical, and process oriented. This definition is widely accepted in teaching leadership to college students and is aligned with the leadership definition and philosophy of both the Council for the Advancement of Standards for Leadership Programs and the programs sampled in this study. Leadership development encompasses almost every form of growth or stage of development that promotes, encourages, and assists in one's leadership potential (Brungardt, 1996). This idea includes how one thinks about leadership, leadership practice, skills, efficacy, and personal leadership identity (Komives, Owen, Longerbeam, Mainella, & Osteen, 2005).

I am not sure why he talks about a "grounded theory model" here. Possibly because he writes in a more practical manner than one that is theory-driven.

In presenting this grounded theory model, the purpose is to provide a foundation for enriching dialogue, idea generation, and action planning that takes place for stakeholders developing new leadership development initiatives and improving existing leadership programs for the sake of student leadership development.

Grounded Theory of High-Quality Leadership Programs

This study identified 16 programmatic attributes of high-quality leadership programs through drawing on the perspectives of stakeholders at four successful leadership programs in the United States. In concert with identification of key attributes, the grounded theory model explicates the connections to enact each of the attributes through actions and corresponding student outcomes. These 16 individual attributes are arranged into three respective clusters: (a) participants engaged in building and sustaining a learning community, (b) student-centered experiential learning experiences, and (c) research-grounded continuous program development. Each cluster will be introduced along with the individual attributes within the cluster that contribute significantly to student learning and leadership development.

Since much of the following analysis is repetitive, I will only include a portion in my discussion.

Cluster I: Participants Engaged in Building and Sustaining a Learning Community

60 plus interviews—it is unusual to have collected so much data. I am not clear whether they were taped and transcribed or how the analysis was actually conducted.

Derived from more than 60 interviews, *participants engaged in building a learning community* is identified as the first cluster of attributes in the grounded theory of high-quality leadership programs. In broad strokes, this specific cluster of attributes speaks to the vital role that the individuals who are a part of the programs play in helping each other to develop as better leaders. Six different attributes were identified within this cluster: diverse and engaged students, experienced and committed practitioners, educators model leadership and support, participants unite through small groups, participants foster a culture of challenge and support, and participants cultivate one-on-one relationships.

This section discusses one of the six attributes.

Eich uses the same pattern for each attribute that he identifies from his study. He names the attribute, discusses the actions taken by the program, and finally addresses the program's effects on students. I find it somewhat disconcerting that he writes in a didactic style that implies his findings are set in stone. I am not quite sure how he gets to the six attributes or how they represent the development of a theory. I have chosen to omit the presentation of much of the data because he follows the same format throughout.

Due to space considerations, I have omitted the remaining clusters. Since the author used the same style and format, I decided that you can interpret the article with what I present here.

I am not sure why this should have been the goal. If he was looking for effective practice, I question why he chose to conduct a grounded theory study.

I do not see how this represents a theory.

Diverse and Engaged Students

Students who participate in a program determine the quality of a leadership program. Indeed, students themselves bring to the "leadership learning table" their previous experience and background. Not only the quality of students but also how they differ from each other and their level of commitment play a great role in a successful leadership development program.

Actions. Stakeholders enlisted diverse and engaged students in the program through two primary means. First, programs use an application and selection procedure to select students who are invested in their own and others' development and are committed to engaging fully in the program. Second, programs recruit from many sources and bring together a mix of students from a variety of backgrounds to create a diverse learning community.

Effects on students. There are two primary leadership development and learning outcomes that students experience from actions taken to enact the *diverse and engaged students* attribute. First, students learn to form collaborations and a network rich in social capital for their leadership endeavors. Second, students acquire new ideas and an enriched understanding through hearing personal experiences and perspectives offered by diverse students in the program.

. . .

DISCUSSION

From studying four leadership programs and learning from 62 stakeholders, new knowledge and understanding was gained about effective practice through programming for student leadership development. This knowledge and understanding is expressed in this grounded theory of high-quality leadership programs. In broad strokes, it was learned that high-quality leadership programs engage in continuous program development. This development systemically integrates student-centered experiential learning experiences for diverse program participants who together engage in building and sustaining a leadership learning community.

Put simply, this grounded theory, in a sense, is about the program "walking the leadership pedagogy talk." The theory shares with programs how to model and teach the kind of leadership they value through engaging in the leadership of the program for the purpose of developing leaders. High-quality programs actually practice the kind of inclusive, empowering, purposeful, ethical, and process-oriented leadership for positive change that they advocate to their students. This practice is reflected through all of the clusters of the theory from the engagement of the participants, to the student-centered learning experiences of the program, to the continuous research-grounded program development. It is a "lived leadership" that is reflected throughout the teaching and pedagogy of the program.

Students learn about leadership in the process of understanding themselves, others, and the world around them. The factors that facilitate this learning include the participatory students themselves, the environment in which they learn, the activities they do, and the systems approach of the program that leads to improvement. Put another way, high-quality programs are spaces that help students do leadership and understand what they are doing along with others. In creating a space for this to happen, leadership programs that integrate and enact attributes of this theory demonstrate not only that leadership can be taught and learned but that leadership development can be fostered and accelerated as a result of a program educational intervention rather than leaving leadership development to chance through life experiences.

Normally an author integrates the literature into his discussion. But this very brief section seems more like a summary than a discussion.

Significance of Findings

This grounded theory model of high-quality leadership programs can be applied to enhance leadership development in our institutions and help programs to innovate for the sake of improved student outcomes. In short, the model can guide the design of programs and participants' learning by helping participants grow through self-discovery, personal development, and collaborative leadership with others. Because this grounded theory of high-quality leadership programs identifies and connects program attributes and activities to outcomes, it represents a new contribution to the current leadership education literature.

Do you think that the writer did this? I don't.

Implications for Practice

This study was undertaken with a vision that it could be readily applicable to practice. It was a study of practice for the improvement of practice. A grounded theory of the attributes of high-quality leadership programs has numerous implications for a variety of individuals who seek to advance student learning and development. The grounded theory can provide a foundation to develop new leadership programs or enhance existing ones. It can also catalyze ideas for innovations to the way leadership education is delivered. Each attribute offers opportunities to take associated actions to affect leadership development outcomes or offers knowledge to generate new ideas for program features. Program developers can use this theory as evidence for the value of creating new programs. They can justify that when created and implemented properly, programs can have tremendous effects on student learning and leadership development, which are central to the mission of many institutions.

Source: Eich, D. (2008). A grounded theory of high-quality leadership programs: perspectives from student leadership development programs in higher education. *Journal of Leadership & Organizational Studies, 15*(2), 176–187. Reprinted with permission from SAGE.

Summary and Review

I initially chose this article for you to read because it is an actual study and purports to be a study using a grounded theory approach. But as I reread the study in greater depth, I found it did not help you to understand what grounded theory is really about. The research cited about the approach is cursory at best, and the author does not choose to comment at all about it. He used buzz words, but he didn't offer any in-depth presentation. I am especially troubled that he reports his results as though they are based on an analysis that in some way is reproducible, but he doesn't explain how he did his analysis at all.

This research represents one style of writing using a grounded theory approach. Unlike some of the other approaches you have read about, the writing tends to be of an objective and scientific bent. It is almost as though the researcher wants to do a quantitative study but for some reason chose not to. Some researchers using a grounded theory approach do not bring up topics like reflexivity. In fact, the role of the researcher in gathering and analyzing the data seems to be somewhat obscured when Eich talks about triangulation and member checks. You don't really hear the voices of those being studied. The writer does not include any quotes.

Nothing is mentioned about getting permission from those in the study or going through a human subjects review process. I find the presentation of data very repetitive and not necessarily believable. I wish the author had tied in the related research more to the findings he presents. Of course, it is up to you to be the final judge.

Finally, if you return to the four questions I posed at the beginning of this chapter, you can see the extent to which this article was successful. In my opinion, Eich's work offered interesting insights about leadership programs. His writing was not always clear. As for whether it illustrates elements we expect to find in a study using grounded theory, this is an area in which Eich was not especially successful. I leave you to draw your own conclusions with regard to the fourth question.

- Does it provide new information and insights related to the topic?

- Is it engaging and written in a clear manner?

- Does Eich generate new theory from his data?

- Do the positive aspects of the article outweigh the potential drawbacks?

Article 2.2. Using Grounded Theory to Research Parent Participation (2006)

Imelda Coyne and Sarah Cowley

My Expectations

Although initially I thought the article would be a study of parent participation and I would expect to see it follow a traditional way of doing grounded theory, I quickly learned that the authors have written an article that helps readers know more of the mechanics of doing such a study. Since at times researchers have little to go on in terms of analyzing the data, I looked forward to reading some details about the process.

Initially, I was reluctant to use this article because it appeared in the *Journal of Research in Nursing*, and not in a journal in the educational field. However, once you get into it, you will see how applicable it is to education and to an understanding of grounded theory. In many articles (like the one you just read by Eich), so much of the "how to do something" is left unsaid. Writers use words and make statements, but I can't really tell quite what they mean. This is definitely *not* the case in this article.

You are in for a treat here so now it is time to reread the title, and read the abstract and headings.

The abstract makes clear the goal of the article. It makes use of data on a study of parent participation (a topic educators certainly will find interesting) to illustrate how to do a grounded theory study. So while the study uses data collected for another reason, its emphasis is on how to do a grounded theory study. As you have seen, one of the criticisms I have of the Eich study is that he provides very little explanation of how he did what he said he did. This study addresses many questions you might have had either in reading Eich's work or in trying to design your own study. Coyne and Cowley begin with an Introduction. As I have said in other places, it is by no means a requirement to use the heading Introduction. My preference— leave it out. Since the purpose of this study is to explain the use of grounded theory as a research approach, the authors provide a brief overview of the approach and the controversies surrounding

Abstract

There are many interpretations and applications of the grounded theory method which have contributed to different understandings of grounded theory and different versions of how the key components (theoretical sampling, constant comparative analysis and theoretical saturation) should be implemented. The esoteric terminology coupled with the matrix style of the analysis process can be challenging for new researchers. This paper uses data from a study on parent participation to illustrate the application of the key components of grounded theory. Grounded theory provides clear guidelines on how to analyse qualitative data and so is a rigorous method that provides structure and direction to the researcher. However, theoretical sampling with vulnerable groups can be problematic and requires further discussion and debate from other users of grounded theory.

Introduction

Grounded theory is an inductive research method that develops theory through constant comparative analysis. The goal is to develop theory that will explain the dominant process in the social area being investigated. It is underpinned by symbolic interactionism which focuses on the nature of social interaction and, essentially, is a theory about human behaviour that sees humans as both actively creating the social environment and being shaped by it. A person's response to an event is determined by their understanding and interpretation of the meaning of the event and the ability to communicate this meaning using language (Blumer, 1969). Since the publication of it. Note how short the information is under the literature review heading. They do not provide a literature review on the topic of parent participation because that is not the purpose of this article, but they make an important point. They say that a literature review is usually "contraindicated." I would have chosen a different term here, but you get the idea. Some people believe that doing a literature review puts the researcher in a box and narrows his or her thinking about the topic. But, as the authors suggest, there is no general agreement on this point. In Eich's article, he included a brief literature review, but did not integrate it into his discussion.

Glaser and Strauss' seminal work on grounded theory in 1967, there have been many interpretations and applications of the method and disagreements over how the key components should be implemented (Chenitz and Swanson, 1986). Several researchers have criticised grounded theory reports for the mixing of methods and muddling of theoretical perspectives (Baker et al., 1992; Becker, 1993; Sandelowski, 1993; Stern, 1994; May, 1996; Wilson and Hutchinson, 1996) which has led to concerns about rigour (Sandelowski, 1993; Chiovitti and Piran, 2003). The main criticism appears to be that many studies have not adhered to the critical components of the method, resulting in studies that are descriptive rather than with conceptual depth (Becker, 1993).

Disagreement arose between Glaser and Strauss themselves with the publication of *Strauss and Corbin's Basics of Qualitative Research* in 1990. In Glaser's opinion, this text advocated a forcing of the data to form theory, rather than letting the theory emerge from the data, which he termed as "full conceptual description" rather than grounded theory. Glaser's criticism of Strauss and Corbin's description of grounded theory and his central argument about the emergence of grounded theory has received support from other scholars (Stern, 1994; Robrecht, 1995; Melia, 1996). These authors provide excellent critiques of the key issues in this argument, therefore this paper does not intend to revisit this discussion in detail. It is an important distinction that Glaser allows the data to reveal the theory, whilst Strauss and Corbin look for every contingency, whether it appears in the data or not. It is also significant that the two grounded theorists are seen as demonstrating differing epistemological premises for the method (Annells, 1996). Therefore, it is the belief of this researcher that one should adhere to the original premise of grounded theory, which is that theory emerges from the data, thus this paper reflects a Glaserian approach.

The connection to symbolic interactionism is often overlooked. Some believe that this theory is the underlying theoretical underpinnings of grounded theory. But not all writers agree.

The authors state their purpose very clearly here.

Given that grounded theory is a complex method and the language can be esoteric, many researchers often experience difficulty using the method. Practical "worked" examples help to explain the process and particularly the method's central components. To this end, this paper will use data from a study on parent participation to illustrate the data analysis process of the grounded theory method. It will draw on Glaser's (1978) description of grounded theory because it provides clear steps on the key principles of the method.

The authors make a very important point here. Some believe that a literature review influences the direction of data

LITERATURE REVIEW

With a grounded theory study, the researcher usually begins with a broad aim and a literature review is usually contraindicated.

interpretation, and argue that a review should not be conducted prior to collecting data.

However, others would argue that a literature review is necessary as it helps to identify gaps in knowledge on the topic (Stern, 1980; Cutcliffe, 2000; Chiovitti and Piran, 2003). The aim of this study was to explore the topic of parent participation in the hospitalised child's care from the child's, parents' and nurses' perspectives. Hence a literature review was conducted which revealed that, although there were many descriptive qualitative studies in this area, none had used a grounded theory method to research this topic, and there was a lack of explanatory theory on the subject. It showed that the child's view had been omitted in studies of parent participation. Thus the literature review was very useful as it provided justification for another study in this area and for the particular approach that was taken.

Because the central purpose of this article is not a study of parent participation but rather of how to do the data analysis in a grounded theory, the authors did not report any information about the literature on the former topic.

DATA COLLECTION

Data Collection is only a brief paragraph. Unlike Eich, who described in great detail how he selected his sample, these authors just say a very little bit about where, from whom, and how many were involved in data collection.

In a grounded theory study the data may be collected from interview, observation or documents, or from a combination of these sources. The data were derived from in-depth interviews (n = 33), three questionnaires (children only), informal observation, documents (ward philosophies, care plans) and literature. The bulk of the data were from interviews with parents (n = 10), their children (n = 11) and nurses (n = 12) selected from four paediatric wards in two hospitals in England. The type of observation was "observer as participant" in that the predominant activity was to observe the participants, locations and potentially to interview (Streubert and Carpenter, 1999). Throughout the study, the researcher kept field notes of all observation periods, contacts with participants, discussion with health professionals in the field and reflections on interview data.

Data Analysis Process

You might be wondering why I selected this article for you to read. It is the section that follows that represents the strength of the article. The data analysis process is described and illustrated in great detail. Various stages lay out the process. A section on theoretical sampling is followed by the conclusion.

Table 1 illustrates 4 stages in the analytic process. Notice how the stages move the analysis from detailed coding into categories and ultimately to the generation of theory.

The process of generating theory is one of deconstruction and reconstruction of the data, and the principal strategy for achieving this is the constant comparative method of analysis (Glaser and Strauss, 1967). The steps in the analysis process are grouped into four stages which are outlined in Table 1.

The stages listed in Table 1 imply a linear process, but the method actually involves a matrix with several processes in operation at once (Stern, 1980). For example, as codes were compared, more data were collected, categories were merged, memos were written and compared, then more data were collected. Memos were written at different stages in the analysis and the memos built on previous memos and also captured new insights into the data. Interview transcripts were read and reread throughout the study as

Table 1   Stages of the Analytic Process

Stages	Procedure	Purpose
1	Listening to the interview tapes Transcription of interviews Creating a database	Heighten awareness of key issues Recording data in word format System for managing the data
2	Line-by-line substantive coding (Writing codes in the margin of the transcript) Put incident and codes on cards Write theoretical notes on cards	Labelling the substance of the data Breaking data down (fracturing the data) Keeping record of analysis Capturing ideas about fragment of data
3	Compile list of codes Group codes into categories	Forming categories Abstraction from the data Integrating the codes
4	Constant comparison of the codes Movement of codes Compare and contrast with previous codes Memos on categories Identify theoretical codes Mapping of categories Using literature as data	Discovering and building categories Building and developing categories Integrating the data Capturing ideas and documenting recurring themes Conceptualising how substantive codes relate to each other (developing links and relationships between categories) Visual representation of categories and relationships Developing the categories

This discussion is an example of an iterative process and theoretical sampling.

The next section provides a detailed explanation of the stages of the analysis.

Figure 1 provides a graphic pathway through the data collection and analysis process. You will note that the process begins in a linear order but provides for an iterative process cycling back through gathering information, developing codes and categories, integrating the literature, and—most

the categories were developed. This "checking back" is a method of confirming or disconfirming that ensured that the categories were grounded in the data rather than "flights of fancy" or pet ideas. This is the strength of the grounded theory approach: the conceptualisations are grounded in the social world of participants. The data analysis was a series of overlapping steps that were revisited at different points (see Figure 1). Thus the analysis process contained both linear and circular dimensions that allowed for a logical systematic analysis and also allowed for introspection and ruminating.

STAGE 1: CREATING A DATABASE

A simple computer package called Filemaker Pro (Claris-Corporation, 1992) was used only to manage the data. As incidents were coded on the transcript, each incident was then entered onto a card on the database, along with the codes attached to it and any memos (thoughts) on the particular incident. These cards could be compared and contrasted. The interview tapes were listened to,

Figure 1   Matrix of the Data Analysis Process

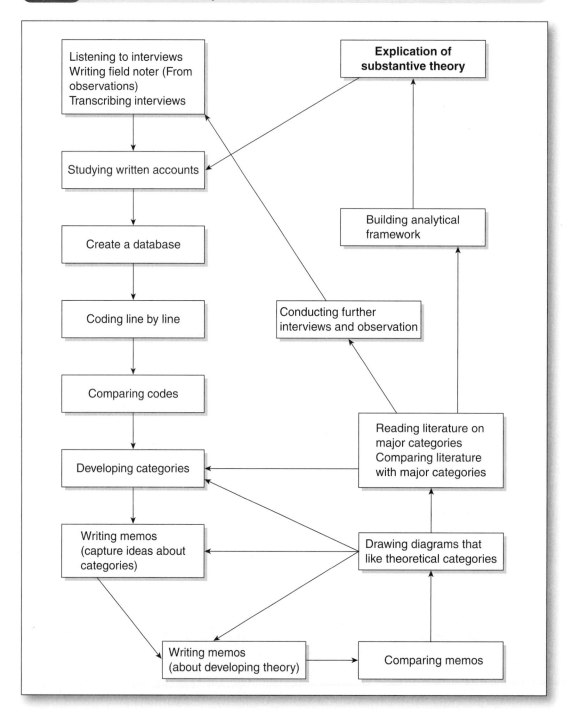

important—gathering additional information through observations and interviews.

Most researchers today would tend to use a computer to keep track of things. This is especially true if there is a large amount of data to organize.

broad themes were recorded and then the tapes were transcribed verbatim. Although Glaser (1978) recommends that each interview be analysed before proceeding to the next interview, at times this was not possible. On such occasions, listening to the tape and compiling broad themes ensured awareness of issues prior to the next interview. Interviews were labelled with codes to protect respondents' identities and were prefaced with a front sheet that contained relevant demographic and observation details. Field notes were written up after every visit to the wards and the data were used to provide background to some of the interview data.

STAGE 2: CODING PROCESS

Much qualitative research, not just grounded theory, claims that the process is dynamic and moves between data collection and data analysis. In my experience, though, researchers tend to follow a linear process: first they collect the data and then they analyze it.

Again, do not assume it is only this research approach that involves such detailed coding. Many approaches do.

In grounded theory, the analysis begins immediately with the first interview and also guides further data collection. The interview transcript is read line by line and paragraph by paragraph, looking for incidents and facts, and is coded for anything and everything that seems potentially relevant. This coding is very detailed and time-consuming, yet it is critical as it forces the researcher to be open to all possibilities in the data (the discovery in grounded theory) and to systematically conceptualise the data. This is the deconstruction of data as the data are cut into meaningful segments and coded with one or more substantive codes. The fragments of data may vary in length and may contain a variable number of substantive codes. According to Glaser (1978), the length of the fragment is not important; what matters is that it is meaningful. The database record contains space for theoretical notes, which are the researcher's thoughts and impressions about the fragment of data. Table 2 provides an example of an incident and coding.

. . .

STAGE 3: FORMING CATEGORIES

Notice we have moved from codes—stage 2—to categories—stage 3.

Through constant comparative analysis, the substantive codes are then developed into categories, and the categories are finally integrated into theory. It is the code rather than the data itself that the analyst works with, thus achieving a level of abstraction from the data. Categories are "simply coded data which seem to cluster together" (Stern, 1980). For example, as each transcript was coded, the generated codes were summarised in one file, thus making "laundry lists" of substantive codes from the data which were then compared with codes from previous interviews (Chenitz and Swanson, 1986). The interviews from the children, parents and nurses were initially analysed within their grouping. For example, each interview (from a nurse) was coded line by line, then compared with codes from previous interviews (from nurses) and then collated into one file in the database. Then as the next nurse transcript was coded, these codes were compared with the first list of codes. The same process was conducted with the parents' and children's transcripts.

STAGE 4: DEVELOPING THE CATEGORIES

In Stage 4, the categories are narrowed and integrated.

As categories are formed, the process of developing and integrating the categories is occurring concurrently. This process is somewhat like trying to put the pieces of a puzzle together without having the picture available. Glaser (1978) suggests several strategies to help the researcher through the process: constant comparison and reduction; theoretical sampling; theoretical coding; writing memos; drawing diagrams; and using literature as data.

One distinguishing feature of the grounded theory approach is what is called the constant-comparison method: the number of categories is reduced by comparing one with another until the researcher sees how they fit together. The redundant ones are eliminated or joined with others.

Constant Comparison and Reduction of Categories. Categories are reduced by comparing and contrasting categories to see how they cluster or connect together. This process helps to build, densify and saturate the categories and is also a vital step in discovering the core categories that will form the "scaffolding" in the final substantive theory. The formation of categories is characterised by fluidity because, as more data is collected, the categories may change, or become part of another category. As Stern points out, "the researcher may hypothesise that data belong in a certain category and may prove or disprove the hypothesis of categorisation by collecting more data" (Stern, 1985). It is a process of fitting categories together and, as linkages emerge, categories collapse and form more theoretical categories. The categories were compared and contrasted (reduction of categories) until the major categories were identified for each group (nurses, parents and children). Then these categories were developed and integrated through use of theoretical coding, memos, diagrams and literature, to identify the core categories for the substantive theory. The developed theory must be integrated, which means that all parts must fit together and the core category should account for most of the variation in a pattern of behaviour that is both relevant and problematic for the participants involved (Glaser, 1978).

Theoretical sampling is another key element of the grounded theory method. Here the authors explain how this is done.

Theoretical Sampling. Theoretical sampling is a process wherein the researcher jointly collects, codes and analyses the data, and decides which data to collect next and where to find these data, in order to develop the theory as it emerges (Glaser, 1978). Thus the type of sampling is selected according to the developing categories in the emerging theory, rather than a concern for variables such as age, class or characteristics of the sample. Hence, theoretical sampling is an integral part of the data collection and analysis process.

The sampling in this study may be seen as comprising four phases that represented different forms of theoretical sampling.

PHASE 1

If you do not read carefully, you might get confused between Stages of the analysis and Phases of the theoretical sampling approach.

Initially the sample is purposefully selected from an area where the phenomenon is found to exist (Coyne, 1997). The broad subject area was "parent participation in hospitalised child's care," therefore the intention was to interview children, parents and nurses because they represented information-rich cases who had experience by virtue of their involvement. The only criteria for the children were that they were aged seven years upwards and were physically able to cope with an interview situation. The initial participants were from Ward A (dermatology—chronic illness) and from Ward B (medical and surgical—acute illness). At the start of this study, unstructured interviews were used to collect data in the participants' own words, to gain a description of situations, and to elicit detail using the minimum of control. The interview schedule contained a set of general questions which served as prompts if the case arose. Most of the time, when parents and children were asked the opening question, they proceeded to "tell their story" with minimal prompts from the interviewer.

PHASE 2

Additional sample drawn to modify category identified earlier during coding process.

Theoretical sampling is also used as a means to test, elaborate, and refine a category and/or to test the validity of a category (Glaser, 1978). Thus, particular participants may be selected because of their characteristics and the format of the interview may alter according to the dictates of the emerging categories. The data indicated that the category "time" could be a significant condition linked to categories termed "relationships" and "knowing." The linkages were tentative, which indicated the need for further sampling. Therefore it was decided to collect data from another research site, where the children would experience lengthy admissions (longer that four days) in order to develop and extend the category of time. After observing three more wards, Ward C was chosen as it provided treatment for children with orthopaedic problems. The selection of another site also enabled the comparison and contrasting of data with data on ward culture from the previous two sites.

As the study progressed, the interview schedule became more focused because of new questions related to the developing categories. The format of the interview still remained relaxed, in that the researcher followed up on cues and leads provided by the participants. This does raise the issue of bias, in that concern may be expressed over the possibility of "leading" the respondent. In clarification, Glaser (1978) points out that the categories emerge from the analysis of the data, so these are sensitising concepts produced by the respondents that are used to uncover more data rather than verify possible existing theoretical biases of the researcher. Therefore the interview guide was reflecting the developing categories rather than any preconceived ideas from the researcher. For example, the issue of "disruption" and "parenting role" was evident throughout the first few nurses' interviews, but it soon became clear that there were gaps about the links between these two categories and the related conditions and consequences. Therefore open questions on these categories were incorporated into the interview guide with subsequent nurse respondents.

This is a very interesting insight. In my experience, asking participants to speak of something that happened to them last week yields much more direct and meaningful information than asking them about events that are more remote. It is important to remember you are trying to understand what participants are feeling and not just get them to respond in ways they think you want to hear. These authors rightfully disclose certain problems that arise when interviewing children. Keeping things on a concrete level typically results in more meaningful data than going abstract.

However, pursuing specific lines of inquiry with the children proved to be more difficult. For example, most of the interviews ended when the children decided that they had said enough, as evidenced by the length of the interviews (ten minutes to one hour). Pursuing other lines of inquiry met with non-committal replies and nonverbal signs of "switching off." When attempts were made to probe certain issues by asking about feelings, some children either ignored the question, or said, "I don't know how I feel about it." Similarly, other researchers have found that requests for accounts of recent experiences elicited fuller responses from the children than directly asking for opinions or evaluations (Backett and Alexander, 1991; Alderson, 1993). The demands of theoretical sampling were balanced with the need to ensure that the children were not stressed by the interview, and to uphold the principle of beneficence. It was possible, however, to ask questions on some emerging categories without causing discomfort to the children. For example the "importance of school" and "making friends in hospital" emerged from the interview with child 1A. Thus with subsequent interviews, questions were posed about school and friendships in hospital which elicited good data that helped to elaborate those categories. Further interview data produced other categories such as "knowing the nurse" and "concern for parent," and efforts were made to direct questions around those categories to enhance elaboration and saturation.

PHASE 3

Phase 3 illustrates the interplay between data collection and data analysis.

The data analysis at this time also indicated that additional data needed to be collected in a theoretical manner to clarify the properties of the main categories. The criterion for judging when to stop sampling the different groups pertinent to a category is the category's theoretical saturation. At this stage of the analysis, the major categories appeared to be: "being there," "uncertainty," "disruption," "environment," "involvement," "knowing," "trusting," "relationships," "balancing" and "controlling." The links between the major categories needed to be checked with more nurse participants. Therefore, three more interviews were conducted with nurses from a Ward D (medical and surgical) in a second hospital. In these interviews, the questioning was more focused, as the purpose was to clarify the properties of the major categories and develop hypotheses with nurses from a different site.

PHASE 4

Phase 4 involves additional review of data already collected. It is used to combine or eliminate redundant categories.

This phase did not involve more data collection from participants. However, according to the dictates of grounded theory method, it was a form of data collection as the data already obtained was theoretically sampled. For example, the emerging theory appeared to involve the major categories that were "being there," "balancing," "knowing" and "trusting." It seemed that, from the children's and parents' data, "finding a balance" was a core process that appeared to integrate the major categories and explain the data. However, the nurses' data suggested that "trying to get a fit" was the core process that explained the underlying action in the data. The category of "time" was evident in all the data, but it was not clear how time was related to the overall theory. Therefore the researcher re-read all the interview transcripts and theoretically sampled for the properties of time (a major category). This helped to identify the linkages between time and the major categories as time emerged as a subcategory of the categories that were "being there," "disruption" and "balancing." This stage helped to clarify that knowing and trusting were both properties and subcategories of balancing. Concurrent with the theoretical sampling of the data, the sampling of the literature helped to clarify the core processes in the study.

Developing Categories Through Theoretical Coding. To further assist in the development of theoretical codes that describe the links and relationships between categories, the researcher can apply a variety of analytic schemes to the data to enhance their abstraction. Theoretical codes are thus much more abstract than substantive codes and therefore provide a way of thinking about the data in theoretical rather than descriptive terms. To assist in the process of theoretical coding, Glaser (1978) provides many examples of theoretical codes, which he calls "families." One of these families he calls the "range model" which is a simplified version of the more complex "Six Cs" family of theoretical codes (see causes, contexts, contingencies, consequences, covariances and conditions, 1978: 74). In this range model, the researcher looks for all the possible causes and consequences of the phenomenon. Table 4 provides an example of theoretical coding of categories from the children's data.

Notice here how we have moved from coding (first level) to categories (second level) to theoretical coding (third level).

The next sections offer alternative ways of developing categories. The first alternative uses memo writing, the next uses diagrams, and the last uses the literature. These are interesting ways of using other data, and not using interviews as the only source of data.

This table lists the codes as they appeared at one stage of the study, but the full range of conditions under which these causes and consequences occur still required further development. However, developing theoretical codes helped to conceptualise how categories relate to each other and are integrated into the theory eventually. The analysis is tentative at this stage as there is constant movement of the categories throughout the analytic process.

Developing Categories Through Memo Writing. In the early stages of the data analysis, the researcher can quickly feel overwhelmed by the proliferation of data produced by the line-by-line coding. To avoid losing track of the analysis, Glaser (1978) suggests writing memos that help capture ideas, note linkages between categories and document the recurring themes and categories noted in the data. This process encourages the researcher to be creative and ideational. Memos were used extensively in this study and helped to (1) keep track of the analysis by documenting what the data were saying about different codes and categories, (2) capture relationships between categories, (3) enhance the theoretical ordering of the categories and (4) integrate existing memos.

The initial memos appeared to be very descriptive and repetitive of the actual statements of the participants, which indicated a difficulty in writing at a theoretical level. According to some grounded theorists, memos should not be redone on the grounds that the researcher felt that her/his skill was poor or that the memos are unclear (Glaser, 1978; Stern, 1985). The important issue is to build upon the memos as the analysis proceeds, rather than present a neat, compact summarisation of the issues. As the study progressed, confidence grew with handling the data and, consequently, the memos became more theoretical, which helped to raise the data to a conceptual level. Figure 2 provides an example of some memos on trust written over a period of time.

Writing memos helped to identify the relevance of the category "trusting" and some possible linkages to other categories, such as "knowing" and "relationships" which indicated that more detail was required on this category and its properties. Therefore, when the issue of trust was mentioned by further participants, the researcher used the opportunity to clarify some of the properties and conditions associated with the category. Second, memos were used to capture relationships between categories and these types of memos are termed "hypothesizing memos" (Chenitz and Swanson, 1986). For example, the terms "standing back" and "taking steps" were repeated frequently by parents and nurses in relation to parents' involvement in care. These terms conjured up the image of participants "dancing around" each other, which was captured in a rough memo. This imagery helped to capture the tentative ideas in a memo that later proved quite useful in understanding the relationship between parents and nurses. The significance of this

Figure 2 Example of Memos on Trusting

Memo 1

This nurse described a situation where the nurses used strategies to remove a parent from bedside in order to develop relationship with a child. The nurses found it difficult to know the child because the mother had a "disapproving" presence. She described how consequently she weighs up the "pros and cons" of involving parents in doing care. Developing the relationship was important in order to build up child's self-esteem and enable trust to develop between child and nurses. This implies that nurses may find it difficult to establish a trusting relationship with a child due to parents' presence.

Memo 2

It is important to "build up" trust with patients as this makes it easier to explain care and deliver care. This implies that trust is important in the formation of relationships and delivery of care. Building trust appears to be a process. Involving parents in care appears to help the trust relationship with child and parents. Why is building trust with the child so important and how does it occur? Do nurses build trust with parents and children?

Memo 3

It seems that nurses are "strangers" to both parents and children, therefore nurses need to work at building a trusting relationship. Parents' presence provides support and security to their children as the children know and trust them. This implies that parents and children may start an admission from a position of distrust or wariness perhaps.

Memo 4

Involving parents in care reassures the child and helps nurses "get the children's confidence." This implies that nurses need parents as it takes time to gain child's confidence. Children who are unaccompanied need to be able to relate to a nurse that they can trust. Trust makes it easier to explain and deliver care to [children] which was mentioned before. Talking and relating to children daily helps nurses to gain their confidence. Children "trust you better" and this helps with the delivery of care. This implies that building trust is a gradual process influenced by time that helps with the delivery of care.

memo did not become apparent until much later in the analysis, when it was linked with the strategy of "trying to get a fit" and "finding a balance."

Third, memos were used to integrate existing memos, which is very important as it is from memos, compiled and sorted, that the analyst derives the material to write up the final theory. Memos were written constantly on all the data from nurses, parents and children, which meant that towards the end of the data analysis, there was a large collection of memos on different categories and issues.

You will find that memo writing is extremely helpful. These illustrative memos should give you some ideas you can employ in your own work.

Initially the researcher began writing by referring to unsorted, but very rich memos, but eventually the write-up stalled. Indeed, not surprisingly, Glaser warns that memo sorting must not be skipped or hurried since: "if the analyst does omit sorting, he will indeed have somewhat of a theory, but it will be linear, thin and less than fully integrated" (1978: 116). Hence the process of writing yet more theoretical memos about existing memos enhanced the sorting of the memos and helped to clarify the linkages between the major categories and the core concept. For example, this process revealed that "time" was a condition rather than a major category and was related to other conditions that were "knowing" and "trusting," which influenced the process of "finding a balance." This led to a re-examination of the database on the codes and categories, a re-reading of the interview transcripts and the production of more memos. Glaser suggests that, although memo writing begins during data collection, coding and analysing of the data, and peaks as coding saturates, *it is never over* until the final draft is complete. This example of memo sorting clearly illustrates the "back tracking" matrix nature of the data-analysis process in grounded theory.

Developing Categories Through Diagrams. In addition to writing memos, the mapping, linking and ordering of categories were developed through the use of diagrams. This helped to capture creative thoughts on the data and provided a method of documenting tentative hypotheses. Diagrams enhance the conceptualisation process by encouraging the researcher to see theoretical codes related to properties, conditions, strategies and consequences (Glaser, 1978). Constructing diagrams helps to show how the categories relate to each other to develop the theoretical codes. Through the diligent use of diagrams, the researcher may discover relationships that may not have been readily apparent and examination of a diagram may also indicate gaps in the analysis where the categories or emerging theory needs further development. In this study, diagrams also made a strong contribution to the final formulation of the substantive theory as considerable effort was directed towards providing a pictorial representation of the theory so that the core concept was clearly outlined in relation to the main categories. This diagram was the most difficult to compile and underwent several redraftings until it accurately represented the substantive theory. Interestingly Orona (1997) suggests that "if the researcher is unable to graphically depict "what all is going on here" he or she is probably not genuinely clear of the process yet" (1997: 181). This may not be true of researchers who dislike drawing and thus struggle to capture ideas in graphic form. The diagram of the substantive theory may be seen in Figure 3.

Developing Categories Through Selective Sampling of Literature. Glaser and Strauss (1967) recommends examination of the literature on the area under study once the analytic core of

| Figure 3 | Integration of Core Categories |

Process	FINDING A BALANCE		
Participants	Children	Parents	Nurses
Strategies	Disruption of being ill Relying upon parents Re-establishing routine 'Fitting in' Helping with care	Disruption of being there Feeling responsible Re-establishing routine 'Fitting in' Providing care	Relying on parents being there Re-establishing parents role Socializing parents and children Maintaining routine
Conditions Knowing	⟵⟶ Trusting	⟵⟶ Time	⟵⟶

Figure 3 provides a detailed example of how categories can be integrated. These concrete examples provided throughout the article should help make the analysis process more transparent and easier to follow.

categories has emerged. The literature is searched for different insights or ideas about some of the categories in order to develop and extend the categories. The literature was used to further the process of constant comparative analysis, through seeking similarities and differences to the categories identified in this study, thus acting as a secondary source of data by forming another comparison group with the data. For example, the category of "being there" was developed through comparison with nursing literature on presencing (Gilje, 1992; Taylor, 1994), and caring (Morse et al., 1990; Gaut, 1992; McCance et al., 1997; Edwards, 2001). This literature revealed that there were different meanings to the category "being there"; it had links to issue of trusting and that there were different dimensions to "being there," such as being there as a reliable presence rather than just being present on the ward. This information enhanced understanding of the data from the parents in relation to their presence on the ward, and guided the inquiry process in further interviews with nurses and parents. Some of the categories were also identified in qualitative studies on parent participation (Darbyshire, 1992; Callery, 1995), in a paediatric grounded theory study (Price, 1993) and in a grounded theory study of caregivers for elderly relatives (Shyu, 2000). The categories also led to the examination of unexplored literature on social order theory, disruption theory, humanistic psychology and role theory.

THEORETICAL SATURATION

Participants were recruited until theoretical saturation of data was achieved. In grounded theory, data saturation occurs when the categories

This section provides a very good example of how to reach theoretical saturation.

are saturated, elaborated and integrated into the emerging theory. The process appears quite straightforward, but in practice it involved considerable work using the tools outlined above before the core concept emerged. It became clear that "finding a balance" was the core concept as it recurred frequently in the data, accounted for most of the variation in a pattern of behaviour identified in the data, and helped structure all the major categories into a workable theory that explained the major problem under scrutiny (Glaser, 1978). Saturation is defined as "data adequacy" and operationalised as collecting data until no new information is obtained. However, other researchers have questioned the notion of "absolute" theoretical saturation, as findings are forever tentative and open to modification through the findings of other researchers or one's own subsequent research (Gilgun, 1992; Morse, 1995). Thus saturation of data may be the "best" that is achieved at a particular time. Gilgun (1992) recommends that having confidence in your data is what matters and ensuring that the findings are grounded in data, that the concepts and hypotheses extracted from the data have been tested many times within and across cases, and they have been linked to previous research and theory.

CONCLUSION

Much of the grounded theory research is difficult to follow. These detailed illustrations point out a way to move from the actual data through various steps to reach a theory grounded in the data.

This paper has demonstrated how data may be analysed in a grounded theory study. It is not intended as a blueprint; rather, it is offered as just one example of how grounded theory may be used. Each researcher who uses grounded theory will develop their own style depending on their interpretations of the method. What is important is that researchers adhere to the central components of the method. The advantage of the method was the logical systematic research process which resulted in the production of a theory that was relevant. The matrix style of the analysis process can be particularly challenging for new researchers. Furthermore the numerous stages involved in the data analysis process and the theoretical sampling of participants and literature can be very demanding and requires close supportive research supervision.

Using the literature as another data source when the major categories have been delineated significantly contributes to the data analysis process. However, there is a danger that one can become enthralled by existing frameworks which seem to offer a quick solution and end up trying to force the data to fit. Of course the constant comparison process will quickly reveal that this is a problem and hence is quite self-corrective. But considerable time could be lost if one is not careful with the use of literature as another data set. The final point which should be considered is that theoretical sampling is not easy to achieve with children, and could potentially place undue pressure on them. Grounded theory is a method that is not easily understood, there are disagreements about its central premise and there are many different interpretation of the method. Consequently it is important that researchers publish their techniques of using grounded theory to provide guidance and structure for new researchers.

Of course, other disciplines also make use of the grounded theory research approach. Education is an excellent example of one such discipline.

Key Points

- Grounded theory is a popular research method for the study of nursing phenomena.

- Different versions of grounded theory and the lack of agreement among the originators, can cause confusion.

- It is important that researchers adhere to the central components of the method and not take shortcuts.

- Theoretical sampling with vulnerable groups such as sick children can be problematic.

- The matrix style of the analysis process can be challenging for new researchers thus close supervision from a grounded theory expert is essential.

Source: Coyne, I., & Cowley, S. (2006). Using grounded theory to research parent participation. *Journal of Research in Nursing, 11*(6), 501–515. Reprinted with permission from SAGE.

Summary and Review

Did you find this article helpful? It lays out very specific procedures you can follow when doing grounded theory. The authors' examples should help guide you as you begin thinking about your own analysis or as you read other grounded theory research.

As a practical matter, I doubt many researchers actually go through the iterations that the authors describe. Also, computer software such as NVIVO can facilitate and manage the process. But beware: You cannot really just pick up the software and learn how to use it. Once you master the learning curve, you will be delighted. I don't think that keeping track of data on cards will serve you well in the long run.

Finally, if you return to the four questions I posed at the beginning of this chapter, you can see the extent to which this article was successful. In my opinion, Coyne and Cowley introduced specific ideas about conducting grounded theory and they wrote in an engaging style.

- Does it provide new information and insights related to the topic?

- Is it engaging and written in a clear manner?

- Does it emphasize the data analysis process of grounded theory?

- Do the positive aspects of the article outweigh the potential drawbacks?

FINAL COMMENTS

In this chapter, I provided you with a completed grounded theory study and an article about how to conduct the analysis when using a grounded theory approach. I was quite critical of Eich's study. My criticisms were with the application of the research approach to the study of leadership programs. It is important to understand that Eich published the article in a journal that focuses on leadership rather than a journal that is specifically devoted to qualitative work. The Coyne and Cowley article should be helpful if you plan to conduct a grounded theory study of your own or as you read other research that uses the research approach.

You can access the complete articles at www.sagepub.com/lichtmanreadings.

Chapter 3

READING PHENOMENOLOGY

By now you have read examples of ethnographies and grounded theory. In this chapter, I introduce you to published studies using a phenomenological approach. I have selected two examples. Technology and online communication are the subjects of both studies. The first, by Christopher Hines and his coauthors, uses principals as the primary study group. The second, by Cynthia Bambara and her coauthors, looks at community college students.

Phenomenology emphasizes the subjective lived experiences of individuals. It has its roots in the philosophical writings of Edmund Husserl, Martin Heidegger, and, more recently, Clark Moustakas. Some would argue it is a philosophy, while others speak about it being a methodology or method. It is closely associated with hermeneutics (the study and analysis of the written word). It is important to understand that a good phenomenological study moves beyond just a description of the experience: it strives to arrive at the essence of the experience. I suspect many researchers use the term, but most probably spend time just with a description of various experiences rather than with the underlying essence of experience.

It turns out that finding articles that are written using a phenomenological approach is quite daunting. I started down a number of pathways only to discover that several articles I selected did not exactly fit the bill. One turned out to be a part of a much larger study using a mixed methods approach. The second got so bogged down in the finer nuances of different kinds of phenomenology that I was concerned that you would stop reading before you really started.

KEY ELEMENTS OF PHENOMENOLOGY

- Phenomenology describes and tries to understand the lived experiences of individuals who have experienced a particular phenomenon;
- ultimately looks for the essence of the experience;
- is a research approach that relies heavily on philosophical underpinnings; and
- uses bracketing (setting aside preconceived ideas about a phenomenon) as an important component.
- Much of the work in phenomenology comes out of the field of nursing.

The first article you will read is by Christopher Hines, Stacey Edmonson, and George Moore. The authors are employed in schools, colleges, or universities. All have extensive school experience and write their article from the perspective of practitioners in the field. If you work in a school system, you know only too well that technology has come upon us in a fast and furious manner. Often the students are more up to date and have better equipment than the adults who lead the schools. I think the topic is especially timely. I also want you to read articles written for different types of audiences.

There is a wide range of research studies that calls itself phenomenology. Some are quite complex, and some are fairly simple in design. The Hines and colleagues study falls under the latter category. It is a study of 10 principals and academic leaders as they experience technology. The research is written in a traditional format. After a brief introduction, it includes a review of literature on school leadership and networking. It next introduces the heading *Data Resources.* In fact, what follows that heading is a description of the educational leaders in the study. An extremely short paragraph called *Method* mentions that the research is phenomenological, but says almost nothing else about the research approach. The bulk of the paper consists of the findings that have been organized into 12 themes that the authors present in a simple table.

In the second article, the authors, who are employed at colleges or universities, take a close look at 13 community college students who take online courses. Their study leads them to conclude that the essence of the phenomenon under study leads to a delicate engagement—vulnerable threads of academic and social involvement that permeated the academic experience.

Advance Preparations

I have provided various formats in my comments. In some articles I include detailed comments prior to the article; in others I include more of my comments within the article. In either case, it is important that you anticipate what you will find prior to your reading the article. These anticipations—or advanced organizing principles—assist you in reading in a thoughtful manner. Because the nuances of the differences between and among research approaches are sometimes subtle, you might find yourself lost in details. Setting the stage in advance for your reading will assist you as you try to understand key elements of qualitative research approaches.

Begin by reading the title and the abstract, then flipping through the article and reading the major headings and subheadings. Once you have an idea of the article's structure, go back and read through the article carefully. When you finish reading, you will need to decide the extent to which the article is successful. To do so, ask yourself four questions:

- Does it provide new information and insights related to the topic?
- Is it engaging and written in a clear manner?
- Does it illustrate elements you would expect to find in phenomenology?
- Do the positive aspects of the article outweigh the potential drawbacks?

Article 3.1. The Impact of Technology on High School Principals (2008)

Christopher Hines, Stacey Edmonson, and George W. Moore

My Expectations

I am now ready to look at the first article in depth. I anticipate that it will be a study that looks at the ways principals who are involved with technology experience the phenomenon. I will look for the ways the authors move from the data to amass themes or concepts and ultimately to reach the essence of the phenomenon.

ABSTRACT

The purpose of this study was (a) to research the impact of electronic communication on the role of the principal and school leaders and (b) to investigate patterns of unanticipated consequences or phenomena that have developed within the organization along with the widespread use of electronic media. Twelve themes were identified and grouped into two main categories of the principal's role and computer-mediated communication.

The abstract doesn't convey too much information about the article.

This is straightforward information that really doesn't tell you, the reader, anything you do not know already. Perhaps more factual data here would have been illuminating.

The title talks about technology, but so far the thrust is about electronic communication. I see these as two discrete subjects. I wonder if the authors will distinguish them.

This quote seems to be about e-mail, which is obviously not the only form of electronic communication. Will the authors bring in instant messaging, Twitter, and so forth?

I am confused. Now the authors say they want to address the impact of electronic communication on the role of the principal, a position not mentioned in the title. I think that might be very different from looking at the essence of the lived experiences of someone who has encountered a particular phenomenon. The second purpose, to investigate

There is no question that electronic communication has enabled administrators to solve many of the communication problems they faced only a few short years ago. Time and distance are now less important factors in communication. Ten years ago, cell phones, e-mail, Palm Pilots, wireless networks, and even voice mail were not common tools in the education environment. Today, administrators utilize all of them. The emergence of widespread technology has tremendously impacted the way school leaders perform their jobs and the way they manage information.

The use of electronic communication has grown so rapidly that for more than a decade, "electronically distributed communication supplants the postal service, telephone, and even the fax machine" (Boudourides, 1995, p. 1). As a result of this growth, the impact of electronic communication "on the lives of individuals should be explored to help understand the positives as well as the negatives of e-mail use" (Wilkinson & Buboltz, 1998, p. 1). The astonishing proliferation of electronic communication means that we can no longer ignore its impact on society, organizations, families, and individuals. The purpose of this study was (a) to research the impact of electronic communication on the role of the principal and school leaders and (b) to investigate whether patterns of unanticipated consequences, or phenomena, have developed within the organization along with the widespread use of electronic media and what those patterns might be.

REVIEW OF LITERATURE

Electronic communication is changing the way school organizations communicate. The amount of information at people's fingertips is exploding, and the role of the administrator is changing.

patterns of unanticipated consequences, is also confusing to me.

Why and how is the role of
the administrator changing?

This section is called *Review of
Literature*, but this first paragraph
does not have any literature in it.

These two paragraphs seem
to be introductory, and not a literature review. They include only
one reference. The topics they
introduce do not seem related to
the purpose of the study.

Administrators have observed a steady increase in the number and
types of electronic communication and have found that a growing
amount of time to respond to electronic communication and an
exploding amount of information is now required. This requires
more time at the computer.

The emergence of electronic communication has brought about
many unanticipated consequences, or phenomena. To deal with
these, there is a need for more staff development in the area of managing electronic communication. Owens (2001) pointed out that
while schools have tended to mimic the values and views of industry and commerce, it is becoming more apparent that schools are
distinct and unique types of organizations. As a result, schools
require thought processes, styles of leadership, and administrative
practices that are unique to them. He noted that the uniqueness of
schools as organizations is in their educational mission that demands
that they be growth-enhancing institutions. Schools foster personal
learning and growth, and development of students. Schools encourage processes of maturing, enhancement of self-esteem and self-
confidence, satisfaction, taking initiative, and seeking responsibility
for one's actions. Education organizations seek to increase the personal and interpersonal competencies of the organization's participants, to constantly develop the skills of the group in collaborating,
to enact cooperative group behavior that is caring and supporting of
others, and to manage conflict productively and without fear. Owens
viewed educational leaders as persons who strive for a vision of a
school as one that seeks to be engaged in a never-ending process of
change and development, a race with no finish line. Education organizations may benefit from the added collaboration available from
technology.

School Leadership

Houston (2001) described the leadership of the future as a change
from managing the killer Bs—buildings, buses, books, budgets, and
bonds—to that of the crucial Cs of connecting, communicating, collaborating, child advocacy, curricular choices, community building,
and being courageous champions of children. Goodlad (1993)
referred to these as collaboration, connectedness, and community.
McFadden, Mobley, Burnham, Joyner, and Peel (2003) noted that the
competencies required for public school principals have changed
dramatically over the past decade:

> Academicians and practitioners alike are continually being challenged to
> examine the nature of contemporary school leadership as well as the
> preparation and practice of educational leaders in today's public schools.
> (p. 389)

Skrla, Erlandson, Reed, and Wilson (2001) summarized 21 performance domains identified by the National Policy Board for Educational Administration that define the basis for exemplary principal performance. Information collection is identified under the functional domains of (a) gathering data, facts, and impressions from a variety of sources about students, parents, staff members, administrators, and community members; (b) seeking knowledge about policies, rules, laws, precedents, or practices; (c) managing the flow of information and data; and (d) classifying and organizing information for use in decision making and monitoring. In the interpersonal domains, the principal should possess interpersonal sensitivity, demonstrate oral and nonverbal communication skills, and have a mastery of written expression. Furthermore, worth noting is the work of Mayer-Guell (2000) who argued that organizations establish the norms on how employees communicate and by which media. Principals play a major role in establishing the communication norms of their campuses by selecting the medium that best reflects the social presence desired:

> The social context often has a profound impact on media selection and usage. Within an organization, members' media choices may be affected by contextual factors and previously agreed-upon symbols. Their choices may be constrained by factors such as distance, expediency, structure, role expectations, organizational culture and time pressure. (p. 74)

In short, part of the effectiveness of a principal is the ability to choose the medium that best meets the demands of the situation. For example, a principal may call a faculty meeting to share an unexpected death of a student, whereas the size and distance of the parent audience requires a note be sent home. In today's environment, depending on the need for expediency, principals may even send electronic communications, often reaching parents at their place of work. The principal's ability to match the task with appropriate media selection may play an important part not only in establishing the principal's effectiveness at communicating but also in creating the culture of the organization. Thus, the supervisor (principal) sets an example for how employees (teachers, staff) use electronic communication (Mayer-Guell, 2000).

I do not find this literature review to be particularly compelling. I wish the authors had said more about research.

Networking and Social Interaction

After studying a networking community project for 2 years, Hampton (2003) refuted the idea that communication technologies disconnect people from their social networks and reduce public participation. His findings supported the idea that weak social ties benefit from the use of the technology by creating large, dense networks of relatively weak social ties through the use of communication technology. Hampton's study adds credibility to the notion that a school organization might benefit from the availability of electronic communication as a means for becoming a more connected community that collaborates and works together to fulfill the mission of the organization.

Is the emergence of electronic communication impacting the way members of organizations interact with one another? The shift in the interpersonal relationships is having an impact. One of the unforeseen complications is the reduced face-to-face interaction that results from the emergence of technology. The importance of face-to-face interaction is supported by Sproull and Kiesler (1991), who found that 93% of people's intent in a message was communicated by facial expression and tone of voice. As a result, it would seem that a text-based electronic communication would not readily "convey regulatory and social context cues" (Lieb, 1995, p. 23). Riva (2002) argued that "if face-to-face conversation occurs in a cooperative environment constantly regulated by mutual adjustment and correction, CMC [computer-mediated communication] occurs in a much less cooperative environment because of special conditions imposed by the medium itself" (p. 581). Face-to-face interaction uses a complex system of turn taking and yielding behaviors that are not readily present during CMC.

DESCRIPTION OF DATA RESOURCES

This descriptive study sought to establish how the phenomena related to electronic communication have impacted the role of the principal. For the purpose of this qualitative study, 10 educational leaders were interviewed in order to capture data and to shed light on the phenomena in question. Participants were interviewed in their place of work in order to study the phenomena in its natural context. Participants were varied based on gender, ethnicity, years of experience, and location and size of schools and/or districts in which they are employed. Three elementary principals were selected and interviewed, as were three junior high school principals, one ninth-grade campus principal, and three high school principals. The sizes of the districts represented ranged from fewer than 7,000 students to districts with more than 50,000 students. Although there was a desire to have participants with a variety of years of experience, it was of particular interest to identify participants who have experienced the changes that may be a result of the growing use of electronic communication. For this purpose, school leaders with fewer than 5 years of total education experience were not included. Experience levels

---

Do the authors plan to study this topic?

An impact on what?

The literature review does not seem to be very well focused. I do not know what points the authors intend to make. This last section, which introduces ideas about face-to-face connections, is based on quite old work. Today, given Facebook, MySpace, YouTube, Twitter, instant messaging, web cams, and so on, I suspect that these arguments do not necessarily hold true. I wish the authors had done more than report a few studies. They do not comment on them, nor do they relate them very well to their own study.

The authors should tell us how the participants were selected. For instance, were they volunteers? I suspect so.

The authors seem confused about how studying in a natural context is used. Usually this is done in an ethnographic study.

Since the authors do not speak to how the participants were chosen, one can assume only that they were purposefully chosen to reflect diversity by educational level and district size as well as demographic information mentioned above. In addition, do you think experience with electronic communication could have been a relevant criterion?

Here the authors seem to be getting at selecting participants who might have been in the business for some time and therefore had been involved in schools without electronic communication. I wonder if the authors are going to define what they mean by electronic communication. Are they limiting themselves to e-mail?

This statement seems to be at odds with what they have just said. Presumably someone who has been in the position only two years would not have experienced change. I think the authors are confused here. I do not know what they are talking about when they discuss change.

I don't know why the authors chose this way of describing their sample. They do not plan to generalize to a population of principals—at least they shouldn't be doing so since that is not the purpose of doing a phenomenological study.

The table below does not seem relevant to a description of the participants. For example, the category rating (of the school or the principal) does not seem relevant to anything related to technology or online communication. I suggest you avoid making a table unless it has some real meaning.

While I recognize that this journal is for practitioners, this oversimplification of a very complex method does not assist the reader. Using only two references

as a campus principal ranged from 2 years to 20 years. Ages ranged from 40 to 59 years. According to data provided by the Texas Education Agency (2007), there are 1,227 school districts in Texas; however, 64% of all students are enrolled in just 85 of these districts. Thus, our sample included principals from primarily large school districts. Because it was impossible to mirror an exact representation of the student population and the schools serving these students, we selected a typical case sampling of principals that reflected a diversity of gender, ethnicity, and experience (Gall, Borg, & Gall, 2006). Table 1 describes the specific demographic information for each participant.

Method

This was a phenomenological study, or a study of the lived experiences of the participants. Specifically, phenomenology is a specialized method within the interpretist paradigm for describing the different ways in which people conceptualize the world around them (Manen, 1990). One-hour interviews were conducted with each participant, and it was assumed that the responses were dependable and accurate to the best knowledge of the participants. Pseudonyms were used to protect the identity of the participants as well as the school district in which they worked. The interviews were recorded and transcribed verbatim. Subsequently, each interview transcript was read and analyzed for major constructs and common themes (Creswell, 2006).

FINDINGS

All 10 participants acknowledged that they, as principals, and their school organizations communicate differently as a result of electronic communication. There were many common themes that emerged from the discussions with principals. The time now required at the computer was an issue. This idea also emerged in a few principals' observations that they believed that there is a very real risk of being tied to the computer in one's office all day. As a result, there were obvious concerns expressed by many of the participants regarding the importance of maintaining face-to-face interaction with staff and parents. Related to the concept of time at the computer was a very clear perception that electronic communication has made it easier, even necessary, to work longer hours. Another observation that emerged was the realization that the volume of communication that principals now receive is increasing. In addition, the ability to send and receive large amounts of data and information electronically is adding to the growing demands of the medium. Nine of the 10 principals interviewed reported that they

| Table 1 | Summary of the Participants by Gender, Age (in years), Ethnicity, Campus Grades Served, Campus Size, and Academic Excellence Indicator System (AEIS) Rating |

Principal	Gender	Age	Ethnicity	Grades	Size	Rating
A	male	57	White	9–12	2347	exemplary
B	female	59	White	9–12	1895	acceptable
C	female	50+	Hispanic	10–12	2106	recognized
D	male	51	African American	9	918	acceptable
E	female	50	African American	7–8	1174	acceptable
F	female	53	White	7–8	1160	acceptable
G	male	48	African American	7–8	969	acceptable
H	male	40	Hispanic	PK–4	690	recognized
I	female	50+	White	PK–4	681	exemplary
J	male	48	White	PK–5	804	recognized

is not helpful. The explanation makes everything seem too simple. I would suggest the authors need to explain more fully how this study is a phenomenology.

The writers seem to have lost track of the idea that a phenomenological study deals with the essence of the lived experiences of the participants.

send communications electronically to their staff with the exception of Principal E, who still utilizes paper communication:

The only thing that I e-mail to the whole school is something that comes from Central Office like a posting—they are posting a position. And rather than use paper for that I will just forward it on to the staff. But it's generally something from the central office saying, please notify your staff of this, and then I will forward it on to them. But as far as my generating e-mails about particular situations or something I want them to do, a directive, it goes paper to them.

Finally, some of the principals interviewed for this study acknowledged the ability of electronic communication to enhance the communication within the organization and to foster a stronger sense of community, while others perceived the emergence of the Internet and electronic communication as having retardant effects on staff interaction. Interestingly enough, the perceptions of principals reinforce the two popular views that have emerged regarding electronic communication described by Wilkinson and Buboltz (1998). They noted that relationships that develop through the use of electronic media are, on one hand, shallow, often hostile, or even impersonal, while on the other hand, these relationships can be enhanced by reducing obstacles of physical location and time, resulting in genuine and personal relationships. In sum, 12 themes emerged from the analysis of the interview transcripts of the 10 principals. These themes can further be categorized into two main types: (a) principal role themes, which directly relate to the actual work and role of the principal, and (b) computer-mediated communication themes, which are more closely associated with general attributes and characteristics of computer-mediated or electronic communication.

Examining these 12 themes in a simple manner is no longer possible. What became clear from the interviews was that different people had different names for the same thing and different individuals had different views of the relationships. Thus, these themes represent broad ideas and perceptions, but they were very real, in varying degrees, to the 10 principals interviewed. In addition, each of these themes involves both positive and negative implications. Table 2 summarizes the 12 themes.

The writers identify 12 themes and then write a paragraph about each one, six under Role and Work of the Principal *and six under* Computer-Mediated Communication.

Principal Role Themes

Six major themes emerged as being specifically related to the role and work of the principal. These principal role themes are described below.

Volume of information. The first theme was the volume of information and communication that principals must now process in their jobs. Included in this theme is the concept of extraneous information with which principals now regularly find themselves saturated. Phenomena specifically discussed by participants and related to the notion of increased volume of information and communication include carbon copies, blind copies, forwarding, and junk mail. Also related to this discussion is the change in the filtering of communication that is reported by several of the participants. Since 9 out of the 10 principals interviewed open their own e-mail and the attached files that often come with them, there is also a change in the way principals process information and use their secretaries or administrative assistants. In fact, every single principal interviewed emphasized the tremendous amount of information that is shared via electronic communication and how that has increased the demands of the daily job. While principals are privy to information that might have been much more difficult to obtain in previous years, they are also overloaded with information that is often not necessary to their actual job performance.

This type of explanation of emerging themes sounds more like a grounded theory study than one of a phenomenological nature. I would be looking for the essences of the lived experience. I do not find that in the description here.

Time at the computer. The second major theme to emerge from the discussion related to the role and work of the principal is the amount of time required by principals to work at a computer station. This, perhaps, is what inspired one principal to warn of the danger of becoming chained to the computer. Complications and phenomena

Table 2   Summary of 12 Themes Related to Computer-Mediated Communication Identified in the Study

1. The volume of communication/information being sent and received
2. The increase in the amount of time being spent at work stations
3. Time spent at work
4. The ease of accessibility
5. Training for aspiring principals
6. Training for staff
7. Staff interaction
8. Style and syntax
9. Immediate and impulsive properties
10. The absence of social presence
11. Rate of speed of communication
12. Complications related to open records, legal issues, and student privacy

specifically related to this theme include the importance of face-to-face interaction, principal visibility, and stress and anxiety that result from the immediate and often impatient nature of electronic communication. As principals are required to spend more time at the computer sorting and sifting through information, our participants raised the question as to whether these "new" principal jobs were actually replacing tasks that would have previously been done by a staff member either on a typewriter or by phone. As one participant stated, "They [parents] get frustrated when they make a telephone call because we're not in. E-mail is easy because they can do it whenever they want. They can write it at night, any time they want to, and we'll respond at some point."

. . .

Computer-Mediated Communication Themes

Six major themes emerged from the interviews that related less to the role of the principal and more directly to the unanticipated consequences of e-mail itself. These six themes appear as Themes 7 through 12 in Table 1. Again, like the first six themes, several of these ideas were overlapping and closely related, but each presented a uniquely important set of consequences.

Staff interaction. Theme 7 encompassed the changes in patterns of staff interaction and the school community that resulted from the widespread use of electronic communication. Several principals

It seems almost too convenient that there are 12 themes that are organized into two main categories. I think calling the main categories "themes," and then the topics within "themes" is quite confusing. The authors should have chosen different terms here.

reported that their campuses now have different dynamics as a result of being connected electronically. For example, teachers communicate with each other and with the administrative team electronically rather than in person; as a result, teachers may generally spend more time in the classroom than before. As Principal A noted,

> They're in their room e-mailing, on the Internet, or doing something. I hear that over and over because teachers now will tell you they have to pull a lot of time in their day just to answer e-mails from parents. They've got e-mails from the teachers on the campus. They've got e-mails from administration. They've got e-mails from counselors. Instead of putting a piece of paper in a box asking how this kid is doing, they're e-mailing them, "Let me know how this kid is doing."

There are also new patterns of communication available to staff members and new expectations regarding these opportunities. Principal B noticed that electronic communication has kept more teachers in their classrooms, yet allowed these teachers to expand their circle of communication and network: "That is a great thing because, yes, it has allowed them the opportunity to communicate with each other and multi-task to complete things in their classroom and yet really communicate with other people in their department or across curriculum and do some things." Principal G also observed changes in the way his staff communicates with the emergence of electronic communication: "When they have paper memos, I could be guaranteed they were going to get it because it was physically in their box. There are people in the building who don't check their e-mail on a regular basis. Some teachers may not check it like they would their box on their conference period."

. . .

IMPLICATIONS

Here is where you would look for some connection between what was found and the literature that was reviewed. I do not see evidence of any such connection. When the authors say "only 10 principals," they seem to be apologizing for having only a few participants. You will recall that qualitative researchers often have small numbers of participants.

What are the implications of these findings based on the perceptions of only 10 principals? Technology has changed the way school leaders and their organizations communicate. The flow of that information is changing. Principals are changing the way they work as a result of technology and electronic communication. In simple terms, principals are now processing more information than ever before as a result of electronic communication. The volume of information being exchanged is growing at an alarming rate. The rate of communication is accelerating. The time required to work at a computer is increasing significantly as computers play larger roles in the day-to-day duties of principals. Successful principals must be able to deal with large amounts of information and they must be able to

This section might be more effective if it actually dealt with implications and did not simply state obvious facts.

manage it accordingly. Principals are working longer hours to keep up with the increase of communication. Principals are more accessible to parents, students, and staff. Principals need to know how to manage this aspect of their jobs. Many principals received little, if any, training in the area of technology management.

Staff dynamics may be impacted by electronic communication. Stress and anxiety may be a result of greater work demands, greater awareness, and accessibility. Principals tend to communicate electronically in ways that are different from more traditional forms of communication. They are now dealing with complications and benefits that are the result of electronic communication including the asynchronous nature of electronic communication, the lack of social boundaries, the impulsive properties of electronic communication, the rate of speed of electronic communication, and the legal issues that stem from electronic communication. Principals are starting to provide more training for their staff members as a result of complications mitigated by electronic communication.

RECOMMENDATIONS FOR PRACTICE

The findings from this study support important considerations for school leaders. One recommendation is to develop a staff training to prepare staff members for the complications and benefits of electronic communication. Several of the principals reported that they had already done this. This training was in addition to the "acceptable use" guidelines largely put in place by the school districts. Training should include legal reminders and warnings about responding emotionally, etiquette, policies, procedures, expectations regarding use, and discussions about the properties associated with this medium. Besides establishing rules, expectations, and guidelines for staff members, there should be a similar attempt to educate parents regarding use of the medium. Perhaps this is the one area that was not touched upon by principals. One suggestion might be to place information in the student handbook or to include discussion in a parent newsletter.

I think the authors would be better served by discussing the essence of the lived experiences.

Another recommendation for practice is to set up routines. Many of the principals interviewed had developed a structure, or pattern, to help them deal with the huge volume of information and communication they received. For example, principals described having set times for checking their e-mail such as before school, after school, and at lunch. Many principals purposely scheduled time to be out of their offices to ensure that they were visible on the campus. Many principals had developed working relationships with their secretaries to ensure that information could be managed as efficiently as possible. An additional recommendation for practice is to exercise caution in using e-mail. Pay particular attention to what is being sent and to whom. In general, it is recommended that one avoid putting anything into an e-mail to anyone that one would not want to see read in the newspaper. Another recommendation is to not engage in activities that one does not want staff to engage in such as copying, blind copying, forwarding, and including reckless content.

RECOMMENDATIONS FOR PRINCIPAL PREPARATION PROGRAMS

Although much research makes recommendations, these do not seem appropriate in this type of study.

Principal preparation programs are faced with the challenges of preparing school leaders for the world in which they will practice. These programs must begin to recognize the demands that principals are now facing in the area of managing information as part of preparing principals for the real challenges they will face in their day-to-day duties. The feedback provided by the 10 principals who participated in this study supports the need to include the management of information and electronic communication as part of the preparation of principals.

Principal preparation programs must help candidates to develop strategies to manage their time carefully, to effectively use their personal communication devices, to broaden their accessibility, and to better utilize their staff. Prospective principals should be prepared for the possible complications that may result from electronic communication and how to deal with extraneous information. Principals should be prepared to anticipate phenomena such as bypassing the chain of command, decision-deferring by subordinates, and potential legal complications created by electronic communication. Moreover, principals should be prepared for the political properties of e-mail and be on guard to its uses. Preparation programs should also help candidates to develop strategies for working with the volume of blind and carbon copies and the occasional angry e-mail that was written late at night or in the heat of the moment by the parent who would communicate differently in person.

Principals will deal with an accelerating pace of communication and larger amounts of information. Above all, principals must be made ready to deal with the change that is an inevitable part of their job skills. Technology has become the catalyst for change in so many areas related to school leadership, whether it is the gathering and analysis of data, the processing of information, the delivery of instruction, or the completion of administrative tasks such as managing budgets, completing evaluations, or simply generating reports.

Current textbooks on school leadership must provide more attention to this complex interaction. Specific recommendations include developing a curriculum designed to comprehensively evaluate the changing role of school leaders as it relates to communication and technology. Another recommendation is to continually evaluate the skills required of successful principals and to continually evolve the coursework needed to prepare these principals. What courses are still being taught that are now less important to the day-to-day challenges facing school leaders? Another important aspect of these preparation programs must focus on the development of capacity. The current role of this researcher includes the selection and hiring of school principals. One of the most critical of qualities sought in applicants is the capacity to learn and change with the ever-changing role of the job.

This study began with the simple observation and experience of the researchers that the job of a school principal has changed significantly in only the past few years and that, somehow, electronic communication was one of the catalysts for this change. The increase in communication places demands on principals to manage time, information, and perhaps most importantly, relationships.

I think this section should be strengthened.

RECOMMENDATIONS FOR FURTHER RESEARCH

Here the authors' comments, reflect their misunderstanding about the purpose of doing this kind of research. It is not intended to generalize as one would from a random sample. If the authors had been clearer on the purpose of doing a phenomenology, they probably would not have made this statement.

First, it is important to consider that the limited number of participants makes it difficult to generalize these findings. However, the research does open up discussion that is worth continuing. In addition, there are additional questions that are worth further study. Additional research on the impact of electronic communications on the role of the principal might wish to focus on some of the particular issues that only began to emerge from this study. Are there significant differences in perceptions depending on the size of the campus? There was some indication that larger organizations may experience the phenomena described to a greater degree. Are there differences in perceptions based on the gender and ethnicity of the principal? The small sampling indicated very little difference, but this question might be worthy of further exploration. Are there differences in perceptions based on the age and experience of the principal? This study had a fairly similar population in terms of experience. It might be beneficial to look at a broader range of principals in terms of years of experience. Are there differences based on the socio-economic makeup of the community of the campus? There were indications based on the interviews that those campuses serving communities that had higher socio-economic factors related to the number of free and reduced student lunches utilized electronic communication to a greater extent and had more experience with some of the phenomena discussed. Issues related to the digital divide that may exist between these communities might also be worthy of further study.

It seems as though the authors are making typical statements about doing additional research based on other obvious possible comparisons. I do not think this enhances the article.

An interesting question that may also be worthy of investigation revolves around the changing roles of school secretaries, or administrative assistants, as a result of electronic communication. As more and more principals directly engage in their own correspondence and as technology changes the patterns of work, are secretaries performing different functions? And, if so, what are these functions and how do they relate to supporting the role of the principal?

Also worth exploring is the question about stress and anxiety associated with the work of principals. Does electronic communication add to the stress and anxiety of principals? Is the already difficult job made more so because principals now have more things to worry about? Has the pace of work accelerated as a result of electronic communication? Are the long hours that principals already put in growing even longer? Are the skills required to be a successful principal changing? This study would indicate that principals perceive that the skills required to be successful are, in fact, changing with the demands of technology.

Another question to be explored might include the relationship between the principal and the campus use of electronic communication. Does the principal influence the overall campus use of electronic communication? If so, how? As a result of this study, we would like to gain a better understanding of the impact that electronic communication is having on the staff interaction. Are campus staffs becoming more isolated or less isolated? We heard perceptions from the principals on both sides of the argument. What are the changes in the way that staff members interact as a result of electronic communication? Are schools becoming a stronger learning community or more fragmented and isolated as a result of electronic communication?

A question that evolved from the discussions with principals is related to characteristics associated with successful principals. What do the best principals have in common in terms of practices? As data were collected, it was tempting to draw conclusions as to whether the principal was strong, or less so, based on the way he or she responded to questions. Of particular insight was how principals structured their day, their perceptions of work, their desire to embrace change, their openness to new ideas and technology, their ability to deal with multiple tasks, their ability to deal with large amounts of information, their ability to manage stress, and their ability to communicate with constituents.

Again, this idea of using quantitative research to "validate" qualitative research is an old one not normally held today by most researchers.

In addition, this study could be validated by a quantitative study. The 12 emerging themes that have been placed into the two categories of principal themes and computer-mediated communication themes could be studied further by creating an instrument that specifically deals with these themes. The results could be quantified and used to validate this study. Furthermore, the surveys might be given to teachers to check any difference in perceptions between principals and staff.

Additional studies could focus on each of the 12 emerging themes individually. For example, the style and syntax question could be asked and answered by examining thousands of e-mails, looking for patterns. The lack of social presence and complications associated with this could be examined further. A study of legal issues might be in order. One of the points made in the review of literature was that e-mail is perhaps the most political of media because of its properties such as forwarding, mass mailing, blind copying, carbon copying, and so on. How political e-mail is in school systems is a question that might deserve more attention.

Source: Hines, C., Edmonson, S., & Moore, G. (2008). The impact of technology on high school principals. *NASSP Bulletin, 92*(4), 276–291. Used with permission from SAGE.

Summary and Review

While I recognize that the authors are writing for a journal aimed at people in the field rather than researchers, in my opinion they are somewhat confused in their understanding of the underlying research approach. In the last page, they speak about emerging themes. This is a concept you would expect to find in a grounded theory study, not one that follows a phenomenological approach. And more troubling for me is their comment that the study could be validated by a quantitative study. This certainly represents thinking about qualitative research as a less worthwhile or important way of conducting research than if one used a quantitative approach.

Overall, I am disappointed that this article does not really represent a good example of a phenomenological study. I think the authors selected a topic that is of interest and perhaps importance. They offered some interesting findings. But I believe the study would have been much stronger if they omitted the idea that it was a phenomenology and just presented it as a study of the views of principals about technological communication. The study has a 2008 publication date, yet the authors did not really reflect the various new insights into new ways of communication that certainly are here to stay.

Finally, if you return to the four questions I posed at the beginning of this chapter, you can see the extent to which this article was successful. I think the authors introduced a few new ideas, but would have been more successful if they had broadened the nature of the questions they asked. The authors wrote in a very didactic style that doesn't really engage the audience. Although they state that they were doing a phenomenological study, it seems to be lacking in many elements. Although the authors began by addressing a potentially important problem, I think the published study was not particularly successful.

- Does it provide new information and insights related to the topic?

- Is it engaging and written in a clear manner?

- Does it illustrate discussion of the lived experience you would expect to find in phenomenology?

- Do the positive aspects of the article outweigh the potential drawbacks?

Article 3.2. Delicate Engagement: The Lived Experience of Community College Students Enrolled in High-Risk Online Courses (2009)

Cynthia S. Bambara, Clifford P. Harbour,
Timothy Gray Davies, and Susan Athey

My Expectations

I continue to look for excellent examples in the published research that illustrate a particular research approach. The Hines et al. study left me somewhat disappointed. I am beginning to believe that researchers choose a particular research approach but are not necessarily clear on what constitutes its essential elements or why they chose it. I wonder why a researcher decides to do a phenomenology rather than a grounded theory. As I write my detailed comments, I now change my expectations and think that many researchers choose one approach without a clear understanding of why.

This article follows a fairly traditional style of presentation. After a short introduction that includes the specific research question at hand, the authors provide a literature review about online courses. Following that, they present brief information about the research approach of phenomenology, and how data were collected.

I am intrigued by the engaging title. The first part of the title—delicate engagement—is appealing. The other part of the title introduces the term "high-risk online courses." I wonder if the authors mean that the course is high risk for students to fail, perhaps because of difficult content. I think I know what a high-risk student is, but I have to confess that I do not know what a high-risk course is. I expect that the authors will clarify both points shortly.

ABSTRACT

One of my questions is answered almost immediately: I see that a high-risk course is one with a withdrawal or failure rate of at least 30%. Lest I jump to the conclusion that it was the subject matter or the teacher, I quickly learn from the abstract that in-depth interviews were conducted on 13 students from four different courses. I am not yet sure if

This article reports the findings of a phenomenological study that examined the lived experience of community college students enrolled in high-risk online courses (HRCs) at a community college in the American Southeast. HRCs were defined as college courses with withdrawal or failure rates of 30% or more. In-depth interviews were conducted with 13 students enrolled in four different HRCs. Isolation, academic challenge, ownership, and acquiescence emerged as structural themes that framed the experience of participants. These structural themes intermingled in discrete ways that led to the survival or surrender of these HRC participants and formed the essence of the phenomenon that is referred to as delicate engagement, which these students were those who dropped out or completed the course. An explanation of the delicate balance, while provided in the abstract, will need to be explained more completely.

In contrast to the article by Hines and colleagues, this introduction offers some hard data to support contentions about increased enrollment in online courses.

The next paragraph is a brief but well-supported introduction to the purpose of the research.

I hope they explain what they mean by "challenging."

Was the objective to see if participants shared a common experience or was it to see if they could describe and understand that experience?

This approach to writing usually works well. They essentially tell you the pathway the article will take and make it easier for you to follow along.

speaks to the vulnerable threads of academic and social involvement that permeated the HRC student experience.

Nationwide, the number of students enrolled in online courses has grown at a rapid rate. Student enrollment from the fall of 2004 to the fall of 2005 increased from 2.3 million to nearly 3.2 million (Allen & Seaman, 2006). The 2005 online enrollment represented 17% of all higher education students. Allen and Seaman (2006) found that 96% of all higher education public institutions provided opportunities for online learners. Associate's degree granting institutions, such as community colleges, enrolled more than half of all online learners.

Online courses provide many community college students with new opportunities to participate in postsecondary education (Cox, 2005; Dalziel, 2003; Kozeracki, 1999; Young, 2008). Online courses are especially attractive to many community college students because work and family obligations limit attendance in traditional synchronous, on-campus classes. Some students enroll in online courses to expand their schedule of classes or limit the cost of commuting. Health-care workers, fire fighters, and police officers find online learning compatible with their dynamic shift schedules. In addition, parents of small children can reduce child care expenditures by taking online classes.

As online learning options expand, however, these new opportunities are accompanied by higher attrition rates (Berge & Mrozowski, 2001; Carr, 2000). Carr's (2000) inquiry into online learning at several community colleges indicated that student attrition increases when the instructor and the student are in different locations. Studies of online student attrition and persistence conducted at individual community colleges confirm Carr's findings, reporting dropout rates that are 15% to 50% higher in online classes than in the same synchronous face-to-face options (Crabtree, 2000; Kennedy, 2001; Pedone, 2003; York, 2003). As community colleges continue to expand opportunities for students through online learning, it is essential to understand why large numbers of these students withdraw or fail these courses.

This article reports on a qualitative study that used the phenomenological method to examine the lived experiences of students enrolled in challenging online courses at a community college in the American Southeast. Our main objective was to determine if participants in such online courses shared a common experience that superseded their individual successes or failures. We discuss our study in the following manner. First, we briefly review the relevant literature on community college online learners. Second, we explain our research method, phenomenology, and discuss data collection and analysis procedures. Third, we present and interpret our findings in a section that outlines four structural

By including this guideline, the authors provide the reader with the means to easily grasp the overall structure of the article. I suggest you use such a technique in your own writing.

themes that describe the experiences reported by our student participants. We then describe and explain the essence of the phenomenon that we refer to as a "delicate engagement." Finally, we close with a summary and recommendations for practice and research.

LITERATURE REVIEW

General information on distance education but not directly related to this study.

The literature regarding distance education at the community college has confirmed its rapid growth. Kozeracki's (1999) research provided a baseline for examining the early development of distance education at community colleges. Kozeracki based her work on several sources, including statistical data from United States Department of Education reports and documentary data collected from community college course listings, catalogs, and enrollment reports. She found that in the late 1990s only a small portion of the curriculum was offered via distance technologies. However, she reported that between 58% and 79% of the institutions surveyed in two national studies offered at least some courses via distance technology. More recently, Cox (2005) examined the adoption of online education at 15 community colleges in six states. Cox's work, based primarily on documentary and interview data, found that the institutions' adoption of online courses was driven to a large extent by myths regarding the utility of online courses as a means of satisfying student interests and demands, the need to adopt online education to survive greater competition in the higher education marketplace, and the notion that online education was enhancing students' technological literacy. Cox maintained that these myths were not supported by empirical data and instead reflected context-specific institutional forces and interests. These two studies (Cox, 2005; Kozeracki, 1999) showed how researchers are attempting to describe and understand the development of this important innovation in the community college curriculum.

Why do you think they single out dissertation research as a separate category? Does it have less value? Is it more recently completed? I do not know the answers.

Since Kozeracki's (1999) study, the literature has focused more specifically on various aspects of community college online courses and on the students enrolled in them. Dissertation research has reported on student performance (Bangurah, 2004; Crabtree, 2000), the experience of student learning (Harbeck, 2001; Pedone, 2003; Schilke, 2001), student satisfaction (Aljarrah, 2000; Reed, 2001), and student retention (York, 2003). Research concerning student performance in online courses at 4-year colleges and universities is progressing along similar lines (e.g., Dupin-Bryant, 2004; Morris, Wu, & Finnegan, 2005; Schreck, 2003). For example, Schreck (2003) reported on efforts made by one university's faculty and staff to retain students in online courses. Morris et al. (2005) described their work to identify student record variables that came closest to predicting retention in one university's general education online courses.

Researchers in both community college and university settings are still seeking to identify and then understand the variables most likely to predict retention (e.g., Dupin-Bryant, 2004; Morris et al., 2005) and the complex life experiences of students enrolled in online courses (e.g., Harbeck, 2001; Pedone, 2003; Schilke, 2001). Our specific interest was in understanding the life experiences of community college students enrolled in high-risk online courses (HRCs), that is, courses in which 30% or more of the students withdraw from the course or earn final course grades of D or F (Pascarella & Terenzini, 2005). An extensive review of the literature revealed no research on this topic.

The authors use the literature to build up and make a case for why they are doing their own study. Do you think they are successful?

Method

We selected phenomenology as our qualitative method for research. This approach allowed for an in-depth inquiry of participants sharing a common experience (Moustakas, 1994). Phenomenology also afforded us an opportunity to examine the interrelated dimensions of the human experience and address our universal research question: What is the lived experience of community college students enrolled in HRCs?

Like the other article you have read the authors say very little about the research approach of phenomenology. I wish they had written another paragraph or two on this topic.

The community college selected for our study published a distance learning research report providing an analysis of enrollment in all online courses offered in 2003–2004. The report compared 25 courses delivered online and on campus. Following Pascarella and Terenzini's (2005) definition of an HRC, we identified 13 online courses in which 30% or more of the students withdrew or earned final course grades of D or F. From the list of HRCs, we selected the four courses with the highest rates (40%–76%) of withdrawal or final course grades of D or F. The HRCs selected for this study were the following: principles of accounting I, precalculus, statistics, and basic computer skills.

Presumably they chose a school to which they had access. I note that one of the authors works at a community college. We do not know if the college they studied was the same one. In fact, though, I don't know if it makes a difference.

All students enrolled in these four HRCs from the spring of 2005 through the summer of 2006 were sent an e-mail invitation to participate in the study. All participants were required to be enrolled in a program leading to a degree or certificate at the college. Thirteen students who met this criterion volunteered to participate in our study. Our primary researcher collected data through private, face-to-face, in-depth interviews to gain a rich understanding of their experiences (Fontana & Frey, 2000). Interviews lasted 60 to 90 minutes each. A standard but flexible protocol with broad discussion topics was used to guide the interviews (Moustakas, 1994). Questions asked participants to describe their experiences as community college students enrolled in an HRC, what the experiences meant for them, how the experiences

Here the authors provide some details about how they conducted the study.

Do you think it is reasonable to take comments from the same students about different courses? I don't.

Similar to the first study, this research ended up with 10 participants. Just a coincidence. Do not extrapolate that most phenomenologies use that number.

These experiences could be described more fully. I doubt you could figure them out on your own.

The article is silent on the role of the different authors. Did everyone do everything? Did they check each other? Did they do the analysis independently? I think this would have been a good place to lay out more about the process. At the same time, I recognize that the purpose of writing the article is not to explain phenomenology but to try to understand why students complete or drop out of online courses. Some would say that by including details of the process the reader is better able to judge the extent to which data can be relied on.

The authors state that they have found four structured themes. I am not sure what a structured theme is. The themes identified are isolation, academic challenge, ownership, and acquiescence. Apparently all students experienced the theme of isolation. The first study you looked at had 12 themes. Do you think it is reasonable to have only four themes here? Many authors

affected them, and what opportunities and obstacles were encountered in the HRC. E-mail and brief telephone conversations were used for follow-up conversations with participants to clarify and check data for accuracy.

Of the 13 community college students who participated, three had experience in two HRCs. This allowed us to collect data from sixteen course experiences. Eight participants were women and five were men. Participants ranged in age from the early 20s to the early 60s. Eight participants completed their HRCs and two of the eight completed two different HRCs. This allowed for a total of 10 completed HRC experiences. Five participants withdrew from or failed their HRCs. The participants' experiences included both completion and withdrawal or failure in principles of accounting I, statistics, and basic computer skills. One experience in precalculus was reported; in this instance, the participant withdrew from the course.

The interview transcriptions and follow-up e-mail messages were used to create typed, electronic data sets for all 13 participants. Pseudonyms were assigned to each participant, assuring confidentiality. Moustakas's four major processes were used to analyze and interpret data: epoche, phenomenological reduction, imaginative variation, and synthesis of composite textural and structural descriptions. As we followed these processes, we developed a procedure to organize, analyze, and synthesize the individual portions of our data. Adaptation of Moustakas's method allowed us to articulate our participants' collective voices and the essence of the phenomenon that emerged in those voices.

FINDINGS AND INTERPRETATION

Participants' voices (presented here through pseudonyms) combined to form four structured themes that defined the participants' lived experiences in their HRCs. These were isolation, academic challenge, ownership, and acquiescence. All participants experienced isolation and academic challenge in some way and to some degree. Where they differed, however, was in how they responded to these experiences. Data analysis revealed that some responded through ownership. Others responded through acquiescence.

Isolation

The structural theme of isolation describes the loneliness participants felt as they experienced their HRCs. Data analysis confirmed that four dimensions of the students' HRC experience contributed to would say that narrowing the initial data into three to five major ideas is preferable to having too many themes. Recall that the ultimate goal of phenomenology is to arrive at the essence of the experience.

Don't be confused here. The authors first talk about four structured themes, then they talk about four dimensions of the experience that contribute to this theme of isolation. If you read too quickly, you might get lost in the details.

This sounds like the fault either of the instructors or the type of content that did not lend itself to a lively dynamic place. You will notice that the courses they studied tended to be in the math or science domain.

In a fairly typical manner, the authors begin by presenting their findings and explanations related to them. They intersperse the explanation with relevant quotes from participants. I think the choice of quotes illustrates the points the authors are making. I am beginning to think the problem with the classes rests squarely with the instructors or with the format the instructors might have been required to use. Although a phenomenology is about the lived experiences of those being studied, I might have had a deeper understanding if I had more information about the details of the online courses. I was surprised about the comments regarding technology issues. But we have no information about the platform used for transmission, the kind of computers and Internet access students had, and

their sense of isolation: the surreal HRC classroom, the lack of–instructor interaction, the void in student-to-student connections, and the possibility of a different experience.

The surreal HRC classroom. Participants' voices portrayed the HRC classroom as a surreal and intangible place. They articulated the difficulty of interpreting an abstract concept in a virtual world and then attempting to apply it in their real world. To make the classroom feel real, they needed to connect the virtual world to their real world through an inanimate object, a computer, and intangible technology. As they logged in to their course management system, their connection to this virtual world occurred through downloading course documents, interacting with other students on the class discussion board, interacting with their instructors through the courseware e-mail, and dropping assignments into a digital drop box. Many participants knew the virtual classroom could be a lively, dynamic place, but it was not so in these HRCs. On the contrary, these virtual classrooms were static. Participants reported that the discussion board was used minimally with no meaningful student or instructor interaction. Responses from instructors to e-mails or discussion board postings were often cryptic and incomplete. Without a requirement to interact with other students or the instructor, many participants downloaded the course documents and essentially took the class offline. Alyson and Carly both said, "It's not the same as being in a regular class, you don't have a teacher." Sandy described the isolation she felt by saying, "I thought that it was a lot of teaching myself . . . I was by myself a lot. I remember feeling left out." Samantha added, "I don't feel like HRC is a real class." Tom echoed, "What class? What professor? What assignments? . . . The online courses seem almost surreal." The experience of isolation tempted HRC participants to believe there was no class at all.

The lack of student–instructor interaction. Struggling to find life within their classrooms, participants reached out to establish a relationship with others. Unlike traditional campus classes where, as Keith said, "there are other people around you to talk to, [where] you can figure out what is going on," HRC participants did not see anyone, and they did not have a sense that anyone was present. David explained, "I don't feel like there was an instructor present . . . I don't feel like there was anything that I was learning from the instructor. The instructor was simply there as a Web administrator or as a grader." When our participants tried to contact their instructors, some received very limited and unhelpful replies. Geraldine explained that whenever anyone would ask a question, the instructor would respond monosyllabically: "It was so 'yes, no.' . . . It was a two-word answer . . . you sort of felt slapped." In some cases participants received no reply at all. In many instances, the only feedback they received on class assignments was a score in the electronic so on. I think the authors might have gathered or reported more information.

course grade book. Participants reported that the interaction between the instructors and participants decreased as the semester progressed, leaving the students with a greater sense of isolation. Keith said:

> It is kind of like leaving home for the first time and Mom and Dad aren't going to help you . . . you learn it on your own . . . you figure it out . . . you are on your own. And that is how I felt . . . Good luck!

The void in student-to-student connections. Participants explained that they had little or no contact with other students in their HRC classrooms. There was no chance to hear the perspectives of others, no opportunity to learn from each other. Geraldine summarized the importance of student-to-student connections, "I think the interaction among students is everything!" David echoed the value of student to student connections and said, "Not only are you learning from yourself, from the manual, from the instructor, but you are also learning from the other people in the class." What our participants found was aptly described by Samantha as follows: "No interaction between the students, student interaction is nonexistent! I know nothing about these people!" They had no sense of community within the HRCs, no peer interaction. Geraldine remarked, "I was just sort of on this island, all by myself." David echoed her sentiments when he said, "I felt like, specifically in that [HRC] class, I was alone and adrift." For some participants, the need to have a student community was in David's words "ultimate," and for others like Julie "a huge obstacle to try to overcome." The void in student to student interaction intensified the sense of isolation felt by our participants.

The possibility of a different experience. Through their experiences in other online classes, many participants realized virtual classrooms could be vibrant, interactive, and filled with life. Participants knew there were ways to reduce the feelings of isolation that ran rampant throughout the HRCs. The remedy for their isolation was human interaction. Participants saw the instructor–student interaction and student-to-student connections as the conduit to reduce the isolation and bring life to their virtual classrooms. When they did not find the human element within their HRCs, their feelings of isolation became an important aspect of their experience.

Academic Challenge

Academic challenge articulates the sometimes overwhelming feelings participants faced as challenges were posed by course content and delivery. For many participants, expectations for their HRCs were not realized. In most cases, they believed the academic content would be easy to understand. Instead, they often found course material unfamiliar, complex, and nonintuitive. In addition, participants reported that the content of the HRCs was cumulative. To progress, participants often needed to grasp and understand the content in sequential order. The way HRCs were organized affected the learning experience of participants. In addition, technology hurdles surfaced for many participants throughout their HRC experience. The nature and extent of the problems varied. Academic challenge emerged as a structural theme defined by four areas in participants' experience: unrealistic expectations, academic content, course organization, and technology frustrations.

Unrealistic expectations. The participants' unrealistic expectations framed their experience of academic challenge within the HRCs. Many participants believed it would be easy to understand course content and navigate the online environment. For example, Alyson was very direct about her unrealistic expectations: "Honestly, I didn't know how difficult it was going to be." David made a similar observation when he said, "I didn't know that the HRC was going to be so tough for me . . . I didn't have a clue . . . I didn't really know what I was getting into." Participants entered the HRCs thinking, as Julie did, that the course "would be a breeze." Instead they found that the classes were far more complex and difficult than they had expected.

Academic content. Participants were challenged by the academic content of their HRCs, and this was evident in four respects. They struggled with new terminology, nonintuitive content, sequential content, and in some cases, a disdain for the course. As Helen expressed, "It is hard . . . when you don't understand what the words mean. So, that was a big problem for me." Without a background in the subject matter or a context in which to ground new information, some participants struggled to understand course content. The absolute, nonintuitive content also was difficult for some participants to master. Tom described this aspect of academic challenge when he said the following:

> With the HRC course . . . there is only one way to do it. There is a right or a wrong way . . . when you are taking an online course, it is very difficult to determine what [that] is.

The cumulative nature of the course content was problematic when participants did not focus on thoroughly learning the material in sequence. They were unable to complete advanced material when they did not master foundational content. Sandy, who completed two HRCs, said, "If I hadn't done well at the beginning, I know I definitely would not have been able to grasp the end." Finally, several participants entered their HRCs with a distinct disdain for the subject matter. Carly commented, "HRC and me do not get along." Keith echoed, "HRC and me, we just don't play nice together." Helen

Again, the authors identify four areas. Do not be misled: this is just a coincidence and is not usual or expected.

The authors use repetitive terms here. This sometimes makes it difficult to follow the findings.

was anticipating the challenge of her HRC and said, "I think that is why I have avoided it." She was clear about why she saved her HRC for last: "The HRC was the hard course . . . it is my least favorite. Anything dealing with HRC . . . I avoid the things I don't know, and what I am afraid of. I just hate HRC." The sentiments from Carly, Keith, and Helen expressed the discordant attitudes of some participants toward their HRC. The lack of interest in the content presented a barrier to their learning.

...

Technology frustrations. Our participants told us that a myriad of technology hurdles surfaced throughout their HRC experience. Some related to academic assignments and others to more general issues concerning software and hardware. A challenge for some was simply navigating the course management system. Participants were especially vulnerable when technology issues occurred in the beginning of the semester. Technology concerns left them feeling anxious, and this threatened their ability to keep pace with the course. These difficulties caused frustration among participants, adding to the other areas of academic challenge that they were experiencing.

The academic challenge experienced by participants as they attempted to learn the academic content left them surprised by their unrealistic ideas of what to expect in the course. They were overwhelmed by the difficulty of the content, inundated and confused by aspects of the course organization, and frustrated by technology challenges.

Ownership

On the other hand, ownership explains how some participants prized their HRCs and how they embraced the demands of the course. Although the experience of ownership was not always associated with success, it usually was, and it was less common with those students who failed or withdrew from their HRCs. Participants demonstrated their HRC ownership in two ways: a positive stance toward the HRC and the investment made in the class. The positive stance of participants was reflected as they described their motivation, commitment, independence, self-direction, and resourcefulness. Participants invested in their HRCs through preparation and a commitment of their time, effort, focus, and organizational skills. Participants' personal stances toward their HRC, combined with their investment in the course, enabled them to prize and own their experience.

A positive stance toward the HRC. Participants illustrated their positive stance by explaining how their motivation, commitment, independence, self-direction, and resourcefulness enabled them to

I like the use of quotes to support the points the authors are making.

The report of findings given in the next few pages is typical of the way some authors report data. Remember, the themes are based on coding of data obtained from participants. There is no right or wrong about which themes or how many of them to report. Following this presentation the authors move to a discussion of the essence of the experience.

survive and in some cases thrive in their HRCs. As Kay said, "It takes a lot of motivation to take time away from your kids after not seeing them all day." Keith described his commitment to his HRC in his statement, "I started it and I had to finish it." The independence described through several voices propelled the self-direction and resourcefulness of HRC participants. Samantha articulated independence when she said, "I am independent by nature anyway, so it's not a huge thing for someone to say, here is the book, you need to learn this." Although some participants perceived working alone as a debilitating feature of the HRC (as mentioned above in the discussion of the structure of isolation), others like Samantha were also motivated by this independence.

Our participants also articulated the need to be self-directed learners within their HRCs. To complete the HRCs, they needed to teach themselves. Tim described his learning experience as "having to piece it all together myself." He went on to say, "It was basically something that was all going on with me." Sandy added that her instructor was not "linking the material very well. I remember things if I write them down. So, every chapter I would outline and then go through all of the problems. I thought that it was a lot of teaching myself." Alyson described a similar perspective and observed the following:

> I like being self-driven . . . I like to work on my own instead of having someone stand over me and tell me OK, this is what you are doing. I just like for them to say, OK, this is what you need to do, and leave me alone.

Resourcefulness also emerged as a personal quality that contributed to the positive stance of participants within their HRC experience. Geraldine shared, "one thing I learned by taking an HRC was, really, what you need to learn, if you are patient enough, you can usually find your answers on your own." We found that those who were resourceful in finding the help they needed to solve problems independently were able to progress in the course. Participants equipped with a positive stance toward their HRCs—a stance marked by motivation, commitment, independence, self-direction, and resourcefulness—completed their courses. Those without such personal qualities did not.

. . .

Acquiescence

Acquiescence emerged as a structure that described the subtle ways participants submitted to their HRC and slowly surrendered to their experience. The experience of acquiescence was not always associated with a student's failure or withdrawal in the HRC, but this was usually the case. Acquiescence was seen in three ways: silent submission, compromise, and loss.

Silent submission. Silent submission was experienced and represented through the quiet self-acknowledgement of lost motivation, a sense of diminishing returns, lackluster commitment, and a realization that there was no going back to a time without the HRC experience. For example, David voiced how he lost motivation and commitment for the course when he said, "I honestly believe it was a much harder challenge for me to do the HRC. I found the time that I was putting into it was less enjoyable. Yes, that certainly has an effect on my motivation." Similarly, Julie stated, "Motivation is a very big issue for me. I did not have the motivation." Some were not able to adjust to the independence and self-direction required to complete their HRC courses. Julie also offered,

> Learning from other students as well as from what the instructor is providing for you, and the textbook. To me, that is a huge learning thing . . . and a huge obstacle to try to overcome . . . with not having contact with other students.

The retreat to acquiescence was imminent when participants' investment in their HRC did not reap tangible rewards. This led to erosion in personal commitment to the HRC and a sense that the effort invested was not producing the desired returns. David explained this aspect of his experience when he said "It was just taking me a lot of time. That was a growing source of frustration for me because I knew the more time that I was putting into HRC, the worse my grade was getting . . . the more important that time was to me to be able to put into other [classes] where I was strong."

When participants realized that their effort was not rewarded with satisfactory learning and good grades, they began to see the experience as a losing proposition and pulled back in their effort and commitment. Whether evidenced by a lack of motivation, a sense of diminishing returns, or lackluster commitment, students recognized that the HRC was not what they bargained for and they responded by silently submitting to the requirements of the course and their experience.

. . .

DELICATE ENGAGEMENT

Here the authors show how they moved from the four primary themes to extract the overall essence of the experience. They choose to use the term "delicate engagement" to represent that essence.

The four structural themes of isolation, academic challenge, ownership, and acquiescence framed the HRC student experience. These structures interplayed in positive and negative ways that led participants to survive or surrender to the HRC experience. We characterized survivors as either empowered or compromised. Empowered survivors successfully completed their HRCs. They persevered through the experience of isolation and academic challenge and responded by successfully taking ownership of the courses.

It would be helpful to know how many of the people they studied were survivors and how many surrenderers.

Compromised survivors also successfully completed the HRCs but did not respond positively to the isolation. Although they took some degree of ownership of the HRC, their experience also was characterized by acquiescence.

We characterized surrenderers as either reluctant or misplaced. Surrenderers did not complete their HRCs successfully. Reluctant surrenderers responded positively to their experience of isolation but were unable to meet the academic challenge posed by the HRC. They did not exhibit ownership and ultimately demonstrated their acquiescence to the experience of the HRC. Misplaced surrenderers responded negatively to both isolation and academic challenge and, in the end, only exhibited acquiescence, therefore leading us to conclude that of all four groups, these were the students who never should have enrolled in the HRC. They were truly misplaced. Table 1 illustrates the ways in which participants responded to the four structures of the phenomenon under study.

The subtle ways the structures of isolation, academic challenge, ownership, and acquiescence intermingled formed a delicate engagement, the essence of their HRC experience. Delicate engagement speaks to the strength and resilience of participants who brought ownership to their experience and embraced the isolation and academic challenge of the HRCs. Delicate engagement also describes the fragility and vulnerability of those who retreated to acquiescence, unable to overcome the isolation and academic challenge of the HRCs, and ultimately surrendered to their HRC experience. In addition, delicate engagement also describes the vulnerable threads of academic and social connection that permeated the experience of HRC participants. It represents how only some were able to persevere with a lack of contact with others. For many, this void adversely affected the quality and satisfaction of their learning experience. Our participants valued interaction with fellow students and with their instructors, and without such meaningful associations, many participants expressed dissatisfaction. Connection to the HRCs was fragile, and for some the engagement was too delicate to retain their involvement.

SUMMARY OF FINDINGS AND RECOMMENDATIONS

Table 1 is a little too simple for me. What purpose does it serve?

Online learning is rapidly expanding in community colleges. It is also a relatively new form of distance education delivery, and relatively little is known about the community college student experience in online courses. The literature reports high rates of student withdrawal and failure in community college online courses. This study focused on how one group of community college online students experienced their HRCs. To be sure, this research cannot be generalized to a larger population of community college students.

Table 1 Delicate Engagement

Structure	Survivors		Surrenderers	
	Empowered Survivors	Compromised Survivors	Reluctant Surrenderers	Misplaced Surrenderers
Responded positively to isolation	Yes	No	Yes	No
Responded positively to academic challenge	Yes	Yes	No	No
Exhibited ownership	Yes	Yes	No	No
Exhibited acquiescence	No	Yes	Yes	Yes

But, of course, this was not our objective in conducting a phenomenological inquiry. Instead we sought to understand if in-depth interviews with a small group of students might help illuminate an overarching experience that was shared by those who were and were not successful in completing an online HRC. Our findings indicate that for these students at one community college, a shared experience did reflect a discernible phenomenon. Insights gained from the study allowed us to offer recommendations for practice and future research.

Recommendations for Practice

Like the previous article, this study makes recommendations for practice and future research.

In our study, we examined the experience of HRC students who completed their courses and those who did not. By looking at both groups of students, we were able to gain a holistic understanding of this shared experience for both completers and noncompleters. This was an essential feature of our study. The following are recommendations for practice and are intended to aid all students who might enroll in HRCs, that is, those who are well prepared and those who are not:

1. Identify HRCs and develop targeted retention programs for students enrolled in them.

2. Provide prospective students with orientation sessions that alert them to the course expectations and the personal investment of time, effort, and focus required to complete the HRC.

3. Examine institutional policies and practices to ensure student services and academic support programs are prepared for a range of students enrolled in HRCs.

4. Provide mentoring for HRC instructors and require participation in professional development that promotes best practices in instructional design and delivery of online courses.

The recommendations above are only some of the ways online opportunities for community college students can be maximized and obstacles minimized. Continued assessment of courses and services can provide community college administrators and faculty members additional strategies to enhance the student experience.

Recommendations for Future Research

The findings of our study demonstrated a need for additional research and we suggest inquiry along the following lines:

1. There is a need for research examining how community colleges can mitigate the isolation experienced in HRCs while also enhancing student ownership.

2. There is a need for research examining online teaching strategies along with associated high and low completion rates in HRCs. Such studies could identify both effective and ineffective teaching strategies.

3. There is a need for research examining how student advising, learning communities, and other student learning and support strategies affect retention and positive completion in HRCs.

4. There remains a need for research examining the relationship between enrollment in HRCs and degree completion and successful transfer.

CONCLUSION

In this research we provided a forum for participants to share their perspectives of what worked for them in their HRCs and a chance for them to voice their ideas on what can be improved in HRCs. Their willingness to share their experiences provides a valuable contribution to the future of community college online learning. The importance of these student experiences was heard through their voices as they shared why they enrolled. For some, the HRCs and other online classes were their only access to higher education. For others, these classes afforded the chance to better manage their many obligations and responsibilities. The insights gained through the voices of HRC participants offer all of us an opportunity to identify ways that might improve the quality of the online learning experience for future community college students.

Source: Bambara, C., Harbour, C., Davies, T., & Athey, S. (2009). Delicate engagement: The lived experience of community college students enrolled in high-risk online courses. *Community College Review, 36*(3), 218–238. Used with permission from SAGE.

Summary and Review

This study is quite successful at employing some of the principles of phenomenology. I particularly liked the way the authors reached the essence of the lived experience: the delicate engagement. Online teaching has become quite prevalent at the college and university levels. This study should have appeal to many readers.

Finally, if you return to the four questions I posed at the beginning of this chapter, you can see the extent to which this article was successful. The article provides some interesting information about online teaching. While it is reasonably clear to follow, it adopts a neutral objective tone. Overall, I think this was a successful example of a phenomenology.

- Does it provide new information and insights related to the topic?
- Is it engaging and written in a clear manner?
- Does the study move toward a discussion of the essence of the lived experience?
- Do the positive aspects of the article outweigh the potential drawbacks?

FINAL COMMENTS

These two studies illustrate different ways researchers approach phenomenology. Both are published in nontechnical journals. An article by Michelle Byrne should help you understand this research approach more completely: "Understanding life experiences through a phenomenological approach to research," *AORN Journal,* April 2001, by Michelle M. Byrne. You can access it at http://findarticles .com/p/articles/mi_m0FSL/is_4_73/ai_73308177/?tag=content;col1.

You can access the complete articles at www.sagepub.com/lichtmanreadings.

Chapter 4

READING CASE STUDIES

A s we have seen, qualitative research uses different approaches to design. You have read about ethnography, grounded theory, and phenomenology. In this chapter, I introduce two articles using another approach: case study methodology. In the first article you will read, Emily Bouck focuses on two self-contained special education classes in rural secondary schools. The second article, by Michael Watts, deals with his reflections on the art of case study. As such, it is not truly a report of a case study but rather a collection of ideas about conducting case studies. Both authors wrote these articles when they were graduate students.

Usually when a researcher plans a case study, he or she thinks about drawing boundaries related to the following:

What or who do I want to study?

On what aspect of the whole do I want to focus my attention?

What time period can I reasonably cover?

The defining characteristic of a case study is that it is an examination of a particular group or event or program. The researcher's responsibility is to identify what is to be studied. For example, it might be the study of a specific phenomenon. The phenomenon can be major and significant (e.g., Hurricane Katrina or 9/11), or it can be a small event such as the championship football game between two small rival high schools. It can also be the study of a particular program. It can be a large program such as the charter school movement, or it can be a small program, such as the way Ms. Smith organizes and manages her new high school math program.

In addition to being the study of a phenomenon or a program, a case study can also be about a person. The individual might be well known or prominent in sports, the arts, or politics, or known to only a few people in his or her immediate circle. A case study can also be about a process. How is an organization transformed? How does a community join together to keep a school system from closing a school? How do a group of people at the grassroots levels change a troubling situation?

Once a particular case has been identified, it is up to the researcher to establish additional parameters:

- A case study can target a particular aspect of the whole (e.g., forming friendships, getting the job done) or it can look at many dimensions.

- It can cover many years or be limited to a short time.

- It can look at many individuals connected with the case or at just a few or even one individual.

All the decisions regarding what to study—what time span will be covered, what documents or individuals will be studied, and so on—rest with the researcher. Gaining access to the case and individuals and documents or artifacts connected with it are challenges to the researcher. Availability of members connected with the case is another dimension to be considered. As with all research, the researcher must consider time in planning and conducting a study—the time of the researcher and the time of those who participate.

KEY ELEMENTS OF A CASE STUDY

- Case studies focus on an intensive examination of particular group, program, or project;

- are concerned with the identification of the case size (small, medium, large, multiple cases);

- are concerned with selection of the case type (typical, exemplary, unusual, unique);

- are concerned with definitions of boundaries, aspects, and time frame;

- are concerned with selection of individuals involved in the case (all, some, a few, or one member(s)) of a group); and

- are concerned with determination of the period covered (such as a year, a week, several years).

- Case studies in education are common.

I have selected two articles for you to read. The first, a traditional case study, is by Emily Bouck. It takes place in two rural high school classrooms in Michigan. Teachers, some students, and paraprofessionals were observed and interviewed. Bouck collected the data, often shifting between observing and participating in the class. Like an ethnographic study, her role in the classes changed as she became more familiar with the students and teachers.

The second, by Michael Watts, is not exactly a case study. Instead, it is an article about doing case studies. He writes in a challenging and engaging manner. Watts reflects on the work of Robert Stake, one of the major writers in the field of case study. In 1995, SAGE published his book, *The Art of Case Study Research*. Ten years later, SAGE published Stake's *Multiple Case Study Analysis*. I suggest you locate these books and review them as you read the Watts article. Watts's article is written in a very different style and uses a different structure from almost everything else you have read. There is no abstract. There are no headings. There is no traditional review of literature, although there is a reference list and there are citations in the text. I do not see any reference to data collected or analyzed.

But first let's get you started on reading a completed, traditional case study.

ADVANCE PREPARATIONS

Begin by reading the title and the abstract, then flipping through the article and reading the major headings and subheadings. Once you have an idea of the article's structure, go back and read through the article carefully. When you finish reading, you will need to decide the extent to which the article is successful. To do so, ask yourself four questions:

- Does it provide new information and insights related to the topic?
- Is it engaging and written in a clear manner?
- Does it illustrate elements you would expect to find in a case study?
- Do the positive aspects of the article outweigh the potential drawbacks?

Article 4.1. Exploring the Enactment of Functional Curriculum in Self-Contained Cross-Categorical Programs: A Case Study (2008)

Emily Bouck

My Expectations

In this article, Emily Bouck presents her study of two self-contained special education rural secondary schools. Her particular interest is in functional curriculum. In this research, she presents two cases from two schools.

The first section briefly explains case study research. Next, she turns to a discussion of curriculum. You are certainly familiar with the term, but might not know what Bouck discusses here. Since this is a study about special education, you should not be surprised that she includes a discussion of the research on that topic. The next several headings are typical of a traditional structure to reporting research. After introducing the topic, she includes a section on methodology (setting, participants, role of the researcher, procedures followed, and data analysis). Next is a section on results, with several attention-grabbing headings, such as *Where Everyone Knows Your Name*...and *More Than Meets the Eye*...You should anticipate that she will include some quotations in this section. A discussion follows, and Bouck reuses the headings from the section on results. This time, however, they are not presented in quotations. The paper concludes with limitations and future directions.

Abstract

Notice how she limits her study of the classrooms to functional curriculum. This makes her task manageable.

Little research has been devoted to studying functional curriculum in secondary special education programs, self-contained cross-categorical programs, or curriculum enactment in special education, which warrants study of the culmination of these issues. This article presents a case study that attempts to answer, "What is the nature of the enactment of functional curriculum in rural self-contained cross-categorical programs?" The study occurred in two rural secondary self-contained cross-categorical programs with two teachers, four paraprofessionals, and 15 students. The findings suggest that the curriculum was enacted in

I'm not quite sure what she means by "enactment." Apart from that vague term, the abstract provides a good overview of the study.

the moment, was relative, and created tensions between special education and general education. The findings also suggest that the enactment had to be very encompassing and that it developed a community within each programs.

CASE STUDY RESEARCH

"A case study is an examination of a specific phenomenon, such as a program, an event, a person, a process, an institution, or a social group" (Merriam, 1988, p. 9). As a methodology, case study attempts to understand "the complex interrelationships among all that exists," (Stake, 1995, p. 37) or in others, a case study attempts to understand particular nuances about a case, which in education, can be a student, a school, etc. (Stake, 2006). It involves an examination of a bounded system, which is the case or multiple cases one chooses to study (Creswell, 1998). Each case study is bounded by both time and place as well as the actual case being explored (Creswell). Case study research is a form of qualitative research, focused on interpreting a particular phenomenon. Thus, case study methodology studies the particulars and complexities of a case as opposed to trying to generalize to a larger group, with a central focus of interpretation (Stake, 1995).

I suggest that it is almost impossible to study all that exists. Bouck limits herself to studying one aspect of the classroom.

Notice here Bouck's reliance on Stake's work. In the next article you will read, the author describes Stake in detail.

I am not sure why she includes this comment. I think you might find it confusing.

Qualitative case study research is just one form of qualitative research, and there are several different types of case studies within the qualitative tradition. Within the case study "family" there are ethnographic case studies, historical case studies, and psychological case studies. Case study research methodology can also be parsed by its end product. Case studies can be descriptive, where a detailed account of the phenomenon is presented; interpretative, in which thick description is presented to either illuminate, support, or challenge previously held theoretical assumptions; and evaluative, which focuses on judgments (Merriam, 1988).

Notice three purposes of case studies—descriptive, interpretive, and evaluative. Some writers spell the second term "interpretive," while others spell it "interpretative." I prefer the former spelling.

Case study methodology, particularly interpretative, was used in this study because the method fits the questions being asked (Merriam, 1988). It is an "ideal design for understanding and interpreting observations of educational phenomena" (Merriam, p. 2), in which a case in education can be a class, program, teacher, or another bounded educational phenomenon. A lack of previous research or exploration on a topic might warrant qualitative research, particularly a case study approach (Naumes & Naumes, 1999; Stake, 1995). Case studies typically consist of varying emphasis on data collection by observations, interviews, and document or archival reviews, in which triangulation among the data is sought to reduce the likelihood of misinterpretation (Stake, 1995).

The triangulation concept is not used widely today.

CURRICULUM

The question of what constitutes curriculum has been frequently asked, and its answer sought (Nolet & McLaughlin, 2000). It has been referred to as long-lasting educational programs, materials used in classrooms (i.e., textbooks), and experiences that students receive while in school (Morrison, 1993; Nolet & McLaughlin). However, curriculum is not singular. It is comprised of the written, enacted, and received curriculum. The written curriculum "is the official or adopted curriculum often contained in state or district policy" (Nolet & McLaughlin, p. 15) and represents what students are expected to learn (Cuban, 1992). The enacted curriculum "is the operationalization of the intended curriculum" (Nolet & McLaughlin, p. 16). It reflects teachers' decisions in implementing the written curriculum and encompasses formal and informal lessons and activities as well as teachers' behaviors, groupings, management strategies, beliefs, and comments (Cuban; Nolet & McLaughlin). The received curriculum "is what students actually learn as a result of being in the classroom and interacting with the intended and taught curricula," and includes the written and enacted curriculum as well as the unintended consequences (Nolet & McLaughlin, p. 17).

Some scholars have felt that the enacted curriculum was more encompassing. Synder, Bolin, and Zumwalt (1992) expanded the definition of enacted curriculum to include the co-construction of educational experiences by teachers and students. They suggested that enacted curriculum is a transactional process where teachers and students interact, construct, and make meaning of the curriculum and educational experiences within context. Yet, their expanded definition may still be too narrow. Enacted curriculum is a transactional process, co-constructed by the current situation and histories of teachers, students, the schools, communities, legislation and policy, and curriculum materials.

. . .

RESEARCH STUDY

This research sought to understand the enactment of functional curriculum in two rural secondary self-contained cross-categorical programs through the use of case study methodology. A functional curriculum is a curriculum that teaches functional life skills, or in other words, the skills necessary to live, work, and have fun in an inclusive community (Brown, McLean, Hamre-Nietupski, Pumpian, Creto, & Gruenewald, 1979; Falvey, 1989; Snell & Browder, 1987).

. . .

Here she talks about the question I raised earlier in the abstract.

Do you think she makes her point?

Notice the style of writing in this study—objective and impersonal. Case studies can be written in a variety of styles.

Here she sets the boundaries for her case.

The article is part of a larger study. I am not sure why it is necessary to tell you this is part of a larger study. I don't think it helps your understanding.

This article depicts one aspect of the study of the enactment of functional curriculum in these programs. The larger study sought to understand the enactment of a functional curriculum both in terms of the emerging themes surrounding enactment as well as the pre-determined factors that impacted the enacted. This study specifically focused on the themes that have emerged regarding the enactment, whereas the other aspect not reported in this article focused on the pre-determined factors that were hypothesized to influence the enactment of a functional curriculum (e.g., teachers, students, school) Thus, this article essentially reports half of the larger study, which was too large to report in one article. The two articles from the study were logically separated along two different foci: emerging themes following the qualitative tradition and alignment of the qualitative data to pre-determined factors hypothesized to impact the enactment. The study sought to answer the question, "What is the nature of the enactment of functional curriculum in rural self-contained cross-categorical programs?"

METHODOLOGY

Setting

The sentence about purposeful sampling is not necessary. Some qualitative researchers struggle with the dictates of quantitative research. One aspect that causes difficulties is concerned with selection of what or whom to study. Quantitative research assumes that samples will be drawn from a population in such a way that generalizations can be made about the population. Those kinds of samples are considered random. However, qualitative research does not—I emphasize does not—have as its intention generalization to populations. But many qualitative researchers seem confused about the issue. Bouck, like a number of other studies you have read, falls into this quandary. This case study is a type of cross-case comparison. You can either select a similar case

This project involved two rural high schools in the state of Michigan. Purposeful sampling was used to select the schools. The schools were chosen because: (a) they had a self-contained, cross-categorical program in their high schools to educate students with disabilities, (b) they were located in the same county to minimize the differences across schools (i.e., geographical location, resources, socioeconomic status), (c) they had similar school profiles (e.g., similar rates of special education, low socioeconomic status, diverse populations), and (d) they represented a convenient sample for the researcher to access (i.e., where within driving distance from the researcher's institution). The first school, Harborville High School, had a student count of 622, a special education rate of 14.1%, an economically disadvantaged rate of 10.3%, and was 97% Caucasian (Standard & Poor's, 2004). Purposeful sampling was used to select the second school, River Bend, which was located in the same county. It had a student count of 807, 11.8% special education rate, and 16.9% economically disadvantaged rate. It was also a relatively racially and ethnically homogeneous school district (96% Caucasian; Standard & Poor's).

Participants

Teachers

One teacher in each district participated in this study. The teachers were selected because they were the only teacher in the or a contrasting case for such a comparison.

Concerns with logistics are a reality when doing research that involves intensive time in the setting.

She selects three types of participants: teachers, students, and paraprofessionals. It is up to the researcher to decide who will be studied. What other groups might she have chosen? In addition to interviews and observations, what other types of data might she collect from these groups?

Researchers use a variety of ways to identify schools and teachers. Many school systems have elaborate processes to gain access to their classrooms—the larger the system, the more complex the process. Since these schools were in rural areas, I suspect the researcher had access through her own connections.

She chose to give information about their IQ since the classes were special education. However, I question whether providing an average IQ that is so precise is appropriate. Perhaps it might be better to say "all functioned at the XX level of ability."

Researchers often enter a system as an observer. Initially, their intention is to observe what is happening; they do not plan to interact with those in the study. However, some find that their roles often become that of a participant as they become comfortable in the setting and participants become involved with them. This often occurs when conducting a long-term ethnographic study. In this case study, Bouck uses many techniques often associated with ethnography. You can see how

respective districts selected that taught a self-contained cross-categorical high school program. Each teacher started her respective self-contained cross-categorical program and had been teaching the program for five years. River Bend teacher Paula had been a nontraditional teacher education student, returning to college to earn her teaching certificate after 25 years in the business world, and prepared to teach elementary special education. Katie, the Harborville teacher, had been a traditional teacher education candidate and focused her preparation on secondary special education. The teachers were separated by age, but had similar teacher preparation training, as they attended the same institution at approximately the same time.

Students

The students in this project were selected because they were the students educated in each of the two programs studied. All students were invited to participate, but not all students had parental consent or gave student assent. Katie had seven students participate in the study: one senior, two juniors, two sophomores, and two freshmen. Three of the seven students were labeled as having a learning disability, two as having a cognitive impairment (mild), one as Autistically impaired, and one as otherwise health impaired. The average IQ across the students was 77.6. One of Katie's students was female, the other six were male. Paula had eight students assent to full participation: one senior, three juniors, and four freshmen. Four of her students were female and four male; four of her students were classified as having a cognitive impairment, two as having a learning disability, and two as emotionally impaired. The average IQ of Paula's students was 68.5.

Paraprofessionals

Each program had two paraprofessionals. In River Bend, one paraprofessional worked in the morning and the other worked in the afternoon. In Harborville, one paraprofessional was assigned to the program, and the other was assigned to work with two students with Autism in general education classes. Each program also had a transition/job coach, which assisted and supervised with work experiences. A transition/job coach is typically an individual hired by a school district to help students with and without disabilities acquire job experiences, gather skills to be employed, and to supervise these students to help ensure a positive work experience while in school.

Role of the Researcher

The role of the researcher was that of a participant-observer. At the beginning, the researcher attempted to maintain more of an some of the research approaches are not especially "pure." In fact, researchers often choose techniques that are commonly used with many types of research approaches. Participant-observer is one type.

Often researchers face this problem as they conduct studies in classroom settings.

Do you think this influenced the way the study was conducted?

I wonder how she handled the fact that only some students could be interviewed. Obviously, during her class observations she looked at all students.

Do you think she was able to keep her own ideas about curriculum outside the study? I doubt it. But I don't see that as a drawback.

Many contemporary authors choose to write in the first person. By using the style in this article (third person), I think the author tried to show she was remaining objective and distancing herself from the study. At the same time, through her language she reveals that she at times participated in the workings of the classroom.

In this section, Bouck reveals a dilemma many researchers face. They select something to study that is of great interest to them. They believe they know the "right way" to do some things. In a sense, Bouck's study had a political agenda often found in action or teacher research

observer role. However, as observations continued the role shifted to more of that of a participant. At different times, the researcher had to assist with instructional activities and intervene for behavioral reasons. The participation was at times sought by the teacher or students. It was also unsolicited at times, but student safety or the lack of instructional assistance to a struggling student necessitated involvement.

The role along the participant-observer continuum was attempted to be structured based on the realities of the classroom and the constraints upon the teachers, actively trying to understand and respect their role within this collaborative research project (LeCompte, 1995). For the project, the researcher tried to set herself as different from the teachers as well, so that she would not have that role attached to her for the purpose and ease of having students participate in interviews (Corsaro, 1985). The students knew the researchers as Ms. Bouck or Emily, depending on the program and the teacher's preference.

The researcher was interested in this topic, given the decreasing emphasis on a functional curriculum in research and practice, despite her belief that this curriculum was beneficial to the education of students educated in self-contained secondary programs (see Bouck, 2004). She was further interested because use of a functional curriculum for secondary students having particular needs is one of her passions, and she feels that often this population is not given the curriculum it deserves because too much is focused on high-stakes tests and achievement in the general education curriculum. The passion emerged from the researcher when she was working in the field of special education as practitioner and felt too many students within this population were not being properly served by the education field, particularly in light of the curriculum they were receiving. The researcher hypothesized that a functional curriculum would result in better post-school outcomes for this population, but felt that before correlational or intervention research could be conducted that it was important to understand what was occurring. Hence, a qualitative research project was developed to understand the enactment of a functional curriculum.

Procedure

Data from the case study was collected through multiple means in an effort to triangulate (Stake, 1995). At each site data was collected through full school day classroom observations for two days a week for three months (Bogdan & Biklen, 2003). A total of 85 hours was spent at Harborville and 70 hours spent at River Bend. During classroom observations, the researcher took fieldnotes and observed the events within the classroom. Decisions about what to observe and when were based on purposeful sampling (Patton,

I'm not sure what the CA-60 files are.

This seems contradictory. She said she did not receive approval to interview all students. Did she have approval to use test score data?

Earlier in the article, the author said that she did not receive permission for all students to participate, yet here it appears that she interviewed all students. This seems contradictory to me.

1980), such that observations were selected to present the greatest opportunity to understand and gain insight into the case (i.e., each program). In addition, document reviews were conducted. Students' CA-60 files were analyzed and data was gathered on students' IQ, achievement test scores, disability classification, years in special education, age, and other pertinent information. Prior to any data collection, the researcher collected student assent and parental consent for the collection of all data.

Teachers in the study were interviewed formally and informally. A semi-structured interview protocol was used in the formal interview and focused on how curriculum became enacted as well as factors influencing the curriculum. All students who participated were interviewed as well. They were asked about curriculum choices implemented in class and their ideal curriculum. Students were also asked to respond to questions regarding their high school experience, and what they were learning in the program. Paraprofessionals in both programs also participated in an interview, focusing on the program from their perspective.

Data Analysis

This is the first mention of a research question.

Data (interviews, field notes, researcher reflection notes, and archival review notes) were read and re-read, and then divided by the research questions, the specific one for this paper being, "What is the nature of the enactment of functional curriculum in rural self-contained cross-categorical programs?" (see Appendix D). Data analysis began by organizing the hard copy of the fieldnotes, researcher reflective notes, and interviews in chronological order by school site. The researcher then read each site's hard-copy fieldnotes' notebook and noted patterns. The researcher also condensed and expanded the patterns emerging around the question, including both adding to the themes and deleting themes that seemed less relevant. Key and/or typical analytical vignettes were located within the data to support assertions being made. Parsing the data by emerging patterns occurred for each school site separately and then comparisons were made between the two sites. Overarching patterns were noted that cut across both field sites. These overarching patterns were then organized with the analytical vignettes as well as any negative case analysis.

This is a general and typical manner of doing data analysis.

Earlier I said that triangulation is a concept not generally in use today. However, some research approaches appear to rely more heavily on the idea than others. Those that try to be "objective" make use of the construct more than other approaches.

Triangulation was sought among the multiple data sources (i.e., observation fieldnotes, researcher reflective notes, teacher interviews, student interviews, and paraprofessional interviews; see Appendix E). Observations formed the main source of the data and interviews were used to support or challenge what was observed in the classrooms. Archival or document reviews were also used to support and challenge the data from both observations and interviews. The focus on observations, and then document reviews and interviews, to triangulate data occurred because of the challenge of interviewing the students (see limitations section of this article). Furthermore, given that there was not a formal written functional curriculum (as noted below in the results) analyzing the written curriculum proved challenging as well. Thus, observations formed the main data along with the other data collected (e.g., interviews).

Most researchers choose multiple sources of data.

RESULTS

The case study approach does not prescribe any particular way of analyzing or presenting data. This study's approach is fairly typical of the way people analyze and report data from qualitative studies.

The findings from the research question regarding the nature of the enactment of functional curriculum were parsed into five overarching themes. The first major theme indicated that functional curriculum was found to be relative, as the functional part was "in the eye of the beholder." Next, the enactment occurred in moment-to-moment interactions. The enactment of functional curriculum created a community within the programs, and it was found to be more than what met the eye, as it had to be everything to everyone. Lastly, tensions between special education and general education were formed from the enactment of functional curriculum.

"Eye of the Beholder"

Many writer choose quotations that are "catchy" as headings. I think this gets the reader's attention and is effective. The author then follows with a general paragraph and supporting information, including quotations or sections from fieldnotes. Some of the reporting has been omitted.

Initially both teachers stated that they used a functional curriculum, which was the major criterion for inclusion in the research project. However, in interviews, River Bend teacher Paula described her curriculum as "a mixture of academic and work-related" (Interview, March 15, 2005), although she indicated that she considered it functional. She suggested her curriculum's functional nature was evident through the spelling words she used in her language arts class, as they were words related to employment stating, "I want students to read words and know what they are when they go for a job" (Interview, March 15, 2005).

Paula's focus on academics and work was revealed through her statements.

> I struggle because I have them [students] for four years. Technically, they should be out of my room junior and senior years and placed in jobs in the community or work sites. That would be ideal if there was money, and resources, and jobs. (Fieldnotes, January 31, 2005)
>
> . . .

Moment-To-Moment Enactment

The enactment of functional curriculum occurred within the moment-to-moment decisions in both programs, and was associated with the flexibility demonstrated by the teachers, students, and other individuals with the program. Teachers had to be flexible to what students brought into the classroom, to what other school personnel might ask of the teacher and/or students, and finally to their own changes and spontaneity. Students had to be flexible to changes the teachers and other school personnel made, as well as changes their own peers influenced.

The teachers repeatedly used the word "flexible" when discussing their programs. For example when Paula's program at River Bend was visited by middle school students joining the program next year, she created activities to integrate her current students and the new students. However, shortly into the visit the principal stopped in and asked Paula if her class could clean the outside of the school. Paula then changed her plans and sent the incoming students off with current students and an adult to clean outside the school. At the conclusion Paula commented, "See, it's about being flexible" (Interview, March 28, 2005). In another instance, Paula received a phone call from the office at the end of the day asking her students to stuff, fold, and address parental updates for the school. By agreeing, Paula's curriculum changed for the next day and she stated, "So much for my lesson plans tomorrow" (Fieldnotes, January 28, 2005).

. . .

"Where Everyone Knows Your Name . . ."

The enactment of functional curriculum created a sense of community within the programs, constructed through the deliberate and purposive decisions of each teacher as well as through the unintentional and inherent features of the program. Because the majority of students spent almost all of their school day within the self-contained cross-categorical programs together, this contributed to the development of community. In addition, most students had minimal acceptance in the larger school community. Their social or peer community was more likely limited to students within their programs, or at least in special education.

Students' lack of acceptance within the larger school community at Harborville was supported by Brenda, a paraprofessional, who commented that not everyone was equally accepted. Katie confirmed that few of her students were accepted within the larger school community and stated that her students' acceptance was "sometimes really good and sometimes they are just that special education group." Katie said that there were "always a few in my class that just naturally stick out more and take the beating; some just naturally stick out more and take the heat," meaning that some students were picked on and less accepted (Interview, June 14, 2005).

. . .

More Than Meets The Eye . . .

In this section, the author integrates her findings with other research.

The enactment of functional curriculum in both programs was "more than meets the eye." A large aspect is that the enacted functional curriculum had to be everything and to everyone. Powell, Farrar, and Cohen (1985) coined the term "shopping mall high school" in the 1980s, and stated that high schools represent a unique place, as "no other social institution has the task of serving such matured diversity at the same time and in the same place" (p. 2). Within their shopping mall high schools, they discussed different aspects of curriculum, namely horizontal, vertical, extra-curricular, and service curricula.

Powell and colleagues (1985) also proclaimed that special education classes were specialist shops within the *shopping mall high school.* However, the nature of the programs and the enactment of the functional curriculum involved having to be all to all, including the horizontal, vertical, service, and extra-curricular curriculum. Rather, these programs were most like "one stop shopping centers," the Super Targets of today. They were everything, curriculum-wise, to every student who entered.

Horizontal Curriculum

Powell, Farrar, and Cohen (1985) described horizontal curriculum as the surface of what was available (i.e., the variety of subjects offered). In both programs, a variety of subjects were offered; and remarkable similarity existed between the two programs Both Katie and Paula's programs had social studies, math, language arts, employability/practical business, and life skills/life management classes. Because most students spent the majority of their school day in these classrooms, they had to cover a wide variety of subjects (academic and functional). Paula discussed the three year rotation she used with her curriculum areas, as she taught English and math every year, but alternated the other subjects (i.e., geography, history, life management, personal management, health, and advocacy). Katie's program kept the same core classes every year; social studies, math, language arts, employability, and life skills, but varied the content across years.

. . .

Vertical Curriculum

Powell, Farrar, and Cohen (1985) considered the vertical curriculum to be the range in difficulty within a particular subject. A vertical curriculum was evident within both programs, as historically the field of special education was built upon individualization and accommodating materials to help students access the content. However, one could question the amount of individualization that occurred within these self-contained programs.

. . .

Service Curriculum

These programs also had to encompass service curriculum, which Powell, Farrar, and Cohen (1985) considered the academically or educationally relevant emotional or social needs that students might face. While both programs were observed to address "service curriculum," the teachers felt constrained and indicated this was an area lacking in their program and the whole school.

. . .

McCutcheon stated, "By curriculum, I mean what students have the opportunity to learn in school through both the hidden and overt curriculum, and what they do not have the opportunity to learn because certain matters were not included in the curriculum" (as cited in Morrison, 1993, p. 84). The enactment of curriculum includes not just what was apparent (i.e., socially constructed and blatantly enacted), but also what was hidden; not just what was intended, but also what was unintended or missing.

Paula often spoke of what was missing from the enactment of her curriculum. While she mentioned resources and facilities to teach aspects of functional curriculum, such as laundry and kitchen facilities, she primarily spoke of institutional constraints from the school or district. Paula stated that the master schedule of the school took precedent, meaning that scheduling her students and their educational needs took a backseat to the concerns of the entire school. Paula also discussed that opportunities to enact a functional curriculum were missing because of the location of the school. The high school was located outside of town in the already rural community and, according to Paula, the location impacted the opportunity for her students to have work experiences in the community or for Paula to use community-based instruction within her program. The final component Paula discussed as being missing was freedom to structure her day. Paula suggested that for her program confinement to class periods was not appropriate. Paula wanted the freedom to do spontaneous trips to see and experience things that her students would benefit from, stating, "It sounds like a small thing, but it's a big thing to me" (Interview, March 15, 2005).

. . .

This is an example of how the author wove the related literature, her interpretations, and comments from interviews or fieldnotes into a coherent whole to support her results.

"Grass Is Always Greener . . ."

The enactment of functional curriculum in both programs created tensions, particularly between the pull-out classroom and general education classes. Students were torn between these two "places and spaces." Students implied the grass was always greener wherever they were not, whether that be general education or special education.

Students in Katie's program expressed concern over being in special education; yet, they did not want to do the work in the general education classes. Students' tension could be seen in comments regarding Katie's program expressing, "it is a crazy class," "I feel like I am in first grade," and suggesting that there were "weirdos" in the class and concern over being associated with them. These stood in contrast to their comments such as, "I don't do book work," refusing to actually do written work in their general education classes, or selecting an ideal curriculum based on classes that would require no homework.

. . .

Summary of Nature of Enacted Functional Curriculum

Overall, the nature of the enactment of functional curriculum was found to occur in the moment. The enactment of functional curriculum was not the same in both programs; however, its functionality was relative. What was functional to Katie was not necessarily functional to Paula, and vice versa. While both teachers indicated they enacted a "functional curriculum," they were not enacting the same thing. Despite some negative implications, the enactment created a community within each program, providing students with a peer group and a place to feel safe.

Although both teachers indicated they enacted a functional curriculum, the phrase does not begin to describe what was enacted; as the curriculum had to be more than what met the eye, meaning that the curriculum had to be more than what was just presented. The curriculum could not just be academics or vocational or life skills, but had to be all and it simultaneously had to be at an appropriate level for every individual student. Finally, the enacted curriculum created a continual tension around being in special education versus general education and vice versa. Despite what students verbally indicated about wanting one placement over another, their actions and behaviors revealed different wants and needs.

DISCUSSION

The nature of the enactment of functional curriculum emerged from the themes that cut across the two programs: (1) functional curriculum was in the eye of the beholder, (2) enactment occurred in the moment, (3) enactment created a community, (4) enactment generated opportunities and affordances that were more than meets the eye, and (5) enactment created tensions between general education and special education (see Appendix F).

In this next section, Bouck takes five themes and provides a discussion based on the results.

In the Moment

Functional curriculum in both programs was enacted in the moment, meaning teachers, students, and other personnel associated with the program had to be flexible. Katie and Paula often used this language to describe their program and those within it, implying that flexibility was inherent within the program. The flexible nature of the enactment was met with appreciation and resistance. For example, teachers' comments expressed resentment ("So much for my lesson plans tomorrow") and appreciation ("It is nice to have that flexibility").

The flexible nature enabled moment-to-moment interactions and dynamic assessments as well as positioned the programs to alter their written curriculum to meet the demands of school personnel. Paula was asked to alter the curriculum on short notice and to perform tasks such as cleaning or stuffing envelopes, jobs generally outside of the everyday school activities of a "typical" high school student. Individuals also asked Katie's program to adjust their curriculum to stuff bags for a fundraiser, a task asked only of Katie's students.

While one could suggest that these altered enacted curriculum activities and could be used to teach students both vocational and social skills, one needs to consider the messages being sent to students, teachers, other school personnel, and parents when these students are asked to perform tasks that the requester would not ask of other classes or programs at the schools. One possibility is that school personnel did not see much value in these programs' curriculum and assumed changing it would not be as difficult or as damaging to students' academic achievement or success on state tests. This raises the question of positioning one type of learning over another, and suggests perhaps "book learning" was more important than "practical learning," or even that the education of students in the pull-out programs was not as important as the education of other students. However, rather than completely dismissing these activities and their potential for functional skill acquisition, they should be turned into teachable moments.

The purpose of this section is to talk about the meaning of the results. Some authors weave the related literature into the discussion.

In the Eye of the Beholder

The functionality of the enacted curriculum came into question when considering different agents' perspectives, and crafted the question if "functional" was in the eye of the beholder. While both teachers believed the curriculum they tried to enact was functional, they expressed subtle resistance to calling it that. This resistance acquires meaning when one considers Morrison's (1993) point that, "how we define curriculum makes a difference in how we think about it and how we plan it." Both teachers were quick to highlight the academic part of their functional curriculum programs. Paula preferred to call her program a "mix of academic and work-related," and Katie repeatedly stressed the importance of math and reading. Their word choices may have been spawned by the current political climate which stresses academic achievement and rigor. Despite the value both teachers placed on work experiences and daily living skills, they illustrated an awareness that these were not supported in policy.

The enacted functional curriculum in each program could also be analyzed regarding if "enough" of certain components were included or taught. For example, were either Katie or Paula allotting sufficient time to the components of self-determination or social/relationship skills? Both teachers spoke of social/relationship skills as an area that was being slighted in their programs. Katie discussed how in her ideal curriculum she would have a school social worker within her program to help her students address issues which may be impacting their relationship skills. Paula also devoted class time throughout the day to addressing issues related to social/relationship skills. However both teachers did question the enactment of social/relationship skills in their programs. Insufficient emphasis of social skills is important, whether the lack comes from teacher controlled factors or other personnel impacting the enactment of this component. Halpern (1985) stated that personal/social relationships skills were the most important of all transition goals because they impact all facets of life.

The teachers discussed the value of self-determination and indicated they enacted it; yet observations indicated aspects were overlooked, such as an emphasis on post-school plans, course selection, and programmatic decisions (Zhang, Katsiyannis, & Zhang, 2002). Neither teacher employed a formal, commercially-available self-determination curriculum model, either as a stand-alone or embedded within a functional curriculum model. Thus, the lack of a formal, commercially available curriculum model suggests that the teaching practices the teachers did employ failed to incorporate research or even perhaps theory on best practices towards this domain. Zhang and colleagues found secondary special education teachers did not pay enough attention to self-determination.

Students' comments supported the need for a greater emphasis on self-determination. For example, Katie's student indicated to the researcher an interest in taking a Spanish course, but confessed that he had never asked to take it. This implies that the student was unaware of his need to advocate for himself and had difficultly problem-solving the situation. There were also instances when students tried to express themselves and demonstrate self-determination, only to be "shot-down" by an adult. This occurred with one of Paula's students when he stated he did not want to clean inside or outside of the school. He advocated for himself to Paula and ended up being sent to the school's time-out room.

Overall this theme raised questions: (a) What is functional within a functional curriculum? (b) Who does, and who should, define what functional curriculum is and is not? (c) How does the functionality within a functional curriculum relate to students' post-school success?

Even in light of the data from this study, the field needs to consider these issues.

. . .

More than Meets the Eye

This section is another example of how Bouck weaves the related literature into her discussion.

The two programs in this study were more than what meets the eye. They had to be more of everything to everyone who entered. Unlike other programs or classes, Katie's and Paula's programs could not stop at academics. The teachers, and the programs, had to extend their repertoire of skills to be more than just academically oriented, or even functionally oriented in this case.

The observed programs included extracurricular aspects, which involved components not normally able to be enacted within the four walls of the classroom (i.e., community access, leisure and recreation, and real-life application of social skills). The extracurricular components served to define students differently, by others and how they viewed themselves. Particularly important was the emphasis on vocational classes and activities within the community. Vocational settings allowed students to demonstrate their strengths and be a more knowledgeable other. Yet, concerns existed for structured or formal vocational opportunities for students of these programs. Katie indicated that many of her students struggled in the vocational programs at the county vocational center, as that they could not keep up in these non-special-education-supported classes.

Concern over students' access to formal vocational programs is consistent with data from the Second National Longitudinal Transition Study (NLTS2; Wagner, 2003). Data from the NLTS2 indicated that between the first National Longitudinal Study conducted in the mid-1980s to the early 1990s and the early 2000s, students with disabilities enrolled in vocational courses dropped seven percent, which was correlated to an increase in academic courses for students with disabilities (Wagner). The NLTS2 found that a lower percentage of high school students with disabilities were enrolling in occupationally specific vocational classes as compared to their general education peers (52.2% vs. 64.2%); and more general education students were taking any type of vocational courses than high school students with disabilities (79.5% vs. 61.2%) (Wagner).

In addition, today's formal vocational programs appear designed to serve general education students, and are not necessarily tailored for supporting special education students. Cameto and Wagner (2003) found that more than 85% of special education students reported the same vocational experiences as their general education peers when considering curriculum, instructional materials, instructional grouping, and classroom activities. For students in self-contained cross-categorical programs, who may be several grade levels behind in reading, as well as have challenges with social skills, the lack of individualization or differentiation can be problematic. It may be that students, like those that Katie and Paula educate, are being "phased out" of formal vocational programs and left with only vocational opportunities that can be offered within their pull-out programs.

. . .

LIMITATIONS

It is not the purpose of a case study to generalize. I find that many qualitative researchers inappropriately make apologies for the small or nonrepresentative sample they choose to study. The concept of generalization and representation belongs to quantitative research approaches.

Of course, any case must have limitations on the period. I am not sure why she sees this as a limitation.

Saturation is a concept from grounded theory.

Perhaps there could be other ways to gather data from such children.

This study presented several limitations. One limitation involved the cases, as the study consisted of two rural self-contained cross-categorical programs, and whether or not the results of this study might appropriately transfer to other locations and different school programs. Another limitation is that the two cases were observed for a bounded period of time prior to ending observations. Additionally, the cases were not observed for the same amount of time. Although the data did become saturated More hours of observation were recorded at Harborville High School, Katie's program, than at River Bend High School in Paula's room. This resulted from the teacher at River Bend High School getting sick, the school having snow days, and students being away on field trips.

Limitations also arose in the data collection. Not every student in both programs returned parental consent forms. Little is known regarding the students for whom consent was not obtained, in terms of their personal and school data as well as their perspective of the enactment of functional curriculum. Student interviews posed a limitation. Some students had difficulty understanding some of the interview questions. Even when students did appear to understand the questions, their responses were limited to a few words rather than expanding their thoughts even when prompted by the researcher.

Future Directions

Research needs to continue to explore the enactment of functional curriculum in multiple settings. In general, greater research is needed across all of special education areas; self-contained cross-categorical secondary programs, functional curriculum, and curriculum enactment in special education. Research needs to explore the enactment of curriculum before the field can begin to analyze the relationship between curriculum usage and post-school outcomes, which should be the ultimate goal of research related to special education curriculum.

Research needs to explore inclusive versus pull-out settings. The data from this study added to the current equivocal literature, but additional research is needed. And within that research, students' voices need to be reflected. In addition, researchers need to increase the attention paid to vocational education and the benefits it brings to students primarily educated in self-contained cross-categorical programs.

Source: Bouck, E. (2008). Exploring the enactment of functional curriculum in self-contained cross-categorical programs: A case study. *The Qualitative Report, 13*(3), 495–530. Used with permission from Emily Bouck and Nova Southeastern University.

Summary and Review

Bouck's case study is well written and easy to follow. We don't really know how and why she decided to study the topic she did, however. Perhaps she had access to the teachers or the classes. Perhaps she had been to these schools before. We know that she had a passion for the topic because she says so. I think she does a good job of laying out what she did and how she did it.

Using a case study approach presents interesting challenges for researchers. She seems to have drawn ideas about collecting and analyzing data from other qualitative research approaches. For example, she speaks about participant observation—a concept typically addressed by ethnographers. She talks about saturation of data—a concept associated with grounded theory.

In her style of writing, use of some statistical information about the classes and students, her apologies for small and nonrepresentative samples, and mentioning of triangulation, I think she is trying to position her article as objective and "scientific." Many writers do this—Bouck is not alone.

Finally, if you return to the four questions I posed at the beginning of this chapter, you can see the extent to which this article was successful. I believe you can respond in the affirmative to each question.

- Does it provide new information and insights related to the topic?
- Is it engaging and written in a clear manner?
- Does it illustrate aspects of a functional curriculum in a special education setting?
- Do the positive aspects of the article outweigh the potential drawbacks?

Now I would like you to turn your attention to reading Watts's reflective piece about doing case study research.

Article 4.2. They Have Tied Me to a Stake: Reflections on the Art of Case Study Research (2007)

Michael Watts

My Expectations

As I mentioned earlier, this article is not a report of a completed case study. It is about doing case studies. The article begins with a title that is meant to be a play on Stake's name and the word "stake." I notice that the text is written in different fonts, so you will need to pay attention to that.

Watts writes this opening almost like notes from a journal he may have been writing or thoughts he might have had while in class. Perhaps you have experienced the same kind of confusion that he did. This is an excellent demonstration of the kind of self-reflexive strategies that some contemporary qualitative researchers use.

Have you asked yourself this very question?

You had to see it to believe it. I mean, we're sitting there, thirty-odd people in this new class, and I really can't think I'm the only one here wondering what exactly qualitative research is all about and why has he just walked in carrying a box of coat hangers? Why? And what has any of this got to do with this book he wanted us to read? He stands there for a while without a single word of explanation and then he quotes some guy called Stenhouse and says "I have a fear of lecturing lest you believe me." And suddenly my interest is piqued because I'd read that book he'd recommended and, to be honest, I hadn't liked it. I had no real idea what it was saying or why it wasn't saying it. It was like—Oh, I don't know. Like it had just been scribbled down because the publisher's deadline was up. That's it: it was unfinished and I figured that there had to be more to it than that. It's funny, but one of the reasons I read English as an undergrad was that I wanted to find out more about literature than just how the book ended. And here I was with this thing and here was the chance I'm wondering what the hell is the

"Wretched book!" I think he is trying to get your attention!

point of this charade that's dressed up as a lesson? I mean, we've been told to read this wretched book that's supposed to tell us all about case study research and it's utter nonsense. But now he's telling us that he's not going to tell us anything about it, you know, so it looks like it's going to be down to me to figure it out for myself and I suppose that's what this story is all about: what do I think of qualitative research after reading Stake's Art of Case Study Research? *In its own way, it's about change: change of attitudes*

What is the central point of this introduction, which is in italics? I had difficulty knowing how to read the first page.

and a look at whether it's possible for these different attitudes to exist side by side, like they're following the same lines of thought and sometimes just veering off on their own and sometimes merging back again.

This article is written as a response to my reactions to Robert E. Stake's (1995) *The Art of Case Study Research*—first introduced to me through a postgraduate course on qualitative research—and, in

To clarify, Watts read Stake's work, which is a case study of the Harper Elementary School.

We learn Watts's purpose following this short introduction. Do you agree with Watts's comment that Stake's work on case study represents "the qualitative research"? I don't agree with it. Watts introduces issues about self-reflection here when he says, "a response to my own self . . . where I had been coming from and of those values." His view that research is value driven may not be something you have considered in the past.

Writers sometimes use their own journal notes for data.

Watts now introduces how he has narrowed his topic: he is limiting it to literary devices and fiction in writing case studies. Do you think he is justified to use such devices? There is quite a discussion about this in the literature. Can something be too much of a story and not enough of a report? Do you believe that if something is written in an interesting fashion and tells a story that it is not really research?

particular, to the report on Chicago's Frances Harper Elementary School contained within it (Stake, 1995). As such, it draws together some of my reflections on case study research and attempts to trace the development of my own attitudes toward the qualitative research that has, for me, been symbolized by Stake and his report. At the same time, it is a response to my own self, an auto/biographical reflection on my understanding of where I was and where I had been coming from and of those values I had brought with me and was developing (Stake, 1995, 2006). Within this second enquiry, drawn from a (self) research diary and class notes kept throughout the course, this article also represents an exploration of myself—including myself as a qualitative researcher with a fascination for the auto/biographical. This attempt to present and re-present these entwined reflections— on qualitative research and on myself—has a third purpose here: to explore the re-presentation of this developing understanding (see also, e.g., Ely, Vinz, Downing, & Anzul, 1997; Stronach & MacLure, 1997) and tell others something of what I might not otherwise have included (Stake, 2004). I apologize if the results seem merely pretentious.

The sources for this story are primarily my own, mostly taken from a diary that noted some of my extempore reactions to and reflections on various aspects of qualitative research. These are referred to within this article as "Stake *x*" and are included, complete with numbers, to mark the passage of the time within which my understanding, such as it was, developed and progressed. In effect, they are a series of interviews with myself. These interviews were recorded and purposely left unamended—even down to the odd typographic error. They were subjected to annotation without amendation (tempting as that sometimes was), and this article is, in effect, yet another series of annotations. The temptation, even now, is to annotate it further—but that would be to spoil the story.

Although I had raised other issues with myself and with others during the course of study, I have limited myself here to an exploration of the uses of literary devices and fiction in the writing of case studies. For me, particularly as I had read English as an undergraduate, these were sources of discontent and satisfaction: I had simultaneously wondered "what the hell is the point of this?" and had my interest piqued. In an early consideration of the report I had suggested that it was "a case study of Robert E. Stake at Harper School" (Stake 1) and objected to the intrusion of literary devices: It was too much of a story, not enough of a report. I recognize the irony of writing my own report now in the form of a story as this article becomes a case study of myself considering "the case study of Robert E. Stake at Harper School." However, I believe that there is a validity in this as such a case study addresses the question of whether there is, as had been suggested in the very first class, "some intelligent reason to change the way of doing things in one's own professional life" (class notes). The "first objective of a case study is to understand the case" (Stake, 2006, p. 2) and in trying to present and to re-present the explorations of my own self I have had the opportunity to submit my reflections to what I had heard called "the alternative interpretation test" (class notes) and thereby locate the sources of my discontent. As I subsequently came to appreciate, this was not only a part of my own "self-correcting system" (Stake, 2004, p. 22) and my commitment to skepticism (Stake, 2004) but an acknowledgment of the ethical responsibility to identify influences on my interpretation of the case (Stake, 2006).

I have deliberately eschewed the literature of case study and qualitative research in this story, other than that written by Stake, shared with me in the classes or included in the notes I have written in response to Stake's work because this is intended as a personal approach to case study. It is not intended as an abstract examination of the uses of fiction in qualitative research, for that would "not involve the reflection that Stake has pushed me towards" (Stake 16). Instead, this is an attempt to forego the "ease of relying upon the authority of others—whether for confirmation or to argue . . . Do I want to know (explore) what I know or what I don't?" (Stake 16). However, just as Stake had taken his "experience in program evaluation" into the unfamiliar milieu of urban schools (Stake, 1995, p. 140), so I carried my experience of literary criticism (shaped by my responses to the "authority of others") with me as I explored the unfamiliar milieu of case study research. Such literature as informed my experience informs this story.

Given the extent of self-reflection, does this article have any worth? Although acknowledging the potential for solipsism, I believe that it does. During the course of study I found myself tied to my own stake, for Stake and his report on Harper School informed the course of these notes throughout. The pun in the title, however, has a more serious point. Aware of the pitfalls of assuming my own knowledge in others—be it in terms of a single word such as "catharsis" (Stake 2) or to the canon of medieval literature (Stake 13)—it may be worth putting this quotation into some sort of context. Its significance may become clearer by seeing it in relation to this article where it lies in my growing appreciation of qualitative research: "If I'm to use such research then there is a value in having come to appreciate (at least some of) its methods heuristically" (Stake 5). And so, if I had tied myself to a stake, then this represents my attempts to fly from it. To understand. Shakespeare's "Scottish play" where Macbeth cries these words as the unrelenting course of action that had been initiated after his meeting with the three witches draws to its inevitable end. Having seized the Scottish throne by force, the consequences of his actions are now laid before him. He does not recognize his own culpability—after all, it is "They" who have tied him to the stake leaving him no more room for maneuver—and defiantly, heroically, gloriously unrepentant

Do you agree with his decision to stay away from the literature of case study and other qualitative research? Remember this author is British. While the word "eschew" may seem stilted to you, perhaps it is more common in Britain. Why do you think he avoided including other literature? How do you feel about his argument that he wants to forgo the ease of relying on others or on authority? Do you trust yourself enough?

Since the author's background is in literary criticism, it is difficult for him to write in any other frame. So terms such as "solipsism" (which means that the self is the only thing that can be known and verified) tend to creep into his writing.

to the very end of the play that bears his name, he is killed in the next and final scene. Claims have been staked, and it behooves me to explore them.

My immediate reactions to case study research, particularly as the art form suggested by the very title of Stake's book and through his report on Harper School, were unfavorable. Two annotations, made at the time of my first reading the report, suggest this. Alongside the passage, "A 20-page case study is likely to run 50 if the researcher doesn't 'ruthlessly winnow and sift'" (Stake, 1995, p. 121) there are pencil marks, thickened with frustration, and the single comment "precisely!!!" On the first page of the report itself (Stake, 1995) I have written "Is this a paradigm for qual. research?" Although I believe that some words carry their own emotive meanings around with them (Stake 6) those quoted here do not appear to do that. Looking at them isolated in print they remain obstinately neutral even now. Without the preamble of frustration they could, particularly amid the data gathered since then, suggest fervent agreement and genuine inquiry. My own claim to Stake, then, is as genesis of and mediator between these two positions of frustration and agreement through inquiry.

To be honest, I was getting more and more confused with the whole case study as art thing. And that business of describing coat hangers just didn't help. I mean, what do you say? They look like coat hangers. They're designed as coat hangers. You know, things you hang your coat on. They're hangers for coats, aren't they? Well, they didn't help me at all with the book. So I went up to him afterwards and said to him, "Look, I don't get it. There's got to be more to this and I just don't get it. It reads like a story and it's not even a very good story It doesn't tell me anything. It's a piece of crap." I mean, obviously I said a bit more but, between you and me, I was rather expecting that the persuasive force of my logic would soon swing him round to my point of view. Well, alright. No. Looking back to it I was probably hoping that he'd get all defensive and then I'd kick in with a devastating argument that would prove my point. But do you know what he said? He thought about it taking his time like he was interested, then he said, "That's interesting. Why don't you write something down?" And I thought, "Right. I'll do that. I'll show you what I mean." And that's where it all started, I suppose.

I rejected the report for being "too literary" (Stake 2): I objected to the style of the report and, through its stylistic presentation, its content. Indeed, I wondered whether a "whole piece of work [could] be dismissed because of just one of its components—in this case, that the entire report, including its content, may be dismissed because of a negative reaction to its stylistic presentation" (Stake 1). The central narrator offered inconclusive description rather than definite prescription. It was not what I considered to be a report (Stake 3).

I think it is interesting that he acknowledges his negative view about case study research.

Do you think Watts is guilty of the same excess he dislikes in others?

Again, his personal reflections might just be something with which you can identify. Of course, if you haven't read Stake's book, then it is somewhat difficult to follow all the details that Watts includes here.

Here Watts expresses his initial frustration and annoyance about having to read and accept the Stake work as something to be considered. By his own writing, I think he leads you to think that perhaps he changes his mind.

By the way, one type of case study research is a descriptive narrative.

Do you feel sometimes that qualitative research is nothing but a story?

It was, in short, a story: instead of being told whether or not the Chicago School Reform and the school's own School Improvement Plan were working or not, I was told about Professor Stake's outing to a Chicago school. And I did not like that.

It was not the language that I had reacted to. I have revisited enough of my own work to appreciate a report being readable. With Stake it was what the "readability" represented that concerned me. Comparing it to "a bad novel by Don DeLillo" (Stake 1), I dismissed it out of hand because, with its descriptive narrative rather than prescriptive conclusions, it was a story that "fails to adequately address any of its own stated goals" (Stake 1). The problem was that I wanted answers to, not insight into, the problems addressed by these "stated goals." I put style above content. It is small consolation if I am not the only one "guilty of that" (Stake 12). Interestingly (or not) reflecting on this paper helped my understanding of my appreciation of DeLillo's (1994) work in general and the "bad novel"—*White Noise*—in particular.

I had picked out and focused on one sentence: "I reach to the ground and pick up a spent casing" (Stake, 1995, p. 142). I chose to read it, "with its blandness and (seemingly) sudden incongruous juxtapositioning," as a "*mimesis* of the very situation" that I interpreted as my picture of the scene (Stake 1). Safely wrapped up in the language of literary criticism, I criticized him for not drawing proper attention to evidence of gun use on these school grounds. The suggestion that "one purpose of this research is to make the familiar seem strange so that attention can be drawn to it" (Stake 1) indicates the potential for literary devices in the writing of such reports. It allows the reader to determine the import of the matter according to his or her own understanding of the situation—as does much literature. It says: "Here is the situation. Make of it what "you will" (Stake 6). . . . This use of a literary dissonance contributed to my original dismissal of the report as nothing but a story. My problem with the use of a literary style is not necessarily that it does render "the findings of [such an] enquiry . . . 'woolly'" (Stake 6) but that the association with literature can render them such. Although I can explore the nightmare scenario of *White Noise* and suggest that "Life cannot be reduced to a series of questions with definite answers" (Stake 8) I clearly had great problems applying that same consideration to Stake; and, through Stake, to qualitative research. I believe that this problem lies in "what I see/saw as the purpose of literature" (Stake 9). Yet, looking ahead to my engagement here with another work of literature—Pat Barker's *Ghost Road* (1995)—I can appreciate the suggestion of a reasonable, and reasoned, approach to life by seeing in the fictional character of Billy Prior a ludicrous type who must split his personality in two to maintain the inflexible code he tries to live by.

Acknowledging the dangers of making sweeping statements, I will risk the suggestion that whereas qualitative research is concerned

Do you agree with this assertion? Can qualitative research move beyond particularities? Should it?

with particularities, literature is concerned with generalities that are illustrated through the particular. Blake (c.1804/1989) summed it up rather well when writing of seeing a world in a grain of sand and holding infinity in the palm of your hand and so on. Common humanity—or Sartre's (1981) notion of the universal singular by which every person is like every other person because of the universality of social experiences and processes and yet like no other person because they are single instances of those same social experiences and processes—allows the audience to meaningfully relate to the generality of the literature. It may be worth pausing here to look at an example. So, a novel, a particular favorite of mine that you might also know, a story such as Joseph Conrad's *Heart of Darkness* (1902/1973) "can illustrate the human condition. Francis Ford Coppola then took it up, and did so brilliantly, to show the madness of the Vietnam War in *Apocalypse Now* which became a commentary on the sheer madness of War, of all war" (Stake 9) even more so "after has been saved from the obscure tedium of a modern anti-imperialist dogma (which so obviously fails to recognize the reality of turn of the century Empire) by the film *Apocalypse Now.* "I mean, who can forget those helicopters going into battle with the surfboards and with Wagner's *Ride of the Valkyries* blaring out? And it's used to show the inevitable consequences of human vanity and thirst for power in a glorious and heroic depiction of necessary justice. It's brilliantly done even though there was all that aggravation with the helicopters which had been sold by the US to the Philippine government then borrowed by Coppola before being requisitioned back to put

You will notice he uses many literary references.

down the insurgents" (Stake 7). What is strangest here: truth or fiction in film?

With too much of the story in it, the truths that I first saw in the report on Harper School were generally applicable rather than particularly so: I saw the story of Harper School from the premises looking out rather than in. They were liable to dismissal in terms of the school because they were not objectively reported. I wanted

This is a concept that qualitative researchers grapple with, especially those who were trained in the quantitative tradition.

"confirmation and got this instead" (Stake 3). Yet I can smile at Shakespeare's (c.1601/1975) Olivia giving out the divers schedules of her beauty and, if I can put aside the canon of "great literature" for the moment, I have laughed out loud when the meaning of life, the universe and everything has been given as 42 (Adams, 1986). I can quite gleefully agree with Wilde's (1891/1970) suggestion that people did not notice sunsets until Turner started painting them and that the artist is, indeed, a critic. However, in reading Stake I had a great deal of difficulty in accepting that I could notice the consequences of the Chicago School Reform at Harper School. I had (with apologies to Wilde and Stake) difficulty in recognizing the researcher as critic, never mind as artist.

Do you have these same struggles?

In fact, I am not sure that I even recognized the researcher—in the sense that I recognized his authority to comment upon urban schools. My impression "was of a white upper middle-class male being unduly surprised at finding a spent cartridge on the grounds of an inner-city school in Chicago" (Stake 1). I wondered whether it was simply this picture that I had drawn of him that had led to my resenting his authorial intrusion. What could he know of urban schools? What could he as an outsider tell me with my inner-city experiences about urban schools? Had this perception further prejudiced my reading of the report? Stake (1995) himself answers the first question: "most" of his experience is "not in urban schools" (p. 140). Yet my experiences are also limited: I have worked in inner cities, but I have not lived in them. If I saw him as a middle-class inner-city colonizer (as opposed to me with my 9–5 anticolonialism) it was because he knew enough (unlike myself at the time of these early musings) to define his limits "so that I can make my own mind up from his experiences. Not only has he given a voice to the voiceless, he has given me a picture of the particular school and the CSR that allows me, if need be, to 'determine an alternative in the light of [my] own experience'" (Stake 8). Moreover, in declaring his own limitations of experience he had given me the advantage of knowing "where he is coming from" so that I could take that into account when applying my own experience to his observations. He knows enough to not comment, to not give why is he there, speaking for others and not letting them speak out and up for themselves?" (Stake 4). Instead of such presumption, surely he could just get to the point and get on with giving me the firm conclusions I sought. Of course, such conclusions and commentary would ultimately be the judgment of one who has little experience of urban schools and would have to be accepted or rejected accordingly.

Yet, for all Stake's attempts to preclude such judgments, I made my own and found it difficult to recognize the validity of the report's content. I did not recognize his story as an account of Harper School under the CSR and its own School Improvement Plan. I may be able to recognize that life cannot be "reduced to a series of questions with definite answers" (Stake 8) but only if, it would seem, life is neatly bound up within the safety of a literary story. I could not approach life through case study research in the same way. My problem with Stake (and, through Stake, with qualitative research) was that I failed to recognize the potential of fictive and literary devices in his report. My problem with myself was that I had failed to bridge the divide I had made between fact and the fictive style. This was where the source of my discontent was located. Case study research, I was beginning to realize, like literature, is concerned with illustrations rather than definitive answers; but whereas literature may be concerned with the ideal, such research is concerned with the real and the particular. But that was then. Now, bridging the divide I had once seen, I had found that I was able to recognize the potential of fictive and literary devices as they are used in Stake's report. It has required

Here Watts makes a very important point. The researcher's acknowledgement of his own influences enables the reader to see such a report not as a neutral account or a biased account, but an account. The reader then brings his or her own experiences from the past to the reading of the report.

Here again Watts shows his initial impatience with Stake.

Perhaps this is the intent of Watts's article. He admits he failed to see the potential of using certain kinds of devices. Do you now begin to think that perhaps Watts really finds value in the Stake work?

This is self-awareness on the part of Watts.

He acknowledges that he finally came to see the value of using fictive and literary devices.

Okay. Now we have it.

What do you think?

This point is critical in understanding Watts's take on this type of research. This article shows how his own insights developed over time. But they involved a considerable amount of thinking—not just a quick glance.

me to locate myself within the source of that discontent as I have brought what I know to bear on what I have been presented with in his study. There are answers in the stories told by Stake and by myself. And this is the thing: propose (through the abstraction of these common human experiences as they are realized, with more or less skill, in literature) a working hypothesis capable of defining the lack of definition held out here by Stake. And it is this: there are answers in the plural—not just the one. The story allows the writer or researcher to hold out a choice so that the reader can pick and choose what is appropriate to the circumstances. The reader can determine the truth as he or she sees it.

And so I put the book to one side. Anyway, the course was getting a lot more interesting. He got this speaker in to talk about the uses of "personal stories for professional learning" I think it was. You know, what really got me with that was that she brought in an excerpt from Pat Barker's Ghost Road, *the last of her Great War trilogy. I felt on more secure ground with that because I know this stuff. I think I even wrote that down somewhere. Yes, here it is: "There is a fascinating amalgam of fact and fiction here. Billy Prior is a creature of Barker's own making, but he could have been there. Rivers, Sassoon, Owen, they were all there. Real characters, people who existed and who recorded their own thoughts, have been brought into a work of fiction and their backdrop is the mess of events and propaganda that was the Great War. Four years of fighting between fact and fiction." Yes, that's it. It's from Stake 4. And how many of these facts find their way into truths told by Prior? Truths that the others may not have told? You know, where does the truth lie in all of this?*

But as Pontius Pilate asked 2000 years ago at the beginning of another story: *Quid est veritas?* What is truth? And where does the fiction become a fact? Can facts and fiction interwoven together tell a truth? "Can a story avoid the limitations of what may be seen as something definitive and still contain a truth?" (Stake 8). This suddenly came to me appearing as "contain the definitive truth and then tell it in a fictive style?" (Stake 8). And this, I thought, must surely "be the question I need to put to the answers I've given myself" (Stake 8). A story can contain a general truth, even if it is not an actual and factual report of events. "*Gulliver's Travels* did not happen, but the story does not lose its significance for this oversight of Swift's (1726/1967). Indeed, it can be argued that the message would have been missed if satire had given way to mere reportage" (Stake 4). But *Gulliver's Travels* is clearly a fictional story. What of Stake's story of Harper School? "What I find interesting now," I later wrote, "is the recognition that I can carry all my critical analyses, carefully nurtured, to a piece of fictive literature or writing, but have difficulty in applying the same to non-fiction. And the Harper's School Report in particular. Yet when I read fiction, I don't particularly want to be told that 'This is the answer!' I want to reach my own conclusions based upon the evidence I read" (Stake 11). Stake's "story" did happen, but it had not happened for me.

In a poem, perhaps? "My friend, you would not tell with such high zest / To children ardent for some desperate glory, / The old Lie: Dulce et decorum est / Pro patria mori" (Owen, 1920/1990). Quid est veritas? What? To illustrate the point being made? But pausing to consider this carefully surely the answer or the hypothesis or report or whatever you want to call it should be enough without an illustration? . . . Or am I missing it?

I began to see that the prescription that I had looked for in the Harper School report could tell me nothing if I have no knowledge of the school: "If a novel can reveal this human element as it is affected by outside elements, can a report that is written in the style of a novel do the same? The answer, surely, is *Yes* . . . The narrative form, the storytelling does not obscure this" (Stake 5). And why should I have such particular knowledge? I have a general knowledge of inner cities and of their schools, but not in the U.S. and particularly not of this one in Chicago: "Stake's report is a facet of the School [and] certainly the only part of it that I am likely to access" (Stake 11). I "know" DeLillo's *White Noise* and Barker's *Ghost Road* trilogy. But I wasn't there. In carrying my own limited knowledge into the report, had I been creating my own ludicrous type, unable to relate reality to an inflexible code? And why should the audience for whom the report was first intended, and whom I had originally written off as probably unfamiliar with the reality of inner city schools (Stake 1) have such a knowledge?

But what is the reality? Is it the casual visit of an academic, or is it the daily grind of the Chicago School Reform in action? Or is it both? After all, the academic visited the school and reported on that: "Stake's report, Stake's truth, contributes to the whole that is the perception of the school . . . If I want to consider how CSR is working, then I must have my Stake in it" (Stake 11). I returned to my own experiences, to my own knowledge of literary criticism to reach the answers that I believe I now have. They may not be the answers that others have, but they are answers nonetheless. And to frame them within some matrix of truth it was necessary to indicate the relevance of and to my own self, to posit myself as narrator—as Stake had done.

Quid est veritas? What is truth? Truth, suggested Vàclav Havel (1990), "is not simply what you think it is; it is also the circumstances in which it is said, and to whom, why, and how it is said" (p. 67). Here, the truth, my truth that had been recorded in a series of observations made over a course of study, is presented as a composite story: a truth in action. That story tells of my objections to the style of a particular case study, of how I reacted to a story told by someone I considered unqualified to tell it. Through the story, those

Watts reflects on this article and the journey he has taken in preparing it.

He realizes he has changed.

observations are condensed in to an identification of the problems I had in approaching the report as story. What had changed? What began that process of change?

I suspect that it was a disturbed peace: the peace of unquestioned assumptions disturbed by the "sudden incongruous juxtaposition-ing" of a story (about which I had some knowledge) presented as truth and a truth (about which I knew nothing) presented as a story. But what were those assumptions? And where were they located? "What is the status of the story? What is its relation to 'reality'?" (assorted class notes). Here were questions underlying my assump-tions; and here was an opportunity to explore the divide I had cre-ated between fact and the fictive style rather than simply fall over into it. Two questions in quick succession following rereadings of and returns to *White Noise, The Ghost Road,* and Havel's *Disturbing the Peace* suggest the beginnings of this exploration: "did it really happen like this?" and "does it really matter?" (Stake 4). Do the small accuracies and their depiction really matter if they illustrate the greater truth?

I think this is the central point for Watts. "Truths can be told through fiction."

What was crucial, I believe, was the realization that truths can be—and, indeed, are—told through fiction. Words that are put in the mouths of fictional characters who speak their truths can bring the reader up against unpleasant or unexpected truths told through a story. It was dawning on me that they can "make the familiar seem strange so that attention can be drawn to it" (Stake 1) and that these words "may not have been spoken [but] what is the story without them?" (Stake 4). What indeed? For these words are the story—even though they may not have been spoken. These words "make the story [and] give it its significance" (Stake 4).

As for Stake (1995), in placing himself as narrator within the report, he made clear that he had done little research in urban schools (p. 140). And, by way of compensating for this recognized lack of experience, he explains that it "is always important for me to make myself visible to the reader so as to establish the interactivity between researcher and phenomena. I try to provide lots of incon-testible description but still remind that these views are my views" (Stake, 1995, p. 140). Yet I had dismissed his report because of the inclusion of literary devices—as if it were a story. There was noth-ing in it, though, that I dismissed as untrue. I do not doubt, for example, that he did pick up a spent cartridge. I merely objected to the way that he presented that particular truth. Here, though, in sto-ries that were far cries from Chicago's inner-city school, were indi-cations that I *was* able to appreciate the inclusion of literary devices to enhance the truth—or a truth, at least—to make if affective: pre-scription without description of the unknown does "little to convey the sense of the subject" (Stake 3). Havel (1990) presented stories, plays with truth in them, DeLillo (1984) told truths in *White Noise* and Barker (1995) used a fictional character to tell truths about the

Great War. More than this, though, and even allowing for Havel's absurdist drama, they tell these stories as if they were true, and they tell stories within true events as if they, too, were true. You have, as it were, to see it to believe it. Take DeLillo. He tells stories that I have no particular affiliation with so perhaps my defensive association disappears and leaves me free to realize that, one way or another, you have to be there to appreciate the import of the fictive moment.

In my original consideration of *The Art of Case Study Research* I had suggested that it "may be that as perceptions of the content change, then so too will the perceptions of the style" (Stake 1). At the time this was a comment on the nature of qualitative research; and there was a sense in which I felt that the more I learned of qualitative methods of conducting research, the more I may come to appreciate the style in which it was presented. However, in focusing on the style in which it was presented, I had come to appreciate the content more. My problem with Stake was that I had allowed the "could have" element of fiction to impinge too much and lost sight of the "what is": in seizing on one or two elements of the fictive style, I had dismissed the report as being close to fictitious. "What would I tell in my own story? And what would I leave out? I don't know" (Stake 2). What would I want to tell? How would I begin the telling?

> What an interesting, unexpected outcome. Although this article is concerned with the style and literary devices used by Stake in his case study presentation, the writer discovered that the content became important as well.

You had to see it to believe it?

Perhaps. But as this story began with the words of Lawrence Stenhouse, and as I have attempted to put them to use here in this exploration of my reactions to the writing of case studies it becomes, perhaps, appropriate that I should close with further words of his: "Public funding should not be used to finance the writing of bad novels" (class notes).

> What do you think Watts means here?

So we're talking about this and, out of the blue, he's telling me about some lecture notes of Stake's that he's got. Don't know where he got them from. Certainly don't know how he got hold of them. To tell the truth (but what is truth?) it doesn't seem important now. But what's important is that they're annotated notes. It's important because, you see, apparently Stake had been adding these annotations on the plane as he was heading off to the lecture he was giving. And that's the whole point, I suppose, as it made the jolly old Art of Case Study Research *a lot clearer. Apparently it took him about 14 years to write it and I suddenly had this picture of him sitting on the plane adding yet more notes to an already prepared lecture. I don't know if they were annotated or not, but I don't think it matters because it was the picture I created that made me think this. Anyway, I see him in this picture tinkering away, and suddenly the publisher is saying to him "Submit that manuscript!" Of course, it wasn't "complete" then because if you think of him on the plane with those lecture notes, it'll never be complete. I mean, it can't be as there will always be more stories to tell and different ways of telling them to different audiences and so on because just about goes and sums up everything I've been trying to say about this wretched* Art of Case Study Research. *I mean, take a good look at it. There he is and he's supposed to be on his way to this lecture and he hasn't even bothered to prepare his notes properly. You know, it's just so obvious he's left it all to the last minute and here he is trying to palm this book of his off on gullible students like there really is "more to this case study research than meets the eye" (Stake 8). And if you don't keep your eyes open, you're going to miss this whole point. Or not, as the Case may be.*

Source: Watts, M. (2007). They have tied me to a stake: reflections on the art of case study research. *Qualitative Inquiry, 13*(2), 204–217. Used with permission from SAGE.

Summary and Review

This is an unusual article, one that you have to read with some thought to get the author's point. What are your reactions? Do you think Bouck would find it useful?

Because of the unusual nature of this article, I have not written a traditional summary or analysis.

FINAL COMMENTS

Case study research is somewhat different from the approaches you read about in the first three chapters. It does not have any specific guidelines for gathering or analyzing data, nor does it address how information should be presented or written. Rather, it emphasizes the study of a particular phenomenon. Bouck's study does that. Watts writes about case study research and provides his own frustrations on a journey of understanding.

You can access the complete articles at www.sagepub.com/lichtmanreadings.

Chapter 5

READING ACTION RESEARCH

Like many other types of qualitative research approaches, action research means different things to different people. Most agree

- action research occurs in a school setting,
- it is often used when individuals look for solutions to common problems about which they can take some action,
- the problem being solved often relates to school improvement,
- action research is practitioner based, and
- it usually involves collaboration among key players.

Often it is a teacher who uses systematic and disciplined inquiry with the intent of changing and improving practice. What makes it a form of research is that the inquiry is disciplined. The topics are specific and current. The intent is for school improvement. At times the inquiry may go beyond one specific teacher; in fact, at times the inquiry can center on an entire school improvement project. What is important to keep in mind is that the intent is school improvement.

Action research fell into disfavor during the 1950s when the scientific movement in education was so strong. This type of research was seen as soft. While it has been in and out of favor, currently action research is on the upward cycle.

Action research does not have a philosophical basis, as does phenomenology. It does not follow specific strategies, as does grounded theory. Rather, it uses a general approach to identifying problems, gathering data, and interpreting the data. Its ultimate purpose should lead to some specific action. Since school personnel conduct this type of research, it tends to follow general qualitative strategies and avoids the use of complex research designs, hypothesis testing, and statistics.

There is considerable overlap between action research and teacher research. I do not discuss the latter in this book of readings.

KEY ELEMENTS OF ACTION RESEARCH

- Action research emphasizes decisions about educational programs;
- is closely associated with teacher research;
- tends to be straightforward; and
- involves key decision makers.
- Action research usually is used in schools to address a particular educational problem.

I have selected two articles for you to review. In the first article, Maya Miskovic and Katrina Hoop provide an example of two individuals (themselves) collaborating on two research projects. Both authors were students when the projects were conducted. They take a very strong position on the role of critical pedagogy (which they connect to action research) at the beginning of the article. I hope this is a study that relates to your own practice. The intent of their two projects was to get children involved in civic life and to raise awareness of social inequality—no small task, I would say. What are the special issues and flags that researchers need to be aware of when studying something in which they are intimately involved? You might ask yourself, can you be both objective and neutral? The very premise of action research is that the projects studied involve action.

Kath Fisher and Renata Phelps present their action research study in the form of a play. In this series of readings, my purpose has been to present to you a variety of research approaches as well as styles of writing. Here I take the opportunity to present a play. The authors explore the challenge of the principles of action research and the demands of the academy for more traditional writing. You will note that they are affiliated with a university in Australia.

ADVANCE PREPARATIONS

Begin by reading the title and the abstract, then flipping through the article and reading the major headings and subheadings. Once you have an idea of the article's structure, go back and read through the article carefully. When you finish reading, you will need to decide the extent to which the article is successful. To do so, ask yourself four questions:

- Does it provide new information and insights related to the topic?
- Is it engaging and written in a clear manner?
- Does it illustrate elements you would expect to find in action research?
- Do the positive aspects of the article outweigh the potential drawbacks?

Article 5.1. Action Research Meets Critical Pedagogy: Theory, Practice, and Reflection (2006)

Maya Miskovic and Katrina Hoop

My Expectations

You learn from reading the abstract that the authors examine participatory action research (PAR) and critical pedagogy. You need to anticipate what they might say about these two topics. A quick reading of the headings reveals that the initial section deals with collaborative research as an educational practice. You might not be too familiar with the research on this topic. Be on the lookout for PAR. The literature review is several pages long and is academic in structure and writing. The topic critical pedagogy is also reviewed, in particular how it relates to PAR.

ABSTRACT

This study brings together several concepts: collaborative and action research with critical pedagogy. Critical pedagogy and theory (concepts from Paulo Freire) are concerned with helping students to question and reflect.

This article describes and critically examines the collaborative research process between an urban university's research center and its community partners. The authors link the theoretical framework of collaborative research, participatory action research, and critical pedagogy to their personal experiences involving two collaborative research projects in which they participated. The projects were designed to foster engagement of youth in civic life through social research and to raise awareness of social inequality and injustice. The authors critically examine various phases of research with a particular focus on the following challenges: recruitment and attendance issues, development, language and methods issues, and the university and funding agency–driven push for a "product." The authors point out the strengths and weaknesses of the collaborative approach and problematize issues not visible in the final research reports. Finally, strategies for enhancing the quality of the collaborative research involving youth are proposed.

We learn that the emphasis is on examining collaboration between a university and a community organization. We will have to look for how critical pedagogy is connected.

This article is a description and critical examination of the collaborative research process between an urban university's research center and its community partners. We link the theoretical framework of collaborative research, participatory action research (PAR), and critical pedagogy to our personal experiences involving two collaborative research projects in which we participated. During these projects, we both worked as graduate research fellows at the university center and were involved in the research collaboration from the initial phase of designing the research to the end phase of writing the report. Both projects were designed to foster engagement of youth in civic life through social research and involved the university research center and different educational and political institutions and agencies in the greater Chicago metropolitan area. Drawing on experiences from community-university collaborative research projects, we critically examine different phases of collaborative research and our role in the process. We point out the strengths and setbacks of the collaborative approach involving youth and problematize issues not visible in the final research reports. Certainly, this article is written from our perspective and might not reflect the impressions of other actors involved. Finally, we propose strategies for enhancing the quality of the collaborative research process that involves youth.

These ideas should be stimulating.

COLLABORATIVE RESEARCH AS AN EDUCATIONAL PRACTICE

Notions of collaborative research and PAR are used simultaneously in this article because a review of literature revealed great similarities in defining the terms (e.g., Brydon-Miller, Greenwood, & Maguire, 2003; Greenwood & Levin, 2000; McTaggart, 1997). What those definitions have in common is the idea of university-trained researchers and community representatives working together on all the phases of the research process and generating knowledge that promotes social justice for groups that have been traditionally excluded from the process.

Here you see a political agenda.

In their fierce critique of university-based produced knowledge that bears little or no significance to the everyday activities of the communities in which the universities are embedded, Greenwood and Levin (2000) proposed praxis-oriented research that is not abstract, self-referential, and distributed within a narrow disciplinary circle; instead, such research is highly contextual and focused on "real problems" in the communities. By developing "cogenerative inquiry" (Greenwood & Levin, 2000, p. 86) where trained researchers and community stakeholders collaborate in all phases of research, the process becomes democratized, done "*with* the community, not *to* it" (Nyden, Figert, Shibley, & Burows, 1997, p. 7).

The idea just presented might appeal to many of you.

PAR as theorized in this article has six key features, adopted from Kemmis and Wilkinson (1998): PAR is a social process whereby actors in an educational and social setting learn how they are connected to social structures. PAR is participatory and practical because the actors involved are not passive subjects but rather, active agents working toward social action. PAR is emancipatory and critical as individuals examine and challenge the role of larger social, political, economical, and cultural conditions that shape their identities and actions. In this process, research inevitably touches on the issues of power, domination, and hegemony. Finally, PAR is reflexive because participants are encouraged to critically examine their own role in research.

Some of these concepts are appealing to those who find that research is remote from and irrelevant to their own work.

Collaborative research could have an empowering effect for those involved, such as community groups. By including community activists on a university-trained research team, the research process is demystified. In addition, community members acquire skills to conduct research pertinent to local issues. The idea of empowering the powerless by including them in the research process is not a novelty; the topic is well documented in research literature (Fine, Weiss, Weseen, & Wong, 2000; Greenwood & Levin, 2000; Kemmis & McTaggart, 2000; Suarez-Balcazar & Orellana-Damacela, 1999), as well as on the World Wide Web (e.g., Aspen Institute Roundtable on Comprehensive Community Initiatives at http://www.aspenroudtable.org, Community Tool Box at http://ctb.lsi.ukans.edu/, United Way Outcomes Measurement

Do you think inclusion alone results in demystification?

Tools at http://www.national.unitedway.org/outcomes/). However, this process presents many challenges, especially when young people are included in the research process.

The idea of engaging students in classroom activities that stimulate the research process from formulating research questions to data collection and analysis is not a rarity, but situations that apply this newly acquired knowledge for solving problems in the community are rare (Atweh, Christiansen, & Dornan, 1998). Manuals, textbooks, and other written sources dedicated to PAR in schools are mostly aimed at teachers as researchers in the classroom (e.g., Cochran-Smith & Lytle, 1993; Mills, 2002; Tabachnick & Zeichner, 1991). In their comprehensive analysis of studies that involve teachers as researchers, Baumann and Duffy (2001) delineated a portrait of a "typical teacher researcher" as such:

> A reflective elementary, secondary, or postsecondary classroom teacher identifies a persistent teaching problem or question and decides to initiate a classroom inquiry. This teacher reads theoretical and applied educational literature, including other teacher-research reports, and decides to work collaboratively with a colleague. Using primarily practical, efficient, qualitative methods recommended by other teacher researchers, with perhaps a quantitative tool added in, the researcher initiates a study. (p. 611)

School children involved in this type of research are usually recipients of research practices developed by their teachers, such as case studies of teachers assisting an English-as-a-second-language learner (Schoen & Schoen, 2003) or when fourth-grade students evaluated, through interviews and group discussions, materials studied in the classroom (McCall, 2002). In both cases, adult figures were initiators of classroom activities. In their study of teachers and autistic children interacting, Schoen and Bullard (2002) assessed teachers' actions as successful, but when students themselves needed to initiate behavior that teachers introduced, only "modest accomplishments" (p. 39) were observed.

Another common type of PAR involving children depicts teachers and parents working together to develop strategies that support students with emotional and behavioral disorders (Cheney, 1998), to create a program for parents that enhances reading abilities in children with developmental disabilities (Kay & Fitzgerald, 1997), or to establish a school-family partnership with economically disadvantaged and racially and ethnically diverse families (Ho, 2002). A common feature of this type of PAR is the role of children and young adults in the process: Students are participants in research, but only indirectly—their role is limited to the receivers of some strategy, practice, or program that was created, implemented, and evaluated by adults.

Have you ever thought of including children in the research process?

Why is it so difficult to involve school children as active agents in research? Discussing action research that takes place in schools, Feldman and Atkin (1995) argued that research is riddled with difficulties even when all the actors involved are adults. Research ideas usually originate from university researchers, whereas schoolteachers are assigned to "assistant" status. Such relationships could be successful and collegial, but the major intellectual impetus comes from the university. Furthermore, once the research is completed and the university researchers leave the school, teachers are rarely compelled to continue with further inquiry. In addition, researchers outside academia must rely on university insiders who understand academic jargon that often does not have sympathy for context-laden research but rather adheres to the post-positivist research paradigm; furthermore, researchers have to deal with institutional review board requirements or local school boards, all of which contribute in developing a dependent behavior in teachers (Zygouris-Coe, Pace, Malecki, & Weade, 2001).

They may not have the time or the skills to continue.

Even when teachers feel confident enough to pursue their research agenda, they continue to face a power imbalance between themselves and university researchers (Zigo, 2001). Also, teachers report lack of time and interest for research among their colleagues, who can feel threatened by the research process that in turn can result in alienation and hostility toward the teacher researcher (Lloyd, 2002). These issues are mentioned to stress even greater challenges to PAR when on one side we have university researchers and on the other, school children or young adults. The PAR projects we participated in involved youth aged 13 to 15, with an aim to assist them in developing critical agency through participation in social research and active involvement in their communities. These goals resonate with the theoretical framework of critical pedagogy, a topic we address next.

CRITICAL PEDAGOGY AND ITS LINK TO PAR

This discussion about democratic change has not occurred in the other articles you have read.

The theory of critical pedagogy has similar goals to PAR. Brydon-Miller et al. (2003) claimed that action research aspires to contribute to the well-being of individuals and communities, promoting large-scale democratic change. Like critical pedagogues, action researchers are critical of a positivistic view of knowledge that regards valid research as objective and value free. Brydon-Miller et al. continued,

> Instead, we embrace the notion of knowledge as socially constructed, and recognizing that all research is embedded within a system of values and promotes some model of human interaction, we commit ourselves to a form of research which challenges unjust and undemocratic economic, social and political systems and practices. (p. 11)

Similar to PAR, critical pedagogy addresses the challenge of providing students with the capacity for critical judgment, social responsibility, and a sense of public commitment (Giroux, 2001). It has also been associated with critical literacy, "the capacity to decode, demystify, and deconstruct the taken-for-granted narratives, symbols, metaphors, and tropes that guide the production of truth within texts" (Carlson, 2003, pp. 46–47).

Having emerged in the 1980s in the United States, critical pedagogy has been inspired by various sources: Latin American philosophies of liberation (Freire, 2001), the Frankfurt school of critical theory (see Kincheloe & McLaren, 2000), feminist theory (Luke & Gore, 1992), and neo-Marxist cultural criticism (McLaren, 1998). It also encompasses the discussion of multiculturalism (Gay, 1995) and antiracist education (Ng, Staton, & Scane, 1995). Therefore, critical pedagogy is not a homogeneous concept but a broad tenet that includes sometimes-disparate discourses. Even its name is a source of debate; for instance, Gore (1998) used the term "radical pedagogy discourses" (p. 272), Lather (1992) wrote about "emancipatory pedagogy" (p. 122), and Rezai-Rashti (1995) employed the notion of "transformative theorists" (p. 5) to include theoretical approaches that, despite their differences, have a common goal: to practice the "teaching/learning intended to interrupt particular historical, situated systems of oppression" (Lather, 1992, p. 121).

Critical pedagogy has similar goals to PAR in that it is aimed at drawing on "indigenous knowledge" rather than knowledge rooted in those who have power to claim authority, such as academic scholars and university-based research sites (Greenwood & Levin, 2000; Kemmis & McTaggart, 2000). Both approaches have transformative potential, demanding equality, diversity, and social justice. Educators and researchers using PAR and critical pedagogy challenge the educational system on many fronts, such as policy-related issues, stereotyping, and oppressive practices within the school setting. In addition, teachers address educational content that reflects authoritarian positions, fostering individuality, critical empowerment, critical literacy, and instituting multicultural education materials and activities that reflect demographic shifts throughout the world. Although each student's background experiences are respected and honored, they are also taught to critique and respond to the many texts and resources they are given.

Has critical pedagogy fulfilled its goals? Educators who have attempted to implement the principles of critical pedagogy in their classrooms have reported success on various fronts, such as developing students' capacities to read, write, and use language to consider how they perceive themselves in the world and what choices they make (Ball, 2000); challenging university students' beliefs about race and class, while simultaneously being attentive to their own role as multicultural educators (Obidah, 2000); or leading

These views reflect a philosophical position of critical theory or pedagogy.

students to use their imagination and critical thinking when addressing abstract social issues such as globalization and its effects on everyday life (Bigelow, 1998).

Still, reviewing some earlier critiques (Ellsworth, 1989; Lather, 1998) and the recent writings on critical pedagogy (Giroux, 2000, 2001, 2002; McLaren & Farahmandpur, 2001a, 2001b, 2001c; Wardekker & Miedema, 1997; Weiler, 2001), the impression is that critical pedagogy, once a promising and prominent paradigm, has been seriously flawed, if not completely failed. Apparently, critical pedagogy, along with its partner multiculturalism, has become rearticulated and domesticated by its ideological enemies, the politics of neoliberalism, and corporate global capitalism, prompting an explicit and vocal anticapitalism turn in the field, although offering different solutions (Giroux 2000, 2001, 2002; McLaren & Farahmandpur, 2001a, 2001b, 2001c). Because of the intellectual and moral paralysis of postmodernism, critical pedagogy has been redirected toward identity politics, in which social class lost its crucial place in the discussions on difference (Scatamburlo-D'Annibale & McLaren, 2003).

Rather than focusing on the postmodern equivalence among different forms of oppression, McLaren and Farahmandpur (2001c) proposed a "strategic integration of different yet equally important struggles . . . in which race and gender antagonisms can be addressed and overcome within the larger project of class struggle" (p. 143). Critical pedagogy, or what has been left of it, could be salvaged by a revolutionary Marxist pedagogy that

> must be able to endorse the cultural struggles of workers and coordinate such struggle as part of a broader "cross-border" social movement unionism aimed at organizing and supporting the working-classes and marginalized cultural workers in their efforts to build new international anti-capitalist struggles. (McLaren & Farahmandpur, 2001a, p. 12)

It is questionable, however, that critical pedagogy could be rescued by historical materialism and calling on a socialist revolution. We are not debating here the "end of history" or "end of ideology" ideas but are highly suspicious (one of the authors of this article experienced socialism, East European style) of most educators envisioning no less than socialist revolution when contemplating the possibilities of improving the educational system in the United States. McLaren and Farahmandpur (2001a) wrote,

> A turn to socialism in no way diminishes the importance of industrial, postindustrial or technological development, which we believe must continue. However, in our socialist vision, *individuals would contribute labor according to ability, and the material means of life would be distributed according to need* [italics added]. Ideally, a redistributive socialism would be followed by the managed obsolescence of the money exchange. (p. 13)

The comments in these last several paragraphs are quite different from what you have previously read. Much of what you have read previously seems to adopt a stance of objectivism and neutrality. These authors reflect their own experience and viewpoint, however. While you may not agree with it, I want you to consider how it informs the authors' own design of research.

Despite McLaren and Farahmandpur's eloquent and poetic indictment of the exploitative nature of capitalism, those who have lived under East European socialism remember these sentences as empty slogans memorized and recited in classrooms and displayed on banners in factories. At the end, the revolution did eat its children and those who survived seem to have immersed themselves happily into mind-numbing consumerism. Regardless of the broken promises of a get-rich-easily capitalist mantra, one needs only to take a stroll through the streets of Moscow or Belgrade to see youth (who can afford it) enveloped, often to the grotesque extent, in designer clothes and accessories, which are supposed to symbolize high life à la Hollywood.

We do not accuse McLaren and Farahmandpur (2001a) of being "naive, impractical or hopelessly utopian" (p. 13). However, if the United States is ever to reach socialism, we hope this time it will be devoid of tactics so mercilessly employed by East European socialist ideologues for half of the previous century, namely, exploitation, manipulation, and outright inhumane treatment of its citizens. If the "metaphysical turn" of postmodern, postcolonial, and cultural studies has led to the abandonment of theory as a tool for concrete political action (De Lissovoy & McLaren, 2003), we think there is a danger that critical pedagogy as a Marxist project could fall into the same trap.

We believe that the idea of critical pedagogy is not superseded; and in searching for solutions toward its renewed relevance, we agree with Henry Giroux (2002), who asserted that "we need to reject both neoliberal and orthodox leftist positions, which dismiss the state as merely a tool of repression, to find ways to use the state to challenge, block, and regulate the devastating effects of capitalism" (p. 1154). Giroux went on to claim that we are missing a language and movement that does not equate democracy with consumerism and market relations. It is extremely difficult today for both youth and adults to articulate their private concerns within a public discourse, because the private has become the only space where we can imagine a sense of hope or possibility. In such an atmosphere, capitalism's very fuel is consumerism, where prosperity and safety are addressed by consumption. The key here is to teach youth how to become "skilled citizen[s]" (Giroux, 2002, p. 1153) who can use critical thinking skills to understand that the principles of democracy should not be coupled with corporatizations of private and public life. It seems more realistic that solutions be pursued within the system we live in, using all avenues where critical identities are created.

Because critical pedagogy is concerned with the social embeddedness of education and its inevitably political character (Wardekker & Miedema, 1997), its commitment to social justice remains a valuable platform from which educators and practitioners can speak and act. At the end of the 20th century, Carlson and Apple (1998) addressed the importance and urgency of critical education in "unsettling times." Post-9/11 United States presents such times again with national homogenization, political and ideological divisiveness, subversion of civil liberties, and military expansion and imperialism. Patriotism is measured by the level of consensus, in which "symbolic capital and political power reinforce each other through a public pedagogy produced by a concentrated media" (Giroux, 2004, p. 207), and it is not surprising that youth, and many adults as well, have difficulties in breaking from this dictum. Not immune to these cultural shifts, the American Association of University Professors (2003), representing academic establishments, has extensively addressed the pressure and scrutiny to defend academic freedom.

. . .

In such a climate, here and abroad, we deem the framework of critical pedagogy and practice of action research as crucial components of a democratic educational system to penetrate and challenge systems of control. Despite the differences between various critical discourses and their often-complicated relations with critical pedagogy, at this historical moment—when debate *in and of itself* is threatened—the right for critical voices to safely and rigorously be heard must be defended. Not to conclude on a pessimistic note, we take with hope the words of Darder, Baltodano, and Torres (2003), who "in the light of a long-standing historical tradition of progressive educational efforts in the United States," asserted that the "underlying commitment and intent of critical pedagogy will continue as long as there are those who are forced to exit the conditions of suffering and alienation, and those who refuse to accept such conditions as natural evolution of humankind" (p. 21).

Two collaborative projects we participated in resonate with the main ideas of critical pedagogy. The creators of the projects did not evoke the philosophy of critical pedagogy—at least its name was never mentioned; however, as participants in these projects, we came to realize that our mission had a lot in common with its principles. Our projects enacted the framework of critical pedagogy in our desire to educate youth to question the principles of social and political life and equip them with strategies to shape and change social, political, and economic constraints in their environment. Equally important, both projects understood youth as community assets rather than problems to be dealt with. The projects illustrate the difficulties of implementing this framework of what happens when researchers are faced with a "reality check." Our two projects were designed to assist youth in developing their capacities to become more active social agents, and although the process was riddled with challenges, it was a worthwhile attempt to involve youth in social research and foster their awareness.

You might think much of this is a diatribe and not relevant to the research of the study. I leave it for you, though, to consider how the views and beliefs of researchers strongly influence what they do. In this article, the views are made explicit. In many other articles that you have read and will read, the views are not mentioned.

Does this seem strange to you? These writers adopted the critical pedagogical stance even though it was not the overt premise of the study in which they were involved.

I really like the concept that youth can be community assets rather than community problems.

CIVIC ENGAGEMENT OF YOUTH:
TWO CASES OF COLLABORATIVE RESEARCH

In this section, we describe the collaborative research process between a university research center and its community partners. At the time of the projects, we were both graduate research fellows at a university research center and involved with everything from the implementation of the collaboration idea to the final phase of writing a research report. We are White middle-class women closely related to the university and its culture; our community partners and students that participated in research reflected the urban milieu of racial and economical diversity. Although we participated in these projects independently, our roles were common: to teach teenagers how to conceive, develop, research, and report on important social issues for them and their communities. The nature of collaboration in the two projects reflected the principles on which our university center works: Although the university and community partners collaborate closely during all phases of the research process, there is a "division of tasks" approach that shifts the element of activity toward one side as research unfolds.

It is not until almost halfway through the article that you finally encounter a description of the actual program with kids. I know: this makes it seem like it is a case study. This is an example where the approach to research taken by authors is by no means pure.

The first case involved a university research center, Chicago schools, and the City Educational Institute (CEI).[1] Faculty members of the five Chicago schools implemented a 16-week Empowerment Workshop—developed by CEI and evaluated by a university research center—to bring service learning and leadership development into the educational experiences of school children. As community partners, CEI developed a course curriculum and a method of evaluation, whereas teachers implemented the curriculum and distributed evaluation tools. University researchers helped the community partners refine their evaluation instruments and served as support when the teachers experienced difficulties. The majority of students who participated in this program were Latinas and African American females, aged 13 to 14. Teachers used the workshop both in and out of the classroom setting. The workshop was designed to allow students to explore their own leadership potential, build positive relationships with their peers, develop leadership skills, explore and understand community issues and strategies for action, and ultimately design and implement a service project based on their interests. These interests included racism, disabilities, homelessness, and violence, to name a few.

The second case involved collaborative research with a university research center and the For Safer Neighborhoods (FSN) organization. FSN is an organization in Chicago that works with neighborhoods on issues such as affordable housing, civic engagement projects for youth, judicial reform, and neighborhood safety policy. Youth from FSN, a year earlier, had challenged a Chicago-based antiloitering law, deeming it unconstitutional, and won. University researchers established a connection with FSN after learning about its affiliated youth group that had been active in Chicago political and civic issues. The funding for this project was part of a larger grant on youth civic engagement and hoped to address and challenge the notion that young people are detached from and disinterested in civic and political issues. With the promise of critical pedagogy in mind, this project had the potential to challenge the image of disengaged youth and illustrate the importance of action research. The goals of this project were to (a) involve youth in policy research by helping them identify and research issues salient to them and their neighborhoods and (b) teach youth how to work with their host organization—FSN—so that they could independently conduct policy research in their communities. However, although the researcher going into this project was "equipped" with the goals listed above, there was no "step-by-step" handbook on how to deal with the challenges this project faced. All the participants in this program were 15-year-old African American females.

PROJECT CHALLENGES

Although fully aware of the interrelated nature of various stages of a research process and the issues emerging from it, the challenges discussed in this section are separated for analytical reasons. The three areas we discuss include recruitment and attendance issues, development, language and methods issues, and the university and funding agency–driven push for a "product." We faced challenges on both projects within these areas.

Recruitment and Attendance/Rapport Issues

As members of the university research center, we assumed that youth participation would be plentiful, as had been demonstrated with their past activism. From the start of the FSN project, however, the university staff failed to interest more youth than it was hoped for. Many of the older youth who had worked on projects did not attend the first meeting. A group of 15 youth—mostly junior high school students—attended the first meeting. At this meeting, our primary goal was to "hook" them into the idea of the project. We brainstormed ideas for project topics and explained how the process of research worked. From the beginning, we explained that this project would be *their* project; we were there to work with them. However, at the next meeting, 3 girls showed up; we did not "sell" the idea as affectively [sic] as we had hoped. Although 3 young women eventually continued with the project, we failed to gain more

In this section, a brief page and a half describe the two projects. The authors concentrate on several challenges they faced. If you have been involved in projects in such situations you might not be surprised that one issue they address is recruitment and attendance. I am less clear on what they mean by "development, language, and method issues," but I hope to understand more after I read this section.

youth participants at our first meeting. Many of the young teens were new to community work and viewed these gatherings as purely social in nature. Had we established a stronger rapport by spending more time with the youth and by fostering activities that would help capture their interest, our group would have been larger. In addition, the civic engagement process would have fostered and supported the heightening of critical consciousness. In retrospect, it is very likely that the youth perceived our initial meeting as too academic: dry and structured. At the second meeting, researchers were able to form a close rapport with the teens, which was crucial to the sustainability of the project. We talked to them without interruption, unlike the first meeting, where distractions cost us the chance to gain interest and connect with youth on a personal level. At this meeting, the researchers brought in academic articles about gangs and violence. We discussed whether the articles represented their experiences at school (in many ways, yes) and what other topics were of concern to them. We met in different places for 6 months—often because of scheduling difficulties—which also contributed to the "unpredictability" of the project. However, spending more time with the participants at our university would have helped them gain better research skills on topics of their interest. One of the goals of the FSN project was for youth to acquire technical skills, such as computer research, but this did not crystallize because of the limited time of the project and the challenge of transporting the participants to other parts of Chicago.

On the CEI project, student participants for the Empowerment Workshop were recruited by their teachers, who clearly sent a message to the students that their participation was a desirable outcome. In this way, all the actors involved on the project were satisfied: The students made a good impression on their teachers, the teachers satisfied the test makers, and the university center had enough data to conduct data analysis and write a final report.

The question remains whether the approaches employed in these projects—both involving civic engagement—truly reflect the theory of PAR and critical pedagogy. Although the FSN project failed to recruit more participants, those who stayed involved expressed some level of action and it is hoped, developed an insight into how research can make a change in their community. The young women learned interviewing skills, interviewed each other on topics related to their neighborhoods, and were later involved in planning and hosting a small youth conference. The CEI research project, on the other hand, operated on a mass scale (more than 200 students participated), and students' gains from the research were more in accord with the business-as-usual school praxis. Adults proposed and organized the workshop that they believed would be useful to students and by choosing a quantitative approach to evaluate the workshop, failed to engage students in a more meaningful and active way.

Having completed the workshop, during which they could exercise some sort of personal involvement and activity through dialogue and class exercises, the testing situation returned students back to passivity. Students could have written a newsletter, organized an exhibition in their schools, or produced a video record of their activities.

Instead, the community partners wanted the university center to evaluate the course impact in a traditional way, namely, through testing. As program evaluators, we did not have insight into instructional material, nor did we have an opportunity to observe students and teachers in the classroom. From the evaluators' position, what was actually happening in the classroom remained a "black box." The effectiveness of this workshop was understood strictly as a test score. This is not a critique of the community partners' decision but, rather, a reflection of how in a new era of accountability, educators are forcefully pushed into the single direction of pursuing and justifying research with quantifiable results.

. . .

Another challenge they address is a drive toward the product.

The authors reflect on some weaknesses in this type of collaborative research.

Drive Toward the "Product"

Another constraint common for both projects was the drive to end with a "product." The fact that a research study is funded adds "a spin on the issues" (Cheek, 2000, p. 409). Receiving funds for the study is not a neutral act, it implies a certain relationship between the funder and researchers in terms of obligations, responsibilities, and expectations. In the FSN project, all our meetings needed to be accounted for with a finished result, such as a paper or a research piece. We were constantly cognizant of this requirement and wondered who should write these weekly pieces: Did the authorship belong to the university researchers only or should the youth have some impact on the shape and content of the texts? This constraint was compounded by the fact that the youth involved in the project had weak writing and researching skills. Although they were interested and eager to carry out interviews in their community and discuss the results, we, as university-trained researchers, had the impression that they enjoyed the meetings more for the social aspect than the strictly research-learning component. This experience pointed to the assumption that PAR often has an empowering effect on the participants. We forget, however, that participants may not share our assumptions. Because research within universities is a "product-oriented" process, we often tend to neglect the aspects of research that might seem successful to participants. In this case, it was more social gathering and doing activities different from everyday school tasks.

A related issue to a research "product" is that of offering financial rewards to participants. University researchers may view an intellectual discovery or published article as an intrinsic reward in

The issue of rewards for earning grades is very much in the news as of this writing in 2009.

itself, but for the youth on the FSN project, their highly anticipated reward would come in the form of Old Navy clothing gift certificates. However, a university research center could not offer them this prize for participating and instead, offered coupons for either a grocery store or a bookstore. The youth reluctantly took the coupons for a grocery store, deemed by the FSN project funders as a "reasonable expenditure." This situation illustrates yet another reality check in the work of community-university researchers: differing notions of participation and rewards within a capitalistic economic system. What represented a reward for the university center staff meant little to the participants.

Are you surprised that the authors take such a strong position here?

Regardless of how much students are aware of societal injustices and inequalities, which they themselves experience on an everyday basis, these young women inevitably contribute to and are a part of this exploitive process. Growing up in capitalism socializes young people to desire and enjoy the products of capitalist exploitation, so the wish of our participants to be rewarded with Old Navy clothes instead of books or social research itself is not surprising. After all,

> exploitation through the capitalist marketplace has been so naturalized and the pauperization of the state so dehistoricized and depoliticized that we have learned to accept a certain amount of exploitation and . . . feel that it is an inevitable part of living in a developed capitalist democracy. (McLaren & Farahmandpur, 2001a, p. 6)

The perceived failure of critical pedagogy to engage more educators in applying its principles to their teaching and research practices lies partly in this disconnect between echoing socialist and communist icons and attempting to make them attractive to youth in today's consumerist United States. Regardless of all the injustices and inhumanities that capitalism (Whose capitalism?) brings to human lives, it is questionable whether its alternative lies in socialism (Whose socialism?) and even more, whether that alternative resonates with the lives of North American youth. Various and complex types of capitalism exist (Esping-Andersen, 1990), which makes a valid debate about whether capitalism is necessarily evil and if so, whether the idea of its abolishment is empirically unrealistic.

Do you think the authors were naïve to think the students would write the project results? And, if they attempted to write them, do you think the authors and university community would have accepted the work? Most often in any kind of qualitative research, those being studied have little voice in what is said about them. Of course, some authors use quotations from participants, but do not put them in the role of co-researchers or coauthors.

In the completion of the projects, our university center's staff took control of the research by being the sole author of the research reports. It seems that this role was expected and welcomed by the community partners, because the writing phase may be seen as less "active," more analytical and, therefore, less interesting. The underlying message from the community partners was "After all, you are trained to write, and we'll gladly let you do it." The question, then, is, what should be the research product and who owns it?

McTaggart's (1997) writings bridge the gap in our dilemmas of full collaboration and of research report ownership. He differentiated "authentic participation" from "mere involvement." Although the former implies ownership, or "responsible agency in the production of knowledge and improvement of practice" (McTaggart, 1997, p. 28), the latter denotes a mere co-option and further exploitation of people for the sake of others. McTaggart argued that this is a common practice in community programs that are proclaimed as collaborative but instead, are just another oppressive implementation of some policy. According to Tandon (as quoted in McTaggart, 1997, p. 29), characteristics of authentic collaboration are

- people's role in setting the agenda of inquiry;
- people's participation in the data collection and analysis; and
- people's control of the use of outcomes and the whole process.

Our research experiences do not fit neatly into these determinants. Neither the institutions nor the agencies outside the university were the ultimate research product owners; nor was the university research center just another oppressive body in knowledge production. Again, our experiences are more a reflection of a "task division-of-labor" approach, where community partners proposed the research agenda with minimal interference by the university and where the university was responsible for analyzing the results (especially if the analysis requires knowledge of statistical package) and writing the report. The realization of the research agenda itself fell in the middle: What was actually happening in the classroom or within the youth group was a true collaboration. We fully agree with Kemmis and McTaggart's (2000) assertion that in most action and collaborative research, methodological rigor is exchanged for answering the question whether the data collected make sense to participants in their, not our, context. PAR sometimes "sacrifices methodological sophistication in order to generate timely evidence that can be used and further developed in a real-time process of transformation (of practices, practitioners, and practice settings)" (Kemmis & McTaggart, 2000, p. 591). In our case, a trade-off

Do you think this compromise is reasonable?

between technical and "reality check" issues for the purpose of solving people's real problems was a worthwhile experience.

CONCLUSION AND RECOMMENDATIONS FOR FUTURE RESEARCH

When the two university-community collaborative research projects we participated in were designed, their goals were clear: to include youth in social research. It was believed that participation in the research process could benefit youth in raising their awareness of social issues and prompt them to take action in their communities. Both projects were concerned with students' development of critical thinking on the issues of social justice and equality and their empowerment that would crystallize in taking action. We also have realized that the opportunity to conduct collaborative research with the school children was a rarity for us and that fact also influenced our choice to place a theoretical framework of critical pedagogy within an examination of the research process and our role in it.

Here the researchers recognize a disconnect between what was planned and what actually happened.

Despite the well-defined goals, the research process itself became "muddied" as a result of various dynamics that different people brought to the research table. Thus, our initial goal was to establish a dialogue across class and race. The university researchers failed to attract more youth to one of the projects; however, close rapport with those who stayed was developed. After the bumpy start and searching for language that could bridge the gap across age, social status, and race, we developed a mutual and friendly bond that made our time spent together worthwhile.

The involvement in collaborative research with youth led us to question whether we managed to provide an authentic voice for the youth, and whether our students made a link between the personal and political. Our impression is that students were conscious about their race, class, and gender and that their participation in the research process made them even more cognizant. But they felt inapt (sic) to take action, at least on the scale that was suggested during the research. It seems that the adults, who designed and implemented the ideas of what it means to feel empowered and confident to take social action, did not take enough into account the difficulties that 13-and 14-year-olds might experience when dealing with abstract ideas of difference and social change. It is not that students did not have a chance to link their everyday life with broader societal forces; rather, they missed the opportunity to do something in their communities that was meaningful for them, not the adults.

Do you accept the statement that "their impression" proves that the students were more cognizant? Most researchers would want better evidence than that.

It seems then that the authority of adult figures—equally university researchers, school teachers, and community partners—was not decentered (Trent, 2003), in the sense that we did not question our pedagogical authority enough during the research process itself. That realization came later, once the research reports were filed in the cabinets of the university center and community organizations. This was especially prominent in the Empowerment Workshop project, where the opportunity for the students to express further involvement ended with the completion of the workshop. Given that a chosen method for the workshop evaluation was survey, it asked the students to merely express their level of agreement or disagreement with the statement adults constructed. It is not a surprise that the results were indiscriminative and uniformly positive. Accustomed to testing, students knew what was expected from them.

The power imbalance between students and adults was mirrored by the power imbalance between university researchers and community partners. Both projects reflected a task division-of-labor approach to collaborative research, where university researchers or agencies' research associates still had more power in the process—by having the power to make important decisions—than those who should feel empowered the most: the students.

Although we faced methodological and theoretical challenges that transformed and complicated the research, findings, and reports in unexpected ways, there are a number of important lessons we learned from our experiences. We encourage researchers involved in community-university collaborative research to heed these lessons on future projects so that the process is feasible, equitable, and productive. We offer the following suggestions for future research:

- Find a congruence between the developmental stage of the students and the research goals. Researchers should be particularly sensitive to language and youth culture. We can unintentionally alienate youth by using language that is appropriate in the university setting but not in the social environment of our participants. As our experiences have taught us, this is especially pertinent in working with nondominant and underrepresented groups, where researchers must confront their own power, both as usually White, middle-class, educated persons and institutionally as representatives from university settings. Terms such as *hegemony, social construction of race,* or *gender inequality* are all a part of everyday vocabulary within a university. The real challenge is to translate these abstractions and connect them with the everyday experiences of youth so that they can make sense out of them and realize how these abstractions shape their lives.

- Find appropriate ways to research the problems that are important to youth. Sometimes university researchers assume agency where there is none, such as when middle school children are expected to critically examine social issues and independently take action in their communities. Youth are rarely, if ever, equipped with money, institutional power, and formal connections in their neighborhoods that would assist them in solving major problems. This is not a claim that such projects should be abandoned completely but, instead, is a cautious note for those in collaborative research to understand and adapt to youth's ability to participate in research in a meaningful way. Otherwise, we are in danger of romanticizing collaborative research (Zygouris-Coe et al., 2001) and overlooking the instances where youth's abilities can be better used. Instead of expecting 14-year-olds to grapple with complex social issues on a grand scale—both abstract and practical—it is more useful to focus on smaller projects that would revolve around students' own classrooms, streets, and neighborhood blocks. Although the research topic might appear trivial to adults, it could be meaningful to teenagers. It is important that in working toward social justice, educators find a way to address the issues of race, power, and ideology that reflect the age and interest of the participants. Otherwise, the impression that youth are going to form about social research will reflect the very attributes we are fighting to shed: a highly abstract, ponderous, and technical endeavor that bears no meaning to youth's lives.

- Invest more time and organize more meetings with participants to form a strong rapport. To achieve true collaboration, it is crucial to establish connections with organizations that have the capacity to be fully involved in all the phases of research. In addition to fostering a close and mutual relationship between the university and organization, participants should gather frequently at convenient and comfortable locations, chosen by all who attend. Although it might sound obvious, it is crucial to plan ahead to prevent transportation and meeting place problems. We experienced firsthand these constraints that seriously limited full collaboration. When these problems appeared, it looked only "natural" for the university staff to take responsibility in shaping and redirecting the project the way we thought appropriate. Only in the process of dedicated collaboration can the community partner truly challenge the dominant role of university-trained researchers.

- We join with the researchers who critically address this era of "accountability" in which we live (De Lissovoy & McLaren, 2003; Eisenhart & Towne, 2003; Lincoln & Cannella, 2004). As Lincoln and Cannella (2004) noted, "The language of education has shifted from a discourse of equality of opportunity to one of blame and punishment of those who do not perform appropriately" (p. 9). Randomized clinical trials, testing, and experiments are proclaimed scientific, leaving out contextually rich research. As critics have pointed out, this trend of being academically accountable has turned the process of learning into a cutthroat competitive capitalistic marketplace, pitting school districts and all those involved against each other. Gaining knowledge should remain inherently good, as it stands, and various strands within critical pedagogy can help. Raising the issue of how knowledge becomes marketed should be a part of future research with youth so that youth can become truly engaged in challenging and changing the status quo.

Source: Miskovic, M., & Hoop, K. (2006). Action research meets critical pedagogy: Theory, practice, and reflection. *Qualitative Inquiry, 12*(2), 269–291. Used with permission from SAGE.

Summary and Review

This article is quite different from any you have read earlier in this book. It begins with a strong review of the issues regarding action research, participatory research, and critical pedagogy. The authors state their position quite clearly and use related literature to support their viewpoint. It does not include elements you expect to find in a research article. Information on the type of data they actually collected and how they analyzed it are omitted. It strongly reflects their own viewpoint about power, politics, and global issues of democracy, socialism, and communism. I included it so you can see how some are moved with passion to write about their studies.

Finally, if you return to the four questions you can see the extent to which this article was successful. This is a very interesting example of an action research study. It is written with passion. However, the authors do not give you any details about the process of conducting a participatory action research study. Overall, I found this article very engaging.

- Does it provide new information and insights related to the topic?

- Is it engaging and written in a clear manner?

- Does it integrate ideas from critical pedagogy with participatory action research?

- Do the positive aspects of the article outweigh the potential drawbacks?

The next article is also nontraditional. In fact, it is written as a play. Because I do not want to interrupt the flow of the play, I have included only a few comments in the text. You will see my thoughts at the end.

Article 5.2. Recipe or Performing Art? Challenging Conventions for Writing Action Research Theses (2006)

Kath Fisher and Renata Phelps

My Expectations

I am not really sure I know what to expect when I read an article written in a nontraditional manner such as a play or a poem. Several questions concern me. If the authors chose this format in order to engage the audience, do I find it effective? I also want to know to what extent the information is fact or fiction. I recall that Watts wrote about literary devices when he commented on case study. I also want to know what type of action research was done. How does it compare with the article I just read regarding participatory action research? Do I think the work is somehow "lesser" because it doesn't follow a usual style? Or perhaps I think it might be more successful. I also wonder whether my institution would be sufficiently open to permit a piece of written scholarship in this form and also one that is collaborative. All these ideas run through my mind before I begin to read the play.

ABSTRACT

This article explores the tensions and incongruities between conventional thesis presentation and the principles of action research. Through the experiences of the authors' alternative approaches to thesis structure are proposed which are argued to be more congruent with the epistemological, methodological and ethical aspects of action research. Consistent with our arguments, the article is presented as a play. Act I considers the tensions facing research students wishing to write up their action research in the context of conventional thesis writing requirements; Act II consists of four "scenes," each of which illustrates a key learning arising from our own stories: writing in the researcher as central to the research; staying true to the unfolding research story; using metaphor; and finally, weaving literature throughout the thesis. Act III considers the challenges of examination in the face of breaking with tradition. We conclude with a "curtain call" from the narrator that offers a reflexive engagement with the main themes of the article.

This abstract says it so well. You can see how the authors tried to deal with traditional requirements of presenting research. I suspect Miskovic and Hoop faced similar challenges when writing up their research in the Chicago schools.

What do you think of when you hear the term "action research"? How important is the term "participatory"? Are you surprised that they state, "there is no single way of doing action research"? By now, you should be familiar with that mantra. It seems as though there is variation within research approaches just as there is between research approaches. The point that Fisher and Phelps make is that action research could range from a technical focus on organizational change to emancipatory processes that look at radical social changes in which participants actually become co-researchers. These two ends of the spectrum are discussed later in the paper by one of the protagonists.

INTRODUCTION

As action research and practitioner-based inquiry is increasingly adopted as a basis of doctoral study, issues arise for students, supervisors and examiners alike as to what it means to produce and judge an action research thesis in relation to traditional thesis presentation criteria (Winter, Griffiths & Green, 2000). Indeed, the question of what constitutes "quality" action research has resulted in important paradigmatic debates across the humanities and social science disciplines, debates that problematize the nature of "knowledge" and question the need for uniform criteria of validity (Bradbury & Reason, 2001; Winter et al., 2000). Furthermore, "one of the great problems with all qualitative research is the constant need to seek its justification within someone else's language game and in relation to someone else's definition of suitable criteria" (Green, cited in Winter et al., 2000, p. 30).

The quality of PhD or Masters level research is ultimately judged by the dissertation or thesis; the primary mode of exposition, even in the creative arts. It is this writing task that is our focus in this article. Most research candidates seek advice in relation to this task, to ensure they are meeting the all-important examination requirements.

Have you come across the term "performing art" related to research? You will not find many references to it, I am sure.

Traditional approaches to structuring theses, especially in the sciences and social sciences, have resulted in the familiar "five-chapter model," comprising introduction, literature review, methodology, analysis and conclusions. To borrow Bob Dick's (2002) terminology, this is writing by "recipe" and, as a rule, supervisors will be anxious to ensure their students are following accepted approaches to reduce the risk of alienating examiners. But what of the student who has undertaken action research? Do these conventions apply? Can their less conventional research process be made to "fit" the five-chapter recipe and still be true to its practice? Do they take an unacceptable risk by straying outside the mainstream? Or can they write their thesis more in keeping with the "performing art" that is action research (Dick, 2002)?

In this article we contemplate these questions through the stories of our own experiences as doctoral action researchers. We present some insights which may be of interest to other students undertaking action research who are considering challenging the conventions of the academy. As academics now supervising students undertaking action research and remaining committed to improving our own and our students' research and writing practice, we propose that these insights might also contribute to the ongoing debate about the quality, authenticity and integrity of action research.

I want you to keep your minds open as you think about presenting information in this manner. I recognize it is not traditional. As you read, you might ask yourself these questions: Does it engage the audience? Does it get the message across? What makes this type of writing so interesting is that there is no recipe to follow. These authors are breaking out of the tradition and need to find their own way.

In keeping with the spirit of viewing research (and in our case, writing) as performing art rather than recipe, we have adopted the metaphor of a play to structure our article, playing with the notion of presenting research as a form of performance text. We see our approach in this article as an example of "presentational knowing" (Heron, 1996; Heron & Reason, 2001), which, while rarely seen in academic journal writing, allows the text to "speak out" and challenge convention. A good performance text "must be more than cathartic, it must be political, moving people to action and reflection" (Denzin, 2000, p. 905). It is our hope that our "performance" produces this effect through a deeper and more active reflective engagement with our audience than a more conventional exposition may offer.

A Tale of Two Theses (A play in three acts)

Prologue: In Which the Audience Is Revealed and We Meet the Main Characters

A single spotlight shines on the middle of the closed curtain as the narrator, a figure in top hat and tails, emerges onto the stage.

NARRATOR: Ladies and gentlemen, we invite you to take your seats as we prepare to take you on a journey of intrigue and adventure—some might even say foolishness! Let me assure you, this is not a voyage for the fainthearted. Before we get under way, though, how many of you here tonight are research candidates? . . .

Wonderful! We think there might be some important lessons for you here, if not cautionary tales. What about students doing action research? . . . Excellent! You may find that some of the dilemmas you are facing in the writing of your thesis will be echoed in the stories you hear tonight. Any supervisors in the audience? . . . Aha! If you have been challenged to consider how your students might best structure their action research theses, then this play may provide some inspiration and, perhaps, reassurance.

Now, I'm wondering if there mightn't be an examiner or two out there as well? . . . It's great to see you here! Action research candidates will no doubt be pleased to know that you are interested in being challenged regarding the conventions of thesis presentation. Finally, there might be some action research practitioners out there who are reporting on their research outside the formal academic examination process . . . would you raise your hands? Ah, good. You are most welcome. While this play is more about writing theses than research reports, I'm sure you will find relevance to your own writing context.

Some of you will be fortunate enough to be studying and researching from innovative academic faculties with strong traditions of participatory inquiry and action research. Such places may well already promote creativity and breaking with convention in theses presentation. For you, some of the messages in this play may not be all that new, however, we are glad to have you here with us, and we welcome your participation. I suspect, however, that a good proportion of you will be from contexts where action research is little understood or reluctantly tolerated. We hope our play will offer some alternative strategies as you embark on the significant undertaking of writing your thesis.

In this play we will not be reiterating the foundational tenets of action research, as we are assuming that you have come here tonight with some background already in this area. In any case, action research is discussed extensively in various seminal and current works (for instance, Altrichter, Kemmis, McTaggart & Zuber-Skerritt, 1991; Carr & Kemmis, 1990; Grundy, 1982; Kemmis & McTaggart, 1988; Passfield, 2001; Reason & Bradbury, 2001; Wadsworth, 1998; Zuber-Skerritt, 1996). In producing this play we do acknowledge that there are a range of approaches to action research, from the more technical focus on organizational or educational change (where the researcher is "expert") to emancipatory and participatory processes that aim to engender radical social change, and where all participants are equal as co-researchers. The characters who will be performing here for you tonight each have their own understanding of action research practice and appreciate that there is no one "correct way" to do action research.

The time has now come to introduce the characters and allow them to speak for themselves. The two protagonists in this play are researchers who found that conventional social science thesis presentation constrained the way they wanted to present the complex and non-linear nature of their research. Our protagonists, MCR and CRK, are both higher-education teachers who conducted their (quite different) research projects in the course of their professional work. They will now introduce themselves, describing their research projects and their values and perspectives on action research. Our first is Dr. MCR, currently a teacher of learning technologies to pre-service teachers:

MCR: Thank you and good evening to you all. My thesis is the story of an action research initiative underpinned by my strong belief in the importance of approaches to computer education which foster lifelong computer learning. In my thesis I trace the journey of a reflexive process of change and iterative development in the teaching of an information computer technology (ICT) unit to pre-service teacher education students. Over a period of three years I pursued a central research question, namely: "How can I develop my teaching practice to better facilitate the development of capable computer users?" My research explored the distinction between a "competent" and a "capable" computer user and trialled a range of teaching and learning approaches to facilitate the development of capable computer users (Phelps, 2002; Phelps & Ellis, 2002a, 2002b, 2002c). From the research I developed a metacognitive approach to computer education; an approach which is founded on the premise that adoption of ICT is influenced by an individual's attitudes, beliefs, motivation, confidence and learning strategies and which promotes learners' active engagement in directing the learning process.

In my approach to action research, I concur with Bob Dick (2002) who refers to action research as "meta-methodology." Like Lau (1999, p. 2), I equate doing action research with a "commitment to an underlying philosophy of social science" and deeply relate to the view of action research as a "living practice" (Carson, 1997). While my research certainly represented a process of critiquing, informing and developing my own teaching practice (the "first person" focus), it also represented a significant opportunity for students to self-examine and redefine their relationships with technology (the "second person" focus). A "third person" focus inevitably emerged as we collectively challenged the traditions of directive-style computer training, and ultimately provided a more complex understanding of the computer-learning context.

While my unconventional writing approach was somewhat challenging to my supervisors, they were willing to support it given my fairly persuasive justification of the approach in the introduction to my thesis.

NARRATOR: Our second main character is Dr. CRK, who currently supervises and mentors postgraduate students within the same institution as MCR.

CRK: Thank you—and great to see such an enthusiastic audience here tonight. My PhD explored how economics could be taught within an emancipatory framework to students in two different institutions—those studying welfare at TAFE (Technical and Further Education) and those undertaking social science at university. The TAFE students became collaborators with me (the "second person" focus of the research) in developing an empowering curriculum that demystified conventional economics and introduced students to a range of alternative economic theories. The process of critical reflection emerged as a key research interest for me, which I explored in detail with the university students who were encouraged to reflect critically on how economics impacted on their lives as well as on the wider society and ecological systems (the "third person" focus). One of the outcomes of my personal reflection was to critically examine the role of activism in the face of globalization and how I personally constructed my own activism (my "first person" work), drawing on critiques of critical social science put forward by postmodern writers (Fisher, 2000, 2003a, 2003b).

My philosophy in relation to action research is located in the emancipatory and critical tradition. In my view, critical action research involves a commitment to political action. I concur with Kemmis (Kemmis, 1996; Kemmis & McTaggart, 2000) that a criterion of "success" of an action research process is the politicization of the participants. Thus I perceive the role of the action researcher as an activist who must be critically reflective of her own activist position, being careful not to impose her own "liberatory" agenda (Lather, 1991) on those with whom she researches and works.

I undertook my research in a university department which supported the paradigm of "action inquiry," exemplified in the work of Reason (1988), Reason & Bradbury (2001) and Torbert (1991). My supervisor supported unconventional thesis presentation, particularly emphasising the importance of the subjective presence of the researcher.

The characters and the narrator leave the stage.

—Curtain—

Act I: In Which the Narrator and Protagonists Set the Scene and Describe the "Existential Choices" Faced by Action Research Candidates

As the curtain rises, the audience sees a set on two levels. Towering over the stage, but in the background, is a series of five large symmetrical grey blocks lined up in a row. In the foreground, and at stage level, is a colourful montage of moving and interacting spirals. The narrator walks on, gazing up at the towers and moving in and out of the spirals. MCR and CRK follow, taking up their positions on the opposite side of the stage.

NARRATOR: This is a play about challenging orthodoxy; in particular the orthodoxy of writing up research. Many of you will have consulted, at some stage, the wealth of literature available for research students on how to write a thesis (for example, Rudestam & Newton, 1992; Van Wagenen, 1991). Such "self-help" manuals generally offer what has come to be an accepted approach to writing a thesis; the standard, formulaic "five-chapter" structure—introduction, literature review, methodology, analysis of data, and conclusions and implementations, followed by the bibliography and appendices. While this model undoubtedly provides a valuable resource for postgraduate students learning the research writing process, it tends to be considered by novice researchers as the *only* approach to thesis writing.

But what if the straight-edged, linear blocks of orthodoxy restrict and impair the authenticity and integrity of a research process that is dynamic, non-linear and emergent? How does the PhD student doing action research proceed? Although alternative approaches have been considered by some researchers (for example, Creswell, 2003; Denzin & Lincoln, 2000; Koro-Ljungberg, 2004), candidates submitting the culmination of several years' research for examination by an unknown academic often consider it "safer" to follow established convention. Supervisors, who are likely to have structured their own theses in the conventional way, may feel hesitant in recommending or supporting alternative approaches. Indeed, some action research candidates have run afoul of the examination process (Hughes, Denley & Whitehead, 1998), and one of our main characters, CRK, had a challenging experience of examination in this regard, as we shall see in Act III. Our focus tonight is to present the story of how our two researchers tackled the challenge of presenting action-based research in the context of a still-conservative academy.

MCR: When I was seeking guidance in structuring my PhD, I found little had been written on how to present action research theses. Those papers that did consider it tended to argue that action research be treated like any other methodology and accommodated within conventional structures and university presentation guidelines (Zuber-Skerritt & Perry, 2002). Perry (1994), for instance, noted that sticking with the five-chapter model can allay concerns regarding the "messy" and "inconclusive" impression provided by action research and he recommended including reflections on the action research study in the body and restricting discussion of practical and experiential aspects of the research to appendices.

Within my institution, action research had a strong profile, however, the conventional thesis structure had been widely adopted by action researchers and adherence to convention seemed to be preferred by my own and other action research candidates' supervisors.

CRK: That could be because much action research within our institution was predominantly focused on organizational change, and was technical rather than emancipatory.

MCR: You could be right, CRK. I did find some papers presenting an alternative perspective. Bob Dick (1993, 2000, 2002), for instance, notes that universities often structure higher degrees on the assumption that "good" research is "theory-driven" rather than "data-driven." Acknowledging that some examiners "may be surprised by data-driven research because it does not fit their notion of legitimate higher degree research" (Dick, 2002, p. 160), he provides justification and motivation for action researchers to be creative, arguing that conventional thesis structures do not do justice to action research. Bob's articulation of the "existential choice" that needs to be made by research candidates left a particularly strong impression on me:

"Do you want to be an apprentice who will learn thoroughly, from your supervisor, committee and literature, a particular approach to research? That is, will your learning be primarily propositional? At the conclusion of such a research program you can expect to know how to do one form of research. To overstate the situation, this is research by recipe. Or do you expect to engage in research with whatever resources and understandings you can bring to bear, learning from your experiences? That is, will your learning be primarily through questioning inquiry, with supervisor and committee functioning as mentors rather than as teachers? Such an approach will engage you in examining your assumptions about the nature of knowledge and of methodologies. This is research as performing art" (Dick, 2002, pp. 161–162).

CRK: This is certainly a pertinent quote for our purposes, but I wouldn't want to give the impression that research or even thesis writing falls neatly into one of these two categories. The "academic norm" for research reports is only one possible format and conventions and expectations regarding writing structure have been, and are, continually changing (Winter, 1989). Since action research emerges from a different context and different relationships (collaborative and action-oriented rather than authoritative and observation-oriented), Winter argues that there is good cause for reports of action research also to be different. He proposes two specific variations: a "case study" of the process of the work, in narrative form; and a "plural text" where the voice of a single author is partially replaced by an interplay between the voices of participants in the research. Winter goes further by stating that some stylistic features of academic writing can be seen to be "inappropriate" for action research, particularly where style, tone and vocabulary express an "expert" role or a withdrawal from personal involvement or sustained abstraction from concrete detail.

MCR: Like Winter (1989) I would argue that the ideological aspects of action research cannot be separated from the perceived "necessities" of thesis structure and presentation. To do so would undermine the very foundations of action research and hence the integrity of the thesis which depicts and conveys the research. If action research is truly seen by the researcher as a "living practice" (Carson, 1997) then the life and practice of the research cannot, and should not, simply be "appendicized."

NARRATOR: This sets the scene for our play. Let's watch while our protagonists tell their stories of how they attempted to write their theses more in keeping with the moving montage of cycles and spirals than the fixed and immovable blocks of convention.

–Curtain–

Act II: Scene 1: In Which the Writer/Researcher Takes Centre Stage

The curtain rises to the same backdrop as in Act I, but in the front of the stage MCR and CRK, dressed in plain black, are seated on a comfortable garden seat that overlooks a pond reflecting the surrounding trees and sky. The narrator stands to one side of the stage, in front of the curtain.

CRK: One of the conventions of academic thesis writing that has come under sustained challenge from a number of disciplines is the use of the third person, often in passive voice, which renders the researcher invisible, giving the impression of an "objective," dispassionate stance. The use of a first person active voice in research presentation is now supported by ample precedent and theoretical debate (Onn, 1998), and the contribution of postpositivist and poststructuralist analysis, particularly feminist epistemology, has meant that the "objective" researcher has been revealed to be a myth (Alcott & Potter, 1993; Guba, 1990; Lather, 1991; Reason, 1988; Schwandt, 1990).

In action research the researcher is also "the researched" (Wadsworth, 1998). This requires the researcher to account for the way in which the research both shapes and is shaped by them, not just because they conduct it, but because they *are* it (Sumara & Carson, 1997). Epistemologically it is simply not consistent to write a text which does not bear the traces of its author (Lincoln & Denzin, 2000). How did you confront this challenge, MCR?

MCR: I found it quite artificial to separate my voice as writer and researcher from the action research process and the findings. The centrality of reflection itself made this separation impossible. While some action researchers revert to the use of third person in some chapters, such as the introduction or conclusions, I maintained first person throughout. I'll read from my thesis conclusion to illustrate:

"For me, as teacher, the research has evoked significant growth. Aside from the tangible changes in teaching approach . . . a number of more subtle changes have occurred. The research has necessitated my conscious 'letting go' of teacher control and centrality in the learning process . . . to step back and recognise the importance of explicitly acknowledging the breadth of authentic support structures which are important for lifelong and non-institutionally-based learning and fostering students' help-seeking strategies."

CRK: I also made my presence as researcher explicit from the outset of my thesis. As action research (and, indeed, any research) is inevitably formed and influenced by the researcher's values, attitudes and beliefs, I saw it as important to articulate these. After all, situations do not just happen, they are historically and temporally directed by the intentionality of the participants (Clandinin & Connelly, 1994, p. 417). In the second chapter of my thesis, titled "Positioning the researcher: The constructing of an activist identity," I made my subjective position explicit and articulated the influences that led to my chosen research:

"Embarking on research within the paradigm of humanistic inquiry in which social ecology is embedded meant that from the outset I was required to reflect on personal sources of my passion for my chosen research area. This process itself was revealing as it allowed me to take a particular perspective on my life and identify a "path" that had led me to my (activist) interest in demystifying economics and making a difference in the world. . . . This chapter tracks the sources of my framing of such an activist intention, identifying major family and cultural influences as well as the influence of discourses of adult education, co-counselling, living on an intentional community and Heart Politics."

Such exploration would seem to be an essential aspect of reflexivity (Gergen & Gergen, 2000), as the researcher/writer exposes their own historical and geographical situation, their personal investment in the research and the biases they bring to the project.

MCR: Yes, and I'm sure you'd agree that action research theses can successfully draw on the research traditions of personal narrative (Ellis & Bochner, 2000) and self-research (Bullough & Pinnegar, 2001), within which subjectivity is "the basis of researchers making a distinctive contribution, one that results from the unique configuration of their personal qualities joined to the data they have collected" (Peshkin, 1988, p. 18). In fact, personal narrative can enhance the relevance and impact of the research, allowing readers "to feel the moral dilemmas, think with our story instead of about it, join actively in the decision points . . . and consider how their own lives can be made a story worth telling" (Ellis & Bochner, 2000: 735).

CRK: This idea of using reflexivity within personal narrative is illustrated in this excerpt from the second chapter from my thesis:

"When I reflect on that time in my life [dropping out of a prestigious coursework Masters of Economics at the age of 24], it is clear to me now that I was subjected first-hand to the very same alienating experience of that dehumanised, mechanistic, value-absent ideology that has provided the core motivation for this thesis. Despite my inexperience, my lack of training in critical analysis, my devotion to fulfilling my father's (and others') expectations, I wonder if at some level I recognised that there was something seriously wrong with a social science that seemed so devoid of humanity, spirit, ethics and justice."

MCR: I too defined my position as both researcher and teacher up front in my introduction, and made my values and beliefs very explicit. This helped set the tone of reflexivity throughout my thesis:

> "In my approach to both my research and my teaching I firmly identify as a constructivist. I believe that we can only 'know' through interaction with the world. . . . I have a strong passion for learning and change. I tend to challenge existing practices and to strive constantly towards improvement. . . . I view our social existence in the world as highly complex and . . . challenge the capacity of traditional research to adequately address many social problems."

I also structured reflexivity into my thesis through the device of a brief section at the end of each chapter titled "Stepping back and looking forward" which enabled me to reflect on the chapter and outline how this drove the research forward into the following research cycle.

CRK: I presented my iterative reflexive process through the use of different "voices," similar to Winter's (1989) concept of the "plural text," as explained in the following extract from Chapter 6 of my thesis:

> "The three voices are: first, a relatively 'neutral' reporting voice that relays the 'facts' of what happened; second, the 'reflective practitioner,' the voice I used in conversation with the students demonstrating my reflective practice at the time, informed by the requirements of critical action research and supported by a critical community of peers; and the third voice, the 'critical reflector,' offers a 'commentary' on the sometimes naïve voice of the reflective practitioner from a vantage point that names the assumptions made and reflects on some of the silences and absences in the narrative."

NARRATOR: This connection between reflexivity and narrative leads us into the next scene, which highlights the importance of representing the unfolding research story within the writing process.

–Curtain–

Scene 2: In Which the Thesis Stays True to the Narrative

The curtain rises. The backdrop of grey blocks and garden seat remain, but the reflective pond has been replaced by a semi-circle of listeners seated on the ground at the feet of the characters.

NARRATOR: All research is a form of storytelling (House, 1994), although traditionally researchers shy away from using the term "story" given its connotations of unreliability or lack of rigour. Let us see what our protagonists have to say on this subject.

CRK: I would argue that there is no more appropriate approach to understanding action research than to see it as an unfolding narrative. An action research endeavour *is* the story of individual and/or group change: change in practices, beliefs and assumptions. Personal narrative, and the notion of research as story repositions the reader as an active and vicarious co-participant in the research (Ellis & Bochner, 2000).

MCR: Yes, I agree. Winter et al. (2000, p. 36) has, in fact, stated that one of the important criteria for a "quality" PhD is to "tell a compelling story."

CRK: I would suggest that documenting the cycles of planning, acting, observing and reflecting should be done iteratively since each cycle of the research is only understandable in terms of the systematic and self-critical learning gained through previous cycles.

MCR: Wanting to remain true to the story of my research, I presented the chapters of my thesis in the same chronological order as the research itself. I did not have separate chapters covering the literature review, the methodology or the data analysis. Instead I allowed the research process to unfold for the reader, reinforcing the notion of research as personal, professional, methodological and theoretical "journey." What was your experience, CRK?

CRK: I also utilized a chronological format, finding that without staying true to the changes that I experienced during the research process, I could not demonstrate the emergent nature of that process, which cycle after cycle of reflection produced. I reflected at the conclusion of my thesis:

"The very nature of action research is an unfolding and emergent process, inevitably because of the reflection that is embedded within it. The thesis is therefore framed in a way that mirrors the unfolding research journey. . . . Reflection has permeated every stage and has emerged as a primary focus of the research itself. It seems to me that action research itself invites this—what emerges is what needs to be researched. In a way, this reflects a direct antidote to positivism and its ontology of prediction and control. Engaging the spirit of action research almost demands a letting go of having things go a particular way."

MCR: I believe that this narrative approach also supports validity since it consciously works against camouflaging or failing to acknowledge pragmatic realities, iterative learning and the inevitable weaknesses that frequently remain unacknowledged in traditional research presentation. In my research I explicitly acknowledged that action research represents a journey down many roads, some of which inevitably prove to be dead ends. Sometimes these mistaken paths have been taken for justifiable reasons, while others may be traversed through simple error or mistaken assumptions and beliefs.

CRK: I agree. In conventional research there is a culture of leaving these dead ends unacknowledged—we don't hear about the mistakes that often lead to significant rethinking or insight. In action research, however, these apparent "dead ends" are a critical part of the learning, change and theory development process. As highlighted in Scene 1, reflexivity permits us to reveal such weaknesses or "untruths" and requires us to "own up" to our responsibility in the knowledge construction process (Hall, 1996). Mellor (2001), for instance, refers to his "messy project" (p. 465) as an "honesty trail" (p. 479).

MCR: So for us, a chronological approach to thesis presentation supports the researcher's acknowledgment of this iterative and unfolding learning process and represents a more rigorous and truthful presentation of how the research proceeds.

NARRATOR: This reference to research as a journey is an example of how metaphor can be used productively and imaginatively to enhance understanding. This leads us nicely into the next scene.

–Curtain–

Scene 3: In Which Metaphor Dresses Up the Thesis

The scene is identical, but the characters have changed from their plain clothes into travellers' costumes, complete with suitcases, cameras, binoculars, maps, guidebooks, hats and walking boots.

NARRATOR: As Mason Cooley once said "Clothes make a statement. Costumes tell a story" (Cooley, 1993). The use of metaphors in a thesis is like the wearing of costumes in a play—they bring meaning to the story, meaning that is generated through the image with more efficiency than the literal relaying of information.

CRK: Various writers have explored the use of metaphor and its integral role in the generation of meaning and the construction of social and political reality (for instance, Hovelynck, 1998; Lakoff & Johnson, 1980; Ortony, 1979; Taylor, 1984). In fact, metaphors are among our principal vehicles for understanding, permeating communication and perception at individual, cultural and societal levels (Mignot, 2000). Yet metaphor is often perceived as "unscientific, untrustworthy, a linguistic embellishment" (Mignot, 2000, p. 518), arguments which Lakoff & Johnson (1980) refers to as the "myths of objectivism and subjectivism." Metaphor can provide not only a richer description of research as experienced by the researcher(s) but also allows a deeper exploration of the meanings generated by collaborating participants. You used metaphor to good effect in your thesis, MCR.

MCR: Yes, I found that metaphor provided a powerful vehicle for portraying the "journey," the "adventure," the "saga" that was my action research process. For me the cycles of personal engagement over time represented a personal and professional pilgrimage through both familiar and unfamiliar terrain. The title of my thesis, "Mapping the complexity of computer learning: Journeying beyond teaching for computer competency to facilitating computer capability," established the metaphor from the beginning. I also used my chapter headings to demonstrate the unfolding research journey:

- Charting the context of research and practice (Chapter 1);

- Journey origins and point of departure (Chapter 2);

- Embracing reflection as navigation: Postcards from cycle 1 (Chapter 3);

- Encountering a theoretical bridge: Crossing to a metacognitive approach (Chapter 4);

- Integrating metacognition: Planning for cycle 2 (Chapter 5);

- The journey continues: Postcards from cycle 2 (Chapter 6);

- Encountering turbulence: Postcards from cycle 3 (Chapter 7);

- Complexity as window on the research (Chapter 8); and

- Journey ending as journey beginning (Chapter 9).

I continued to use the journeying metaphor as part of my reflexivity, exemplified by the following extract from my final chapter:

"My research has involved me challenging my expectations and re-designing the maps which I brought to my initially envisaged itinerary. My thesis charts my "discoveries" and individual and cultural encounters. It provides a "diary" of my changes in direction and the influence of my travels on my own assumptions."

CRK: While I described my research as a journey I did not use metaphor explicitly to frame my thesis structure. I wish I had! I wonder if, for many academics, constructing research as "journey" would be considered unacceptable, since the thesis is generally perceived primarily as an "argument"?

MCR: This is likely to be the case for many supervisors. However, I believe such a perception is inconsistent with the epistemic foundations of action research. Action research is *not* about testing preconceived hypotheses or generalizing about research "findings." It is about depicting the context, change processes, resultant learning and theorizing of individuals or groups in a process of mutual change and inquiry. Metaphor is like a costume—it enhances meaning through imagery and colour. The author (actor) can dress her argument in a way that indicates the meaning of the process to her. Using the play metaphor has clothed this otherwise conventional journal article in a way that (we hope) brings the arguments we are making alive to our imagined audience.

NARRATOR: Let's move now to the final scene of this act, a scene in which our protagonists make a case for presenting the literature throughout the thesis, rather than in the single "literature review" chapter, as demanded by the conventional five chapter structure.

–Curtain–

Scene 4: In Which Literature
Is Woven Throughout the Thesis

The curtain rises to a scene of movement. The hitherto passive listeners, who have been seated at the feet of the storytellers, join together with MCR and CRK in a process of dismantling the five large blocks (which are now revealed to be made up of smaller blocks), taking the ribbons that make up the spirals and interweaving them among the blocks to produce an impression of flow and harmony.

CRK: Taking a chronological or narrative approach to thesis writing has implications for the presentation of literature and theory. In conventional research the literature review aims to build a theoretical foundation upon which issues are identified as worth researching (Perry, 1994). However, in action research the issues pursued are those which arise from a cluster of problems of mutual concern and consequence to the researcher(s) and collaborators (Kemmis & McTaggart, 1988).

MCR: This means that in an action research thesis, the explanation of the origin of the research and the justification for its need lie not in the literature but in the personal narrative of the participant researchers. Literature is more important in shaping the ongoing *development* of action research (Green, 1999) than informing its initial foundation or relating its findings to other research.

CRK: In conventional thesis formats, the literature review is presented up front in its entirety, implying that all the literature was familiar to the researcher at the beginning of the research. This is usually a misrepresentation of the research process. The requirement to present an up-to-date literature review at the time of submission itself necessitates that the review is in constant flux until submission. Moreover, it is not humanly possible to expect that a researcher, no matter how familiar they are with their disciplinary context, will have covered all relevant literature *before* they begin their research.

MCR: Action researchers seek theory to partially answer their questions, to challenge their assumptions, to widen their perspectives and to inform their practice. Green (cited in Winter et al., 2000) argues that relevant literature cannot be "predetermined" and that quality action research will show how the writer has engaged with the literature and how this has challenged their views. For this reason there is a good case for presenting the literature as part of the cyclical structure of the research and thesis, situating it temporally in the action research cycles themselves. A similar recommendation has been made by Dick (1993, 2000) who recommended that literature be reported adjacent to the relevant findings. In another paper, Green (1999) notes the value of sharing with the reader the excitement experienced by the researcher in encountering new and challenging literature.

CRK: It is also relevant to note that literature encountered throughout the research will either support the researcher's current actions or challenge their perspectives, assumptions or approaches. As Brewer and Hunter (1989, p. 18) note, "evidence from two sources is intuitively more persuasive than evidence from one." If "evidence" is interpreted as encompassing prior research, then the discovery of research which supports one's own interpretations might be seen as "triangulating" the data, but only where such research was not known to the researcher beforehand. Thus it can be valuable to explicitly acknowledge any literature that has influenced the research process or its interpretation *as it is encountered* in the process. How did you tackle this issue of literature presentation, MCR?

MCR: I consciously presented literature iteratively and chronologically throughout my thesis. For instance, in Chapter 4, I describe a transition that occurred in the research, prompted by encountering a body of literature which acted as a new "road map." I not only outline this literature at that point in the thesis, but I include reflections on the literature, its relationship to the first cycle and how, as a researcher, I perceived its value in shaping my second cycle. Towards the end of my candidature, I embraced a fresh body of literature, complexity theory (Waldrop, 1992), that assisted me in "making sense" of my data and experiences. I chose not to present this literature until Chapter 8; to do otherwise would have detracted from the integrity of my research presentation, implying a theoretical window on the research I did not hold at the time. How did you justify your literature approach, CRK?

CRK: I'll quote from my introduction where I argued for this approach to literature in terms of honouring the unfolding nature of my research:

> "The thesis is framed in a way that reflects the emergent process that was produced through conducting action research. . . . Literature is woven through the developing argument, reflecting how my reading informed different stages of the research process. . . . Th[e] unfolding process of research, reflection and insight leading to further research and reflection provides the framework for structuring the thesis."

NARRATOR: Our protagonists have now finished presenting their case for a different sort of thesis presentation consistent with the spirit and epistemology of action research. Please give them a big round of applause as they leave the stage.

In our final act we will hear how their approaches to thesis writing were greeted by their examiners.

–Curtain–

Act III: Enter the Critics!

The curtain rises to darkness. The narrator enters stage left, illumined by a spotlight.

NARRATOR: One of the objections supervisors are likely to raise against adopting these less conventional approaches to thesis writing is the negative response of examiners, especially those unfamiliar with action research. Let's find out from the examiners of these two theses what their responses were.

Tell me, Dr. A., what do you think of the format adopted by MCR?

Another spotlight lights up Dr. A., MCR's first examiner, standing stage right.

Dr. A.: The candidate makes a persuasive argument for the format of the report and then follows this with a superb demonstration of why her initial decision was appropriate.

NARRATOR: And you, Dr. B.?

Spotlight on Dr. A. fades and Dr. B. is lit by a spotlight centre stage.

Dr. B.: The metaphor of a journey integrates the parts of the thesis in a complete story. This structure avoids an artificially neat intellectual edifice, which would disguise the messy and brilliant process of research.

NARRATOR: Overall, MCR's examiners were well satisfied with her thesis, recommending it for an outstanding thesis award. CRK's thesis, however, received a more mixed reception. Dr. C., how did you find the structure of this thesis?

Dr. C.: The thesis had a linear quality to it while capturing the dynamic dialectic of critical reflection. . . . I kept reading to find the research questions, and realized they were truly emergent . . . the research questions, placed where they were, was like an "aha experience."

NARRATOR: And you Dr. D., how do you respond to its weaving and dynamic quality?

Dr. D.: . . . it is striking in the way the thesis exemplifies the critical reflexivity it sets out to explore. . . . It continually weaves together its analytic threads in a most convincing way. . . . [There] is a good, progressive unfolding of the research, first opening up themes and then deepening the analysis.

NARRATOR: So now to you, Dr. E. I believe you were irritated by the method, interpreting it as sloppy and lacking in rigour.

Dr. E.: I found the way literature was treated in the thesis to be most unsatisfactory. For instance, there was no definition or discussion of the nature of ideology until Chapter 3, and only a superficial discussion of reflection in that chapter.

NARRATOR: And yet, the candidate returned to a more detailed discussion of critical reflection in Chapter 8, in keeping with the emergent nature of the research process, which she foreshadowed in her introduction. The candidate responded in her defence that "[Dr. E.'s] reading of . . . the whole thesis seemed partial and fragmented rather than integrated and holistic. He did not seem to be aware of the connections that were being made throughout and the way the thesis was crafted as a whole integrated entity." Now let us take an example where your perceptions were very different from those of Dr. D.—the use of the different "voices" in Chapter 6 (described in Act II, Scene 1).

Dr. E.: I found this device problematic and thought that the voices were used inconsistently and selectively with no explanation for the choices made.

Dr. D.: I beg to differ, Dr. E. The candidate made her rationale very clear at the beginning of the chapter. I thought her use of this strategy was impressive, very effective and a creative and practical resolution of a key difficulty of practitioner-based research.

The light fades on all examiners.

NARRATOR: Ultimately CRK was able to mount a successful defence against Dr. E.'s criticisms, using the comments from the other two examiners and the support of her supervisor to substantiate her claims.

Our protagonists would argue that the most effective ways to overcome potential examiner resistance are to make strong justification for the presentation format from the outset *and* to choose examiners sympathetic to action research and unconventional formats. Many examiners *do* appreciate freshness and originality, not only in thought and expression, but also in presentation. While there is always the risk of an unsympathetic examiner, by explicitly structuring the thesis consistent with the epistemological, methodological and ethical aspects of action research, postgraduate students can provide a clear and rigorous justification for their choices.

–Curtain–

Curtain Call

The narrator comes to the front of the stage in front of the curtain to converse with the audience.

NARRATOR: Now that we have come to the end of our performance, it is time to take stock and reflect on what has arisen here tonight, in the spirit of a reflexive engagement with our practice. How might these different writing approaches contribute to improved action research practice? Our protagonists would suggest that they contribute to greater honesty and authenticity in the research process; honour the reflective and iterative processes at the heart of action research; demonstrate heightened awareness of self for both researcher and collaborators; highlight the importance of contextual influences; and support increased engagement with complexity at personal, interpersonal and global levels. Furthermore, they would argue that encouraging honest reporting of research and the deep reflection it engenders, builds competencies for all those engaging in research.

However, as our play has shown, flying in the face of academic convention is not for the fainthearted. If you are a PhD student, you may wish to reflect on whether you would consider taking an alternative approach to writing up your research. Is your writing practice consistent with the way your research proceeded? Have you been able to incorporate your own reflective process and that of your collaborators? To what extent has your perspective changed throughout your research process and can you represent that in your writing? How important is it to you to record the research *process* as much as the outcomes or results? How open is your supervisor to a different writing format? Does your research context lend itself to this sort of writing? What would be the main constraints for you in adopting such an approach? How might conforming to convention deaden your creativity? And are the risks worth taking in terms of what you might receive at the hands of power?

Those of you who supervise action research students will be aware of the problems of exposing students' work to unsympathetic examiners. One possible risk is that the thesis becomes too "wordy," with too much narrative detail at the expense of clarity and strong theoretical argument. Examiners may not appreciate the "suspense format"; feeling that they are labouring up an incline to reach the punch-line (Brown, 1994) or they may be surprised by the introduction of new ideas late in the thesis. Another risk is that students overidentify with their own stories and indulge in too much "confessional narrative." As supervisors you might consider: how can I help my student(s) recognize what is worth reporting in their dissertations? How can I help them distinguish authentic inquiry and understanding from indulgent navel gazing? How can I assist in identifying key turning points in the narrative rather than giving "blow by blow" descriptions?

CRK and MCR enter and stand beside the narrator.

To conclude, we are not suggesting that the approaches outlined here are essential for students writing action research theses. We certainly do not want to give the impression that this presentational form becomes a "new potential orthodoxy" (to quote one of our reviewers). We would, however, wholeheartedly encourage you as students and supervisors to experiment with any form that seems analogically appropriate to your research material, being always careful to be aware of how the form you use might preclude certain perspectives and how the form itself may constrain your interpretations. For instance, attempting to maintain coherence within a particular chosen metaphor may lead to being too identified with the metaphor itself and prevent disconfirming "truths" being voiced. We found this an interesting dilemma in re-presenting our article as performance. Did we sacrifice too much by being too enamoured with the form in which we presented our arguments? We found ourselves debating and considering the balance required to walk such a tightrope. Ultimately, we leave it to you, our audience, to judge how well we have achieved this balance.

How successful were the authors in communicating their ideas? Do you think you would find this presentation acceptable at your institution?

As a parting word, in the true spirit of action research, we would encourage a "meta-reflection" on the form of presentation as well as the substance of the research itself. Above all, strive to be simultaneously playful and rigorously reflective. Farewell for now, and we hope to meet some of you on your own adventurous journeying.

All bow. Applause.

–Curtain–

Source: Fisher, K., & Phelps, R. (2006). Recipe or performing art?: Challenging conventions for writing action research theses. *Action Research, 4*(2), 143–164. Used with permission from SAGE.

Summary and Review

I am not quite sure how to summarize this play. Using such an unusual vehicle for presentation, the authors weave their thoughts about action research in the fabric of the three acts. You are not to take the text as a literal presentation of actual conversations or interactions. They use the play as a vehicle to hold the interest of the readers. I think they have been successful in doing so.

FINAL COMMENTS

You have read two very different articles. Miskovic and Hoop present a very strong argument about doing action research with children and how critical pedagogy informs every decision. At times as I read the article I was struck with how idealistic and naïve I thought the researchers were when they expected students to buy into an agenda that really was not connected to their own lives. But I appreciated their thoughtful account about the issues and lessons they learned from the research.

Fisher and Phelps also want to present lessons learned; they do it in the form of a play. Representations of this sort are challenging; some institutions welcome alternative modes while others would not. But you should have been challenged by what you read.

You can access the complete articles at www.sagepub.com/lichtmanreadings.

Chapter 6

READING NARRATIVE

People use stories to make sense of their lives and the human experience. Narrative research is a qualitative research approach that makes use of the study and analysis of such stories as the central vehicle for conveying the information learned from and about others. The stories can come from individuals themselves or from others. It may seem strange to you that many see using stories as a viable research approach. Several academic disciplines—especially history, literary criticism, and philosophy—use the study of stories. The social sciences also use the study of stories as a means of research. The technique gained acceptance as qualitative research and inquiry became an alternative to traditional research methods.

KEY ELEMENTS OF THE NARRATIVE APPROACH

- The narrative approach is based on stories or narrations for the presentation of research findings;

- emphasizes story-telling;

- uses stories that may be factual or fictional;

- emphasizes the use of metaphors in the written presentation; and

- does not make use of specific ways to gather or analyze data.

- Narrative approaches have been used in many of the social sciences.

I have selected two articles to illustrate this approach. Erin Seaton's article is about the stories she learns from eighth-grade students. One unusual aspect of her approach is that she develops a communal narrative. Since she deals with a sensitive topic, you can learn much from the way she handles questions and presentation. She wrote this study while completing her degree.

Tom Barone's article deals with the future of narratives in research. This article was named the outstanding article in narrative theory by a special interest group of the American Educational Research Association. Barone is said by some to be an academic storyteller. His paper concludes with two thought-provoking sections. In the first section, he argues that we need what he calls sympathetic members of a research community who value new approaches, although, of course, we don't want new just for the sake of its newness. In the second section, Barone concludes with the idea that this type of research will go on as we work toward improving educational policies and practices.

I have selected this paper for you to read because you need to be aware of the issues and the potential backlash that you might face if you choose to conduct this type of research. If you want to read additional examples, Barone's reference list will lead you to some good resources.

ADVANCE PREPARATIONS

Begin by reading the title and the abstract, then flipping through the article and reading the major headings and subheadings. Once you have an idea of the article's structure, go back and read through the article carefully. When you finish reading, you will need to decide the extent to which the article is successful. To do so, ask yourself four questions:

- Does it provide new information and insights related to the topic?
- Is it engaging and written in a clear manner?
- Does it illustrate elements you would expect to find in narrative research?
- Do the positive aspects of the article outweigh the potential drawbacks?

Article 6.1. Common Knowledge: Reflections on Narratives in Community (2008)

Erin Seaton

My Expectations

In this study of eighth-grade students in rural New Hampshire, Seaton explores the complexity of narratives. One dimension she includes is development of a communal context. I assume this means that rather than telling individual stories, she somehow weaves them together. From her abstract, we learn that personal stories may become part of a larger communal history. I find it especially interesting to look at ambiguity of memory and the multiplicity of truth. We know from many television accounts that eyewitness accounts are not very reliable. I am not surprised, then, that Seaton talks about the ambiguity of memory. Another issue she addresses is the dynamics of power within a community. We also know we will be challenged when reading this article since she hints at one individual who apparently shares some "unspeakable knowledge." We can only conjecture at this point, and need to read on to see what was shared, how it is described, the therapeutic value of the telling, and the meaning we can get from it.

Abstract

Drawing on ethnographic and narrative research with eighth-grade students from rural New Hampshire, this article explores the rich complexity of narratives built in a communal context. In close-knit rural communities, such as the one at the center of this article, personal stories may become part of a larger communal history. As such, narratives retold as communal stories highlight the relational context in which stories are crafted and underscore the ambiguity of memory, the multiplicity of truth, and the dynamics of power within a community. Here, communal stories strip individuals of the ability to craft individual narratives, as personal stories serve to create a larger communal understanding of events and history. However, for narratives of trauma in particular, as in the case at the center of this article, communal narratives may also serve as therapeutic, lightening the burden of unspeakable knowledge through the shared experience of knowing, remembering, and retelling what might otherwise remain silent. Consequently, narrative researchers must attend to the relational context in which all stories are constructed.

In the preceding sentence, Seaton introduces the idea of the relationship between individual narratives and communal history. You can get the sense that rather than relying on individual stories, Seaton will form a collective story that builds on communal experience.

Not much has been written about how such narratives can take on therapeutic value.

Introduction

My interest in exploring the construction of communal narratives developed in response to my research with eighth-grade students at a school in the rural community of Fairfield, New Hampshire, USA—a tiny town nestled in the eastern foothills of the White Mountains. I had come to Fairfield to hear how these students described growing up in a small community and how rural life influenced their identity development. Because I was an outsider to the community, I spent the first six months of the school year observing the 40 eighth-grade students at Fairfield School and collecting ethnographic data. I attended classes, ate lunch in the cafeteria, observed student government meetings, cheered on the sidelines at athletic events, and met with Fairfield School faculty and community social workers. This initial research helped me to establish a strong sense of rapport with the students and revise my research methods in preparation for narrative interviewing.

During my ethnographic study, I met with the eighth-grade English classes at Fairfield School once a week to lead a reading and

This is one way to gather data for narratives.

Of course, you would need a considerable amount of time to do such a study. As I mentioned earlier, there are no prescriptions for how one gathers data when doing narrative research. Seaton chose to follow procedures associated with doing ethnographic research.

We do not know whether she was paid to do this. Do you think it would matter if she was paid? It seemed as though she had the luxury of spending a considerable amount of time in this community. Unfortunately, many researchers (unless they are full-time students) are involved in professional and work activities that would preclude having such a considerable amount of time.

She doesn't really tell us in what ways her understanding of narrative research methods had been altered. We could anticipate that constructing a communal narrative was one such way.

This is a nice use of metaphors.

What is this new pattern? She seems to be hinting at the communal or group story or narrative, but we don't know for sure.

writing workshop. Reading and writing activities invited students to examine identity formation in novels and biographies and to respond through their own writing. These workshops also provided me with an opportunity to contribute to the Fairfield community. .

One of the readings the eighth-grade teachers and I selected for the workshops was Lois Lowry's (1993) novel, *The Giver.* Lowry's story depicts a utopian society that relieves its members of pain and suffering through a rigid system of sameness and control. In the isolated community presented in *The Giver,* memories are held by a single individual, and the novel underscores the consequences of this, questioning how memories are stored, recalled, narrated, and shared. Throughout, Lowry returns to the central image of the river coursing through the community. In her Newbery Honor Acceptance Speech awarded for *The Giver,* Lowry (1994) commented that she intended the river to symbolize the flow of a community's history, in the way it constantly pushes forward, merging, shifting, changing course, and carrying water from one place onto another. Our reading of *The Giver* and my ensuing conversations with Fairfield students altered my understanding of narrative research methods.

Although I had planned for the eighth graders to discuss their own individual memories in response to *The Giver,* the conversation turned toward the river pulsing through their own community. One student recalled hearing about a devastating fire that polluted a portion of the river. Another student remembered his father carrying him outside in the middle of the night to see the fire engulfing a tannery along the river bank. Although the eighth graders were only four or five at the time of the Fairfield fire, the class became animated around this memory. Several students remembered how the blaze lit up the night sky. Others recalled the lingering smell of smoke for days afterward. One student told the class that her cousin lost his job after the fire. Another student said he still finds scraps of leather in the river when he goes fishing.

As word spread through the school that the eighth-grade students were discussing the Fairfield fire, teachers stopped by the classroom to share their own memories. One teacher recalled losing all the food in her refrigerator as a result of a lengthy power outrage following the fire. Another teacher reminded the eighth graders that some residents had to evacuate their homes due to the chemical vapors spewing from the burning tannery. In listening to the students and teachers share their memories, I began to see a new pattern emerging as I followed the way each story joined with another.

NARRATIVES AS RELATIONAL ACTS

The communal discussion of the Fairfield fire enabled me to reconsider the ways in which narratives might be constructed and

This is a nice illustration of times when details of qualitative strategies emerge or change as the study progresses.

experienced by multiple narrators, particularly in a small and isolated community. In response, I revised my interview strategy, inviting students to participate in interviews with a group of their peers. Undoubtedly, interviewing groups of students—similar to focus group interviews, although actually my groups were not so directly focused—altered the shape of the narratives, privileging the collective voice over that of the individual. Madriz (2003) argues that postmodern and feminist researchers have found that conducting research with focus groups shifts the balance of power away from the researcher. My research, grounded in relational theory (Gilligan, 1982; Jordan et al., 1991; Miller, 1976; Miller and Stiver, 1997), demonstrated the way in which narratives of the self are *relational acts*. Many approaches to narrative research (Atkinson, 1998; Clandinin and Connelly, 1994; Coles, 1989; Gergen and Gergen, 1986, 1988; Labov and Waletzky, 1967; Lieblich et al., 1998; Parry, 1991; Riessman, 1993; Rogers et al., 1999; White and Epston, 1990) emphasize that individual narratives are connected to those of others. My research confirms the relational nature of narratives and reveals the social dynamic through which shared accounts are constructed.

It seems unusual to present a finding at the beginning of the article, although we have seen this in Nukaga's study of Korean kids at lunchtime.

In tight-knit communities such as Fairfield, close connections with others blur the boundaries between public and private knowledge. Narratives about experiences which many community members share mirror this blurring, resulting in stories that are built collectively. In this way, the meanings individuals take from their own experiences are inevitably shaped by others, and, as a result, an individual's sense of identity often shifts to reflect his or her community's values, beliefs, and relationships of power. Communal story-building in personal narratives is far from static. As multiple narrators amend each others' retellings of events, each story reshapes the narrative and complicates notions of linear storytelling. The strength of collective narratives lies in this ability to create meaning from multiple and overlapping storytellers—a powerful force from many streams. Narrating a story in relationship can also mean that other members of the community share in the joy or burden of the telling and retelling. At the same time, the nature of close relationships in a small community proscribes what individuals believe they can vocalize, as relationships with others influence what stories are recognized, valued, or dismissed, or dammed. As such, how a community responds to a narrative shapes an individual's self-understanding and the control individuals have over their own stories.

As with other studies you read, article represents part of a larger study.

Using one example from my group interviews with eighth-grade students, I raise questions about what it means to narrate a story in community, the uses of such a method, how collaborative story-building shapes an individual's sense of self, and the strengths and limitations of this approach.

ETHICAL CONSIDERATIONS IN NARRATIVE
RESEARCH WITH RURAL CHILDREN

My prior work in rural communities and previous study of rural ado-lescence (Seaton, 2004) prepared me for the possibility that narra-tives of trauma might emerge within my conversations with students and necessitated that I take seriously the ethical considerations of soliciting such stories. My research in Fairfield was carried out for my doctoral dissertation, and my explicit discussion of ethical con-siderations needed to pass through the Institutional Review Board (IRB) for academic research involving human subjects. The IRB required that I submit a copy of my permission forms for review; these forms required written permission from a parent/guardian for students to participate in the ethnographic and narrative aspects of my study and the publications arising from this research. I also required individual students to provide their own verbal and written permission to participate in my study.

She relies on her prior experi-ence to anticipate and deal with potential problems.

Diana was the last student to volunteer to participate in inter-views. In my first weeks at Fairfield School, the middle school fac-ulty informed me that Diana had survived a serious trauma and required special learning accommodations, such as being able to move freely during classes or leave class without permission to speak to the nurse. Although it was clear the teachers knew the details of Diana's trauma, I did not ask for more information, in part to protect Diana's privacy, but also to protect myself from knowing. At the time of my research, Diana was already receiving supportive services and counseling in and outside of school.

Why do you think Seaton thought she needed to protect herself? Do you think she was fearful she would learn some-thing she did not want to know?

It is with great caution and the deepest respect that I retell Diana's story here. Diana made it plain that she wanted her story to be known on her own terms, and my discussion of the way in which sto-ries overlap and carry each other within a community highlights her struggle to find her own voice. She fully realized that I was in the school conducting research and that I would "tell" and publish about this, including the story she shared with me about her rape. It is my hope that by retelling Diana's story carefully here, tracing the twist-ing streams joining with her own words, I offer an account that attends to the complexity of narratives as relational acts. I do not mean for Diana's story to flood beyond her control once again, but rather to channel this story into something meaningful and powerful—to carve out a new course for a terrible story so that it might carry its readers and listeners to a place of new understanding.

The author is illustrating the idea of the relational aspect of narrative.

Many different voices contributed in telling the story of Diana's rape, and what follows explores the questions raised by such com-munal constructions of narratives. In an isolated town where resi-dents were bound by close networks of association, Diana's rape was public knowledge within the community. This is an aspect of rural life that Diana and her peers took for granted, but surprised me as I came to see how difficult it was for students to maintain confidentiality in their small community. Likewise, some voices in the community (such as those of teachers and school administrators) carried more authority than others. I believe it was directly because of the dynamics of power and the students' struggles for self-authorship in their rural town that the participants wanted their stories to be known, in their own words. Diana and her classmates expressed deep frustration that their perspectives were frequently dismissed or misunderstood, and they were unambiguous about sharing their stories with me. My role as an outsider offered the girls a fresh opportunity to define themselves when they shared their stories with me, and Diana's story—told in chorus with Eve, Emily, and Cassandra—demonstrates how deeply enmeshed individual narratives may be within a community.

DIANA'S RIVER

My interview with Diana, Eve, Emily, and Cassandra opened with a discussion about experiences when the girls felt they were not heard or believed by adults in their school and community. In response, I asked the girls to tell me a story about a time when they had to talk to an adult about something important and this adult listened to them. The following exchange took place in response:

Emily:	One time when you [looks at Diana] told us, we told our mother, and she did something about it.
Diana:	Yeah. Well,
Erin:	*So, one time you* [Diana] *had a problem?*
Diana:	Yeah.
Erin:	*And you told Eve and Emily?*
Emily:	And we told our mother because we couldn't keep it in anymore. We kind of felt it was wrong.
Cassandra:	Was it about Rick?
Emily:	Rick.
Eve:	Rick.
Erin:	*And you told?*
Emily:	And some other people.
Erin:	*And you told your mom, and your mom helped?*

Cassandra:	What'd your mom do?
Eve:	She called Gwen and she called the police and stuff.
Diana:	No. [inaudible] told Gwen first.
Eve:	Oh yeah.
Erin:	*Who's Gwen?*
Diana:	My foster mom. I call her—I don't call her mom.

The *it* in Emily's first sentence was left unspoken, decidedly ambiguous. Coupled with the glances the girls gave each other, I sensed that we were approaching something deeply personal and did not push for more information.

Cassandra's question, "Was it about Rick?" opened the conversation further, revealing their shared narratives of a story that once was Diana's secret. "Tell her about Rick," Cassandra prompted a reticent Diana. Rather than narrating the story of Rick herself, Diana chose a different course, asking Cassandra to explain in this way:

Diana:	I want Cassandra to [explain who Rick is].
Cassandra:	Can I?
Diana:	Yeah. You can.
Cassandra:	He raped her. [pause]

Notice how important the exact words are in the narrative.

Having Cassandra take over the narrative and give voice to the unspeakable trauma of Diana's story marked a critical turning point in my interview; this act simultaneously took control away from Diana and yet shared in unloading Diana's burden. Cassandra's narration of Diana's story took three words: "He raped her." Cassandra's 14-year-old voice was clear: "He raped her," not, "She was raped," assigning Rick power as agent and holding him responsible for his actions.

"Scaffolding" is an interesting term. In education we often talk about scaffolding as specialized instructional supports to facilitate learning a new subject. The idea came from Vygotsky's work related to the "zone of proximal development." In other words, that zone represents the distance students can cover by themselves on a particular topic or idea and when assistance is needed.

Cassandra's telling loosened something in Diana. Diana explained that Rick was her brother's best friend and had been close to her family for many years. As Diana began to speak, Eve, Emily, and Cassandra provided further scaffolding for the story:

Erin:	When was that?
Diana:	Oh, like a year ago.
Erin:	*So what happened? How did you—what did you?*
Eve:	And then he did it when she was like–
Cassandra:	He's been doing it since she was, like, eight.
Cassandra:	He's been doing it since she was, like, eight.

With her friends' support, Diana revealed the multiple layers of trauma she endured, the repeated rapes, and later the realization of what was happening, her decision to tell, and the aftermath of the videotaped gynaecological examination and questioning.

Diana's narrative had a muddled quality about it that is not unusual in narratives of trauma. Writing about the process of reconstructing a narrative, Herman (1992) and Rogers et al. (1999) both attest to extraordinary use of language that narrators may employ to reconstruct such narratives, often revealing inconsistencies, gaps, reversals, and silences, as in the following:

Does she mean that the time sequence is confusing?

Notice that Seaton uses italics to depict Erin's questions and comments. Why does she do this?

Erin:	*Were your friends helpful to you?* [to Diana]
Diana:	Oh yeah.
Erin:	*Yeah?*
Diana:	I was the one who told 'em. That's how.
Eve:	Me and Emily were the first ones to know. And then we told our mother.
Diana:	Adrianne, too.
Eve:	But it must have been really hard to tell your friends.
Cassandra:	My brother.
Erin:	*It wasn't hard to tell them?*
Diana:	I was, like, hey this kid made me have sex with him.
Cassandra:	My brother wanted to beat him up.
Eve:	You didn't really do that! You had a hard time telling us.
Diana:	She said—
Cassandra:	Yeah.
Diana:	Where were we? Weren't we inside of my room?
Emily:	Our room. Our room.
Diana:	Like, doing Truth or Dare or something, and you guys said, "Truth. Like, have you ever done it or anything with a boy?"
Emily:	Whatever.
Eve:	No.
Cassandra:	I don't know how you told me.
Diana:	I was like.
Eve:	You were crying.

Diana:	Of course I was.
Erin:	*Of course you were!*
Emily:	You were saying that, "Please don't tell anybody."
Eve:	Yeah. That was up in our room and you told.
Diana:	I told you I tell the truth during Truth or Dare.

This is a very important concept—multiple truths.

The dispute over when and how Diana first revealed the knowledge of her rape highlights the relational landscape of narratives, and, subsequently, the way in which truth in the story is defined through multiple perspectives. Where Diana said it was easy to tell her friends about being raped, Eve and Emily recalled that Diana struggled to share her story; Diana could not remember or name the exact context in which the disclosure took place. The girls challenged each other, building off of each other's comments, amending their own versions of the narrative. This moment calls to mind Lowry's image of the river, its shifting currents constantly reconstructing the story, demonstrating that narratives are not static, but alterable, influenced by the context in which stories are revealed and to whom.

The active process of constructing a story was heightened by the way in which the girls built Diana's story as a communal narrative, revealing the layers of their agency, listening, telling, and retelling this story within the story itself. Diana's story hinges on a communal storytelling, in which, as Diana states, everybody in her small town not only knows about the trauma, but also becomes part of the story itself. Following Diana's choice to share the story of her rape with Eve and Emily, her narrative took on increasingly complex layers of disclosure. The thread of Diana's story became woven into the public space of the community, spinning out from Diana to Eve and Emily, their mother, Gwen (Diana's foster mother), the police, Diana's teachers, Diana's other peers, and finally the narrative context of this interview and piece of writing. With every new layer of telling, Diana's story takes on new meanings; revisions and interpretations multiply as every new narrator and listener reconstructs and understands Diana's story in her or his own words. Narrators not only rebuild Diana's story but add elements of their own reactions to the trauma, locating themselves as agents within the story. For example, in making the moral choice to tell Diana's story to their mother, Eve's and Emily's retelling mobilized a response from the adults in Diana's community and, in turn, indelibly altered Diana's story.

Notice Seaton's choice of language in telling the story. She uses "woven," "thread," and "spinning"—all of which create the image of a spider or a weaver spinning a complex web.

In the following passage, Diana articulates the rippling effect of her trauma when she was forced to tell her teachers about her rape:

Erin:	*Were any of your teachers good help?*
Diana:	My teachers didn't know till like a month ago.

Erin:	*And did they help or did they not help?*
Cassandra:	Remember—they talked—they all talked about it at that meeting.
Diana:	Yeah. I had a meeting for my [IEP] plan. And they were, like, talking about it in the meeting, and they made me cry, and I was, like, uncomfortable.
Cassandra:	Wouldn't stop when you asked them to.
Diana:	I was like, "I want to stop talking about that. I don't want to talk about that." And they're like, "Well, we need to."
Erin:	*Wow.*
Diana:	So, I just sat there, listened, left. And Mr. Johnson was talking about my vaginal exam.
Erin:	*That's aw—that must be so uncomfortable.*
Diana:	I really—I really just don't like male teachers talking about my—
Erin:	*Sure.*

Here, the story of Diana's rape shifted to a new public level within her community, despite Diana's active protest. Asked to repeat her story to her teachers, I wondered if Diana's discomfort not only came from the increasing exposure of her rape and her body, but also from the knowledge that with each new layer of telling she is forced to relive the memory of the experience. Diana's remembering and retelling heighten her own awareness of this trauma, and each person who hears Diana's story becomes another person whose presence might remind her of this memory. Although her name was withheld, the story of Diana's rape was even published in a community newspaper, catapulting the communal knowledge of her story even further.

In the face of the public aspect of Diana's narrative, I wondered how difficult it was for her to develop a coherent story of her trauma when she faced challenges from others who believed they, too, had a claim to her story. The murkiness of truth in communal narratives was most evident when Eve asked if Diana was pregnant after the rape:

Diana:	I wasn't, well, yeah.
Eve:	I thought you were pregnant?

Emily:	Yeah.
Cassandra:	Shut up.
Erin:	*Is that for real? Is that true?*
Diana:	Yeah. I got it done, like, before, like, if I was already, like pregnant for, like 5 months, then I wouldn't have, because, I would have known that it already started growing, but it barely even started growing, like inside of me.
Cassandra:	You were, really?
Diana:	Yeah. You didn't know that? I didn't tell you?
Eve:	I thought you were, like, not pregnant at all.
Cassandra:	I think you did tell me, but I think I just forgot.

Here, Diana's story is confusing. Within this passage, she uses the word *it* three times, a repetition that implies metonymy (Rogers et al., 1999), or a condensed meaning that seems to stand for the many unspeakable layers of this passage—the physical rape, the videotaped gynecological exam, and the subsequent discovery she was pregnant. Diana's response, "I wasn't, well, yeah" contains a revision that may come from wrestling with questions and knowledge too terrible for any eighth grader to face. Was she really pregnant? How does Diana define and understand pregnancy? How does this stand against the backdrop of her rape? I believe I hear Diana actively trying to craft a narrative that my question, "Is that true?" only makes more confusing. For Diana, truth is not yet fixed, and the questions and challenges to her story only seem to complicate her developing narrative understanding.

I mark this moment as one of Diana's bravest. She doesn't back away from the complexity of her narrative, the trauma, or the context in which she is retelling this story. Diana knows that I am a mother; throughout my time in Fairfield she asked me questions about my pregnancy. I have no doubt that Diana was acutely aware of the connection we shared, having both been pregnant, and the very real differences in age and circumstance that brought about our pregnancies. Here, again, I might have been another person who believed she had access to one truth about Diana's story. For Diana, then, to give voice to her knowledge of pregnancy and mothering in the context of our relationship seems wholly courageous.

Telling, as Diana knows, alters her relationships. The story of Diana's rape is made more difficult by her family's friendship with Rick and his family. Diana explains:

Diana: [Rick's] little sister was my best friend, too. Now, I don't even talk to her no more. She doesn't call me or anything.

Emily: Well, she used to.

Diana: I mailed her a letter.

Emily: She kept doing it.

Diana: Yeah, but she didn't know.

Emily: Yeah.

Diana: Because we weren't allowed to tell [inaudible] because he was over 18. But the police kind of like, they had to tell him, because they had to know to stop calling our house and emailing us, and stuff. It was starting to become, like, harassment. And, like, we were really getting sick of it. So, they went there, like, and questioned his little sister, and that's when they started putting it all together.

Weaving her way backwards again, Diana reveals another layer in the rippling effect that her rape had had within her community. In such a small town, overlapping relationships between Rick's and Diana's families make contact between family members unavoidable. Living in an isolated, tight-knit community heightens the possibility of Diana's contact with her perpetrator or his family, reminding her that she is neither safe from harm nor free from this story.

For Diana—who has been cut off from close personal relationships and forced to reveal intimate parts of herself in the most public of spaces—questions about intimacy, sexuality, privacy, and her ability to craft her own identity are paramount. In a community where many of Diana's friends, teachers, and neighbors have started to craft their own versions of her story, forging her own identity and story in the face of so many competing voices will require great strength.

STREAMS INTO A RIVER

The rural students I interviewed told stories that revealed how their experiences were enmeshed in community connections. In a small town, individual stories inevitably overlap and influence each other, creating a context in which narratives of the self are built in relationship to others. This is particularly evident in Diana's case, as it is the context of communal storytelling that allows her narrative to open within the interview. While Cassandra, Eve, and Emily assist Diana in speaking what is unspeakable to Diana, their stories also blur the edges of what is real, challenging Diana's story and imposing their versions over hers. Within Diana's community, her story is told and retold, published in the newspaper, and spread in circles of teachers and students, as others speak over Diana's words, rewriting her version of events. In retelling Diana's story again, I, too, propel the flood of this narrative forward, but with her words, her silences, her speaking, as central.

While individual narratives provide an opportunity for researchers to gather information about personal meaning-making, such stories exist as only one piece in a larger puzzle. Narratives of the self, however, are strongly embedded within the culture and voices of the surrounding community. Clearly there are strengths and limitations to listening to narratives told in community. Particularly, this privileges a collective story over that of the individual. In Diana's case, it is easy to see how Diana's words could be lost if a researcher is not careful to document the fact that threads of the communal narrative overlapping Diana's story surround her own narrative, shape her self-understanding, and limit the degree of control she has over this narrative. Relationships between narrators are imbued with power, and researchers must be attentive to the ways in which communal stories contradict, cover over, dismiss, or challenge each other.

However, narratives of common knowledge offer a compelling and richly rendered account of experience and highlight the social context in which narratives are created. There is a risk that giving control of memories to a community may invite differences of interpretation, even conflict. Similarly, in inviting members of a community to narrate a story collectively, researchers relinquish a degree of control and must tolerate ambiguity, because communal narratives with multiple storytellers, perspectives, even contradictory storylines, will certainly diverge from a linear path. However, the richness of communal narratives lies in exactly this. Telling stories of identity and community are not singular acts, and each person articulates narratives shaped by community and context, revision and relationship. It is imperative that narrative research addresses the relational nature of story building. Concerning traumatic events in particular, communal narratives may well lighten the burden of knowledge by sharing the experience of knowing, remembering, speaking, what might otherwise remain unspeakable.

Source: Seaton, E. (2008). Common knowledge: reflections on narratives in community. *Qualitative Research, 8*(3), 293–305. Used with permission from SAGE.

Summary and Review

I suspect you will be drawn to Seaton's account. She reveals a number of aspects about using narratives in qualitative research. Her special emphasis is on the complex interaction of using communal narratives. You can see she relied heavily on methods drawn from ethnography. That is not a requirement of narrative research, but it can be useful. Seaton's article is an example of narrative research. Once you read it, you might ask yourself the question, how is this really research? It seems just like some stories. What makes these stories fit into the framework of qualitative research?

Finally, if you return to the four questions I posed at the beginning of this chapter, you can see the extent to which this article was successful. Seaton introduces some new ideas in this study. I had not heard of communal narratives previously. It is certainly a thought-provoking idea. She writes in a very engaging manner, drawing you in to the story quickly. She explains her method quite clearly. I believe you will feel, as I do, that the article is very successful.

- Does it provide new information and insights related to the topic?
- Is it engaging and written in a clear manner?
- Does it illustrate elements of stories and their interpretations?
- Do the positive aspects of the article outweigh the potential drawbacks?

In the next article, Barone addresses some of the questions you and others often raise about narrative research. You can tell from the title that this type of research might not quite fit into a traditional framework of research that fits the gold standard. Remember, when we talk about the gold standard, we refer to research that fits a traditional model of a double-blind experimental study. Barone tells us in the abstract that data are placed into storied or diachronic formats. (The term "diachronic" refers to phenomena that change or occur over time.) In this article, Barone addresses some specific topics and addresses ways to enlarge the use of narratives as a qualitative approach, especially during a time of political conservativism. I am not sure if the times will change with a more open political approach from the Democrats.

Barone cites the No Child Left Behind Act of 2001 as a specific time in this move toward a conservative stance. Among other things, it calls for scientifically based research. When you read this article, you need to think about the ways in which qualitative research in general and narrative research in particular can position itself to respond to such an agenda. Barone refers you to Ellen Lagemann's 2000 *An Elusive Science: The Troubling History of Education Research,* published by The University of Chicago Press. I discuss this issue in greater depth in Chapter 10.

Article 6.2. A Return to the Gold Standard? Questioning the Future of Narrative Construction as Educational Research (2007)

Tom Barone

My Expectations

The title of this article provides clues that you will be reading an opinion piece rather than the results of a completed piece of research about using narrative. I have been reading some things recently about a move to return to a form of research that is considered traditional or experimental. I know that a gold standard in research is one considered by some to be of the "highest" type. This controversy has surrounded qualitative research since its very entry into the education domain during the 1980s. I anticipate that this article will explore some of the issues. What Barone has to say about the issues will, hopefully, be addressed in the article. I also wonder why he has singled our the future of narrative construction rather than the future of qualitative research. Might other approaches to qualitative research be spared?

ABSTRACT

Notice Barone's comments about the influence of a political agenda.

Narrative construction is an approach to social research in which data are configured into any of a variety of diachronic, or storied, formats. Having recently gained popularity, this approach is now in danger of marginalization (along with other qualitative and quantitative forms of social research) as a result of politically charged attempts to reinstitute a narrow methodological orthodoxy. In an attempt to prompt discussion about the future of this inquiry approach, the author asks questions that highlight recurring issues within ongoing conversations among educational researchers who advocate and/or engage in the construction of narratives. These questions relate to the political character of stories, fictionalization, audience, modalities of representation, quality control, research purpose, and strategies for maintaining and enlarging the space for narrative construction as a qualitative research approach within an era of political retrogression.

You can see from this abstract that Barone plans to address a number of issues

Have those of us who celebrate the potential of innovative forms of educational research, now in this first decade of a new millennium, fallen on times even harder than those with which we are accustomed? Observing the landscape of educational research within the United States, it is difficult to avoid awareness of moves, especially at the level of the federal government, toward a narrowing of the officially sanctioned methodological spectrum. Given the influence of American thought, culture, and government policy over the rest of the globe, residents of other countries who advocate and practice forms of educational research that are not conventionally scientific might also take notice of this narrowing.

The passage of the No Child Left Behind Act of 2001 is the most obvious of these moves. The law calls explicitly and exclusively for the use of *scientifically based research* (a phrase used 111 times within it) as the foundation for many education programs and for classroom instruction. Gardner (2002) suggested that the text of this law echoes a pervasive theme within current discussions of education in America. This theme is the continuing failure of educational research to improve the dire state of the American public educational system. Because the bill was passed with broad bipartisan support, Gardner may be correct in asserting that "at least on the political front," a consensus has been reached regarding a remedy for what ails educational research and therefore American education. The prescription, moreover, is not merely for any kind of "scientifically based research," but for a quite specific sort:

> Educational research ought to [employ] . . . the vaunted National Institutes of Health model. On this analysis, the more rapidly that we can institute randomized trials—the so-called gold standard of research involving human subjects—the sooner we will be able to make genuine progress in our understanding of schooling and research. (Gardner, 2002, p. 1)

The passage of the No Child Left Behind Act represents a clear reaffirmation—indeed, a particularly aggressive codification—of a pervasive and familiar cultural predisposition toward the glorification of the work of scientists and the technologies it produces. I do not intend here to trace in detail the familiar historical roots of this mind-set. Lagemann (2000, pp. 41–70) suggested that in the 1920s and 1930s Charles Hubbard Judd at the University of Chicago and Edward L. Thorndike of Teachers College played critical roles in gaining acceptance of controlled experimentation and statistical measurements within the field of educational research. The resulting monolithic predisposition toward the "hardest" of scientific methods has eroded slowly over the past century. The gradual acceptance and use of a wide array of quantitative and qualitative methodologies stemmed largely out of a recognition of a vast difference in the nature of phenomena under study within the fields of education and that of the physical sciences (Lagemann, 2000). The new maneuvers on the American political scene may, therefore, threaten the agendas of educational researchers of many different stripes, indeed, of any work—correlational studies and surveys, for example—on the research spectrum even slightly removed from the location of the vaunted medical model.

However, for nearly a quarter century, I have identified myself as a member of a community of scholars who delight in claiming the mantle of legitimacy for work that does not purport to be (even "softly") scientific, work that occupies an educational research terrain on an entirely different continent than that of the "gold standard."

Here, he reveals his own stance. You saw the same position taken by Miskovic and Hoop in their action research article.

Polkinghorne's 2007 article "Validity Issues in Narrative Research" addresses some related issues. See Chapter 10.

By emplotting, I think he means presenting the data using a narrative style of writing, as opposed to a more traditional type of written presentation.

Barone reminds us there is a variety of ways to present such a narrative construction. Can you imagine what he means when he talks about shared common characteristics of these different media?

The remainder of the article is organized into sections around questions. Before we look at the details related to the questions, I think you will find it helpful to think about the questions. He begins with a question related to the political. It will help you to recall that some say all research has a political agenda—even research that purports to be objective and neutral. We'll come back to politics in a moment. He then considers the issue of fictionalizing data. Is fact or fiction presented? I would suggest that narrative research is both/and rather than either/or. And remember that in the Seaton paper there is no clear "truth." Who the audience is or should be is also a question Barone raises. How should the data be presented— through what literary vehicle? I think that with various

In this essay, therefore, I ponder the potential significance of the resurgence of this research orthodoxy for an inquiry approach that may (or may not) be among the most vulnerable to its enforcement.

More specifically, I focus on the kind of research that Polkinghorne (1995) has called *narrative analysis*. In narrative analysis "researchers collect descriptions of events and happenings and synthesize or configure them by means of a plot into a story or stories" (Polkinghorne, p. 12). Because this recasting of data into a storied form is more accurately described as an act of textual arrangement than of analysis, I prefer the term *narrative construction* for this research approach.

In the recent past, narrative construction has burgeoned, with researchers in the field of education experimenting with a variety of literary genres for emplotting their data. These include (among others) poetry (Sullivan, 2000), the novel (Dunlop, 1999) and novella (Kilbourne, 1998), the life story (Barone, 2000, 2001b), the short story, (Ceglowski, 1997), social science portraiture (Lawrence-Lightfoot & Davis, 1997), ethnodramaturgy (Saldana & Wolcott, 2001), autobiography and "self-narrative" (Buttignol, 1999), film and videos, readers theater (Donmoyer & Yennie-Donmoyer, 1995), even the "sonata form case study" (Sconiers & Rosiek, 2000). As representatives of particular literary genres the works by these researchers employ certain design elements that distinguish them from each other. However, as narrative constructions they also share common characteristics, several of which are antithetical to the principles, premises, and procedures employed within the kind of research associated with the gold standard.

The deepening chill in the political climate may signal the need for an examination of the current status of this narrative approach to educational research and for reflecting on its future course. In this essay, therefore, I focus on certain recurring issues within ongoing conversations among educational researchers who advocate and/or engage in the construction of narratives. I spotlight these issues not for the purpose of resolving them here. Instead, I have chosen to couch my musings about the field of narrative research in the form of questions—or more precisely, clusters of questions. These questions are meant to prompt consideration of useful directions for the field within these inhospitable times. Issues suggested by these questions concern:

1. the inherently political character of educational stories

2. the fictionalization of storied data

3. intended audiences of narrative research

4. modalities of representation

5. the tension between the need for quality controls and the democratic impulse of story sharing

means of presenting data via the Internet, Barone could add to his discussion. Of what value are the stories? This is an interesting question to consider. When is a story just a story and when is it something more? And finally, why choose one way or another to tell stories?

He presents seven very challenging questions in the list that follows.

Of course, the use of stories is not the only instance of a political agenda in qualitative research.

Do you remember Watts's account of Stake's case study of the school in Chicago (Chapter 4)?

Who do you think should be reading narratives? In Chapter 5, we saw action research represented as a play in the article by Fisher and Phelps.

In the preceding few sentences, Barone contrasts Phillips's view that stories should be judged from a perspective of truth as opposed to views of Rorty and Habermas regarding stories and power relationships. Is this power over truth, or is that too simple an explanation?

6. the ultimate purposes for which narrative research in education is conducted and for which educational narratives are constructed

7. maintaining and enlarging our space within the retrogressive political realities of educational research.

A Place for the Overtly Political?

Should the value of stories be judged primarily on epistemological rather than political grounds? As befitting a postpositivist, Phillips (1994) argues for the former over the latter. He worries that narrativist methodologists have been overly influenced by the likes of Rorty, Habermas, and Lyotard, all of whom would argue, in different ways, that it is less important for research (including storied) texts to earn a badge of truthfulness than for those texts to attend to the power relationships that infuse their creation. Phillips names narrative methodologists and other researchers—including Polkinghorne, Lytle and Cochran-Smith, Jardine, Connelly, Clandinin, and Barone—whose writings, he says, betray an unfortunate lack of concern about epistemological warrants.

I believe that Phillips is correct in his assessment of the prevalence among narrative researchers of a belief in the inescapably political nature of all storytelling. However, about this matter there are more shades of opinion within our field than Phillips suggests. Varying degrees of attention to power relationships within research texts can be discerned. Consider the question: Should the researcher reframe the perspective of what she or he considers a politically naïve outlook of an informant who becomes a character within a narrative construction? At least two different answers have been offered.

On one hand, some deem story sharing to be a deeply personal undertaking with any such reframing the equivalent of a narrative abduction. On the other hand, a progressivist argument assumes that because all human understandings operate within, and are constrained by, sets of power relationships, it is the obligation of narrative researchers to move overtly toward the redressing of imbalances within those relationships. For storytelling to be an ethical undertaking there must be an attempt to make obvious the connections between political forces and individual lives, connections not always immediately obvious to those whose stories are being told. This position usually implies a recasting of the views of participants into presumably more enlightened, usually theoretical and academic, forms of discourse. However, other questions arise about the reconcilability of these two approaches. What forms of negotiation between these two points of view are possible? What new forms of politically aware narratives can we imagine?

hooks' idea about the emancipatory nature of storytelling is
interesting.

A tension is also felt in attempts to blend the political and the aesthetic in narrative constructions. How do we reconcile the opposing
tendencies of political substance and aesthetic form in emancipatory-
minded storytelling, or what bell hooks (1991) has called *critical fictions?* Can narrative accounts be both artfully ambiguous and socially
conscientious? How can a narrative researcher successfully navigate
the line between blatant propaganda and stories with ideological
integrity? Can the polemical and the artistic coexist for purposes of
political enlightenment through narrative research? To take a specific
example, how might a researcher construct a persuasive narrative of
the stultifying realities in the lives of teachers and students of the high-
stakes standardized testing movement? How might such a narrative
project embody a deeply held progressivist point of view while avoiding a tedious and self-defeating didacticism?

You can see Barone doesn't
offer pat answers. Rather, he
raises questions and issues for
you to consider.

And finally, there may be disagreements on this question: Is it
wise, at this reactionary moment in educational research history (at
the governmental level), for us to continue explorations into narrative construction that is openly ideological?

FICTIONALIZING THE DATA?

You might recall reading Watts'
account of Stake's case study
about a school. I suspect some of it
was fiction based on fact.

A second set of questions concerns the issue of fact versus fiction in
narrative construction. Indeed, several researchers in the field of
education have considered the advantages and disadvantages of fictionalizing narrative research texts. However, precisely what is
meant by the term *fiction?* More than one definition can be found
within the works of literary and social theorists. Some would argue
for a comprehensive sense of what can count as fiction. For
example, Geertz (1974) has suggested that all anthropological writings are "fictions in the sense that they are "something made,"
"something fashioned"—the original meaning of *fiction*" (p. 15).
Such a broad notion of the term seems to place all human institutions and artifacts—including projects of science—under its
umbrella.

In opposition to this inclusive definition, postpositivists and certain phenomenologists—strange methodological bedfellows—
support a more circumscribed notion of what is fictional.
Postpositivists argue for truth as a regulative ideal in research, something to be striven toward if never reached. They dismiss texts that do
not aim for the purely factual as subjective and useless. Less dismis-
sive of the value of fiction as imaginative literature, phenomenologists
nevertheless tend to distinguish between literary texts that are brack-
eted off from the mundane world and self-disclose their fictional
nature, from those texts that are not and do not. However, despite their
differences, both groups support a bifurcation familiar to those of us
in Western cultures, the kind that results in the segregation of literary

works into separate fiction and nonfiction best-seller lists and sections of libraries.

Arriving on the scene to heal that conceptual rupture were the genre blurrers. Their work first appeared during a moment of genre dispersion identified by Denzin and Lincoln (1998) as the third stage of qualitative research. This was a time in which "boundaries between the social sciences and the humanities had become blurred" (p. 18). Ever since, experiments in the use of fictional devices have proliferated, recasting the fact–fiction dichotomy into a continuum, one that accommodates the following observation by literary theorist Wolfgang Iser (1993):

> [A] piece of fiction devoid of any connections with known reality would be incomprehensible. Consequently, if we are to attempt a description of what is fiction, there is little point in clinging to the old distinction between fiction and reality as a frame of reference. The literary text is a mixture of reality and fictions, and as such it brings about an interaction between the given and the imagined. (p. 1)

Despite the efforts of the blurrers, a "single drop of blood" mentality lingers, one that deplores genre miscegenation within narrative. Factual texts are seen as tainted by the introduction of even minor, "weak" fictional literary devices such as imagined dialogue and composite characters. Thus, "fiction remains a no-no, a mode of expression . . . that is simply off-limits in conventional academic discourse" and social research in general (Banks & Banks, 1998, p. 17).

Indeed, within the field of educational research, the use of what are conventionally identified as fictionalizing devices remains controversial. A series of American Educational Research Association (AERA) debates between Elliot Eisner and Howard Gardner about the appropriateness of writing a novel as a dissertation stirred the pot, even as examples of dissertations as novels began to appear (Dunlop, 1999; Saye, 2002). Other forms of fictional writing by educational researchers have also found their way into print. For example, Sconiers and Rosiek (2000) collaborated on a case study that was, as they say in Hollywood, "based on a true story." Certain teaching experiences of Sconiers are recast into those of the fictional character named Jerome Jameson, a middle-grades science teacher, and told from his perspective. The aim of the researchers is to explore several critical issues related to teaching science to students of color.

For many of us narrativists, such developments represent an overdue release from a methodological straightjacket, even as others would demand a tightening of constraints. Still, questions surrounding the fictionalization of our texts linger. Questions such as: What are the various promises and pitfalls involved in the fictionalization of narrative constructions? Are different purposes served by a fictional narrative account than a nonfictional one? If so, what are they? Or is

Do you think a dissertation can be a novel? Apparently it can at some institutions.

Barone makes an important point in the preceding comment about being put into a straightjacket, at the same time recognizing there is a concern about the fictional nature of the written narrative. Watts comes to grips with his own concern as he strives to "make sense" of Stake's account of Harper School.

As someone new to the field, you might be frustrated to see more questions than answers.

That sounds to me like an elitist group. Perhaps he could say this in a less pedantic manner. Or does he mean to be sarcastic? I am not sure.

Perhaps he is saying we should rethink this position.

it better to ask: When is fictionalization a useful strategy and when not? Should we think in terms of degrees of fictionalization? What are the various literary devices and textual design elements available to narrative researchers in the fictionalization process? Are some of these same elements employed in texts that are commonsensically classified as nonfictional? Regarding narrative constructions, is there indeed a clearly identifiable border between fact and fiction?

And then: With the noisy arrival of policy makers with the most restrictive of methodological straightjackets in hand, is this moment a propitious one for continued experimentation with strongly fictional texts whose elements of design and research purpose so highly objectionable to those advocates of "scientifically based research?"

BROADENING THE AUDIENCE?

A third set of questions relates to issues of audience. Traditional social scientists have been relatively free of confusion about intended audiences for their research texts. A common identity as social scientists has meant possession of the expertise needed to generate trustworthy knowledge and to communicate it in a language accessible primarily to coinhabitants of their tightly bounded community of discourse. Educational researchers' texts must be, foremost, informative and persuasive to professional colleagues. These texts may be subsequently translated, primarily through the press and other media, for those outside of the research class, including educational practitioners, policy makers, and even members of the general public (Barone, 2000).

Although we occupy similar academic spaces as our more traditional researcher colleagues, narrative constructionists have tended to be less clear about intended audiences. Unlike traditional research texts, storied texts often appear to be written for (or at least accessible to) school people residing within the research setting whose educational beliefs, values, and practices are portrayed, or toward school people in analogous settings who might gain sustenance from the sounds of voices similar to their own. Whether out of thoughtless habit or studied deference to traditional notions of scholarship, we educational narrativists rarely craft our stories toward people who are not professional educators.

Should we reconsider our intended readership? This question seems apt at this moment in educational research history and, indeed, in the larger history of American education. In my view, a prejudicial educational imaginary about public schools and school people dominates educational discourse and the processes of educational policy making (Barone, 2002a). The result has been, in many places, a nearly unparalleled diminishing of the professional status of teachers and the demonization of the children whom they teach. McNeil (2000) and Sacks (1999) suggest that for many thoughtful and dedicated teachers this is a time of despair and even terror, for themselves, their students, and for the larger culture. Adherents to a marketplace ideology have successfully promoted a frenzy of high-stakes testing that is severely narrowing and distorting the curriculum, dramatically increasing student dropout rates, exacerbating a teacher shortage, and desecrating the meaning of education (McNeil, 2000; Sacks, 1999).

This paragraph is an example of how the author reveals his own political agenda.

Should our narrative research agenda not include an attempt to rescue ourselves from this terror? Should we seek out a wider band of allies for doing so? Should parents, other laypeople, the intelligentsia, and educational policy makers at all levels, be afforded direct access to the stories of those whom the imaginary has stereotyped and mischaracterized? And if the answer to those questions is in the affirmative, then how do we compose stories that persuade lay people and educational policy makers to ask themselves serious questions about the nature of teaching and education? And how do we respond to the inevitable resistance of those whose image of the appropriate audience for our scholarship is more traditional?

Or should we postpone discussion about and efforts toward audience expansion until a less politically sensitive moment?

Through What Media and Modes of Representation?

In Chapter 5, you read a play by Fisher and Phelps as they presented their take on action research.

Another risk-taking venture for narrative researchers involves the use of visual media and the performing arts in our storytelling. Theatrical, film, and video productions are indeed narrative-based endeavors. Dance, opera, and music also contain narrative dimensions. Even photographs, sculptures, and paintings may be said to suggest stories. What might result from explorations of these art forms as media of disclosure in narrative research?

Issues of audience may reassert themselves here. Some would argue that the use of the plastic and performing arts for conveying research findings might prove as bewildering and alienating to members of a general audience as are traditional texts that employ the queer (to them) idioms of the scientific monograph. Still, our postmodern culture has sometimes been described—like the educational imaginary—as image based. Might issues of educational policy and practice be more powerfully explored through the electronic media, video, film, staged drama, and CD-ROMs (Bagley & Cancienne, 2002)?

Image-based and performance-based precedents within the social sciences are rife. For example, playwriting and ethnography have collaborated within works variously described as *performance ethnography* (Turner, 1982), *ethnodrama* (Mienczakowski, 1995), or *performance texts* (Conquergood, 1991; Denzin, 1997). Saldana has recently coauthored and staged what can be called educational ethnodramas (Saldana, Finley, & Finley, 2002; Saldana & Wolcott, 2001). Visual ethnography is even more commonplace, in the forms of photographs, videos, and films. In support of the latter, Marcus and Fisher (1999) have noted that

> perhaps the ethnographic film cannot replace the ethnographic text, but it may indeed have certain advantages over it in a society where visual media are strongly competing with written forms for the attention of mass users, including intellectuals and scholars. (p. 75)

The above statement is hardly news to scholars in the field of cultural studies. However, what would it mean for narrativists in the field of education to take this observation seriously? Are the tools of the visual media really more capable than the printed word of persuading an audience beyond the walls of the academy to entertain deep and difficult questions about matters educational? Or do the many potential obstacles, difficulties, complications, dangers, and trade-offs involved in using the visual and performing arts render them poor candidates for future possibilities for narrative researchers?

Or perhaps, as with issues of the overtly political, the fictional, and audience expansion, we should merely wait for a more accommodating climate for probing into the possibilities of alternative modalities of representation?

HOW CAN STORIES BE WORTHY?

Perhaps in our misunderstood need to be objective, rigorous, and scientific, we have failed to give voice to those very people in our schools who have so long not had their views heard.

It was not so long ago that the American Educational Research Association (AERA), the major professional association of educational researchers, was dominated by white men. When I first joined the organization in the 1970s, it was overwhelmingly such a group. Today, in contrast, women and/or people of color have taken major leadership roles, including the presidency.

Next we turn to the ongoing tension between the democratic thrust of the narrative research movement and notions of excellence within the craft. We understand that the move toward narrative research in education has resulted in part from the long overdue recognition of the sound of silence, a sudden painful awareness of the extent to which human voices have been systematically excluded from the kinds of traditional research texts. These texts revealed disinterest, even disdain, for the experiences, and therefore the stories, of all sorts of school people, especially those from members of social categories whose marginalization has extended far beyond the arena of educational research.

The democratic impulse of narrativists to rectify historical wrongs though a widening of the discursive space is easily understood. However, is diversity among storytellers a sufficient criterion for the publication of educational narratives? Thoughtful members of the educational community have expressed concern about a kind of narrative overload that may be at hand. Maxine Greene (see

Ayers, 1995), generally sympathetic to the notion of narrative research, has wondered about the ultimate point of the diversity afforded by narrative constructions. Greene is not interested in newly strengthened voices contributing to a pointless and futile cacophony of individual interests. Diversity, she has commented, is important, but "we need to think hard about where we go with the multiple voices" (Ayers, 1995, p. 327).

How do we judge whether a particular narrative construction is useful? How do we know whether it is worthy of dissemination? What degree of literary achievement must it evidence? How compellingly and artfully composed must a narrative be to deserve publication? Should we as a research community strive toward consensus about goodness criteria for narrative research? And if so, what are the practical concerns related to the application of those criteria in specific venues such as conferences, dissertation committees, and journal publications?

Again, more questions are raised.

More traditional commentators, less sympathetic to narrative than Greene, have also been heard on this issue. Perhaps predictably, some have raised the issue of relativity. A colleague recently suggested to me that in our democratic zeal to welcome new sorts of stories "narrative researchers risk a backlash because they seem to think that anyone's story is just as worthy as anyone else's." This comment, of course, reflects the skepticism (even antagonism) toward narrative and other research methodologies found at the heart of the resurrected research orthodoxy.

Do we, therefore, as a result of our seeking out and welcoming new sorts of stories, risk the freedom to pursue narrative research in the future? If so, should we not be concerned as a research subcommunity about the issue of quality in narrative construction? However, while our anxieties about returning to an era of silencing run deep, should fear be our motivation for extending or limiting our intramural debates about which educational stories are worth sharing? Or is it out of a sense of responsibility to our audiences that issues of diversity and quality demand our continued attention?

WHY TELL STORIES?

A sixth set of questions involves our reasons for doing narrative research. Why do we construct educational narratives? Are our purposes as researchers similar or identical to those of authors of imaginative literature? Are we primarily interested in publicizing perspectives about educational issues and practices that cannot be obtained though other sorts of research? Or are we mainly interested in the validation of teachers' stories of their professional lives? Or in assisting educational practitioners in securing (self) respect by communicating their own *personal practical knowledge* (Clandinin,

1985)? Is our primary purpose to deflect a romanticism that distorts educational practitioners' stories by placing them into a sociopolitical context, thereby recasting them into histories of disempowerment? Is our aim then to empower schoolteachers from the outside? Or is our main purpose to challenge educational practitioners and policy makers by questioning the taken-for-granted and perhaps deficient values that support prevailing policies and practices? And perhaps most important, how is the function of narrative construction fundamentally different from the purpose of research that honors the gold standard?

I think he tries to offer some answers here.

My own response to the latter question is that most narrative constructions do indeed serve quite different ends than do projects of traditional social science. Researchers of each sort tend to be predisposed toward achieving contrasting research purposes. Cronbach (1982) suggested that projects of social science generally aim to reduce uncertainty, to approach (if never reach) truth within a particular paradigm, framework, or world-view. Valid data secured through the methods of social science enable us to explain, predict, and sometimes control similar future events. Such data provide guidance about how to argue about how to act. Controlled experiments represent the research methodology most carefully designed to further the reduction of uncertainty.

That is an important point. He acknowledges the validity of traditional research approaches.

Elsewhere, I have suggested that this quest for certainty is evidence of a particular predisposition shared by most traditional social science researchers (Barone, 2001a). This quest for valid knowledge may be fueled by a need shared by all human beings for at least temporary closure to the issues that plague our lives. I recognize the importance of this impulse. Unlike skeptical postmodernists, I do not seek to undermine the fundamental presumptions and claims of traditional, modern social science (Rosenau, 1992). I do object, however, to the exclusivity of this predisposition toward a single research end. Indeed, I see an exclusive identification of educational research with social science as according with a totalizing master narrative. In this master narrative, science is depicted as the sole source of reliable knowledge and the arresting of ambiguity as the only legitimate goal of inquiry.

As a human being *and* an educational researcher who engages in narrative construction, I am also predisposed toward a *second* research purpose. Although I do occasionally feel the need for research texts that guide me toward conventionally valid propositions, I also appreciate texts that offer varied (sometimes even conflicting) renditions of educational phenomena (Barone, 2002b). These are narrative constructions with the power to lift the veil of conventionality from my eyes as they subtly raise disturbing questions about the necessity and desirability of comfortable, familiar educational discourses and practices. These are the products of an educational research that refuses closure to redirect an ongoing conversation.

However, this may be merely the outline of one of many rationales to be presented in defense of the work that narrative researchers do. How might it be refined? What are some other, additional rationales for justifying our work? Then again, these questions may call forth an even more fundamental, and (for this essay) final set of questions.

SAVING NARRATIVE FROM THE NEW POLITICAL REALITIES?

How can we narrative researchers, in this era of ideational retrenchment, secure space for our work? How can we revise the prevailing master narrative about what counts as research, the scientistic metastory that denigrates the artistic and literary, that denies the possible significance of the narratives we construct, that disputes our right to pursue our work?

Can the articulation and dissemination of rationales enhance the likelihood of this revision? Are rationales desirable and necessary in the defense of narrative construction? Is each analogous to a creed that strengthens the faith of true believers, increasing a sense of solidarity within a mutual identity? For members of an already marginalized educational research subcommunity who are feeling increasingly threatened, do our tight and tidy arguments offer nothing more than the collegial comforts of a common intellectual meeting place?

However, for skeptics about the legitimacy of narrative as research, are rationales merely the products of defensive posturing? Are deep-seated dispositions about the purposes of educational research likely to be touched through appeals to reason? Do elaborate arguments not reveal participation in a kind of abstract linear discourse that cuts against the nature of the work that we do as storytellers? Are those who have been professionally socialized to participate in the prevailing metanarrative about research amenable to reeducation through logic? Or may they best be lured into our worldview through encounters with specific examples of our work, seduced through our acts of storytelling? Or more basic yet, need we bother with converting the traditionalists?

The new political moves are played out on an academic landscape vastly different from that found in the heydays of the controlled experiment. Will today's postpositivists who have gathered up the epistemological and methodological remnants of the intellectually discredited philosophy of their positivist forebears not also, just like us, recoil from identification with a truth regime that relegates even correlational studies to second-class research status? So if the new political mandates are rigorously enforced, are we less alone than in the past? Will the new moves create allies among educational inquirers with widely differing research predispositions and worldviews?

This paragraph sets forth an important point.

He continues to express his concern about the fate of the narrative. In this paragraph he addresses issues raised by postpositivists.

Note that he acknowledges the aim of narrative research is not to seek certainty [or truth] but to raise questions about policy and practice.

By using an example of a fictionalized film, Barone suggests ways in which narrative can accomplish a political agenda.

You may know that Thomas Kuhn, writing *The Structure of Scientific Revolutions* in 1962, popularized the idea of a paradigm shift or scientific revolution. Such a shift dealt with a change in basic assumptions about how we see the world.

Will a perceived need for alliances cause narrativists to compromise too much? Let us accept for a moment the view I have expressed about the unique purpose of our work that distinguishes it from other forms of educational research: that our aim as researcher-storytellers is not to seek certainty about correct perspectives on educational phenomena but to raise significant questions about prevailing policy and practice that enrich an ongoing conversation. Holding this possibility in mind, we can revisit some of the issues identified in this essay concerning dimensions of narrative construction that make it uniquely suited for prompting interrogations into unexamined educational values. These dimensions—an overtly political stance, fictionalizing strategies, new intended audiences, and historically underused modes of representation—locate narrative construction at the exploratory edge of educational research. Indeed, an example of a boldly avant garde narrative construction might be a carefully researched but fictionalized film intended to raise questions about an important educational issue (retention in grade? the learning of a second language? the practice of high-stakes standardized testing?) through the adoption of an obvious political point of view.

Would actualizing this sort of research vision not involve a plunge into unfamiliar and dangerous methodological waters? Would that plunge risk greater alienation from our nonnarrativist, methodologically pluralistic allies? Would it further jeopardize our standing within the broader research community? Would it increase the likelihood of a backlash against narrative research? Is such experimentation worth the risk?

Or should we even care about cultivating allies in striving for our own space? To what extent have we needed allies in the past? It is not possible to detail here the developments that brought us to the methodological diversity that currently flourishes in the field of educational research. Suffice it to say that the narrative turn in the social sciences and the humanities arose out of complex set of developments in academic culture. Prominent among them were the prior legitimation of qualitative research, the successes of postmodernist theory, and the incursions of literary criticism into the field of philosophy.

Against this backdrop, a few pioneers in the field of educational research led us to where we find ourselves today, coexisting in an era of methodological innovation by some, benign neglect by others, and polite but sustained opposition by traditionalists. The heroes persuaded sympathetic members of the research community of the value of new research approaches. They also begat and empowered like-minded graduate students who begat others, until the changes in the field seemed somewhat analogous to an inevitable and permanent Kuhnian-style paradigm shift.

Will We "Go On"?

From the ancient Greeks, mythos—a religious view of the world—contrasts with logos—a rational view of the world

However, is our healthy future as a research subcommunity ensured? Are past accomplishments not jeopardized by a wider, more ominous, cultural shift, a change that permits or even encourages a nostalgic return to a former Zeitgeist? Is it too defeatist to suggest that, because mythos inevitably precedes logos, the outcomes of our professional ratiocinations will be determined by larger cultural forces? Or should we direct our efforts toward the gargantuan task of altering the mythos, and the political landscape that it decorates, in accordance with our own aesthetic?

Perhaps things are not as bad as they seem? Do the new political moves really represent a return to a prior era, or is the gold standard merely a corruptible, disposable mythological ideal of a scientistic culture? Have we narrativists not already managed to survive and even thrive in a quite arid cultural climate? For example, we have managed to sponsor Winter Institutes under the auspices of the AERA, claimed much meeting space (especially under Division B and two special interests groups) at AERA and on the programs of other professional conferences. Publications of and on storytelling as research have proliferated. If our counter-hegemonic work has rarely lent itself to the securing of grants from politically influenced, scientifically oriented funding agencies, the careers of many of us have, nevertheless, hardly been harmed by our interests in storytelling.

So what about the future? There are numerous ways in which narrative construction as a research approach is unlike the kind of scientific paradigms about which Thomas Kuhn (1962) has written. However, for the sake of questioning, let us substitute the term *research approach* for *paradigm,* and *researchers* for *scientists,* in his following passage:

> If [supporters of a new paradigm] are competent, they will improve it, explore its possibilities, and show what it would be like to belong to the community guided by it. And as that goes on, if the paradigm is one destined to win its fight, the number and strength of the persuasive arguments in its favor will increase. More scientists will then be converted, and the exploration of the new paradigm will go on. (p. 159)

I agree with Barone that encourages a variety of approaches to educational research and not one that is better or more acceptable than an other.

Finally, I repeat that, as a narrative researcher, I am not interested in the establishment of a counter-hegemonic research "paradigm." I favor a kind of research ecumenism that encourages continued exploration into and with an array of educational research approaches. However, does Kuhn's statement above not suggest that, for our research to "go on" in the face of a return to exclusionary political sanctions, we should continue to do what we have been doing? That we researcher-storytellers continue our conversations about how certain dimensions of our research approach might advance our mission to improve educational policies and practices? That we do so even as we engage in constructing narratives aimed at that mission?

Just asking.

Source: Barone, T. (2007). A return to the gold standard? Questioning the future of narrative construction as educational research. *Qualitative Inquiry, 13*(4), 454–470. Used with permission from SAGE.

Summary and Review

Barone provides more questions than answers. I hope he got you thinking about the value of narrative research as a way of answering educational questions. Since Barone does not present an example of a research study it is not appropriate to address the four questions. I hope he got you thinking about some of the important issues educational researchers face today.

FINAL COMMENTS

Seaton offered an interesting example of what she called a communal narrative. I hope you found it helpful to read the detailed interviews that she included. Barone offered his take on the place of narrative research in today's political climate, although he offered more questions than answers. I think, by extension, that you might substitute qualitative research for narrative in his comments.

By now you have read a dozen articles that serve to illustrate different types of qualitative research approaches. You can see how there is some overlap among the approaches.

In the last chapter of Part I you will see what some researchers have done. They have developed the idea of using quantitative and qualitative research approaches in the same study. It is time for you to continue reading about these ideas in the next chapter.

You can access the complete articles at www.sagepub.com/lichtmanreadings.

Chapter 7

READING MIXED METHODS

I thought you might like to begin reading this chapter with an editorial written by John Creswell. I know Creswell primarily through his popular text *Qualitative Inquiry and Research Design: Choosing Among Five Approaches,* originally published in 1998 and revised in 2007. When I began teaching from the first edition of this book I was not aware that he had been a proponent of mixed methods research for so long. Knowing Creswell's views about how qualitative research can fit into a mixed methods perspective helps me understand his approach to qualitative research in general.

KEY ELEMENTS OF MIXED METHODS

- A mixed methods approach makes use of both quantitative and qualitative data in the same research study;

- often emphasizes quantitative analysis and display of data;

- uses a generic qualitative approach rather than a particular approach such as ethnography or grounded theory; and

- uses a writing style that is objective and neutral.

- Mixed methods are becoming widely used in education.

I want to look at some of the issues that Creswell raises. He begins with the question that he immediately addresses as to why we need a map at this time. Although he lists 30 topics being addressed today, I don't think you will want to read about all of those. Instead we will look at the four topics he chose for special attention. According to Creswell and others, the field has changed very rapidly within the last few years.

Many of the studies that are called mixed methods include very complex statistical analyses. The article by Caitlin Scott and Rosemary Sutton does not. I selected it to illustrate a very recent mixed methods study. It is based on Scott's dissertation. Since many of you are or have been teachers, you should find it very interesting to read about professional development and teacher emotions.

Article 7.1. Editorial: Mapping the Field of Mixed Methods Research (2009)

John W. Creswell

My Expectations

As I think about reading this article, I reflect on the other material that I have been exposed to. Since this is an editorial and written by one of the major figures in the field, I anticipate he will help me understand the central issues relating to mixed methods research. I am a little uncertain whether I agree that mixed methods—somehow combining both qualitative and quantitative research—is a good thing for qualitative research. For so long, qualitative research has taken a back seat to quantitative research. My own position is that it stands on its own—and is not lesser than quantitative. I also expect that Creswell will help me understand the connections and pathways between the two and how I arrive—that is what a map is supposed to do.

ABSTRACT

Since Creswell is a central contributor in this field, you should find it helpful to read his very current views in this editorial.

The intent of this editorial is to advance my list of topics currently being discussed in the field of mixed methods research. As one who has been involved in the mixed methods field since its beginning 20 years ago, I have some sense of the topics that have evolved and that hold center stage in mixed methods discussions. Furthermore, as one of the founding coeditors of the *Journal of Mixed Methods Research* (*JMMR*; and outgoing editor after June 2009), I have been privileged to have examined close to 300 manuscripts submitted to the journal in the past 3 years, and I have taken notes on what I have seen as potential contributions of these manuscripts to the field of mixed methods research.

My discussion will first address why we, as researchers, need a map of the field at this current time. Then I will advance a list of 30 topics that are being discussed today in the mixed methods literature.

Thirty topics seem like too many. I hope he narrows his discussion so I can focus on what is critical to the discussion.

I reflect on how Creswell uses data he has collected in his role as journal editor and then cross-checks the accuracy of his list with information from another source. A common practice among some qualitative researchers is to "cross-check" or "verify" their data by comparing with others. You should understand, however, that treating data in this manner fits more into the mold of a quantitative researcher than one who comes at data from a purely qualitative perspective.

Four is a much more manageable number of topics.

To crosscheck the accuracy of my list, I will reflect on the topics that were discussed last summer at the 2008 Mixed Methods Conference at Cambridge University, UK. I will note differences and similarities between the papers presented at the conference and my list. Then I will select four topics from my list, discuss the development of the topics, and note recent insightful contributions that have emerged in the literature. Finally, I will end with some thoughts about the future of mixed methods research. I hope that by reading this editorial you will learn how one individual constructs the field of mixed methods today, obtain a glimpse into what topics current writers presented at the Mixed Methods Conference last July, and assess how your mixed methods manuscript might make a contribution to the field.

WHY WE NEED A CURRENT MAP

We need a current map of the field of mixed methods to help authors who are submitting manuscripts to *JMMR*. As a coeditor of *JMMR* (and I do not speak here for Abbas Tashakkori, the other coeditor), I often ask authors, "Please rewrite your manuscript with attention to how it contributes to the mixed methods literature." As I examine their manuscripts, I like to note in my logbook something about "here is the contribution of this manuscript." But, of course, the author is not before me to respond. The author might ask,

> What does a contribution mean?
>
> Just tell me how it adds to the literature.
>
> What literature?

Take a hypothetical professor from political science with a specialty in public policy. She or he knows the research on public policy quite well and perhaps also has a good grasp of research methods in political science. In response to this individual's question about the literature, the following conversation could unfold:

> Have you read any articles about mixed methods in the social sciences?
>
> Not really. You see, I am content specialist in public policy in political science and I am quite familiar with the methods that we use in political science.

Perhaps the scenario unfolds now that the author retracts the manuscript because it is not suitable for publication in *JMMR*. Perhaps the author begins reading the mixed methods articles, chapters, and books that have been written over the past 20 years. It seems to me that this professor could profit from having a map of the mixed methods literature so that they could position their study within the existing discussions.

Assume that this professor inquires further:

What do you mean by a "contribution"?

It means adding something new to the literature.

But I quickly add,

But also your study might replicate existing literature, test a theory, raise the voices of the underrepresented, provide an explanation for the meaning of experiences, promote social justice, or even represent your own personal transformation gained through your research.

I do believe in all of these reasons for publishing an article in *JMMR,* as is discussed within a previous editorial on ways of contributing to the literature (Creswell & Tashakkori, 2008). Right now, however, I want to focus on developing a map of the mixed methods literature and consider how a manuscript may contribute to this growing picture.

This is an example of how the field is rapidly changing. What were core issues in 2003 might not be core issues in 2009.

Another reason for the need for a current map is that maps available in the field are rapidly becoming dated or are too general to use. For example, in 2003, Tashakkori and Teddlie, in their 26-chapter *Handbook of Mixed Methods,* announced the six core issues of the field.

1. The nomenclature and basic definitions used in mixed methods research

2. The utility of mixed methods research (why do we do it?)

3. The paradigmatic foundations for mixed methods research

4. Design issues in mixed methods research

5. Issues in drawing inferences in mixed methods research

6. The logistics of conducting mixed methods research

Did you realize the issues had changed so much?

This *Handbook* provides a nice map of the field. But it is now 5 years old (a new edition is in the planning stage) and I feel that much of the explosion in interest in mixed methods has occurred during the past 5 years Alternatively, we could turn to the dimensions of the field identified in a *JMMR* article by Jennifer Greene, published in 2008. This article was adapted from her keynote address to the Mixed Methods Special Interest Group Business Meeting at the American Educational Research Association conference in April 2007. She created a generic framework for the components of any social science methodology and she applied this framework to mixed methods research asking, What do we know? What have we accomplished?

And what important questions remain to be engaged? Her four domains of this framework were as follows:

1. Philosophical assumptions and stances

2. Inquiry logics (methods, sampling, design, etc.)

3. Guidelines for practice (empirical guidelines, such as how to mix)

4. Sociopolitical commitments (interests being served, situational politics)

These domains provide a good, general map, but they too provide insufficient guidance for specific topics and areas in need of further development in the mixed methods field. We need a more detailed map.

A MAP OF RECENT TOPICS IN THE MIXED METHODS LITERATURE

So I began thinking about designing a map of the field as it currently stands. I have a small notebook and, for every manuscript that I review for *JMMR,* I faithfully log a statement about the potential contribution of the manuscript to the field of mixed methods. Recently I went through this notebook and assembled a list of 30 topics that represent the contributions of recent mixed methods manuscripts. Then I aggregated these topics into five domains. Once this was done, I went through the 2008 program for the Mixed Methods Conference held in July 2008 at Cambridge University, UK, and assigned the papers to my list of topics. In this way, I could see the coverage of the conference topics. I apologize to presenters if I misassigned their papers to one of my topics. Indeed, some papers addressed several topics on my list, and I chose to assign them only to one. Also, in this editorial I cite only the lead authors and their general topics rather than reference all of the papers presented at the conference. The reader is directed to the conference Web site for exact titles (see http://www.mixedmethods.leeds.ac.uk/pages/information/confarchive.htm).

MY MAP AND THE CONFERENCE PAPERS

(Table has been omitted.) Creswell identifies five major domains in this table: philosophical and theoretical issues; techniques of mixed methods; nature of mixed methods; adoption and use of mixed methods; and politicization of mixed methods. He arrived at these domains by sorting and coding all the data he

Table 1 provides my list of domains, topics, and my assignment of conference papers to the topics. In my map of the field, I listed four topics under philosophical and theoretical issues: combining philosophical positions, worldviews, and paradigms; the philosophical foundation for mixed methods; the use of qualitative theoretical lens in mixed methods; the false distinction between quantitative and qualitative research; and thinking in a mixed methods way (mental models; Greene, 2007) . . .

collected when he was a journal editor and from the conference he attended. This is another example of how he provides you with a model that organizes his original data. He codes and categorizes the separate pieces of data to construct the table. You can think of this process as a qualitative analysis.

I listed numerous topics under the domain of techniques of mixed methods. These range from unusual blends of sources of data, to specific elements of the process of research, and on to validity and ethics . . .

Topics related to the nature of mixed methods reflect the ongoing discussion of defining the field, creating a language for it, and using it as a stand-alone design or in conjunction with other designs and methodologies. At the conference, the use of mixed methods in existing designs, such as case studies, formative evaluation in experiments, and action research, attests to an emerging trend toward incorporating mixed methods procedures into traditional designs . . .

Many fields are adopting and using mixed methods . . .

The topics of funding, deconstruction, and justification under the politicization of mixed methods are not surprising, and as the field grows in visibility, more papers are predicted for future conferences. We had few papers in this area at the 2008 Mixed Methods Conference. However, at the Qualitative Inquiry 2007 Congress in Illinois recently, several audience members asked for my mixed methods presentation (Creswell, 2007) [and] expressed keen interest in the deconstruction of terms in mixed methods, such as *mixing*. They were especially interested, too, in the Freshwater (2007) article on a postmodern critique of mixed methods presented in *JMMR*.

SELECT TOPICS AND INSIGHTFUL CONTRIBUTIONS

He does not offer any particular reason why he chose these topics. Do you think he should?

Now I will take four topics on my list, briefly discuss some history about each topic, and then talk about recent insightful contributions that I believe will extend the conversation about the topics.

Incorporation of Mixed Methods Into Other Designs

(Figure has been omitted.)

I think he has just put forth an important idea of having some connection between the two methods rather than a kind of war. You can read more about these issues in Chapter 9.

In terms of discussions about research designs, I often begin with a general introduction to mixed methods. As shown in Figure 1, mixed methods was originally viewed as two separate strands of research—quantitative and qualitative—with a clear division between the two. In the mid-1990s, the discussion seemed to change from the two separate strands to how the two strands might be linked, and a connection was made between the two strands. Out of this linkage grew the idea of mixed methods as we know it today. But immediately different perspectives emerged on what constituted the nature of mixed methods (see an earlier editorial by Creswell & Tashakkori, 2007). Some, like myself, focused on the methods of collecting and analyzing data, recognizing that the methods were an integral part of the entire process of research. Others focused on how qualitative and quantitative research flowed into all phases of the research process (the methodologists). Still others focused on

He has just presented three different ideas about what constitutes mixed methods—should it be about collection and analysis of data or about integrating qualitative and quantitative research. Or should it be philosophical? Perhaps it can be about all of these topics—and others as well.

I am not quite sure what he means. Perhaps he means that researchers (both quantitative and qualitative) are moving away from a single research approach toward a combination of approaches. This is a different view from what I have presented in this book. I have provided you with examples of various types of qualitative research approaches. I have also suggested that approaches are not especially "pure."

The "incompatibility argument" was popular in the 1980s. The gist of the argument is that the two main ways of understanding research represented different assumptions about how we see the world and come to know about it—a researcher could accept either one or the other, but not both.

Creswell suggests that in order for the quantitative and qualitative to exist together some have adopted a stance of pragmatism; others have taken a position that he calls "transformative." He doesn't really explain the latter. But as you continue reading, you will see that he and his colleague adopt still a third way of thinking about "mixed methods."

How do you feel about his idea of linking paradigms and methods? Does he tell you enough so that you really understand what he means?

philosophy. Now we are seeing yet another group emerge—those who combine mixed methods with more traditional designs. So we have ethnographers using mixed methods procedures as well as case studies researchers, experimental health science investigators, and narrative researchers (Eliot, 2005; LeCompte & Schensul, 1999; Luck, Jackson, & Usher, 2006; Sandelowski, 1996). The use of mixed methods procedures within existing designs and procedures has tremendous potential for making mixed methods relevant to many areas in many disciplines, including visual methodology. I am writing an article now on how an award-winning documentary developer combined quantitative and qualitative data and used one of the mixed methods designs in composing a documentary on immigrants (Creswell & McCoy, in press) . . .

Paradigms as Beliefs of a Community of Scholars

I am tired of the "incompatibility" argument that one cannot mix paradigms. It is as if a particular researcher's worldview is a fixed trait that cannot be examined, changed, or combined. Furthermore, mixed methods research can be conducted by teams that include specialists in quantitative and qualitative research. It is required that members of these teams listen to each other. When the issue of incompatibility arises, it seems to be a conversation stopper. If we cannot mix paradigms, so the argument goes, then mixed methods research is untenable. Fortunately, we have moved beyond this thinking. We now have mixed methods writers talking about the possibility of using multiple paradigms in research, and yes, sometimes they may be in tension, and such tension is good. The dialectic between opposing ideas can contribute to new insights and new understandings (Greene & Caracelli, 1997). Then there are those who have searched for the single underlying paradigm for mixed methods research. Many have found this paradigm in a traditional U.S. philosophy, pragmatism (Tashakkori & Teddlie, 2003). Others, such as Mertens (2008), believe in the use of a transformative worldview. With my colleague, Plano Clark, I have taken a different perspective (Creswell & Plano Clark, 2007). We see a link between paradigms and methods. Perhaps one paradigm (like pragmatism) serves as an adequate foundation for concurrent or parallel types of designs, while paradigms may shift during a sequential design in which one starts from a postpostivist perspective (quantitative) and then moves to a constructivist (qualitative) worldview (Creswell & Plano Clark, 2007). This linking of paradigms and methods is not appreciated by qualitative researchers who have taken the stance that many different kinds of methods can fit with each type of paradigm (Denzin & Lincoln, 2005). I respect this view but, in practice, I still believe that many researchers choose their methods because of their paradigms that either explicitly or implicitly frame their research.

An exciting new development recently in this paradigm discussion is the emergence of the community-of-scholars idea that has been discussed by Morgan (2007) and Denscombe (2008). I recommend David Morgan's *JMMR* article to you. It is a brilliant piece of scholarship and it was presented at the Cambridge Mixed Methods Conference in 2005 as the keynote address . . .

I also recommend Denscombe's (2008) recent *JMMR* article in which the community-of-scholars idea was reinforced and expanded. He outlined how communities may work using such ideas as shared identity, research problems, networks, knowledge, and informal groupings. I am excited about this line of thinking. It leads to a better understanding of the trend toward fragmentation of the mixed methods field in which various disciplines adopt mixed methods in different ways, create unique practices, and cultivate their own specialized literatures . . .

New Thinking About Research Designs

There has been much development on the topic of mixed methods research designs. I have learned that designs used in practice are much more subtle and nuanced than I had first imagined. When my colleague Vicki Plano Clark and I wrote an introduction to the field for beginning mixed methods researchers (Creswell & Plano Clark, 2007), we discussed four types of designs. Triangulation (or concurrent) designs involve one phase of data collection gathered concurrently. explanatory or exploratory designs require two phases of data collection, quantitative data collection followed sequentially by qualitative data collection (or vice versa). Embedded designs, in which one form of data are embedded within another, may be either a single- or a double-phase design with concurrent or sequential approaches. Along with these designs we now have a notation system (Morse, 1991), visual diagrams, and guidelines for constructing the visual diagrams (Ivankova, Creswell, & Stick, 2006). We now know that these designs are not complex enough to mirror actual practice, although I would argue that they are well suited for researchers initiating their first mixed methods study.

One kind of design with concurrent collection of data.

Another kind of design with consecutive gathering of data.

Complex designs have come to my attention through evaluation researchers. For example, Nastasi and colleagues (2007) have introduced complex evaluation designs with multiple stages and the combination of both sequential and concurrent phases.

This level of detail goes beyond what you need to know to understand a mixed methods approach.

    . . .

He now discusses a different way of thinking about mixed methods.

Another way of viewing designs is to look at mixed methods procedures not as designs but as a set of interactive parts. Based on systems theory, Maxwell and Loomis (2003) conceptualized the interactive five dimensions of the research process consisting of the purpose, the conceptual framework, the questions, the methods, and the issue of validity. Thus design, in their approach, gives way to the process of research for a more full, more expansive view of the way to conceptualize and design mixed methods research. Another approach is the innovative thinking of Hall and Howard (2008). They advanced a synergistic approach in which two or more options interact so that their combined effect is greater than the sum of the individual parts. The core principles of this approach are that the sum of quantitative and qualitative is greater than either approach alone. Instead of looking at mixed methods as a priority of one approach over the other or a weighting of one approach, the researcher considers the equal value and representations of each. Instead of unequal importance of the two approaches, the two are viewed from an ideology of multiple points of view, instead of differences. Collaboration on a mixed methods project means researchers share their areas of expertise. The researcher also balances objectivity with subjectivity. These are all important principles in design.

> In practice, I do not find many examples of the complex designs he discusses here.

The synergistic approach along with other challenges to typological perspectives contribute to a softening of the differences between qualitative and quantitative research, provide answers to questions about dominance of one method over the other (e.g., Denzin & Lincoln, 2005) and honor the formation of research teams with diverse expertise. In the future, I will need to rethink how I am looking at designs for mixed methods researchers.

Advocacy Through Extramural Funding

We have at least 15 books on mixed methods research, and several more are in production. We have several journals devoted to mixed methods research—*Journal of Mixed Methods Research, Quality and Quantity, Field Methods,* and the online journal *International Journal of Multiple Research Approaches.* For *JMMR,* the reception has been outstanding in our 2 years of publications. From January through May 2008, for example, we had 58,000 hits on the journal Web site. According to our publisher, Sage Publications, *JMMR* is tracking like a long-established journal, and the number of table of content alerts (8,900) for every issue is the highest for Sage journals except for one other journal (personal communication, Leah Fargotstein, Sage Publication, June 2008). Mixed methods research is expanding internationally . . .

CONCLUSION AND THE FUTURE

These specific topics are only a few areas in which I feel that future researchers should devote their attention as mixed methods continue to grow. Scholars looking to write a manuscript that contributes to the mixed methods literature may want to start by examining this map and considering where their work may contribute to our current understandings of the field. Undoubtedly, some will criticize my efforts as attempting to fix the field and limit conversation. To them I say that we need my list as well as the lists of topics of many others. This is only a start of the conversation.

As we look into the future, I am reminded as to how the *Handbook of Mixed Methods* (Tashakkori & Teddlie, 2003) ended on a note predicting the future for the field of mixed methods research. Now, 5 years later (and many *JMMR* manuscripts later) I would like to make some predictions about some of my topics and the future of mixed methods research. Here is what I see.

The field of mixed methods will continue to expand across disciplines and fields so that my hypothetical professor in political science that I spoke of earlier will have a discipline-based literature on mixed methods. Generic books about mixed methods will no longer be needed; instead, we will have discipline-based books, such as the recently issued book on mixed methods for nursing and the health sciences (Andrew & Halcomb, 2008). The critics of mixed methods will always be present but the concerns about identity will quiet down. Splinter groups will emerge with specific interests, such as feminist mixed methods researchers or mixed methods software developers. The "Atlantic gap" will not be a problem because people from both sides of the ocean have worked hard, from the beginning, to collaborate. In my opinion, this is different than how qualitative research emerged during the 1980s.

We will look back in several years and see that it was the graduate students who promoted mixed methods research and who taught their faculty the importance of this approach to inquiry and the value of not adhering strictly to either quantitative or qualitative approaches. The students will be more interested in how best to address their research problems than the politics of methodology. Mixed methods techniques will be refined and expanded. For example, we will have many models from which to choose to construct a joint matrix of qualitative and quantitative data. My list of topics will be seen as too brief and too incomplete, much in the way I have talked about the Tashakkori and Teddlie (2003) and the Greene (2007) perspectives. Mixed methods research will no longer be seen as a new approach.

Perhaps mixed methods manuscript writers of the future will have more guidance as to whether their paper contributes to the literature. For those preparing manuscripts, topics of interest will be clearly before the mixed methods community and investigations

Do you think his prediction will hold true?

I wonder what will replace mixed methods research as the "new kid on the block."

will have a foundation of literature on which to build a new manuscript. The future editors of the *JMMR* will not have to respond
with the question, "How does your manuscript contribute to
the literature?" and authors will state, somewhere toward the
beginning of their manuscripts, "Here is how my study makes a
contribution."

Source: Creswell, J. (2009). Editorial: Mapping the field of mixed methods
research. *Journal of Mixed Methods Research, 3*(2), 95–108. Used with permission from SAGE.

Summary and Review

Like the Barone study you read in Chapter 6, this article is not an example of a completed research
study. Rather it addresses some issues related to conducting mixed methods research. I believe
Creswell successfully lays out the argument and presents some of the recent work. Since he has been
contributing to the field of qualitative research for many years, he is in a unique position to see the
issues from many perspectives.

Now that you have read some thoughts about the growth of mixed methods in the last five years, I
want you to read an actual research study using mixed methods. Caitlin Scott and Rosemary E. Sutton
begin with the argument that we need to add qualitative approaches to the arsenal of quantitative
approaches. In particular, they want to look at professional development and the writing process. You
should pay attention to some of the details in their design. They are fairly detailed and complex. I think
they support my earlier contention that many mixed methods studies tend to take a traditional position
with regard to design elements—whether quantitative or qualitative.

In the method section, you will learn the authors used teacher interviews for the qualitative portion.
It is of interest that they do not identify which, if any, of the qualitative research approaches they used.
It strikes me that when they say "qualitative" they do not get into a long-winded explanation of what
they mean. Let's just collect some interviews with teachers. Rather, they have a design with the rather
cumbersome name "equal-status sequential multitype mixed analysis." They provide a reference to this
elaborately named design, but do not tell you what the reference means.

Indeed, more time is spent describing the writing intervention program, the participants, instrumentation,
data collection, and data analysis in Phase 1 (the quantitative portion) than in discussing the research approach.
I am not going to talk any more about the details of the quantitative portion lest I get away from the intention
of my comments.

In Phase 2 they describe the sampling approach—a modified version of sequential mixed methods sampling. They speak about saturation of the data. You may recall that this theoretical saturation idea comes from
grounded theory. Grounded theory approaches were also used in part of the data analysis. Interviews were
semistructured. They used a technique of content analysis for that phase of the project. It strikes me that they
did not follow a particular approach to qualitative research. Instead, they used various techniques associated
with qualitative research.

I do not know for sure, but suspect they chose these fairly conservative qualitative techniques of
gathering and analyzing data because they were combining their research with a quantitative

approach. I have not conducted a systematic analysis of mixed methods research, but I am struck by how many mixed methods studies are more structured and systematic than other qualitative research approaches.

I find the presentation of the qualitative data somewhat disappointing. The results move into the quantitative realm very quickly, almost as though the actual numbers of participants who felt something were very important. This supports my assertion that whether consciously or not, those who use mixed methods tend to be more "quantitative" even in the "qualitative" component of the study.

Article 7.2. Emotions and Change During Professional Development for Teachers: A Mixed Methods Study (2009)

Caitlin Scott and Rosemary E. Sutton

My Expectations

I am drawn to this study. I have read so much about the professional development of teachers—the title of this study suggests that I will be examining emotions. I know how difficult it is to define and measure emotions. Perhaps a combination of qualitative and quantitative can be fruitful. I am hoping to find some new ideas about how researchers can combine the best of both qualitative and quantitative. I am also wondering whether they will select a particular qualitative research approach or rely on a more general one. It has been my experience that many studies using mixed methods do not quite know how to deal with integration of the two. I wonder whether any of Creswell's insights into combining the two ways that I just read about will be used in this study.

ABSTRACT

The abstract is somewhat confusing. I am disappointed that so much emphasis is given to the quantitative aspect of the research. They barely mention qualitative—just a sentence about interviews. I am also wary because they studied so many teachers. I know that qualitative researchers tend to use fewer participants.

Teaching is emotional, especially when teachers must change their practices. Past research on emotions and change in the general population has been predominately quantitative. Research about teachers' emotions, however, has been predominately qualitative. To draw on both these approaches, this mixed methods study examined 50 elementary teachers' emotions during eight workshops on the writing process, by using repeated questionnaires with scale and open-ended questions, follow-up questionnaires 4 months later, and participant interviews. Quantitative data revealed that teachers' emotions became more positive, but returned to initial levels 4 months later. Quantitative data analysis found no relationships between emotions and change in practice. Interviews, however, revealed mixed emotions related to changes found in the quantitative data.

Emotions and Teaching Writing

We know that teaching is an emotionally charged activity and that changing the way teachers teach is extremely difficult (Fullan, 2001; Hargreaves, 1998; Hinde, 2003; Schmidt & Knowles, 1995). In research and theory, however, emotions have proved notoriously hard to define, and considerable debate surrounds definitions and measurement (Meyer & Turner, 2005; Schutz & DeCuir, 2002; Zelenski & Larsen, 2000). Perhaps because of this debate, much of the research about emotions and change in the general population has been primarily quantitative (e.g., Beck & Frankel, 1981; Bless, Bohner, Schwartz, & Strack, 1990; Danner, Snowden, & Friessen, 2001; Wyer, Clore, & Isbell, 1999) as researchers have attempted to measure and define emotions in ways that can be generalized broadly. Past research on teachers and emotions, however, has most frequently used semistructured interviews (Sutton & Wheatley, 2003). Examples of such studies include Day and Leitch (2001), Van Veen and Sleegers (2006), and Casey and Morrow (2004). Although this methodology could be useful, it captures the teachers' reflections on past emotional experiences rather than their moment-by-moment affect and cannot be generalized beyond those interviewed. Given these limitations, many recommend adding quantitative measures, such as observation, questionnaires, and physiological measures to the data collection toolbox for researchers interested in teachers' emotions (Hargreaves, 1998; Meyer & Turner, 2005; Shultz & DeCuir, 2002; Sutton & Wheatley, 2003).

Similarly, in studying strategies to improve student achievement, such as using the writing process to teach writing, Stecher and Borko (2002) argued that past traditions of using large data sets alone to explore the success or failure of reforms have proved incomplete. Instead, they advocated using surveys, which can be used to make generalizations, and in-depth qualitative techniques that bring these generalizations to life and illuminate survey findings. As in the study of emotions, the study of the writing process has been split between primarily quantitative studies that focus mainly on student achievement in writing (e.g., Fan, Graham, & Berninger., 2005; Goldstein & Carr, 1996; Jarmer, Kozol, Nelson, & Salsberry, 2000) and qualitative studies that examine teachers' perceptions of change related to professional development in writing (Comas & Shin, 2005; Hasheweh, 2002; Pease-Alvarez & Samway, 2005). Recent scholarly textbooks have shown ways of successfully combining tools traditionally used exclusively by either quantitative or qualitative researchers (e.g., Creswell, 2003; Tashakkori & Teddlie, 1998). Such a combination of approaches is now needed to more fully explain how teachers' emotions during professional development on the writing process affects teachers.

It might be helpful to discuss why this quantitative approach to measuring emotions is not helpful.

Observations are usually seen as qualitative, but I think the point of the sentence is that they want to gather a variety of data.

The authors do not really specify how they intend to combine the two approaches. As you can see from the Creswell article, in the last several years researchers have become heavily involved in looking at how qualitative and quantitative designs can be accomplished. Like so much that you have read so far, there are no prescribed, generally accepted ways to do this.

They spell out 3 objectives: trends in emotions of teachers; ways in which emotions were related to certain kinds of teaching methods; and contributions of mixed methods. These seem to me somewhat unrelated to each other.

The purposes of this study were (a) to explore trends in teachers' emotions during professional development, (b) to examine the extent to which teachers' emotions during professional development were related to acceptance or rejection of teaching methods using the writing process, and (c) to determine whether using mixed methods could clarify and enhance previous research findings that relied on predominately quantitative or qualitative methods. Despite the empirical evidence on the benefits of teaching writing through the writing process, past research shows that many teachers do not fully adopt the writing process (Comas & Shin, 2005, Goldstein & Carr, 1996, Kozlow & Bellamy, 2004). Exploring teachers' emotions associated with professional development about the writing process may help researchers and professional development providers understand why some teachers do not fully adopt this useful practice. The study was conducted in two phases.

You learn that the study is accomplished in several phases— first they used questionnaires and then they conducted interviews.

The first phase of the study consisted of repeated questionnaires and was confirmatory, in that it tested emotional theories posited by other researchers. Although consensus on the number and nature of discrete emotions has proved difficult to reach (Zelenski & Larsen, 2000), an emerging common practice suggests that emotions can be conceptualized as positively or negatively valenced (e.g., Csikszentmihalyi & Larson, 1987; Gregoire, 2003; Gumora & Arsenio, 2002). Many researchers and theorists have explored the possibility that negative emotions are related to change (e.g., Beck & Frankel, 1981; Bless et al., 1990; Gregoire, 2003) whereas others have focused on how positive emotions are related to change (e.g., Danner et al., 2001; Fredrickson, 1998, 2001; Fredrickson & Joiner, 2002; Wyer et al., 1999). However, little is known about teachers' positive and negative emotions associated with professional development and the likelihood that teachers will adopt the aims of that professional development. Although a number of researchers have examined resistance to change in qualitative case studies (Comas & Shin, 2005; Hasheweh, 2002; Pease-Alvarez & Samway, 2005), few have applied psychological theories to teacher change on a broader scale or have used quantitative measures to examine teachers' reactions to professional development aimed at changing their teaching practices. To connect teachers' emotions to changes in practice, this phase first establishes the trends in teachers' emotions during the professional development and the extent of their reported changes in practice. Then connections between these trends and changes are explored.

This seems like quite a complicated design. Do you think it would be better if they simplified this part?

The purpose of the second phase of the study, which consisted of interviews, was "complementary" as described in Greene, Caracelli, and Graham (1989). More specifically, the qualitative interviews allowed teachers to reflect on the issues of interest in Phase 1: their emotions during professional development on the writing process, changes in their teaching practice, and how emotions related to these changes. By using this approach, this phase was similar to other qualitative studies of teachers and change (e.g., Comas & Shin, 2005; Hasheweh, 2002; Pease-Alvarez & Samway, 2005). However, because these reflections elaborated on the findings in Phase 1, at times providing illustrations and at times clarifying results, the findings were much broader and deeper than a typical study using interview data alone.

This study has an overarching mixed methods question, as well as subquestions for each phase of the study, as recommended by Tashakkori and Creswell (2007). The overarching question was what trends appear in teaches' emotions during professional development and how do these emotions relate to acceptance of the writing process based on a mixed methods design. Subquestions included:

> The authors seemed to apply techniques they learned about conducting mixed methods studies.

Phase 1

1. What are the trends in teachers' emotions during the year in which they are asked to use the writing process?

2. What changes do teachers report in their teaching practices?

3. How are trends in emotions related to changes in practices?

Phase 2

1. How do teachers' reflections on emotions and changes in teacher practices illuminate understanding of the relationships between emotions and change in teacher practices as found in Phase 1?

METHOD

The first phase of this two-phase study was longitudinal, consisting of a prequestionnaire, seven repeated questionnaires given weekly during professional development activities, and a postquestionnaire given 4 months later. The questionnaire included scale and open-ended items. In Phase 2, which occurred directly after the postquestionnaire, qualitative data in the form of teacher interviews were collected and analyzed. The study can be considered an equal-status sequential multitype mixed analysis (Onwuegbuzie, Slate, Leech, & Collins, 2007). This design was necessary to address the overarching question of the study because emotions and change in practice needed to be both rated and described during the professional development as well as reflected on after the professional development.

> By "equal status" I think they mean that both quantitative and qualitative data are seen as equal. Earlier, they said they had 50 teachers. Perhaps later they will discuss whether all were included in all phases of data collection and analysis.

School and Professional Development Context

A total of 50 elementary school teachers in the Centennial School District (CSD), an urban high-poverty school, and in the West Linn

School District (WLSD), a first-ring low-poverty suburban school, attended a series of professional development days on the writing process and were invited to participate in the study. The Community of Writers (COW), a nonprofit community organization, provided the professional development. As described on their Web site, "COW is a teacher support program (K-12) with a goal to improve student writing achievement by improving the quality of writing instruction. The heart of the program is a [multi-day] professional development workshop titled Teacher as Writer. Teachers work with professional writers experienced in the classroom" (COW, 2005).

Do you think the authors should discuss how they gained access to the teachers?

Phase 1

Participants. Of the 50 participants who participated in COW, 44 teachers (or 88%) returned both the pre-and postquestionnaires. Return rates on each of the repeated questionnaires ranged from 33 to 40 (or 62% to 78%). Approximately, 18% of participants were male, whereas 82% were female, and 5% were Latino, whereas 95% were White. Grades from kindergarten through sixth were represented.

I assume they lost people to attrition during the qualitative interviews that they collected later on in the project.

Instrumentation. Two numerical scales and several open-ended questions were used in questionnaires for this study. First, the "positive affect scale" was used to examine teacher emotions. This scale consists of seven emotional opposites and asks participants to rate where their current emotions fall between these opposites on a scale of 1 to 5. The paired emotions included the following: peaceful or irritated, happy or grouchy, hopeful or discouraged, confident or worried, comfortable or tense, fine or miserable, and agreeable or angry. Teachers' emotions were expected to have one dimension ranging from negative to positive. The seven items representing emotions in the prequestionnaire and the repeated questionnaires are treated as one scale, and the Cronbach's alphas ranged from 0.84 to 0.95. The factor structure was explored with a principal components analysis with varimax rotation. The first factor consistently accounted for more than 56% of the variance (eigenvalues greater than 1). Furthermore, factor loadings ranged from 0.5 to 0.9, with most items on most questionnaires loading at 0.7 or better. These findings are consistent with other research using this subscale (Csikszentmihalyi & Larson, 1987; Eaton & Funder, 2001; Larson, Raffaeli, Richards, Ham, & Jewell, 1990; Torquati & Raffaelli, 2004).

The writers include a considerable amount of statistical information about the scales used. If you are not familiar with statistics, you probably are just glossing over the information.

The second scale measured the level of teachers' acceptance of using a list of classroom writing activities that COW had employed to evaluate the program in past years. Teachers were asked to rate how frequently their class did the activities on the list in the past year. The elements include the students (a) using the teacher's writing as a model for their work, (b) brainstorming/prewrites, such as idea webs, fast writes, word games, et cetera, (c) writing rough drafts, (d) revising and editing their own work, (e) learning about the conventions of writing, such as grammar, spelling, mechanics, etcetera, and (f) publishing final work. Using a principal component factor analysis with a varimax rotation, the items did not load reliably on to one dimension; furthermore, like items were not consistently grouped into the same dimensions. Therefore, the items were considered separately.

The pre-, post-, and repeated questionnaires also contained a number of open-ended questions that asked teachers to define the writing process and reflect on their emotions about writing over time. These questions included, "If you wish, take a moment to reflect more fully on your feelings by writing in the space below" (8 participants responded on the repeated questionnaires), "In two or three sentences, please describe your current understanding of the writing process" (40 participants responded on the prequestionnaire and 36 on the postquestionnaire), "In two or three sentences, please describe your emotions about teaching writing" (41 participants responded on the postquestionnaire), and "In two or three sentences, please describe your emotions about your own experience with the writing process during the COW workshop" (44 participants responded on the postquestionnaire).

Data collection. Teachers who attended COW's professional development completed prequestionnaires as well as repeated questionnaires during each professional development session. The prequestionnaires were distributed at the first meeting of each group, and the repeated questionnaires were distributed at seven subsequent meetings of each group. These meetings occurred approximately weekly. A postquestionnaire was completed 4 months after the professional development ended. At one school, the postquestionnaire was completed at a staff meeting. At the other, teachers completed the survey at a special meeting explicitly for completing the postsurvey.

Analysis of quantitative data. To address the first question about trends in teachers' emotions, a longitudinal analysis used these dimensions to examine trends in teachers' emotions as reported in the pre-, repeated, and postquestionnaires. To explore the second question of the study, paired t tests were used to determine the significance of the changes in teachers' practices from the pre- to the postquestionnaire. Correlations were then used to examine the third question of the study and determine the extent to which emotions during professional development predicted changes in teaching methods using the writing process, and multiple linear regressions were expected to be used to determine the predictive values of emotions.

Analysis of open-ended questionnaire items. Open-ended items were used to address the first and second questions of this phase of the study. Extended responses about emotions on the repeated and post-teacher questionnaires were recorded and analyzed across cases using classical content analysis with deductive category application for developing codes (Mayring, 2000). Emotions were coded as positive,

The authors are careful to provide many details about how data were collected. This is something that quantitative researchers tend to do. But if you reflect back on some of the other studies you have read, not all qualitative approaches ascribe to this viewpoint.

They just described a systematic way to analyze qualitative data.

This method comes from a grounded theory approach. You will recall that earlier I suggested grounded theory is the qualitative approach most closely associated with quantitative research designs. It is not surprising to me they chose this approach. Do you think that qualitative researchers new to adopting mixed methods might have a tendency to rely on those qualitative approaches that are considered more systematic and objective? Or, alternatively, do you think that researchers that are drawn to using a mixed methods approach might believe that qualitative approaches that are more objective are "better"? I don't have an answer here—I am just speculating.

Data saturation is a concept from grounded theory.

Tables 1 through 6 have been omitted.

negative, both, or other, to determine the frequency with which participants referred to these emotions. The data from these open-ended items about emotions helped address the first question of the study, which inquired about trends in teachers' emotions, confirming or disconfirming the findings from the scale items.

To examine the second question of Phase 1 about how teachers' defined the writing process, the questionnaire items on the pre-and postquestionnaires asking teachers to define the writing process were analyzed using the constant comparison method (Bogden & Biklen, 2003; Glaser & Strauss, 1967). Classical content analysis was then used to determine the frequency with which each participant referred to each theme, confirming or disconfirming the findings from the scale items.

Phase 2

Participants and data collection. All teachers participating in COW were invited to participate in the qualitative portion of the study. This phase of the study used a modified version of sequential mixed methods sampling as described in Teddlie and Yu (2007), in that a convenience sample was supplemented with a purposeful sample based on the questionnaire findings. Eleven participants volunteered, but one dropped out due to illness. The remaining 10 rated their emotions more positively on average than the rest of the final questionnaire participants. Therefore, an additional 6 participants were recruited who as a group had lower-than-average ratings of positive emotions. This recruitment ensured that those with less than positive feelings were represented. These additional participants also helped ensure saturation of the data.

Interviews were semistructured and asked teachers to describe (a) a writing assignment given in the past week, (b) their students' performance on the assignment, (c) their students' emotions associated with writing, (d) their own emotions associated with teaching writing, (e) their emotions associated with participating in the professional development, including emotions associated with their own writing, and (f) changes they had noticed in the way they teach writing and changes in how their students respond to instruction. The characteristics of participants in interviews are compared with those of the respondents to the prequestionnaire in Table 1 .

Analysis of interviews. Data were analyzed across cases using deductive categories focusing on the two broad themes examined in the research questions: emotions and teacher practices. Classical content analysis (Mayring, 2000) was used to determine the frequency of references to emotion and goal themes across all cases to account for each participant's multiple references to emotions throughout the interviews. The data reflecting emotions were coded as positive, negative, or both. In addition, the situation was coded as the teacher teaching, the teacher writing, or the student writing. Teacher practices were analyzed using the constant comparison method with inductive coding of themes (Bogden & Biklen, 2003; Glaser & Strauss, 1967).

RESULTS

As described in the methodology section of this study, Phase 1 data were collected and analyzed first, followed by the data collection and analysis of Phase 2 data. However, to facilitate later discussion of the findings, the results of Phases 1 and 2 are presented here in tandem: Findings related to the first question in Phase 1 are described followed by the findings of Phase 2, which are related to this question, then the findings related to the second question in Phase 1 are described followed by the related findings of Phase 2, and so on.

Phase 1: Trends in Emotions

Quantitative questionnaire items. From the prequestionnaire to the last repeated questionnaire, the means for teachers' emotions decreased indicating teachers' ratings of emotions associated with teaching writing became more positive. The prequestionnaire mean was 2.37, or about at the midpoint, on a scale of 1 to 5, in which 1 was the most positive rating and 5 was the most negative, but by the last day of professional development, the mean fell to 1.81. A longitudinal analysis was then used to examine the strength of this trend.

. . .

Despite this significant change in teachers' emotions, from approximately the middle of the scale to the more positive end of the scale, teachers' positive emotions were not sustained. The mean of teachers' emotions on the postquestionnaire was 2.19. A paired t test showed that for the 41 participants who completed the emotions measures on both the pre-and posttest, the postquestionnaire mean was not significantly different from the prequestionnaire, $t(41) = 1.78$, $p = .08$ (Figure 1).

Open-ended questionnaire items. The qualitative data analysis showed somewhat different results, perhaps because the qualitative questionnaire items allowed a wide range of responses, whereas the quantitative items forced participants to rate emotions on a continuum from positive to negative. On the open-ended questionnaire items on the postquestionnaire, each written answer to each question was used as a unit of text for analysis and the deductive codes "positive," "negative," "both," and "other" were applied. As shown in Table 2, most teachers' written comments in response to these questions expressed both negative and positive emotions in the same response rather than only positive or only negative emotions.

Sidebar:

You have just read an example of the type of quantitative data that the authors present. I have omitted other similar data, but you can get a sense of what the authors included. Although the information is fairly basic, in my experience it is the kind of information that many do not really understand. Do you see that the authors say that teachers did not experience any difference in emotions after the workshop?

Often, teachers began their comment with a positive or negative statement and then added caveats. For example, a typical response was

> I really enjoy the challenges of teaching writing. I feel the most excited when students can't stop writing, when they are drawn into their work. With that said, I also find it quite hard to have students connect/synthesize it all—this can lead to some frustration on my part.

One teacher directly acknowledged the presence of both negative and positive emotions associated with teaching writing. This teacher wrote, "Mixed bag. . . . Some kids love to write, others struggle. Some days things flow, sometimes . . . they don't."

On the repeated questionnaire item asking teachers to elaborate on their emotions associated with teaching writing, one of the eight comments also contained both negative and positive emotions. The teacher wrote, "I'm enjoying teaching writing. I love writing, and I love teaching. Unfortunately, I have students who are unable to speak in full sentences. . . . Writing is impossible." Of the other comments, one was positive and two were negative; the other four mistakenly talked about writing during COW rather than about teaching writing. Of these, three were negative and one was positive.

Here, the authors use quotations to support their claims—a typical way of presenting qualitative data.

. . .

DISCUSSION

The sections omitted provide detailed results. They are presented in a manner similar to the earlier data. For the sake of our interpretations, we do not need to look at all sections.

This very complex study included a large amount of both quantitative and qualitative data.

Phase 1 showed that emotions became more positive overtime but then returned to initial levels and that these emotions were not related to changes in teacher practices. In Phase 2, the qualitative data showed that teachers' mixed emotions were associated with writing during the professional development, with teaching writing, and with increased empathy for students' positive student emotions. The findings from both phases of the study addressed the study's overarching question: What trends appear in teachers' emotions during professional development, and how do these emotions relate to acceptance of the writing process based on a mixed method design? Considered as a whole, data from this study provide the following answer. When represented on a scale of 1 to 5, emotions during this particular professional development became more positive; however, when emotions were described by teachers they were described as mixed, and these mixed emotions appeared to be associated with some changes in teacher practices. Overarching findings about changes in practice; about trends in emotions; about relationships

Do you think it is confusing that the different types of data yielded somewhat different findings? Does it make sense to you that this would happen? How do you reconcile it?

among mixed emotions, empathy, and change in practice and about research methods are discussed in more detail next.

Changes in Practice

In the following sections, the authors discuss some subareas related to changes in practice, trends in emotions, and research methods.

In comparison with other studies, the current study is most like Kozlow and Bellamy (2004), which found that teachers attempted to adopt the writing process but were not fully successful based on quantitative questionnaires about teacher practices. One plausible explanation of the lack of change in teaching some elements of the writing process could be that teachers already used these practices well and did not need to change. However, an examination of the means for the postquestionnaire items indicates that teachers were engaging students in writing drafts and checking their work for errors in conventions about half the time and in prewriting and revising on average less than half the time. This level of reported use is not supported by the literature on the writing process (i.e., Calkins, 1986; Graves, 1983; Heard, 1989; Temple et al., 1982), which indicates that all these practices are important.

Some changes in teacher practice, however, may have been made more difficult, because teachers attempted to integrate the writing process as presented by COW with their prior knowledge of the six-traits writing evaluation rubric used by Oregon and other states to evaluate writing on state tests. As constructivist's theories show, individuals do not learn a new skill such as teaching using the writing process in a vacuum; instead, individuals integrate new knowledge with prior knowledge (Good & Brophy, 1990). In addition, past studies of professional development for teachers found that lack of links to teachers' past learning hindered professional development efforts (Bredeson & Scribner, 2000; Garet, Porter, Desimore, Birman, & Yoon, 2001). For participants in this study, COW's instructions were being added to what teachers already knew about teaching writing and using the six traits from the Oregon state test. Qualitative data from the current study suggest that including the six traits and other elements taught in professional development are important to understanding the impact of professional development in writing and that, in general, researchers studying professional development should carefully account for teachers' prior knowledge and practices as well as the context in which teachers are teaching, including the demands of state assessments and other accountability measures over which teachers have limited control.

Finally, one of the significant changes in teacher practices appeared to contradict the goals of the professional development—the decrease in publishing. Qualitative data from Phase 2 indicated that some teachers shifted their focus from publishing to sharing. Although this study identifies this phenomenon, it cannot determine whether this change had a positive or negative effect on student writing. On the one hand, lack of publishing may result in students missing the crucial step of creating a polished draft. On the other hand, a focus on sharing may help students develop fluency and free them from the pressures that correctness can create, as described by Elbow (1998). More research would be needed to say whether this were a positive or negative effect of the professional development.

Trends in Emotions

This study also has important lessons for examining teachers' emotions and changes in practice. The current study's assumption in the Phase 1 questionnaire scale items that positive and negative emotions occur along a continuum was based on past research using the positive affect scale (Csikszentmihalyi & Larson, 1987; Eaton & Funder, 2001; Larson et al., 1990; Torquati & Raffaelli, 2004) and a large body of research conceptualizing emotions as positively or negatively valenced (e.g., Diener, 1999; Gumora & Arsenio, 2002; Watson & Clark, 1988). However, in the current study's findings, emotions during professional development are not best conceptualized as occurring along a continuum from positive to negative. Whereas the positive affect scale was unidimensional and had good reliability, the qualitative findings of the current study in both Phases 1 and 2 showed mixed emotions. For example, teachers often made both strongly negative and strongly positive statements when reflecting on professional development or on their teaching.

One reason for these mixed emotions may be the context of the study. In past studies using the positive affect scale, participants were typically college or university students whose emotions were sampled during the course of a normal day or week (Csikszentmihalyi & Larson, 1987; Eaton & Funder, 2001; Larson et al., 1990). The current study surveyed teachers during professional development about changing teaching practices, which is an emotionally intense process (Hargreaves, 1998; Meyer & Turner, 2005; Shultz & DeCuir, 2002; Sutton & Wheatley, 2003). A recent study of teachers' enjoyment and anger (which can be seen as positive and negative emotions, respectively) measured these emotions separately and found that they were significantly predicted by different factors in the classroom, suggesting that for teachers these emotions are different constructs, not unidimensional (Frenzel, Goetz, & Pekrun, 2006). Furthermore, teachers have been found to make more frequent emotional statements, both

The authors do a good job of integrating the related research with their own results.

positive and negative, when discussing reforms that affect their classrooms than when discussing reforms in general (Schmidt & Datnow, 2005). The current study's professional development affected teachers' classrooms directly, so these teachers may have had more frequent mixed emotions than other individuals might have had who were simply going about their normal day-to-day activities in a college or university.

The positive affect scale, which contains only seven items, made the current study's questionnaire compact and, therefore, was minimally intrusive during the professional development activities; however, it may not have captured the nuances of teachers' emotions. Another way to measure teachers' emotions quantitatively would be to use an existing scale, which measures positive and negative emotions separately (e.g., Watson & Clark, 1988). An approach grounded in teachers' work would be to examine teacher interviews about professional development and use their statements about emotions to create a questionnaire (e.g., Schutz, Williams, Hong, Cross, & Osbon, 2006). These suggested measurements are more time intensive and intrusive than the positive affect scale, which contains only seven items. Therefore, fewer measurements would have been possible.

. . .

Research Methods

Without the two-phase, mixed method design, findings from this study could have been misleading. In the first phase, the qualitative findings about emotions could have led to the conclusion that teachers' emotions simply grow more positive about writing during professional development and then return to normal, without considering that a different picture of teachers' emotions might emerge if teachers themselves described their emotions without ranking them on a scale from positive to negative. Mixed emotions were discovered in the qualitative data.

This seems to lend support to the idea of using different kinds of data.

Just as the qualitative data informed and refined the quantitative findings, the qualitative data in Phase 2 was dependent on the analysis of the quantitative data in Phase 1. First, additional participants were recruited to be interviewed based on average ratings of emotions during the professional development. Relying on volunteers or a random sample might not have ensured that teachers with both positive and negative emotions associated with the professional development were interviewed. Second, the quantitative data analysis led to a focused exploration of areas of writing practice that changed according to the questionnaire data: teachers' use of modeling and of final products other than publishing.

The current study is an example of how using mixed methods can enhance and broaden research findings. The first phase of the study tested theories of how emotions relate to changes in practice and found that neither positive nor negative emotions were related to these changes. The second phase explored the findings of the first, using a sample based on the results of the first phase and found that participants often associated mixed emotions with change: a possibility that had not been conceived of or allowed for in the first phase. The current study, however, does not clarify our understanding of teachers' emotions and changes in ways that would make mixed methods unnecessary in future research on this topic. Future research needs to continue to use mixed methods to examine teachers' emotions and practices associated with teaching writing, because researchers and theorists still disagree about these concepts and the terms used to describe them. In research and theory, emotions have proved notoriously difficult to define, and considerable debate surrounds these definitions (Meyer & Turner, 2005; Schutz & DeCuir, 2002; Zelenski & Larsen, 2000).

As discussed previously, many measurements of emotion are based on research in social psychology and rely on experiments with college and university students (e.g., Csikszentmihalyi & Larson, 1987; Eaton & Funder, 2001; Larson et al., 1990; Torquati & Raffaelli, 2004) that may not be applicable to teachers. In addition, the current study found that the traditional elements of the writing process examined in the questionnaire did not fully represent the writing process and that instead teachers referred to elements of six-trait writing evaluation and to elements specific to COW. As a result of this emerging language to describe and understand emotions and teaching writing, research questions involving these topics need to examine the meanings that individual participants construct about the topics as well as the generalizability of these constructed meanings.

Source: Scott, C., & Sutton, R. (2009). Emotions and change during professional development for teachers: A mixed methods study. *Journal of Mixed Methods Research, 3*(2), 151–171. Used with permission from SAGE.

Summary and Review

Scott and Sutton provide a detailed example of how a mixed methods study might be designed and executed. The authors write clearly and you could follow the procedures they used, but in some respects I was surprised by the style of writing. I did not find any of the views or perspective of the authors seeping through: the article about emotions was almost emotionless.

I found myself getting somewhat bogged down in details and losing track of which phase of the study I was reading about.

This recently completed study is quite typical of mixed methods studies I encountered. The authors tend to be objective and remote. The qualitative aspects of the study tend to be forced into a quantitative-type of design. In spite of Creswell's comment that many newer designs intertwine both approaches, in my review of studies I did not find this to be so.

Scott and Sutton begin with a very important topic. While I gained some new insights, I felt somewhat cheated that the qualitative aspects of the study took a secondary position compared to the quantitative. I think the authors could have done a better job of integrating the information from the qualitative and quantitative domains. I thought the methodology strongly emphasized the quantitative component. This study illustrates how some researchers attempt to interweave data using mixed methods.

This is the final time I will examine the four questions that have guided my reading and evaluation throughout these chapters. I read each of the studies with them in mind. I suggest that when you finish reading an article, you need to determine the extent to which you have gained information on which you can rely. One way to decide is to judge whether the research follows a design that makes sense and meets the critical elements expected of it. These elements differ depending on which research approach is taken. As I suggest, sometimes researchers tend to mix elements from several approaches. That is fine. Sometimes, however, insufficient information is provided as to how a study was done or why a study was done in a certain way. In such cases, you might feel less comfortable. It is up to you to decide when the positive aspects of a study outweigh the negatives.

- Does it provide new information and insights related to the topic?
- Is it engaging and written in a clear manner?
- Does it illustrate elements you would expect to find?
- Do the positive aspects of the article outweigh the potential drawbacks?

FINAL COMMENTS

I have presented two articles for you to read in this final chapter. Creswell, a leading writer in the field, offered his views about the state of the field in 2009. I suggest, however, that this is not the only viewpoint. You might read Giddings's cautionary article (2006) in which she states, "Rather than the promotion of more co-operative and complex designs for increasingly complex social and health issues, economic and administrative pressures may lead to demands for the "quick fix" that mixed methods appears to offer" (Giddings, 2006, p. 195). She continues, "Clothed in a semblance of inclusiveness, mixed methods could serve as a cover for the continuing hegemony of positivism, and maintain the marginalisation of non-positivist research methodologies. I argue here that mixed methods as it is currently promoted is not a methodological movement, but a pragmatic research approach that fits most comfortably within a postpositivist epistemology" (Giddings, 2006, p. 196).

I think you would do well to read her complete article to get an alternative viewpoint. Although it was not their intention, I think Scott and Seaton's presentation would support Giddings's viewpoint.

This chapter concludes the presentation of individual articles illustrating different approaches to qualitative research. My intention was to expose you to different ways researchers design and present their research studies. Whether you read a study using ethnography or grounded theory, I hope you have gained insight into the myriad ways that research is conducted. One thing you may have discovered is that the different research approaches are not as distinct as you might have anticipated. Sometimes you may have difficulty discerning how the approaches differ from each other. Part II begins with various excerpts from writers in many disciplines that should help you understand similarities and differences among qualitative research approaches.

You can access the complete articles at www.sagepub.com/lichtmanreadings.

PART II

ISSUES AT THE FOREFRONT OF THE QUALITATIVE RESEARCH FIELD

The immediacy and quantity of information available in 2009 is almost beyond our understanding. That you can enter a term in Google or another search engine and almost immediately gain access to information about the topic is astounding. The power of social networking available through the Internet and other electronic devices enables us to communicate instantaneously with those we know and others we may not yet know. The availability of technological gadgets—some so small they can be carried in your pocket—facilitates the visual display of interactions, events, and life in the global world that defies our understanding.

The accessibility of these techniques to all in the world cannot be underestimated. Even when totalitarian regimes try to silence its people, some voices can still be heard. Even when some governments tried to ban news dissemination by blocking Facebook or YouTube, Twitter was on the spot to let voices be heard. The global community saw the faces of those protestors in the streets of Iran. The global community saw the release of two journalists in North Korea who had tried to speak out about human rights and were punished for their statements only to be released following the delicate negotiations between former President Clinton and President Kim of North Korea.

What does all of this have to do with qualitative research? You might wonder. I suggest that it has a great deal to do with it.

The issues I address here have emerged since the year 2000. Some individuals question the value of qualitative research in general. Others relate to silencing of voices other than those in the mainstream—whether voices of students trying to complete graduate school or views of faculty engaging in research through methods not in the mainstream—were quashed. Still others are concerned with the "right" way to do qualitative research and, particularly, who is to decide which way is "right." Yet others are concerned with protection of individuals and ethics of research.

I believe the power associated with instantaneous access by all and the immediate transmittal of information will result in open discussions and dialogue about these issues and concerns as well as others yet uncovered.

THE SPECIFIC ISSUES

I have identified seven issues that emerged from the enormous body of current writing about qualitative research.

Issue 1. Clarifying research approaches. Scholars continue to write about and define different qualitative research approaches. I decided to go outside the field of education to see what other fields can offer. Here you will read excerpts from nursing and other health fields, and from psychology. I emphasize the three major research approaches—ethnography, phenomenology, and grounded theory—that have been written about most often. After you have completed this section, I hope you will have a clearer understanding of the differences among the three approaches. This issue is addressed in Chapter 8.

Issue 2. Qualitative research in the new millennium. Although qualitative research has become an important field, some appear to want it to go away. In this section, I introduce you to some of the contributors to this seemingly never-ending discussion. This issue is addressed in Chapter 9.

Issue 3. Standards for evaluating qualitative research. I am beginning to believe that many fields have those who claim to know the best way to do something. They make themselves authorities and anoint themselves as keepers of what is good and right. I offer you some ideas from the field on this topic. This issue is addressed in Chapter 10.

Issue 4. Review boards, research ethics, and academic freedom. As review boards have become the keepers of approval in the academic community, some have chosen to become watchdogs. They tend to approve research projects that appear to protect individuals against harm. In so doing, these boards at times err on the side of being so conservative that qualitative researchers have difficulty meeting the rigid standards. They try to keep out only those that they deem to be in keeping with the premise that individuals shall be protected against harm when they are involved in conducting research. In theory, protecting individuals against harm is good. In fact, some boards have gone just too far. I have included some detailed accounts of things gone wrong. This issue is addressed in Chapter 11.

Issue 5. Writing up results. The written word needs to be exciting, not boring. Good writing is riveting. People say they can become immersed in a novel and that hours go by, unnoticed, as they read. But is that true of academic writing? I think not. In this section, I provide examples of alternative writing forms as well as offer some techniques for making your writing more interesting. This issue is addressed in Chapter 12.

Issue 6. Reflexivity. Qualitative researchers continue to write about this issue. They do not all agree on specifics, but most agree that qualitative research becomes stronger with the addition of a reflexive stance. I introduce you to some of the current writing on the issue. This issue is addressed in Chapter 13.

Issue 7. Negotiating through graduate school. Most of you are reading this book because you are students. I have selected a few accounts of the journeys students have taken. I wish I had your account to add to this literature. Perhaps in my next edition . . . . This issue is addressed in Chapter 14.

THE PROCESS I FOLLOWED

I began by establishing criteria for selection of issues. I knew that I wanted issues to be current, so I used an arbitrary earliest date of 2006 as my beginning point. However, some earlier references are included for historical purposes. I also knew that I wanted articles that related to qualitative research. Thus, I focused on those journals that tend to publish in that area. I also added some general journals to the mix—specifically *Harvard Educational Review* and *Educational Researcher.*

In order to identify issues of relevance, I reviewed the tables of contents for the following journals for 2006–09:

- *Educational Researcher*
- *Forum: Qualitative Social Research*
- *Harvard Educational Review*
- *International Journal of Qualitative Studies in Education*
- *International Journal of Qualitative Methods*
- *Qualitative Health Research* (2009 issues only)
- *Qualitative Inquiry*
- *Qualitative Research*
- *The Qualitative Report*

When an issue interested me, I read the article and saved the reference to a new file. As I began to see issues emerging, I organized the articles into issues. Once I had selected an article representing a particular topic, I reviewed its reference list. In this way, my search widened and I added articles.

I was able to use the various search capabilities associated with many of the articles. For example, one helpful search device was to click on "Find other related articles in this journal." In this iterative manner, I developed an extensive list of articles.

Once I had decided on an issue, I reopened my search for related articles. In this way, I branched out more fully into allied health, nursing, communications, business, and related fields.

WRITING IT UP

Each of the issues is presented as a combination of others' and my own words. In some sections, I rely heavily on the words of others. For example, in the chapter on writing, I include many examples from others. In other chapters, I include more of my own thinking and use brief excerpts to show you what others have to say.

EXPLANATIONS

The list of issues is mine. Another writer might have chosen a different set of issues. I recognize there is some overlap between and among issues. Hopefully this will not interfere with your understanding.

The selected articles are of my choosing. I wanted to get a mix of those written by established scholars in the field. At the same time, I also wanted to include scholars who have not written before. I know I have omitted some important writers and ideas. For this I take responsibility. It was not my intention to do an exhaustive review of the literature. To the contrary, I wanted to expose you to some of the current thinking on important issues.

I believe strongly in reflexivity. Of course, my imprint is on this work. It is meant to be. I do not intend this to be a neutral objective piece any more than qualitative research is neutral or objective.

THE FUTURE

I welcome your input on these issues. I hope there are not obviously glaring omissions, but I am always ready to learn. I can be reached at MarilynLichtman09@gmail.com or through the university at mlichtma@vt.edu.

Chapter 8

CLARIFYING RESEARCH APPROACHES

A View From Other Disciplines

I write this chapter fully cognizant that you have just finished reading the first seven chapters of this book, where you found examples of different approaches researchers take when they conduct qualitative studies. I suspect, however, that you still might find yourself confused. The confusion is based on several factors. First, you are new to the field and you may not be clear on differences among the approaches. An equally compelling factor is that researchers themselves may not be clear on differences among approaches. In fact, the differences may become blurred when a researcher actually designs and conducts a study.

I think you might find it informative to read what those in related disciplines have to say about qualitative research.

QUALITATIVE RESEARCH IN GENERAL

I think it is fascinating that the health sciences and nursing disciplines have so widely adopted qualitative methods. We can speculate why. Those working in health-related professions deal directly with patients—not just in a diagnostic manner, but also in a supportive and caring capacity. As such, they are more inclined to talk to people and to listen to what they have to say. Helene Starks and Susan Trinidad (2007) suggest that qualitative research methods "enable health sciences researchers to delve into questions of meaning, examine institutional and social practices and processes, identify barriers and facilitators to change, and discover the reasons for the success or failure of interventions" (p. 1372).

Dave Collingridge and Edwin Gantt (2008) conclude on an optimistic note:

> We are confident that qualitative methods will gain further respect and recognition in medical science as investigators more fully appreciate the fundamental standards of qualitative research, clearly

describe their data analysis techniques, and adopt, when appropriate, clear theoretical frameworks for their investigations. (p. 394)

In providing a definition of a qualitative design, Lisa Broussard (2006) publishes the following in *The Journal of School Nursing:* Qualitative research methods can be used to investigate "broadly stated questions about human experiences and realities studied through sustained contact with persons in their natural environments, and producing rich, descriptive data that help us to understand those persons' experiences" (Boyd, 2001, p. 68, quoted in Broussard, p. 212; see also Spradley, 1980).

Collingridge and Gantt (2008) present a discussion in the *American Journal of Medical Quality*. They acknowledge that:

> in recent years qualitative research has been recognized as making a valuable contribution to medical science. The growing popularity of qualitative research is fueled in part by the realization that traditional quantitative research is limited in its ability to capture the meanings people attach to health care social phenomena, and that understanding the experiential and interpretive elements of medical practice that qualitative research is capable of providing is essential to enhancing clinical knowledge and care. (Collingridge & Gantt, 2008, p. 389)

I have to admit: this last statement surprised me. At a time when some researchers in education are questioning the usefulness of qualitative approaches, here we have the medical profession moving in the opposite direction.

You should find it helpful to examine the way some of these authors compare several widely used qualitative research approaches. I found Starks and Trinidad's comparisons especially useful:

> We have depicted the similarities and differences across the three interpretive approaches in Figure 1. The figure approximates an hourglass, in which greater differences are observed at the beginning and at the end of the research project. The approaches converge in the analytic phase, sharing methodologies for decontextualizing and then recontextualizing data. They then diverge again in the postanalytic phase, in which the research findings are framed and packaged for the target audience. (Starks & Trinidad, 2007, p. 1372)

They compare phenomenology, discourse analysis, and grounded theory. They suggest that the three are similar analytically since they all involve taking data out of context by a coding process and then placing the data in another context through a sorting and coding process. Although the details of coding for grounded theory are spelled out more completely than those for other research approaches, the general process is similar across approaches.

We conclude from these several disciplines that qualitative research is useful in various fields. Starks and Trinidad present additional commentary about the ways in which various approaches are similar to each other.

Now I want to investigate ways in which other disciplines have discussed some of the major approaches to qualitative research. I begin with ethnography. You will notice that my selections are drawn from very recent publications.

MORE ON ETHNOGRAPHY

Writing from a nursing perspective, here is Broussard's (2006) statement on ethnography. She relies heavily on Spradley, who was among the earliest writers in the field. His 1979 work on ethnographic interviewing is a classic. A year later he published his seminal work about participant observation:

Ethnography involves studying a group of people in their own environment. The goal of ethnography is to learn from, rather than about, people of various cultures, religions, and ethnic groups (Spradley, 1980). There is a concern with the meaning and actions of the people being studied, resulting in the description and interpretation of cultural patterns. The researcher takes into account the participant's point of view. A major strategy in ethnography is participant observation. Researchers become the data collection instrument through observation and recording of data. The researcher becomes a participant in the "cultural scene," collecting diaries, journals, records, and other cultural artifacts. Ethnographic research occurs in the environment where the participants live. A fundamental characteristic of ethnography involves physically situating oneself in the environment and surroundings of the group being studied. Fieldwork includes journaling by the participant observer to document observations, feelings, reactions, and biases. Also, interviews of group members may be conducted, taped, and transcribed for analysis by the researcher to gain an understanding of people's viewpoints, beliefs, and practices.

With this research method, data collection and analysis are cyclic in nature. As records, observations, and artifacts are studied, the impetus is created for further study. According to Spradley (1980), ethnographic studies end because time and resources do not allow continuation, not because the researcher has completely described a culture. (Broussard, 2006, p. 213)

I am somewhat surprised she draws so heavily on this early work. No accommodation is made for the burgeoning interest in doing ethnography on the Internet or among social networks such as Facebook.

From a medical perspective, Collinridge and Gantt (2008) also address ethnography. They rely on John Creswell and colleagues' 2007 explanation:

The purpose of ethnography is to understand the behaviors and attitudes of a cultural group. Ethnographers seek this understanding by gaining a native perspective from the inside looking around, rather than from the outside looking in. A native perspective is usually obtained by entering the group's environment to interview people and observe objects, events, and symbols that define the culture and give it meaning. Occasionally, where appropriate, researchers may participate in noteworthy communal events. Most well-constructed ethnographic studies generally follow the following format of data collection and analysis: (a) collecting data through natural observation; (b) creating a textual representation of the data; (c) reading through the text and forming initial codes; (d) analyzing the codes to identify themes and patterns; (e) interpreting the identified themes and patterns; and (f) creating a narrative account that describes the people, places, and important objects and social events that define the culture and give it meaning. (Collinridge & Gantt, 2008, p. 392)

From a social work perspective, Patricia McNamara (2009) informs us about feminist ethnography. Ethnography is "the exploration of culture and subculture through application of qualitative research methods designed to produce thick descriptions" (p. 164). From her viewpoint, "continuity and reflexivity to gender is the key to feminist ethnography" (McNamara, 2009, p. 165).

Angela Garcia and her colleagues (2009) examine ethnography as applied to the Internet. According to them, a huge body of research exists on the Internet, but only some is qualitative in general and only a small portion could be considered ethnographic. They suggest ethnographers need to alter their research techniques for dealing with the Internet. They are concerned that, since ethnographers are not physically present, they cannot use interpersonal skills to understand the social world. They discuss issues of gaining access and managing online presence. For those interested in doing such research, the suggestions offered are extremely helpful.

Ece Algan (2009), from the television and news media, makes a plea for continued use of ethnography in his field:

I am willing to bet that the most criticized area in media studies scholarship must be ethnographic audi-ence research. Criticisms begin with and mostly focus on the term *active audiences*. As Ann Gray (1999, p. 25) stated, emerging as the most familiar trope in reception studies, the term referred to work identi-fied as apolitical, naïve, celebratory, and banal. We have treated this kind of work as ethnography, and then, we rightly admitted that it is not ethnography (Nightingale, 1993; Press, 1997). Today, many of us prefer either not to do ethnographic media research or to simply call it qualitative research and leave out important components, such as a discussion of fieldwork experience and informants' accounts, so we are not labeled as engaging in some sort of "soft" research as opposed to "hard" research like the polit-ical economy of media industry. (Algan, 2009, p. 7)

After citing numerous studies using ethnographic methods, he concludes his brief article with a call for a resumption of a dialogue about how ethnography should be done in media studies.

In the communications field, Damion Waymer (2009) uses autoethnography in his study of the ways in which news coverage on crime can affect minorities who do not live in the inner city. Autoethnography is actually a subset of ethnography. You can read the work of Carolyn Ellis and Art Bochner (2000) to learn more about this approach.

What is the distinguishing feature of ethnography? It is the immersion by the researcher into the culture of those studied in order to learn about the culture. The researcher becomes a "participant observer" in the culture. (I do not want to get into the fine points of how some researchers move back and forth between the roles of participant and observer). Ethnography, like many other qualitative approaches, uses interviews and observations to gather data. Ethnographers also apply some form of coding to look for themes. These data collection strategies are not distinguishing elements of the ethnographic approach.

Question: Why would a researcher choose ethnography?

Answer: To understand the interactions and symbols of a cultural group.

MORE ON PHENOMENOLOGY

Broussard (2006) also writes about phenomenology:

The roots of phenomenology date back to the first decade of the 20th century. The philosophical under-pinnings of phenomenology are the basis of this qualitative research method. The goal of phenome-nology is to achieve a deeper understanding of the nature and meanings of everyday experiences. Its central focus is the lived experience of the world in everyday life. The lived experience presents to the individual what is true or real in his or her life, and gives meaning to the individual's perception of a particular phenomenon (Carpenter, 1999).

The foundations of phenomenological inquiry lie in a holistic study of the human experience as it is lived from the perspective of the individual. Areas of interest that are studied using this approach are those central to human life experiences, such as happiness, fear, and caring. There are many ways to proceed with a phenomenological study, and the chosen method is based on the area of interest. According to Spiegelberg (1975), descriptive phenomenology comprises a three step process: intuiting, analyzing, and describing. Intuiting requires that the researcher become totally immersed in the phe-nomenon of interest. It is the process by which the researcher begins to know about the phenomenon as described by the study participants. In the analysis process, the researcher identifies the essence of the phenomenon under investigation based on the data obtained and how it is presented. Relationships are explored and connections are made with related phenomenon. The third step, describing, aims to communicate and bring to written and verbal description the critical elements of the phenomenon. Classification or grouping of the phenomenon provides the basis of description. The holistic perspective and appreciation of experiences as lived by humans make this research approach highly appropriate for the study of topics central to nursing. (Broussard, 2006, p. 214)

Starks and Trinidad (2007) offer the following comments about phenomenology:

Phenomenology is rooted in early 20th-century European philosophy. It involves the use of thick description and close analysis of lived experience to understand how meaning is created through embodied perception (Sokolowski, 2000; Stewart & Mickunas, 1974). Phenomenology contributes to deeper understanding of lived experiences by exposing taken-for-granted assumptions about these ways of knowing.

In phenomenology reality is comprehended through embodied experience. Through close examination of individual experiences, phenomenological analysts seek to capture the meaning and common features, or essences, of an experience or event. The truth of the event, as an abstract entity, is subjective and knowable only through embodied perception; we create meaning through the experience of moving through space and across time. The phenomenological perspective is nicely captured in a remark attributed to Einstein that expresses the difference between embodied time and chronologic time: Put your hand on a hot stove for a minute and it seems like an hour. Sit with a pretty girl for an hour and it seems like a minute. That's relativity. (Starks & Trinidad, 2007, pp. 1373–1374)

Collingridge and Gantt (2008) offer this statement:

The purpose of phenomenology is to understand phenomena from the perspective of those who experience the phenomena. Specifically, the aim is to know an experience the way that the participants know it, to understand the meanings they attach to their experiences, and to capture the essence of a phenomenon as they experience it. This understanding is primarily achieved through interpersonal interviews. "Interviews are particularly suited for studying people's understandings of the meanings in their lived world, describing their experiences and self-understanding, and clarifying and elaborating their own perspective on their lived world." Most well-constructed phenomenological studies generally utilize the following data collection and analysis process: (a) interpersonal interviews with up to 10 people who are willing to share their experiences, (b) transcribing the interview data, (c) locating relevant statements in the transcripts that express self-contained units of meaning, (d) identifying the meanings contained in each statement, (e) synthesizing the meaning units into common themes, and (f) synthesizing the themes across interviews to create a general description of what it is like to experience the phenomenon of interest. (Collingridge & Gantt, 2008, p. 393)

This definition comes from Creswell and colleagues (2007):

In both phenomenology and grounded theory we collect the views of a number of participants. However, instead of theorizing from these views and generating a theoretical model, phenomenologists describe what all participants have in common as they experience a phenomenon (e.g., grief, anger). In this way, phenomenologists work much more from the participants' specific statements and experiences rather than abstracting from their statements to construct a model from the researcher's interpretations as in grounded theory. The basic purpose of phenomenology is to reduce the experiences of persons with a phenomenon to a description of the universal essence (a "grasp of the very nature of the thing"; van Manen, 1990, p. 177). To this end, qualitative researchers identify a phenomenon (an "object" of human experience; van Manen, 1990, p. 163). This human experience may be phenomena such as insomnia, exclusion, anger, or undergoing coronary artery bypass surgery (Moustakas, 1994). (Creswell et al., 2007 p. 252)

What is the distinguishing feature of phenomenology? It is the investigation of the essence of the lived experience of individuals related to a particular phenomenon. The researcher, through interacting with the participants, begins to understand a particular phenomenon. Rather than becoming immersed in the culture as one would do if conducting ethnographic research, , one becomes immersed in a phenomenon when conducting phenomenologic research. Ultimately, the goal is to understand the essence of a phenomenon from the viewpoint of participants.

Sebnem Cilesiz (2009) uses phenomenology to study the essence of experiences at Internet cafés. She provides a detailed description of the process she followed. Here are some of her words about phenomenology:

> I used a phenomenological framework and methodology (Husserl, 1969, 1970a, 1970b; Moustakas, 1994) to study adolescents' lived experiences of educational uses of computers at Internet cafés. A phenomenon is the object of a conscious subject's experience as it presents itself (Moustakas, 1994). Phenomenology dates back to the beginning of the 20th century and includes *transcendental, existential,* and *hermeneutic* traditions (Audi, 2001; Schwandt, 1997). This study uses the transcendental phenomenological framework developed by Edmund Husserl, which I hereafter refer to as *phenomenology*. Phenomenology was a suitable methodology for the purposes of this study for two reasons. First, it is concerned with lived experiences and seeks reality in individuals' narratives of their experiences of and feelings about specific phenomena, producing their in-depth descriptions. Second, phenomenology is the study of the *lifeworld* (*Lebenswelt*), defined as "what we know best, what is always taken for granted in all human life, always familiar to us in its typology through experience" (Husserl, 1970a, pp. 123–124). Everyday experiences of educational uses of computers at Internet cafés are embedded in the participants' lifeworlds. Phenomenology is a systematic attempt to come in direct contact with these worlds, uncover and describe the meaning structures of lived experiences, and arrive at a deeper understanding of the nature or meaning of everyday mundane experience of phenomena (Lauer, 1965; van Manen, 1990). In doing so, it is concerned with the a priori or intuitive basis of knowledge (Crotty, 1998; Husserl, 1969). "An epistemological investigation that can seriously claim to be scientific must satisfy the principle of freedom from suppositions" (Husserl, 1970b, p. 263). This is accomplished by engaging in *epoche* (or bracketing), meaning disciplined, systematic efforts to suspend one's natural standpoint and prejudgments regarding the phenomenon being investigated (Husserl, 1969; Moustakas, 1994). (Cilesiz, 2009, p. 240)

You can see this approach is quite complex and philosophical. I suspect a number of researchers conduct what they see as this kind of study without ever really understanding the writings of some of the major contributors.

Question: Why would a researcher choose phenomenology?

Answer: To understand the essence of a phenomenon

MORE ON GROUNDED THEORY

Creswell (2007) has written extensively about various research approaches. Here is his definition of grounded theory:

Our TI multiple-case study provided an in-depth description and thematic analysis of four counselors. Although each counselor likely approached reporting negative results to clients differently, was there an underlying process common to all of them? If we were to select a larger number of counselors to study, we might develop a theory that explains processes that they have in common, a valuable aid for practitioners in the field as well as for students in training. This theory would be "grounded," or derived from participant data (Strauss & Corbin, 1998). Grounded theory is a qualitative research design in which the inquirer generates a general explanation (a theory) of a process, action, or interaction shaped by the views of a large number of participants. (Creswell, 2007, pp. 248–249; see also Strauss & Corbin, 1998)

Here is Broussard's (2006) statement:

The grounded theory approach to qualitative research explores social processes that occur within human interactions. The goal of grounded theory is to develop theory that is grounded in data systematically gathered and analyzed (Strauss & Corbin, 1998). . . . The task of grounded theory researchers is to discover and to conceptualize the essence of complex interactional processes, resulting in the emergence of a theory that offers a new way of understanding the observations from which it was generated (Hutchinson & Wilson, 2001).

There are five basic steps in the process of grounded theory research: collection of data, formation of concept, concept development, concept modification and integration, and reporting of findings. The researcher collects data through interviews, field notes, and memos. The constant comparison method of data analysis is used in grounded theory, meaning that data are analyzed as they are collected. In grounded theory, each new datum is compared with data previously collected for the purpose of concept formation, which involves codes, categories, and identification of a basic social process. As the concept is developed further, the researcher continues to collect data from participants who will provide more insight and understanding about the concept. Based on subsequent data collected and analyzed, the concept is modified. The existing literature is then studied within the framework of research findings, and a core variable is identified. This provides the basis for the development of the middle-range grounded theory. A major strength of grounded theory as a research method is that it is concerned with how participants create and respond to experiences, rather than what they think or how they perceive the world and their daily experiences, as with ethnography and phenomenology (Morse, 2001). (Broussard, 2006, p. 214)

What is critical about this process is that by using the constant comparison method the researcher gathers data, begins the analysis, gathers additional data, and continues to move back and forth between the tasks until at some point he or she reaches what is called theoretical saturation. If a researcher really follows this process, then the cyclical nature of the analysis is a distinguishing feature of grounded theory.

Starks and Trinidad (2007) also offer their views on grounded theory:

Grounded theory originates from sociology, specifically from symbolic interactionism, which posits that meaning is negotiated and understood through interactions with others in social processes (Blumer, 1986; Dey, 1999; Jeon, 2004). These social processes have structures, implied or explicit codes of conduct, and procedures that circumscribe how interactions unfold and shape the meaning that comes from them. The goal of grounded theory is to develop an explanatory theory of basic social processes, studied in the environments in which they take place (Glaser & Strauss, 1967). Grounded theory examines the "six Cs" of social processes (causes, contexts, contingencies, consequences, covariances, and conditions) to understand the patterns and relationships among these elements (Strauss & Corbin, 1998). Within this approach knowledge of social realities is achieved through careful observation of behavior and speech practices. (Starks & Trinidad, 2007, p. 1374)

From this explanation, you can see that grounded theory is concerned with social processes. However, most authors do not introduce this idea. Collingridge and Gantt (2008) also discuss grounded theory:

> The purpose of grounded theory is to build or expand on theories about human phenomena. Grounded theory research is unique in the sense that it is an iterative process wherein the grounded theorist continually goes back to the field to collect more data and answer new questions. This process continues until no new information is gleaned during the data gathering process. As the information is collected and organized "into a logical, systematic, and explanatory scheme," thematic categories begin to emerge. The categories are eventually organized into a comprehensive whole, thus creating a substantive theory grounded in the experiences of those familiar with the phenomenon of interest. Most grounded theorists generally go along with the following process of data gathering and analysis: (a) interviews with 20 to 30 people who are familiar with the phenomenon of interest; (b) transcribing the interview data; (c) open coding, which involves identifying relevant concepts in the text; (d) constantly comparing open codes looking for conceptual similarities and differences; (e) identifying emerging theoretical concepts; (f) continued sampling and interviewing as theoretical categories emerge and novel questions arise; (g) continued coding and comparison of codes until nothing new is added to the theoretical categories; and (h) synthesizing the theoretical categories in a coherent fashion, including defining core categories, visually displaying relationships between categories, and linking theoretical concepts to the existing literature. (Collingridge & Gantt, 2008, pp. 393–394)

Broussard asserts that of all the various qualitative approaches, grounded theory predominates. Kyung Shin, Mi Kim, and Seung Chung (2009), in their analysis of published qualitative studies, support this assertion. They grouped articles by research approach. Of the 135 articles they examined, 23% were listed as using grounded theory, 14% as using phenomenology, with the rest spread across various approaches.

The distinguishing feature of grounded theory is the systematic technique of gathering and analyzing data that leads to the development of theory. I think what appeals to many about grounded theory is that it specifies ways in which data are analyzed. Whereas ethnography and phenomenology are silent about how to analyze data, a grounded theory approach offers more specific information about coding. It is not always easy to follow how to do the analysis, however. Just when I thought I had identified something that distinguished among approaches, Starks and Trinidad contradict my statement. According to them, "The general methods of interpretation are fairly similar across the three approaches. . . . All three interpretive methods distill textual data to a set of categories or concepts from which the final product can be drawn" (Starks & Trinidad, 2007, p. 1375).

Question: Why would a researcher choose grounded theory?

Answer: To generate theory that is based on data collected from the field.

INFLUENCE FROM PSYCHOLOGY

Although I had read compelling pieces earlier than 2000 (especially Lisa Hoshmand's review of alternate research paradigms in 1989), it was the American Psychological Association's publication in 2003 of an edited volume entitled *Qualitative Research in Psychology* that led me and others to see that the field of education was not alone in finding utility and value in qualitative research.

Some psychology journals have published special sections or issues on the topic of qualitative research. One example is the 1994 special section in *The Counseling Psychologist* and a 2005 issue in the *Journal of Counseling Psychology. The Counseling Psychologist's* March and May 2007 special issues also are devoted to qualitative research. In contrast to publications in the allied health professions, their goal was to address overarching topics rather than specific approaches. It would be well beyond the scope of this chapter to talk about these articles in depth.

In 2007, Susan Morrow asserts that counseling psychology has been in the forefront of psychology calling for greater diversity in methodology. She speaks of the need to explore the depth and complexity of the human experience. She puts her position up front. For her, qualitative approaches offer an avenue to "understand the meanings that oppressed people made of their experiences and give voice to people who had been traditionally marginalized, made invisible, or silenced" (Morrow, 2007, p. 210). It is so interesting that Morrow believes that foundational aspects of qualitative research vis-à-vis counseling psychology are drawn from the fields of anthropology, sociology, and education (p. 212). I believe that education originally adopted models from psychology to use as appropriate research paradigms.

I urge you to read Creswell and colleagues (2007). They compare and contrast narrative research, case study, grounded theory, phenomenology, and participatory action research. This is almost a dizzying array of material to comprehend.

Distinguishing Among Research Approaches

Three research approaches have been the subject of many articles in the fields of nursing, allied health, and psychology. Ethnography, phenomenology, and grounded theory have been discussed to a considerable extent by many authors. In this chapter, I have provided you with many examples by different writers in different fields so you can come to understand the nuances of the various approaches. But I return to the initial point I made at the beginning of this chapter. When you actually read a completed research study, I am not sure you can distinguish the research approach used by the author. Often the researcher includes a section about the approach. In reality, the process or strategy for doing the research is quite similar among the several approaches. Researchers gather data, analyze data, and look for essential themes. While there are some differences in process for those conducting grounded theory (using the constant comparison method, for example), this distinction may not be very obvious.

So where are the differences? They are ultimately in the direction and purpose for doing the research. Ethnographers study culture; phenomenologists study the essence of lived experience; grounded theorists look at theory relating to basic social processes (relying on symbolic interaction).

References

Algan, E. (2009). What of ethnography? *Television & News Media, 10*(1), 7–9.

Bonds, M. (2007). Looking beyond the numbers: The struggles of black businesses to survive: A qualitative approach. *Journal of Black Studies, 37*(5), 581–601.

Broussard, L. (2006). Understanding qualitative research: A school nurse perspective. *The Journal of School Nursing, 22*(4), 212–218.

Cilesiz, S. (2009). Educational computer use in leisure contexts: A phenomenological study of adolescents' experiences at Internet cafés. *American Educational Research Journal, 46*(1), 232–274.

Collingridge, D., & Gantt, E. (2008). The quality of qualitative research. *American Journal of Medical Quality, 23*(5), 389–395.

Creswell, J., Hanson, W. E., Clark Plano, V. L., Morales, A. (2007). Qualitative research designs: Selection and implementation. *The Counseling Psychologist, 35*(2), 236–264.

Ellis, C. & Bochner, A. (2000). Autoethnography, personal narrative, reflexivity: Researcher as subject. In N. Denzin & Y. Lincoln (Eds.), *The SAGE handbook of qualitative research* (2nd ed.) (pp. 733–768). Newbury Park, CA: Sage.

Garcia, A., Standlee, A., Bechkoff, J., & Cui, Y. (2009). Ethnographic approaches to the Internet and computer-mediated communication. *Journal of Contemporary Ethnography, 38*(1), 52–84.

Graves, L. (2007). The affordances of blogging: A case study in culture and technological effects. *Journal of Communication Inquiry, 31*(4), 331–346.

Hoshmand, L. (1989). Alternative research paradigms: A review and teaching proposal. *The Counseling Psychologist, 17,* 3–79.

McNamara, P. (2009). Feminist ethnography: Storytelling that makes a difference. *Qualitative Social Work, 8*(2), 161–177.

Morrow, S. (2007). Qualitative research in counseling psychology: conceptual foundations. *The Counseling Psychologist, 35*(2), 209–235.

Phillips, N., Sewell, G., & Jaynes, S., (2008). Applying critical discourse analysis in strategic management research. *Organizational Research Methods, 11*(4), 770–789.

Shin, K., Kim, M., & Chung, S. (2009). Methods and strategies utilized in published qualitative research. *Qualitative Health Research, 19*(6), 850–858.

Spradley, J. (1979). *The ethnographic interview.* New York: Holt, Rinehart and Winston.

Spradley, J. (1980). Participant observation. Orlando: Harcourt, Brace, Jovanovich.

Starks, H., & Trinidad, S. (2007). Choose your method: A comparison of phenomenology, discourse analysis, and grounded theory. *Qualitative Health Research, 17*(10), 1372–1380.

Waymer, D. (2009). Walking in fear: An autoethnographic account of media framing of inner-city crime. *Journal of Communication Inquiry, 33*(2), 169–184.

Source: All extracts in this chapter are reprinted with permission.

Chapter 9

QUALITATIVE RESEARCH IN THE NEW MILLENNIUM

I
t has been almost 30 years since the original discussion about research paradigms began to appear in the research literature. Beginning in the 1980s, the research community has seen an explosion of journals, books, and articles under the general topic of qualitative research. While initially many researchers equated qualitative research with ethnography, the term "qualitative research" soon became an umbrella term under which many different research approaches, paradigms, traditions, or philosophies could be classified.

One reason it is so difficult to talk about qualitative research is that it is not a single thing. In Part I of this book, I presented examples of research articles that purported to use a particular research design or approach. In fact, as you read the articles you saw there was some overlap among the techniques for gathering and analyzing data. For example, while ethnography focused on the study of culture, it made use of interviews and observations in order to gather data. Similarly, phenomenology—the study of the essence of the lived experiences of individuals—also often used interviews and observations.

Researchers have also creatively combined two or more research approaches in a single study. You may have come across an ethnographic case study, or encountered phenomenology joined with a narrative approach. Some researchers have created variations on these basic research approaches. I have read of autoethnography, existential phenomenology, or performance ethnography.

Some qualitative research does not rely on a research design or approach at all. Rather, its emphasis might be on recognition of power issues or making social change, or on studying marginalized individuals. Other research approaches are concerned with the role of the researcher and issues about the influence of that role on the questions posed, the data collected, and analyses and interpretations. Often called reflexivity, many qualitative researchers address the topic. Here you might read of critical theorists or feminists or participatory researchers.

What is clear, however, is that there are some common elements to all types of qualitative research. I have written about these before, but let me reiterate:

Research is conducted in natural settings.

Research is nonexperimental.

Research is not about testing hypotheses.

Process is inductive moving from data to themes or theory.

The number of participants is usually small.

Participants are usually selected in a nonrandom manner.

The researcher relies on interviews, observations, and records for data.

Statistics usually are not used for data analysis.

Specific procedures for data analysis are not often articulated.

The role of researcher is critical.

Evaluation standards are different from standards for experimental research.

Emerging on the scene within the past 10 years or so is a new movement—a compromise position taken by some. It is called mixed methods methodology. Initially, it was fairly straightforward: rather than doing one or the other, why not do both? As scholars became more thoughtful about the topic, they addressed how the two research paradigms could complement each other. My own view, however, is that qualitative research continues to take a backseat to quantitative research in mixed methods articles.

However, just when it seemed as though some in the academic community had resolved the tensions between qualitative and quantitative research, a kind of backlash emerged.

I think you can take away these key ideas:

- There continues to be a proliferation of different research paradigms under the rubric qualitative research. While this is not necessarily a bad thing, it makes it somewhat difficult for the larger community to get a clear understanding of what qualitative research is.

- Qualitative research is under siege and some in positions of power want it to go away. It seems to me these are old arguments about qualitative research not being scientific, not being rigorous, and not having any clear standards. Some even refer to it as prescientific. The qualitative research community continues to search for ways to address the criticisms.

- In spite of this return toward experimental research, qualitative research is not going away. Its voices are too powerful to be silenced. There is no agreement among the community as to how to proceed, but many believe that multiple voices have great strength.

It is to your advantage to read about some of this history so you can understand how the current state of things fits into the larger context of the development of qualitative research. Judith Preissle (2006) provides an account that spans 4 decades.

In 2006, *The International Journal of Qualitative Studies in Education* devoted its first issue of the year (volume 19, number 1) to a discussion of paradigm proliferations. Its last issue that year (volume 19, number 6) addressed the state of qualitative inquiry. Both issues present articles offering a variety of viewpoints. In 2008, the same journal devoted another issue (volume 21, number 4) to the state of qualitative research in the 21st century.

It might help you to understand if you read a little about the history of qualitative research. Norman Denzin (2008) begins with a discussion of the original wars that emerged in the 1980s. The arguments offered then were that qualitative and quantitative paradigms were fundamentally different from each other in terms of the way they viewed the world. As such, they were incompatible. Part of the reason that qualitative (especially ethnographic) paradigms emerged was that quantitative paradigms did not provide answers to educational questions. Another reason was the rise of the feminist movement, which questioned power issues. Coupled with this was the push by marginalized others to have their voices heard.

By the 1990s, there was a proliferation of published works in the qualitative realm. A compromised middle ground appeared by the end of the last century with the movement toward mixed methods. But Denzin says that there is also another position emerging at this time—one that involves what he calls "critical interpretive social science traditions." Operating during this same period, the movement toward traditional, scientifically based research emerged as a force. Denzin comments—and I agree with him—that this movement took us back to the old debates that led to the incompatibility thesis. Either there is science or there is not.

Denzin suggests we now have another group emerging along with the scientific group and the mixed methods group. He refers to these as interpretive researchers. Labels you might find include critical constructionists, feminists, or oral historians. He refers to "scholars in a different space." They are not concerned with traditional issues of reliability or validity—they are interested in movement and action.

Amos Hatch (2006) argues that changes have occurred historically through four phases. Change begins with a return to conservatism and a backlash against the negative consequences of postmodernism. He talks about a return to what I would call simpler times—what he calls "modern ways of thinking about knowledge, knowing and research methods" (Hatch, 2006, p. 404). He reminds us that positive science is one of "modernity's greatest accomplishments" (p. 404). However, according to Hatch, "Postmodern thinkers deconstructed the illusion of progress and the façade of scientific objectivity. They exposed the inseparable connections between knowledge and power and opened the door to alternative ways of thinking about and doing research" (p. 405).

It would be too simple to suggest that all postpositivists are conservative—they are not, says Hatch. One consequence of the conservative nature of many postpositivists is that the standards of worth that are being imposed have led to a movement to develop standards for qualitative inquiry. Hatch suggests that the mixed methods group has been helpful to catalogue interpretive criteria.

Hatch suggests there has been a kind of postmodern paralysis in which fewer people are actually doing qualitative inquiry. In fact, Hatch wants this group to fight back. He suggests that qualitative researchers need to regain control over what is meant by research.

Several researchers respond to Hatch: Carolyn Clark and Jim Scheurich (2008) introduce the themed issue by suggesting that Denzin's remarks call for a dialogue rather than for the war or call to action proposed by Hatch. While Denzin (2008) does not agree with Hatch's assertions that people are not engaging in qualitative inquiry, he does support the idea of forming alliances among the major groups to work together. Choosing sides is the watchword offered by Handel Wright (2006). He says that in the current state one can either be complicit with or resistant to the government's push toward positivism.

It is clear that this war, dialogue, or debate—whatever you want to call it—is ongoing. It seems to me that qualitative research paradigms are not going away any time soon. There are too many voices, too many diverse viewpoints, and too many global initiatives to allow those who have fought so long for a platform to be silenced.

As novices in this field, it may be time for you to think about your own contribution. This is certainly a field that is fluid, dynamic, and challenging.

REFERENCES

Clark, C., & Scheurich, J., (2008). The state of qualitative research in the early twenty-first century. *International Journal of Qualitative Studies in Education, 21*(4), 313.

Denzin, N. (2008). The new paradigm dialogs and qualitative inquiry. *International Journal of Qualitative Studies in Education, 21*(4), 315–325.

Hatch, A. (2006). Qualitative studies in the era of scientifically based research: Musings of a former QSE editor. *International Journal of Qualitative Studies in Education, 19*(4), 403–7.

Preissle, J. (2006). Envisioning qualitative inquiry: a view across four decades. *International Journal of Qualitative Studies in Education, 19*(6), 685–95.

Wright, H. (2006). Are we (t)here yet? Qualitative research in education's profuse and contested present. *International Journal of Qualitative Studies in Education, 19*(6), 793–802.

Source: All extracts in this chapter are reprinted with permission.

Chapter 10

STANDARDS FOR EVALUATING QUALITATIVE RESEARCH

At times I feel as though we are moving backwards. For so many years, qualitative researchers were in a defensive position, explaining to their more traditional peers that what they were doing had a place in the world of research. Through an evolutionary process, the general field of qualitative research has made great strides since the 1980s. New books, journals, and numerous articles have been written since that time. Although admittedly a hydra, I think qualitative research is here to stay.

Although a number of scholars (many of whom have caught the ear of policy makers in the United States and abroad) have argued that qualitative research is not properly scientific and objective and that we should move away from a qualitative position and adopt this more traditional "scientific" stance, Margaret Eisenhart's (2006) thoughtful article points up some limits of experimental research. Furthermore, she suggests that other forms of research are just as likely as quantitative research to provide useful information in education. But her position is not accepted by those who say we must have proper evidence on which to base our decisions about what works in schools. So we have two camps: One view is that we need to move toward accepting evidence only from traditionally based research. The other view is that traditional research is fraught with problems and is not free from influences of culture—rather, alternative modes of research need to be heard. In this chapter, I offer you some of the writing of those who take this latter position.

There appears to be a conservative movement among some, especially at the federal government level, to return to scientific, controlled experiments. To some extent, the No Child Left Behind Act of 2001 fuels this movement. The movement has also been influenced by the National Research Council's publication in the United Kingdom. The group of articles under *The Debate* addresses these issues.

THE DEBATE

Yvonna Lincoln and Gaile Cannella (2004) comment on this backlash:

> Recent legislative and executive orders that mandate preferred methods for evaluating the No Child Left Behind Act of 2001 signal a much larger movement in the social sciences. Attacks stemming from the

"culture wars" of the 1990s have spread to forms of research labeled "unscientific," including post-modern research and qualitative research. Examination of the sources of the attacks reveals a wide net-work of new and recent foundations with decidedly right-wing political views, the establishment and growing power of the National Association of Scholars, and other well-funded efforts to discredit research that uncovers and exposes deep inequities in social life and schooling on gender, race, social class, religion, and/or sexual orientation. (Lincoln & Cannella, 2004, p. 175)

Perhaps you will find this background that Lincoln and Canella (2004) offer helpful:

Qualitative researchers have long grown accustomed to answering for the kinds of research they pro-duce to a variety of audiences: experimental researchers, philosophical positivists and postpositivists, statisticians, and others, many of whom simply do not understand the purposes, practices, products, or methods of qualitative research. This is not difficult to understand, as many senior researchers were never exposed to qualitative research training in graduate school, had few models to study, and have established for themselves strong reputations using conventional research methods and models. In the same vein, the attachment of educational research to earlier psychological models, which in the begin-ning of the 20th century adopted behaviorism from the natural sciences, creates a social infrastructure that precludes easy acceptance of experimental, qualitative, or any nonconventional paradigms or methods for research. We all continue to have colleagues who believe that the purpose of qualitative research is to provide information for future quantitative studies—who confuse inference and general-izability with constructs such as trustworthiness or credibility—who will go to their graves claiming that cultural studies research in education is not research while at the same time accepting ethnography. (Lincoln & Cannella, 2004, pp.175–176)

This fourth reason for the association of qualitative research with academic "evils" is likely the most powerful reason qualitative research has now become nearly as big a threat to the radical Right as mul-ticulturalism. The deep levels of understanding of social phenomena associated with well-done quali-tative research, as well as the deconstructive, probing nature of that understanding, prove a wedge of support for reform of existing social arrangements. Reform efforts once again threaten to topple extant regimes of power and provide fodder for a right-wing backlash. (Lincoln & Cannella, 2004, p. 181)

Research is not only political, it has never been more politicized than in the present. To the extent that we abandon the Holy Grail of objectivity and move toward understanding the uses to which research is being deployed—both research *qua* inquiry and research as a weapon of policy discourse and policy construction—the more effectively we are able to enter the public discourse arena and defend not only qualitative research but also its ability to penetrate the social veils that mask oppressive, inequitable, and unjust social practices. Recognizing both the political and politicized nature of research discourses cir-culating provides additional sophistication regarding the shape and form of our own discourses and actions, furthers the ability of scholars to "speak in different registers" (i.e., shift discursive structures to vary with the audience being addressed), and has the power to circumvent a one-sided public policy discourse now being dominated by the political Right. (Lincoln & Cannella, 2004, p. 197)

Lincoln and Canella suggest that these attacks can be attributed to right-wing movements aimed at discrediting research findings about inequities of school, especially related to gender, race, social class, and so on. I am not sure if it is really a right-wing conspiracy, although at times it might feel that way. One reason, they suggest, is that understanding social phenomena through a deconstructive qual-itative scheme may lead to fundamental changes in the nature of schooling. They continue speaking about political and power issues. Perhaps by now you might accept that conducting research is not a neutral activity, but that it exists in a larger social and political milieu, and that power and control are part of all research.

Patti Lather (2004) also is concerned with this movement toward conservatism. She lays out her argument in this way:

> In taking on these latest twists and turns in governmental efforts to effect educational research, the reductionisms of positivism, empiricism, and objectivism are assumed. I do not want to rehearse the various critiques of scientism that have arisen in the 30-plus years since Thomas B. Kuhn's (1970) *The Structure of Scientific Revolutions*. Instead, I ask three questions about what I find to be a profoundly troubling situation. First, what is happening to make me willing to return to the scene of my doctoral training in evaluation methods some 20 years ago, to immerse myself in the language of "treatment homogeneity," "setting invariance," the "promiscuous" use of quasi experiments (Cook & Payne, 2002, p. 173), and my favorite, "inadvertent treatment crossovers," in this case of a principal in the treatment condition married to someone in the control school (Cook & Payne, 2002, p. 163)? Secondly, what are the implications for qualitative research of the NRC report, a report that intended a "catholic view toward research methods" in delineating "high quality science" (Shavelson, Phillips, Towne, & Feuer, 2003, p. 25)? Finally, how might the federal effort to legislate scientific method be read as a backlash against the proliferation of research approaches of the past 20 years out of cultural studies, feminist methodology, radical environmentalists, ethnic studies, and social studies of science, a backlash where in the guise of objectivity and good science, "colonial, Western, masculine, white and other biases" are smuggled in (Canclini, 2001, p. 12)? (Lather, 2004, p.16)

You can see how troubled Lather is. She agrees with Lincoln and Canella that we have moved backwards in time. You should read the full article to understand Lather's arguments. She expresses her concern about such a narrow view of science. She sees this current time when, increasingly, questions are raised about the fact that science is a cultural practice and practice of culture. Lather's (2004) conclusions help you understand her viewpoint:

> In short, the Science Wars continue; the line between a narrowly defined scientism and a more capacious scientificity of disciplined inquiry remains very much at issue. In terms of the desirability of degrees of formalization, mathematized and not, generic procedures, and rigorous differentiations, there is virtually no agreement among scientists, philosophers, and historians as to what constitutes science except, increasingly, the view that science is, like all human endeavor, a cultural practice and practice of culture. To operate from a premise of the impossibility of satisfactory solutions means to not assume to resolve but instead, to be prepared to meet the obduracy of the problems and obstacles as the very way toward producing different knowledge and producing knowledge differently. Foucault (1981/1991) termed this "the absolute optimism" of "a thousand things to do" (p. 174) where our constant task is to struggle against the very rules of reason and practice inscribed in the effects of power of the social sciences. (Lather, 2004, pp. 27–28)

You might think that this kind of backlash exists only in the United States. However, Harry Torrance (2008) comments that the trend toward what he calls "evidence-based research" is also seen in Australia, the European Union, and the United Kingdom. He calls it a global movement toward scientific certainty:

> Thus, it can be argued that those working in educational research in general and in qualitative traditions in particular are facing a global movement of neopositivist interest in so-called "evidence-based" policy and practice, where what counts as legitimate evidence is construed very narrowly indeed. . . . Clearly, these various manifestations differ in their origins, orientations, and specific intentions; they are not a coherent and homogenous movement. But equally, they do seem to represent a concerted attempt to impose (or perhaps re-impose) scientific certainty and system management on an increasingly complex and uncertain social world. (Torrance, 2008, p. 508)

Torrance continues with a discussion about randomized control trials, the gold standard of experimental research. He suggests, "it is the appeal to certainty about 'what works' that is claimed to attract policy makers: 'If we implement Program X instead of Program Y, or instead of our current program, what will be the likely outcomes for children?' (Slavin, 2002, p. 18). Such attraction is easy to appreciate. It sounds seductively simple. When charged with dispensing millions of tax dollars on implementing programs and supporting research, one can understand that policy makers would value this sort of help" (Torrance, 2008, p. 509)

How should we deal with standards in qualitative research? Read what Torrance (2008) has to say:

It is not that qualitative research has no standards or even poorly articulated standards. Far from it, the library shelves are stacked with epistemological discussion and methodological advice about the full range of qualitative approaches available, along with what is at stake when fieldwork choices are made and what are the implications of following one course of action rather than another. Reading such sources iteratively and critically, in the context of designing and conducting a study, and discussing the implications and consequences with doctoral supervisors, or colleagues or project advisory groups, is what maintains and develops standards in qualitative research.

At the same time, however, it has been recognized from many different perspectives, including that of the empowerment of research participants on one hand and policy relevance and social utility on the other, that an assumption of scientific disinterest and independence is no longer sustainable. Other voices must be heard in the debate over scientific quality and merit, particularly with respect to applied, policy-oriented research. (Torrance, 2008, pp. 520–521)

The U.S. policy focus on RCTs [randomized control trials] is all the more puzzling in light of these developments and arguments in the United Kingdom. Similarly, the more general scholarly retreat into trying to define the "scientific" merit of qualitative research simply in terms of theoretical and methodological "Standards" rather than in wider terms of social robustness and responsiveness to practice seems to betray a defensiveness and loss of nerve on the part of the scholarly community. We need to acknowledge and discuss the imperfections of what we do rather than attempt to legislate them out of existence. We need to embody and enact the deliberative process of academic quality assurance, not subcontract it to a committee. Assuring the quality of research and particularly the quality of qualitative research in the context of policy making must be conceptualized as a vital and dynamic process that is always subject to further scrutiny and debate. The process cannot be ensconced in a single research method or a once-and-for-all set of Standards. Furthermore, it should be oriented toward risk taking and the production of new knowledge, including the generation of new questions (some of which may derive from active engagement with research respondents and policy makers), rather than supplication, risk aversion, and the production of limited data on effectiveness for system maintenance ("what works"). Thus, researchers and, particularly in this context, qualitative researchers must better manage their relationships with policy makers rather than their research activities per se. This will involve putting more emphasis on interacting with policy and policy makers, less emphasis on producing "guidelines" and "standards" that will only ever be used as a stick with which to beat us. In the conclusion to a new book, *The Work of Educational Research in Interesting Times,* my colleague Bridget Somekh argues that "educational research communities . . . have been socially constructed as powerless . . . and have colluded in this process . . . through an impetus to conformity rather than transgressive speculation" (Somekh & Schwandt, 2007). She further argues that engagement with policy and policy making should include the discussion of "speculative knowledge" (i.e., future possibilities emerging out of research) "to improvise the co-construction of new visions" (p. 340). This seems to me to be a much more productive ground for engagement with policy making. It is not without its threats and challenges, especially with respect to cooption and collusion, but if it is speculative of new policy (and research) and properly cautious about the provisional nature of research knowledge, rather than promising a false certainty and legitimacy for policy, then the dialogue could be productive on both sides. (Torrance, 2008, pp. 523–524)

How do qualitative researchers address this movement toward a conservative stance? Torrance and others suggest we engage with policy makers rather than trying to counter the argument that "one size fits all."

Kenneth Howe (2009) also joins the discussion. His abstract explains his argument. He is especially interested in the humanities:

> The demand for scientifically based educational research has fostered a new methodological orthodoxy exemplified by documents such as the National Research Council's *Scientific Research in Education* and *Advancing Scientific Research in Education* and American Educational Research Association's *Standards for Reporting on Empirical Social Science Research in AERA Journals.*
>
> This article criticizes the new orthodoxy as being a throwback to positivist reductionism and the "two dogmas" of educational research: the quantitative/qualitative incompatibility thesis and fact/value dichotomy. It then criticizes the new orthodoxy for fostering a "third dogma" of educational research cut from the same cloth as the first two: the empirical science/humanities dualism. The article advances the view that no fundamental epistemological dividing line can be drawn between the empirical sciences and the humanities and that, accordingly, empirical research in education should not be cordoned off from the humanities, particularly their focus on values. It concludes with several observations about the problems and prospects for interdisciplinary research in education across the empirical science/humanities divide. (Howe, 2009, p. 766)

If you want to understand some of the history of this debate, I urge you to read the Howe's complete article (2009). First to come are the quantitative/qualitative incompatibility issues:

> The quantitative/qualitative "incompatibility thesis" holds that quantitative and qualitative research methods are incompatible with one another and thus cannot be coherently combined (Howe, 1988, 2003). The source of the incompatibility is typically not located at the level of research "methods" (Guba, 1987) or "techniques and procedures" (Smith & Heshusius, 1986), but in the more comprehensive epistemological paradigms in which the methods find their roots. Quantitative methods are traced to positivism, and qualitative methods are traced to interpretivism, broadly construed. Because positivism and interpretivism are incompatible epistemological paradigms, so, too, are quantitative and qualitative research methods. (Howe, 2009, p. 768)

Howe suggests that a second wave followed—the fact/value dogma:

> The idea that facts and values occupy separate epistemic domains is very deeply entrenched. And it underpins the admonition to social researchers to keep their investigations purged of values, or to at least declare them as biases. Notwithstanding how this positivist-inspired ideal is almost universally disavowed, the belief that the subject matter to which social research applies its tools, as well as the findings it produces, can and ought to remain free of values remains pervasive among social researchers. As Michael Scriven (1983) warned, it continues to "rise from the ashes" (p. 81). (Howe, 2009, p. 771)

He then describes a movement that combines both—what has been called mixed-methods experimentalism. In Howe's description, you can clearly see the backseat that qualitative approaches take. But Howe's article (2009) is about the third dogma of educational research. He is not happy with it, either:

> The dualism between the humanities and empirical social research—the third dogma—is a positivist throwback, just like the first two dogmas. The idea that empirical testability may serve as the criterion to draw a line of demarcation separating science from nonscience is a version of the central tenet— reductionism—on which positivism foundered. In the social sciences, the line of demarcation became

especially blurred with the advent of interpretivist methodology, in which the aims, requisite skills, and vocabularies of the humanities and empirical social science significantly overlap. . . . There is no epistemological justification for setting up the dualism between empirically oriented and humanities-oriented research in education. In turn, there is no justification for culling humanities-oriented concerns, particularly the critical investigation of values, from the conduct of empirical research and policy analysis and, in the process, externalizing them from the content and methodology of scientific research in education. (Howe, 2009, p. 778–779)

Standards of Evidence

I need to be explicit here. I do not believe that we can set standards of evidence in this field. Why? you might ask. First, by now you should understand that qualitative research is not a single "thing." It is multilayered and multidimensional. Second, because it is a dynamic, ever-changing field, standards will evolve as the field evolves. Third, those who set the standards have subtle reasons that are influenced by political, cultural, and social norms. Let's read on to see what others have to say on the topic.

Melissa Freeman and her associates (2007) address standards of evidence.

This article addresses standards of evidence in qualitative research in education. Our premise is that it is neither desirable nor possible to reach consensus about or prescribe standards of evidence in this diverse field. Such prescriptions, we believe, amount to disciplinary action (Foucault, 1975/1979) that constrain the generation of knowledge rather than improve it. We do argue, however, that qualitative researchers both accomplish research of high quality and have a long tradition of demonstrating quality in reports of their investigations. We begin by discussing the importance of this conversation at this historical and political moment in the United States. We then review how validity, a preferred term for the overall merit of a study, has been discussed by qualitative researchers. In this discussion, we consider commonalities in practice across qualitative research communities, describe how qualitative researchers have treated validity in relation to data and evidence, and explain how they have justified their claims. We conclude our review by emphasizing the heterogeneity of qualitative research and cautioning against recent calls for restrictive and disciplinary standards of evidence. (Freeman, deMarrais, Preissle, Roulston, & St. Pierre, 2007, p. 25)

Of interest is the discussion in some of the newer writing about standards of evidence. Freeman and her colleagues (2007) continue:

Only recently have some qualitative scholars begun to explicitly address the issue of quality using the terminology of "standards of evidence." For example, Wilson (1994) proposed five criteria that address the nature of the information, how it is acquired, and how it is interpreted: "evidence should be consistent with a researcher's chosen epistemology or perspective" (p. 26), "evidence should be observable" (p. 28), "evidence should be gathered through systematic procedures" (p. 29), "evidence should be shared and made public" (p. 30), and "evidence should be compelling" (p. 30). Lincoln (2002) offered another set of criteria: (a) "researchers should have been deeply involved and closely connected to the scene"; (b) "researchers should achieve enough distance from the phenomenon to permit recording action and interpretations relatively free of the researcher's own stake"; (c) "claims should be based on an adequate selection of the total corpus of data"; (d) "data should come, at least partly, from publicly accessible observation records"; and (e) "data and analysis should include consideration of inferences and interpretations, as well as concrete phenomena" (p. 9). These are two possibilities for assessing standards of evidence that may fit some qualitative traditions. The introductory texts scholars use to teach qualitative inquiry also offer suggestions for how researchers use evidence to support their claims. Because the relational aspects of qualitative work are so important, scholars value extended time in the field, what Wax (1971) called immersion. "Being there" matters. Qualitative methodologists also encourage member checks: going back to participants and asking them, "Have I got it right?" Working with other researchers—peer debriefers and research groups—to help think about the complexity and ethics of the work is also recommended (Lincoln & Guba, 1985). And because most qualitative research is grounded in descriptive claims about the work, not only are sufficient data to support claims crucial, but researchers must be able to, in Geertz's (1973, p. 10) words, "contrive somehow first to grasp" what is going on before they can represent it for others. (Freeman et al., 2007, p. 28)

As we suggest in the title of this article and throughout, we intend our work here to be the thoughts of one group of qualitative researchers, not an authoritative account of standards of evidence in qualitative inquiry. Although we have described in some depth the many systematic and scientific ways qualitative researchers conduct their studies, we emphasize that we are not advocating for a set of standards of evidence that may be taken up by others and used as a checklist to police our work—quite the contrary. We call on other researchers, both qualitative and quantitative, to resist current political forces seeking to impose a set of restrictive standards on educational research that serve only to control what research gets funded and conducted and, at the same time, to inhibit the creation of new research methodologies. (Freeman et al., 2007, p. 29)

Freeman and her colleagues make a strong case to resist the temptation to respond to the request for a set of standards. As I said earlier, I do not believe there can be one set of standards in judging qualitative researcher.

In their paper discussing the philosophy and politics of quality in qualitative organizational research, John Amis and Michael Silk (2007) discuss criteria for judging research from several viewpoints. After dealing with traditional criteria coming from a foundationalist perspective, they examine neorealist criteria from a quasifoundationalist viewpoint. A new concept for me is what they call free-floating quality coming from a nonfoundationalist perspective. Their conclusion reveals the dilemma within which they currently operate:

Assessing the quality of qualitative research is more than just a technical or methodological exercise. It requires an understanding of the ontological and epistemological bases of the researcher and the research. This, in turn, leads to quite different interpretations of the term quality and how to evidence it in our research—a democratization of quality if you will that loosens organizational research, and indeed the quality of that research, from the shackles of foundationalism. Again, this pluralism is not problematic; quite the opposite, it speaks to the very vitality of the field of organizational studies. For different approaches to qualitative research—and the quality of that research—to coexist alongside that which currently holds the center, and for such (uneasy) coexistence to stir, create debate, and push the boundaries of the field of organizational research, it is important that we judge the quality of such work without being blinkered to the varying interpretations of what this means. In this article, we have only been able to scratch the surface of the important debates over what counts as quality in qualitative organizational research. It remains of crucial importance for continual reflection on how we want to live the lives of social inquirers (Schwandt, 2000); how we grapple with issues of reciprocity, with textual positivism, with interdisciplinarity, with methodological plurality; and the mechanisms through which research can have a progressive impact on an array of communities that organizational research can potentially serve. (Amis & Silk, 2008, p. 475)

Donald Polkinghorne (2007) writes about how social science reformists needed to look at alternative ways of setting standards. He concludes as follows:

Prior to the reformist movement, the social sciences primarily modeled their approach to validation using conventionalist formulas. In this, they believed that the only kind of social science knowledge claims that could be sufficiently validated were those generated from numeric data and statistical analysis. The social science reformists, including narrative researchers, held that social science needed to explore and develop knowledge about areas of the human realm that fell outside the limits of what had conventionally been thought to be accessible to validation. These areas included people's experienced meanings of their life events and activities. Exploration in these new areas required the development of new approaches for the validation of findings about these areas. The creation of these new approaches required returning to the basic idea of validation that underlay the particular validity producing rules and formats employed by conventional researchers. This basic idea of validation placed the judgment of the worthiness of a research knowledge claim in readers of the research. It is the readers who make the judgment about the plausibility of a knowledge claim based on the evidence and argument for the claim reported by the researcher. The confidence a reader grants to a narrative knowledge claim is a function of the cogency and soundness of the evidence-based arguments presented by the narrative researcher. (Polkinghorne, 2007, p. 484–485)

In this chapter, I have introduced you to two main topics. First, I present portions of articles that decry the movement to a gold standard, a more traditional approach to research. Several arguments are presented. Traditional research approaches cannot really claim that their methods are not without the influence of political and social forces. According to some, the progress that has been made since the 1980s in opening up inquiry by alternative means seems to have been eroded significantly. Many believe this is a subtle (or not so subtle) way of silencing those whose voices were not heard before. Scholars urge that qualitative researchers engage with policy makers.

A second topic I present concerns setting standards of quality. The qualitative research community strongly resists establishing a single set of standards to judge diverse approaches to answering questions. This is not to say they do not want to produce high-quality work. Rather, it seems that the issue is who decides what the standards should be and how one set of standards can be applied to such a variety of philosophical and methodological designs.

I urge you to be aware that this debate is currently ongoing, because you might find yourself being drawn into one side or the other.

REFERENCES

Amis, J., & Silk, M. (2008). The philosophy and politics of quality in qualitative organizational research. *Organizational Research Methods, 11*(3), 456–480.

Eisenhart, M. (2006). Qualitative science in experimental time. *International Journal of Qualitative Studies in Education, 19*(6), 697–707.

Freeman, M., deMarrais, K., Preissle, J., Roulston, R., & St. Pierre, E. (2007). Standards of evidence in qualitative research: An incitement to discourse. *Educational Researcher, 36*(1), 25–32.

Howe, K. (2009). Isolating science from the humanities: The third dogma of educational research. *Qualitative Inquiry, 15*(4), 766–784.

Lather, P. (2004). This *is* your father's paradigm: Government intrusion and the case of qualitative research in education. *Qualitative Inquiry, 10*(1), 15–34.

Lincoln, Y., & Cannella, G. (2004). Qualitative research, power, and the radical right. *Qualitative Inquiry, 10*(2), 175–201.

Polkinghorne, D. (2007). Validity issues in narrative research. *Qualitative Inquiry, 13*(4), 471–486.

Torrance, H. (2008). Building confidence in qualitative research: Engaging the demands of policy. *Qualitative Inquiry, 14*(4), 507–527.

Source: All extracts in this chapter are reprinted with permission.

Chapter 11

REVIEW BOARDS, RESEARCH ETHICS, AND ACADEMIC FREEDOM

A basic principle of conducting experiments on humans is that voluntary consent is essential. In the 1960s, the National Institutes of Health (NIH) developed policies for the protection of human subjects. In 1974, the Department of Health Education and Welfare (HEW) adopted regulations in line with NIH's policies. A mechanism designed to enforce the standards was the Institutional Review Board (IRB). In 1981, the Department of Health and Human Services (DHHS; DHHS replaced HEW) revised the standards. Other modifications emphasized basic principles with regard to research on humans: respect for persons (personal dignity of individuals), beneficence (maximizing benefits while minimizing risks), and justice (benefits and burdens be distributed fairly).

Over the years, universities have developed IRBs for the purpose of reviewing research proposed by faculty and students. The boards consist of members from the university community either elected or appointed to multiyear terms. On the surface, it would seem as though having a board charged with reviewing research proposals is a good thing. After all, individuals would be protected. But since 2000, a number of problems have arisen that have a particular impact on qualitative research.

The issue I address here is the relationship between academic freedom and IRBs. Freedom to teach and do research is a tenet of academic freedom. At the same time, institutions are increasingly faced with protecting individuals from harm when those individuals participate in research, so we need to find a balance between freedom and protection. Some scholars believe institutions have hidden agendas—protecting the institution from lawsuit and scandal, marginalizing those whose voices have not yet been heard, and adopting a political stance of conservatism in terms of the types of research that are deemed useful, suitable, and appropriate.

In this chapter, I discuss a number of topics. I begin with introducing you to the context of the problem. Following that, I move to how the field of qualitative research is affected. I then provide you with detailed accounts of several student interactions with IRBs.

Let me be clear: I am not suggesting that IRBs are a bad thing. I believe we need some kind of standards to protect human subjects from harm during the course of the conduct of research. No one wants to see another scandal such as the Tuskegee research study of the last century. But. It is important that qualitative researchers take an active stance in communicating their ideas to those who sit on such boards.

THE CONTEXT

It might help you to understand the issues if you review the context that Yvonna Lincoln and William Tierney (2004) describe so succinctly:

> Any university-based educational researcher who has done research with human subjects/participants has come under the "Human Subjects Protection" process managed by campus institutional review boards (IRBs). Interviews, observations, surveys, and other forms of data collection that do not use data previously collected or archived are caused to undergo review and approval by institutionally created boards. These boards assure compliance with federal laws regarding the protection of human subjects from harm; ensure the right to informed consent to research procedures; and prevent violations of confidentiality and/or anonymity, violations of rights to privacy, and deception. During the course of the 1990s, two issues arose that brought increased scrutiny and sensitivity to the process: concerns regarding privacy (especially of medical and social science data) and violations of appropriate informed consent procedures that apprise subjects fully of the risks involved of participating in research (particularly medical research, as a result of several highly publicized incidents of fatalities). (Lincoln & Tierney, 2004, pp. 219–220)

The issue regarding privacy is important in the context of the conduct of qualitative research. A participant might reveal to the researcher, for example, that she or a family member was being abused. As Lincoln and Tierney (2004) put it, the researcher, although having promised privacy, might deem the information so important that it must be transmitted to appropriate authorities:

> As a result of these concerns, and others, IRBs have now been granted a mandate to oversee research processes more broadly, including the training of graduate students in qualitative research skills (e.g., interviewing, observation) and classroom-based exercises in such skill building. This situation is far less flexible than in the past when graduate faculty could submit syllabi when and if they were changed but otherwise, operated under more or less "blanket" approval for graduate-level training so long as the IRB was apprised of their intent to act as principal investigators for all class members. Thus, approval for conducting such exercises as part of a course requirement and course grade might be granted for a decade at a time.

> Heightened concerns regarding human subjects have changed all that. At the same time, pressure from the political right has intensified to discredit the products of postmodern theorizing, including constructivist theories of knowledge, postmodern epistemologies, Foucauldian analyses, poststructural investigations, action and participatory action research, and other kinds of research associated frequently or primarily with qualitative and/or interpretive research (Bauerlein, 2001; Feagin, 1999; Koertge, 1994; Lincoln & Cannella, 2002). . . . [T]he stances of IRBs have shifted from assuring that human subjects' rights are protected toward monitoring, censuring, and outright disapproval of projects that use qualitative research, phenomenological approaches, and other alternative frameworks for knowing and knowledge.

> Some IRBs are quite clear and aboveboard that their main concern is protection of the institution from damage. This is a fundamental shift from the original purpose of ascertaining risk to human and animal subjects and assuring that informed consent was adequate to prepare human subjects for associated risks. The American Association of University Professors' (AAUP) (2001) "Protecting Human Beings: Institutional Review Boards and Social Science Research" report echoes some of these same issues. Three contexts in which this trend has been especially noticeable have emerged: externally funded projects, student dissertation research, and qualitative research methods courses taught for graduate students. (Lincoln & Tierney, 2004, pp. 220–221)

In the above example, Lincoln and Tierney are concerned there is a limitation on teaching postmodern thinking that might be deemed inappropriate or incorrect. They suggest that the IRBs have shifted emphasis from protecting human subjects to protecting institutions.

How does this affect student research? According to Lincoln and Tierney (2004):

Traditionally, unless research procedures seemed to indicate close supervision to assure the protection of research participants, student dissertations were frequently remanded to the "Exempt" category—that is, highly unlikely to require more than cursory review and unlikely to cause any damage or psychological harm to individual human subjects (even as they are equally unlikely to do any good)—and given review by a subcommittee rather than the full IRB committee. This process was swift, expeditious, and thorough, even though completed by fewer IRB committee members. At this point in time, reviews are taking far longer than the usual 6 weeks; dissertation work that is qualitative is undergoing full-committee review; and at some institutions, qualitative, phenomenological, critical theorist, feminist, action research, and participatory action research projects have been summarily rejected as "unscientific," "ungeneralizable," and/or inadequately theorized (even though they may be descriptive, historical, or exploratory projects and therefore, unable to be theorized at the moment). A variety of strategies have been devised by researchers to overcome persistent rejection by IRBs, including several that actually undermine the work but that have the effect of permitting graduate students to complete their doctorates (AAUP, 2001, p. 64; Confidential, personal communication, February, 2001). (Lincoln & Tierney, 2004, p. 222)

As a consequence of the power of IRBs, qualitative research has come under more serious scrutiny than before. Students might find that it is increasingly more difficult to obtain approval for their qualitative research projects.

What Does This Mean for Qualitative Research?

There are a number of implications offered by Lincoln and Tierney (2004). They suggest qualitative research will take longer to approve because IRBs may have difficulty understanding the level of risk for participants. Since much of qualitative work is conducted in the work or school context and since many participants might be coworkers or students, IRBs may believe participants might be unduly coerced to participate. You can imagine if a supervisor in your school asked you to participate in a study of the administration. If you agreed, you might be concerned that information would not be held in confidence.

Lincoln and Tierney (2004) believe that IRBs are not properly informed about newer models of research,

particularly those that rely on phenomenological philosophy, or those viewed through the lenses of theoretical streams unknown or little understood by IRB members (e.g., feminist theory, race and ethnic theories, critical theories, or postcolonial perspectives). As a consequence, boards constituted with members uninformed about emerging theoretical and philosophical perspectives tend to fall back on definitions of research that ill serve cutting-edge research initiatives. From this perspective, IRBs may well operate, however inadvertently, to abridge academic and intellectual freedom at a time when it is already seemingly under attack. Qualitative researchers (of whatever theoretical perspective) clearly have "a horse in this race." (Lincoln & Tierney, 2004, p. 231)

A number of qualitative researchers believe they should take an active stance in interacting with review boards (Canella, 2004; Lincoln & Canella, 2004). Following up several years later, William Tierney and Zoë Corwin (2007) discuss how these new restrictions affect academic freedom:

> What we are suggesting is that what is being taken out of an individual's hands is the ability to make decisions as an autonomous researcher working within the healthy parameters that the academy previously had established. Instead, in a litigious environment, guidelines are developed that seek to ensure that the institution is not liable to any risk. The individual professor no longer fully decides the research design, who to protect, where to conduct research, or what to ask. The institution determines the answers, and if the individual disagrees, then the research shall not be done. There are many costs with such a stance. (Tierney & Corwin, 2007, p. 397)

The positions I describe above have led a number of qualitative researchers to have great concern about the role of IRBs in the protection of human subjects. What began as somewhat benign rules designed to protect individuals from risk and coercion in becoming involved in research has led to restrictive efforts by IRB. However well intentioned, some researchers believe that academic freedom is being challenged by these efforts.

Equally important are the ways in which this increased pressure toward a strict scientific methodology has affected student researchers.

Listen to what Tara Johnson (2008) has to say:

> As a public high school teacher, I learned pretty quickly how to pay lip service to what was fast becoming the modus operandi of schools in the mid- to late-1990s, the tenure of my teaching: standardized test preparation and its attendant curricular requirements. As long as my students produced acceptable test scores and I fronted what Foucault (1975/1995) terms a docile body, seemingly in compliance with the norms of the school, what happened behind my closed classroom door was unquestioned. I never really felt the effects of disciplinary power until I openly and defiantly challenged the school's practices my last semester of teaching, when I knew I was graduate school bound and untouchable. That is not to say that disciplinary power wasn't operating on me prior to my resistance to it; as Foucault argues, disciplinary power works most effectively when it is invisible:
>
> > In order to be exercised, this power had to be given the instrument of permanent, exhaustive, omnipresent surveillance, capable of making all visible, as long as it could itself remain invisible. It had to be like a faceless gaze that transformed the whole social body into a field of perception: thousands of eyes posted everywhere, mobile attentions ever on the alert. (Foucault p. 214)

> Indeed, the "faceless gaze" of disciplinary power in the form of patriarchy had normalized me long before I became a teacher, predisposing me to docility—to being a "good girl" by obeying the rules. But it wasn't until I questioned the rules that those structures became visible as they mobilized to contain me, to bring my behavior back in line with the school's ideology.

> With the glory days of graduate school serving as a 3-year buffer between the parallel power structures of the public school and the institutional review board (IRB) whose approval I needed to carry out my dissertation research, I had forgotten the necessity of performing docilely. As a student seduced by feminism and post structuralism, I'd learned to unmask the grand narratives that structure society's discourses and trouble the assumptions that undergird my daily living. Privileged as I was to be a student in a department that lauded nonconformity, my unorthodox research agenda of exposing sexual dynamics in the classroom had been wholly endorsed. One professor of qualitative research did warn me that any future aspirations of a dean-ship might be compromised by my choice of research; other than that, my mentors and colleagues affirmed that my work was important and necessary. Although there is a growing body of theoretical work on erotic pedagogy (Barreca & Morse, 1997; Gallop, 1997;

hooks, 2003; McWilliam, 1999) and a smattering of quantitative research on staff-on-student sexual misconduct in schools (Hendrie, 1998; Shakeshaft, 2004), to my knowledge there are no qualitative studies investigating the phenomenon of sexual dynamics in the classroom. My research sought to address this void in educational research through in-depth interviewing of teachers who have experienced desire for and/or from students to trace how these attractions happen and open the door for dialogue about embodiment, desire, and sexuality in education.

Wooed into a false sense of security by my supportive department, I moved forward confidently with the human subjects application for my dissertation research, figuring I might encounter a few obstacles because of the sensitive nature of my research but naively assuming the IRB would agree with my dissertation committee that the proposal itself was fundamentally sound. I was mistaken. Once again I felt the effects of disciplinary power, only this time there was no escape; I was ironically contained in and by the institution that had once set me free. What follows is a narrative of my IRB experience—the story of how I almost didn't get to do research on sexual dynamics in the classroom in the first place.

But first, a caveat: Please read to the end before making any judgments about the people I portray. I debated both internally and among colleagues about the wisdom and ethics of a public accounting of my story because some powerful people are not painted in a positive light—at least initially. As Richardson (2000) writes, "*For the most part* [italics added], I have found no ethical problem in publishing stories that reflect the abuse of power by administrators; I consider the damage done by them far greater than any discomfort my stories might cause them" (p. 932). My "for the most part" here is my concern, much as it is for my research as a whole, that readers will seize on a scintillating scene and unfairly denounce the principal players without considering the context of *the rest of the story.*

Outside the Board Room

Dissertation directors are expected to accompany their advisees to full board reviews, and so my advisor and I arrived 10 minutes early for our 12:45 appointment. The IRB meets monthly from noon to 2:00 to review applications, and mine was the second of four on the docket. My advisor had never had a full-board review for a project, nor had he advised a student who had, so this was a new experience for both of us. As we settled into the chairs that my advisor confiscated from nearby empty rooms—there were only two provided in the hallway, and the first doctoral student–faculty advisor duo on the docket were already seated—I nervously speculated about what the IRB might not condone.

I had met with the IRB's chairperson prior to submitting my human participants application, anticipating the project would require full board review and hoping for a heads-up on potential trouble spots. I had found a way around what I thought was most problematic about my research: protecting my participants' confidentiality. I wanted to ensure there could be no legal ramifications if I learned a participant had had a sexual relationship with a student, and obtaining a Certificate of Confidentiality (COC) from the National Institutes of Health (2004) seemed the best means to do so. . . .

I highlighted this and other aspects of the proposal I expected to be problematic to my dissertation director as we waited outside the IRB boardroom for an audience. In addition to the issue of confidentiality, I thought the IRB might not allow me to include former students of my participants in my data pool. Even though I knew better than to ask to interview current students who would be subject to school and parent approval, I wanted to learn about the other half of the teacher–student classroom dynamic and was hopeful that students who were out of school might be considered safe informants. I also wanted to videotape a focus group discussion of two or more participants engaged in dialogue around my topic. Although I knew video data were problematic, it was worth a try. I thought the worst that could happen was that the IRB would deny me these options for obtaining informed consent and methods of data collection, but I expected these modifications could be routed through expedited review and thus would not significantly delay my work.

And so we waited. Occasional bursts of jovial laughter emanated from within, and the human subjects office secretary crossed the threshold a couple of times, but other than that the door remained forbiddingly closed until 12:45—our appointment time—when the first applicant was called in. As she was from my department, I was familiar with her research; she too was proposing an alternate route to informed consent because the Cherokee tribe she was studying took exception to signing documents. A half-hour later, the door opened and she left crying—definitely not a good sign. My stomach, already in knots, tightened tenfold.

And we waited some more. It became apparent that the IRB first deliberated about a case before hearing it, so I assumed at this point they were discussing mine. By 1:30, the third and fourth applicants had arrived and were chatting desultorily. My nervous bladder cried for relief, but I was afraid to get up for fear I would miss being called. Finally the door opened again and I half-stood, anticipating my turn. But no; we were bypassed for Applicant 3 because, the IRB chair explained, a board member speaking specifically to that case had to leave early. Visibly seething, my director began pacing. I was struck by the power this group of people wielded; to whom could we complain, really? This was it. The last check point before I could embark on my dissertation.

Finally, after an hour and a half wait, we were called in. I was asked to sit with my director to my right, thus closing the square of close to 20 faces focusing their attention on me. I wondered if my conservative, Midwest, Dutch-girl appearance contrasted with the impression they had formed of me based on my application—did I look like someone who wanted to research sexual dynamics in schools? I attempted to adopt a professional, inquisitive mien as I looked around the room of mostly White faces. Although there wasn't a clear hierarchy implied by the layout of the room, one white-haired, aquiline-featured man wearing a white lab coat and stethoscope radiated the markings of authority. Aside from the chair, I recognized two professors at the table, both well-known scholars in the field of qualitative research. I knew them from my coursework; my graduate school institution has an exemplary qualitative research program from which I had taken a number of courses. I smiled hesitantly. After a perfunctory apology for the delay, the IRB chair began with the nonnegotiable items: I was not to talk to former students. I was not to visit classrooms for observation data. I was not to have my participants engage in focus group discussions at all, let alone videotape them. Their reasoning was that any one of these methods of data collection could breach confidentiality: Former students would know whom I was researching, someone could see me visiting a classroom, and my participants could tell on each other if they met. These concerns were not unreasonable or completely unexpected; although I was disappointed, I had been prepared to be reined in.

But then the chair's tone changed.

What had been a clear delineation of points became a series of hedges and false starts as she shifted in her chair. *Okay, what's going on here*, I wondered, my body on alert. We were moving into a gray area—a location of "instability, ambiguity, ambivalence, and contradiction that [delights] postmodernists" (Wolf, 1992, p. 88) such as I—but it was apparently not so pleasant for the predominantly quantitative IRB. The bottom-line concern as it was voiced by various board members was confidentiality, although I suspect, along with Lincoln and Tierney (2004), that the real issue was not protecting participants so much as protecting the university from potential lawsuits and bad publicity.

I realized one mistake I made in writing the application in short order: I gave too much information. In the section describing research participants, I had written that my participants would be about 5 high school teachers recruited through personal contacts, as I had already established the rapport necessary for the sensitive nature of my study. In disclosing that I knew who my participants might be—even though I had no intention of revealing the nature of my relationship to them in the study—the IRB argued that I had already breached confidentiality because *they* were now privy to that information. I needed to recruit more participants, they said—and preferably anonymous ones. How many more? A hypothetical figure of 90 was mentioned several times. One board member suggested I conduct a survey. "But strangers aren't going to volunteer such personal information," I said. "My participants need to know that they can trust me. Besides, I'm looking for dialogue here, in-depth experiences of a few participants, not a bunch of Likert-scale responses." Did they just not *get* it? I mutely appealed to the two qualitative board members for support; surely I didn't need to explain or justify the purposes of qualitative research. They said nothing.

The board was not ready to cede their quantitative solution to my confidentiality problem. One member—who I gathered later is a psychometrician based on my advisor's description of his quantitative clinical studies—provided an elaborate scenario to illustrate the potential danger of my research: "Let's say, 10 years down the road, someone's having a party. One of your colleagues is there and happens to strike up a conversation with one of your research subjects. Your name comes up, and your subject says, 'Oh, I know her! I was in her dissertation study.' Your colleague would immediately be able to identify her."

A number of thoughts chased through my mind. First of all, the likelihood of my colleagues and participants socializing in the same circles is slim. Second, in the unlikely event that such a situation were to arise, I am confident that my participants are savvy enough not to divulge their sexual histories. To what degree is it the researcher's job to protect participants from themselves? If they know the potential costs and still have agreed to participate, isn't it patronizing, a violation of the feminist ethical principle to mitigate the researcher–participant hierarchy (Kirsch, 1999), to decide for them that the risk is not worth it? I wondered how any studies could get done if researchers had to guard against every eventuality. But I am not quick to speak even in congenial settings, so I was hesitant to utter the obvious lest I offend these people who controlled my future. My director came to the rescue. He posited dryly, "But if that scenario were to occur, wouldn't it hold true whether she had 5 participants or 90 of them?"

I was too dumbfounded at this point to be upset; of all the problems I thought might arise in this meeting, it never occurred to me that qualitative research itself would be questioned. I shook my head slowly, trying to take it in. "I'm a qualitative researcher. That's what I've been trained to do here; I'm getting an endorsement for it," I said emphatically, looking meaningfully at the two professors who were in part responsible for that training. "I'm just trying to get my head around how I'm supposed to do qualitative research with 90 participants."

There was a pregnant pause. Then, from one of the qualitative researchers, "Well, I guess you have to decide whether you want to do a qualitative research project or whether you want to do research on sexual dynamics in the classroom."

I couldn't believe it. This woman had been my instructor; she knew my work. Why had she not warned me then that my research would be met with such violence? *What was going on here?*

They were not done with me yet. The confidentiality issue was merely a segue to the deeper problem: sex. If I learned during the course of my research that one of my teachers had sex with a student who was a minor, under human subjects regulations I would be obligated to report it because it constitutes child abuse. This was precisely why I wanted a COC; having one in effect trumps the reporting requirement. None of my anticipated participants were child abusers, but I didn't want to play the role of the sex police in the event that I came across one. However, the IRB was not interested in what a COC could or could not do. I realized then that a COC, although it may well protect my participants and me and ultimately hold up in a court situation, would not protect the university from the fallout if my work were ever contested. "Okay," I said, backpedaling furiously, "what if I made it a stipulation of my exclusion criteria that teachers who've had sex with minors couldn't participate?"

The psychometrician nodded. "I'd feel a lot better about that."

But the man in the lab coat wasn't satisfied. "How would you find out, though? Even if you asked them up front and they admitted they had, that's already part of the research context, and you'd have to report it." He smiled at me gently, patronizingly.

Having hit me with the incommensurables, the IRB eased up a bit with two items that were workable. But even these quibbles spoke volumes to the schism in our mutual understanding. The first was a concern that I had not sufficiently addressed the potential psychological harm to my participants—that there was not just a "slight risk of discomfort" as I had anticipated. I was to come up with a list of counseling referrals in case my participants were traumatized by my research. Mentally, I reviewed the profound relief teachers have expressed to me in having someone to talk to about the unspeakable, in realizing they're not alone; if their well-being were affected at all, these interviews were likely to be salubrious rather than detrimental. I also thought about some of my anticipated participants—women who were comfortable with their sexuality and with whom I had already had conversations about my research. One of them was even in the process of becoming a counselor herself. These women didn't need me to refer them to some stranger–confessor. However, because I was hypothetically going to have a multitude of participants who didn't know me, I conceded the point. (Johnson, 2008, pp. 212–219)

She was told she would hear more from the committee by e-mail and that the full board would review her revised application. I can almost feel her pain as I read the article. Johnson (2008) reflects on what happened:

I was too shell-shocked on the walk back to my office to do much processing of the *event* that had just *befallen* me, although I sensed this moment of collapse was very much going to affect "what might come after." My director assured me that it would be okay, that it was just going to be a matter of writing what the IRB wanted to hear; however, I felt much maligned, betrayed by the qualitative board members who had been in a position to defend, if not me, then at least the principles of qualitative research. I vowed bitterly that if I were ever in a position to be on an IRB, I would certainly stand up for students doing qualitative work. At the forefront of my mind was the delay: I had wanted to start collecting data over the holidays. At the rate I was going, I would be lucky to get approval after the next meeting in 6 weeks.

A week after the initial IRB meeting, I received the chair's e-mail delineating the changes I needed to make: thirteen elaborations, justifications, or deletions on the application form itself, "more specific questions" for the interview protocol, and an additional recruitment flyer and debriefing script ("to mitigate the psychological distress"). I set to making the changes with a determined resignation. As I wrote in an e-mail to my undergraduate mentor,
    I'm resigned to the fact that I can't do the work I want to do—at least not yet, and not in [the South]. But that's okay. As much as I love it here, I just want to get my degree and get on with my life now. (Johnson, 2008, pp. 220–221)

You can read in detail the events surrounding how she received her approval. But she still feels betrayed:

Even though I was successfully carrying out my research, what I had perceived as a betrayal by the qualitative board members still weighed heavily on me as I sat in the conference room for a session on academic freedom at the American Educational Research Association. In retrospect, I know I was fortunate to get a chance to conduct my research at all. As Lincoln (2004) argued in her presentation, the current climate for educational researchers is one of increased surveillance and institutional control. (Johnson, 2008, p. 224)

There was a point after the IRB event fell on me that I contemplated giving up my unorthodox research pursuits in lieu of a safe, tidy teacher education study that would earn me my degree and get me on my way. I suspect I will face a similar predicament in my present situation at a research institution: My work may be interesting, but it's not likely to win grant monies. Herein lies a greater concern, I think: Because the current restrictive climate for educational research discourages edgework and encourages the status quo, the discipline is bound to stagnate. Who is going to engage in risky, cutting-edge research when the stakes are so high? And yet, somehow, the work does go on. Qualitative researchers may be living in dark times, but I am optimistic that the political climate will change. I am hopeful that the answer to Marcus's (1994) title question "What Comes (Just) After 'Post'?" will be a proliferation of alternative methodologies, ontologies, and epistemologies—ways of doing, being, and knowing along with their attendant critiques—that will stimulate the field, support edgework, and open up the possibilities for research in all areas. (Johnson, 2008, p. 229)

I reproduced Johnson's account of her interactions with the IRB in detail. I do not say it is the norm—perhaps it is an exception. But it highlights for you the potential problems and issues you might face as a student who wants to conduct research. I could say that she had several issues with which she was dealing. She selected a controversial topic—she knew that beforehand. She selected a methodology that presented problems for IRBs. But I believe her experience with the IRB is of concern.

Here is Carol Rambo's (2007) account in the form of a performance autoethnography. I am going to begin at the end:

An Unloaded Gun: Negotiating the Boundaries of Identity, Incest, and Student/Teacher Relationships is my story. The chair of the department at that time was wrong to ask me to submit it to IRB. My IRB was wrong to block its publication. My best recourse is to write this story and hope that we, as a community of scholars, can help our IRBs understand the rules and work together to create a safe, defined space where storytelling is permitted without the fear of censorship. The traditional form of scientific knowing is not the only way of knowing. (Rambo, 2007, p. 366)

And here is a brief account of what happened, written as the abstract to the article:

The author's autoethnographic article was accepted for publication and then blocked by her Institutional Review Board (IRB). The overt reasons for the "denial of approval" differ from accounts given behind closed doors. By weaving experience, excerpts from her article, and the responses of others into a narrative, the author creates an ongoing performance ethnography that resists the "tacit norm of silence" regarding discussions of incest and student/teacher attraction. Framing autoethnography as a "breach" of the academic norms regarding scientific inquiry helps her make sense of how IRB as a committee used the resources at hand—the existing religious/political context, their identities, their formal roles, and the written rules they had before them—to co-construct a narrative that rendered her manuscript unpublishable. It is the author's hope that this performance of resistance will help facilitate the creation of a safe, defined space (similar to that of oral history) for autoethnography to occur. (Rambo, 2007, p. 353)

Imbunchar is the ritual ceremony whereby priests or male witches (brujos) steal newborns and bind them up or, in other versions, break or amputate body parts to somehow mark the future of the child. Tortured, with all of their orifices sealed up, these children are raised in a cave with no contact with the outside world. My article, *An Unloaded Gun: Negotiating the Boundaries of Identity, Incest, and Student/Teacher Relationships,* has been subjected to imbunchar. It has been bound up and silenced because the Institutional Review Board (IRB) at the University of Memphis ruled that it was unethical to publish it. It is my fear that my imbunche and others are silently prophesizing a future that faces autoethnography if we do not act quickly to define the situation for IRB and create a space where tales from a researcher's lived experiences can be told. (Rambo, 2007, p. 354)

Annette Hemmings (2006) speaks of the "seemingly intractable" (Hemmings, 2006, p. 12) divide between notions of good qualitative research and ethnography and the ethical frameworks and understanding of basic ethical principles that come from many IRBs. After relaying some of her own experiences in the form of anecdotal accounts, she concludes that the disparate groups can work together to comply with standards and protect human subjects. I suspect that some other researchers are more cynical.

Carolyn Clark and Barbara Sharf (2007) describe their clash with an IRB. As part of a study they were conducting with colleagues at another institution, they planned to analyze online discussions among opiate addicts. Sharf had considerable prior experience with research of this type. However, Clark and Sharf (2007) write:

> [b]ecause the decision to do an analysis of online discourse was a change from the original protocol that stipulated the use of focus groups, we resubmitted an application to the collaborating institution's IRB. Despite the ambiguities of deciding what is the most correct way to proceed with Internet-based research, our stance was to assume rigorous yet feasible protection of the people we would be studying, as I had done previously with breast cancer survivors. Thus, our application stipulated that we would introduce ourselves as researchers and briefly explain our presence within this discussion group. At best, this may be a hit-or-miss endeavor because of membership changes in online interest groups, but it would be a genuine effort to negotiate the unstated privacy norms in a publicly available forum. We also stated that we planned to contact by e-mail individual posters whose words we intended to quote in our resulting analysis; in this way, we would be seeking and obtaining informed consent. Anticipating that this IRB might be unfamiliar with the issues of doing online research, we attached the above cited guidelines (Ess & Association of Internet Researchers Working Committee, 2002; Sharf, 1999) to our application.

> Feeling that we had done our best to honor protection of human subjects and the sensibility of agreed-on ethical standards in this relatively new and still emerging form of scholarship, our team was, therefore, shocked when the IRB refused to approve the application. Instead, it stipulated that our research design could be approved if we participated only in the form of lurking or silently reading and downloading the online interchanges, never revealing our presence and identities. This prohibition to be active participants, of course, prevented the possibility of interjecting questions to the discussion group. More problematic from my vantage point was the refusal of the IRB to let us try to seek informed consent. Its major concern appeared to be the protection of the institution and the privacy of the researchers rather than the people being studied; in other words, it was more important to the IRB to prevent the institution's name (and the names of some of its employees) appearing on an Internet site focused on drug addiction. The principal investigator talked with the IRB chair after receiving the IRB's response, but it became clear that there was no room for negotiation.

> Because adhering to this condition was the only way we could proceed with the study promised to the granting agency, we resubmitted the IRB application, promising to participate only as lurkers, never contacting posters or using the institution's name in this online context. Though we have taken care to protect the identity of any person whose posts we are quoting and feel relatively assured we are not putting any individual at risk for privacy violations, we also felt that our plans for ensuring moral rigor had been compromised by the IRB for reasons that hadn't been explained (though we could guess) and didn't seem defensible. Even after moving on with our work, the underlying ethical dilemma and this question remains: What recourse is available to an individual researcher or research team when their sense of ethics is at odds with the decisions of an IRB? (Clark & Sharf, 2007, pp. 409–410)

Marco Marzano (2007) suggests:

> [d]espite the discontent widespread in the scientific community (Adler & Adler, 1994; Becker, 1982; Bulmer, 1982; Lincoln & Guba, 1989), it is unfortunately not easy to find useful descriptions of the

effects of the action of ethics committees on research, particularly on the work of ethnographers. For this reason, one may presume that in many cases the supervisory work of these bodies does not create serious obstacles against social research.

However, some researchers (Kipnis, 1979; M. D. Murphy & Johannsen, 1990) reported some of the severe dangers that arise from the excessive power of these institutions. Pearce (2003) efficaciously described the many obstacles raised by local research ethics committees (LRECs) against those wishing to conduct qualitative research in British hospitals. Patricia and Peter Adler (2002, p. 34) described with alarm the increasingly difficult climate encountered by qualitative research in the United States. The directives and judgments of these boards have evolved, becoming considerably more restrictive, and they now represent a major bane and obstacle to the active researcher. Although they present themselves as something other than petty, narrow-minded, restrictive bureaucratic "rangers," it is often hard not to suspect otherwise. The Adlers have recounted the vicissitudes of numerous research projects by their students, obstructed or blocked by an increasingly invasive and obtuse system of bureaucratic control on research activity. The situation is made even more difficult by the inconsistency of the criteria used, so that some universities are stricter than others in screening the research projects of students and academic staff. (Marzano, 2007, pp. 423–424)

The Adlers suspected that the real objective of ethics committees is to protect not so much the persons observed by ethnographers as universities and publishing houses, both of which are mainly concerned to avoid any unpleasant consequences of research. (Marzano, 2007, p. 424)

Monica Leisey, a recent social work graduate, is concerned about marginalized voices:

The Common Rule, Department of Health and Human Services (DHHS) Title 45 Code of U.S. Federal Regulations (CFR) § 46.111 Criteria for IRB Approval of Research, the federal policy for protection of human subjects, was accepted by most US Universities in 1991 (White, 2007), making Institutional Review Board (IRB) approval a legal requirement before beginning any research project involving participants in the USA. It is based on underlying assumptions inherent to the biomedical model of research (Johnson, 2004) as well as the analytic framework of principalism, the prevailing ethical system within bioethics (Shore, 2006). Neither of these assumptions is appropriate for interpretive qualitative research. (Leisey, 2008, p. 416)

Here are her conclusions:

Socially just qualitative research has the capacity to bring forward the voices seldom heard as a way to include marginalized groups into our discussion and into our community. Without these voices only a partial understanding of our society is possible. Including members from all of the identified stakeholder groups is imperative to a constructivist inquiry. . . . As researchers it is important to continue to explore ways to bring forward the voices of those seldom heard. (Leisey, 2008, p. 424)

Self-reflection should not only be related to research participants but also to the panelists' values, beliefs, and skills as they pertain to research methodology and subject matter. This reflection would be enriched through the continued education of IRB panel members in regards to new and or alternative research methods and their underlying assumptions, especially those research methodologies that are focused on change.

Simply understanding the tenets of the research being proposed will not be enough. IRBs need to incorporate the potential benefits of the research for participants and the greater community as well as the unanticipated risk of not making interventions available into their risk assessment. This broader perspective may provide opportunities for social change as well as for knowledge generation that has not been possible in the past. (Leisey, 2008, pp. 424–425)

Social science research has continued to evolve. It may be time for a more sophisticated understanding of what protection means within the social-behavioral research community, resulting in the development and implementation of new procedures to ensure participant's safety regardless of the research methodology involved.

While IRBs follow federal regulations and policies, IRB panelists are in the unique position of interacting with researchers and observing the unanticipated consequences of the policies they enforce. Experienced IRB panelists need to share their experiences and observations in order to have policies that do not impede the protection of potential research participants regardless of the research methodology being employed. (Leisey, 2008, p. 425)

I have presented a number of accounts by students about the frustrations they faced in dealing with IRBs. It seems to me that in some way the power of the IRBs has gotten out of hand. Under the guise of protecting individuals, it seems they have become reactionary and perhaps dangerous. Leisey's concern with seldom-heard voices is legitimate. She also suggests that members of IRBs engage in self-reflection. I doubt, however, that researchers will have much success dictating such practices to IRB members.

WHAT TO DO

As you read the various stories told by students and professors, you come away with a sense of challenge. Most writers take the position that qualitative researchers must take an activist stance. They need to become involved with IRBs. If the field is to continue making the strides that it has, all those interested must become ambassadors for the cause.

REFERENCES

Adams, T. E., (2008). A review of narrative ethics. *Qualitative Inquiry, 14*(2), 175–94.

Canella, G. (2004). Regulatory power: Can a feminist poststructuralist engage in research oversight? *Qualitative Inquiry, 10*(2), 235–245.

Clark, M., & Sharf, B. (2007). The dark side of truth(s): Ethical dilemmas in researching the personal. *Qualitative Inquiry, 13*(3), 399–416.

Hemmings, A. (2006). Great ethical divides: Bridging the gap between institutional review boards and researchers. *Educational Researcher, 35*(4), 12–18.

Johnson, T. (2008). Qualitative research in question: A narrative of disciplinary power with the IRB. *Qualitative Inquiry, 14*(2), 212–232.

Leisey, M. (2008). Qualitative inquiry and the IRB: Protection at all costs? *Qualitative Social Work, 7*(4), 415–426.

Lincoln, Y., & Tierney, W. (2004). Qualitative research and institutional review boards. *Qualitative Inquiry, 10*(2), 219–234.

Marzano, M. (2007). Informed consent, deception, and research freedom in qualitative research. *Qualitative Inquiry, 13*(3), 417–436.

Rambo, C. (2007). Handing IRB an unloaded gun. *Qualitative Inquiry, 13*(3), 353–367.

Tierney, W., & Corwin, Z. (2007). The tensions between academic freedom and institutional review boards. *Qualitative Inquiry, 13*(3), 388–398.

Whiteman, E. (2007). "Just chatting": Research ethics and cyberspace. *International Journal of Qualitative Methods, 6*(2), 95–105.

Chapter 12

WRITING UP RESULTS

I want to start with some assumptions:

- The written word will continue to be the primary avenue through which researchers communicate.

- Much of qualitative research writing is tedious, remote, impersonal, and boring.

- Qualitative researchers can communicate in an exciting and stimulating manner without compromising principles of quality.

- Interesting and stimulating communication skills can be taught to and practiced by qualitative researchers.

Let me be truthful: I have been reading research papers and dissertations for a very long time. Much of what I read is humdrum and repetitive—and boring. It is so boring that sometimes I find my eyelids fluttering and my mind wandering. Whether quantitative or qualitative in nature, many published articles take on this characteristic. Studies using statistics are often filled with tables, p values, and correlations that are either difficult to understand or–worse–incorrect. Studies using quotations from participants are overly long and so detailed I lose sight of the purpose of the quotation. I need to force myself to read a student's paper through to the end.

I ask myself, Can I be the only one who feels this way? Aren't there some other voices out there that agree with me? I take a break from reading a research article by reading a spy novel. Then I force myself to go back to the academic reading. Drudgery. I can never set aside enough hours in the day to finish because I get diverted too easily. I have to believe there is some other way to write.

Lest you think these are the rantings of a lone researcher, let me assure you they are not. I call your attention to Darrel Caulley's (2008) article aptly titled, "Making Qualitative Research Less Boring." To be fair, Caulley echoes Laurel Richardson's much earlier comments that qualitative research reports are "boring" and that she had yawned her way through "supposedly exemplary qualitative studies" (Richardson and Pierre, 2005, in Denzin & Lincoln, 2005, p. 959). So, at least some of the research community agrees: qualitative research reports are boring to read.

To take my argument one step further, I ask, Why? Don't researchers know how to write? Are they afraid that by writing in an exciting and stimulating way their work will be seen as less important? Is the content so dull they really have nothing to say about it? I think not. I think this style of writing has been with us for so long we accept it as the norm. We have been admonished not to be personal, and to avoid the use of personal pronouns. We have been warned that our work will not be taken seriously if the writing is not supported with a dizzying array of references and supporting evidence. We have followed an academic and scholarly style that comes to us from a long tradition of "science." Jane Gilgun (2005) concentrates on the "distanced, third-person voices . . . [when she says] . . . that this kind of writing is scientific and that lively, first-person writing is not" (p. 260). The academy will not accept a literary style if our field is scientific. Just the cold facts, please. No personalizing. No editorializing. No embellishing. No flowery language. Follow a prescribed outline. Do not waver.

Although it is not in the mainstream, there has been some attempt to change this. And that is the point of this chapter. Let me share with you what some voices say about how to make the writing interesting and exciting. Perhaps as we in the qualitative research arena move more into center stage, we will find that what we learn from all our studies can indeed make changes in the lives of our children today and the leaders of the future. And by making our writing stimulating, our work will be read and used.

What can we do about our writing? All is not lost. I draw your attention to several ideas:

Caulley (2008) offers many specific suggestions in his very stimulating article about the use of techniques of fiction to convey nonfictional information.

William Tierney (2002) also urges qualitative researchers to build more "fiction and storytelling" into their writing. He urges that more texts be devoted to writing.

Gilgun (2005) is concerned that the impersonal and distanced way in which qualitative researchers write up their results leads, perhaps unintentionally, to the silencing of informants and of the researchers themselves.

Julia Colyar (2009) asks an unexpected question: Why do we write?

Collaborative writing is an idea offered by a number of writers, including Ken Gale and Jonathan Wyatt (2006), Judith Lapadat (2009), and Artemi Sakellariadis and colleagues (2008).

I leave you with some examples of alternative modes of presentation.

AN OLD IDEA RAISES ITS HEAD: WRITING NONFICTION USING FICTION TECHNIQUES

We learn from Caulley (2008) that the idea of using techniques of fiction to write about nonfiction originated in the 1960s and 1970s with "the new journalism." He suggests that this new journalism movement led to an explosion in the academic world. Looks like it took some 20 years for the explosion to occur. Perhaps it was more of a sputtering or simmering. I must confess: I have not seen an explosion, but perhaps I am not reading the same things that Caulley is. Here I want to use Caulley's language to share with you some of his fascinating ideas. The first ideas (not surprisingly) are found in the opening and the first paragraph. Here are Caulley's words: "Open with text that is vivid and vital."

I got off the plane around midnight and no one spoke as I crossed the dark runway to the terminal. The air was thick and hot, like wandering into a steam bath. Inside, people hugged each other and shook hands . . . big grins and a whoop here and there: "By God! You old bastard! Good to see you, boy! *Damn* good . . . and I *mean* it!"

In the air-conditioned lounge I met a man from Houston who said his name was something or other—"But just call me Jimbo"—and he was here to get it on. "I'm ready for *anything*, by God! Anything at all. Yeah, what are you drinking?" I ordered a Margarita with ice, but he wouldn't hear of it: "Naw, naw . . . what the hell kind of drink is that for Kentucky Derby Time? What's *wrong* with you, boy?" He grinned and winked at the bartender. "Goddam, we gotta educate this boy. Get him some good *whiskey*. . . . "

I shrugged. "Okay, a double Old Fitz on ice." Jimbo nodded his approval. "Look." He tapped me on the arm to make sure I was listening. "I know this Derby crowd, I come here every year, and let me tell you one thing I've learned—this is no town to be giving people the impression you're some kind of faggot. Not in public, anyway. Shit, they'll roll you in a minute, knock you in the head and take every goddam cent you have."

I thanked him and fitted a Marlboro into my cigarette holder. . . . (Hunter Thompson, in Cheney, 2001, pp. 16, 17)

The opening aims to involve the reader and to hook them to continue. Conversation can help. Fiction and nonfiction writers know that conversation has the power to hold the reader right from the beginning. A creative nonfiction report that doesn't let us hear human interaction tends to be boring. Note how Thompson appealed to our senses: visual (the runway was dark), tactile (the air was thick and hot, like wandering into a steam bath), aural (the use of "whoop"), and sense of taste (reference to iced drinks).

One way to have an interesting opening is to show someone arriving (as above) or departing. (Caulley, 2008, pp. 424–425).

Caulley continues with suggestions about the first paragraph:

The first paragraph is a crucial one. It indicates the direction and possibly the tone of the work (humor, mystery, violence, romance, or a tough, realistic look at contemporary life) and encourages the reader to continue. In nonacademic writing, this is known as the "hook." Minot (2003) gives two examples of openings that are hooks:
> You never know for sure how you will act in an emergency until you are caught in a burning building.
> My sister was one of the most bossy, obnoxious brats I have ever known. I miss her terribly. (p. 24)

Hooks at the beginning of a piece of creative nonfiction writing grab the reader. (Caulley, 2008, p. 425)

You may not be familiar with Caulley's statement that there are two basic methods of writing: dramatic and summary. In case you think you are poorly informed, I have not heard this distinction either. He calls the dramatic method the "scenic method," by which he means it is the "show" portion of "show and tell." In contrast, he says the summary method is the narrative or "tell" portion of "show and tell." Another way to compare these methods is to use the idea of a close-up shot compared to a long shot in cinematography, to paraphrase Caulley's explanation.

Again, to quote Caulley (2008),

Creative nonfiction writers will typically conceive of their report as a series of scenes connected by a series of summaries—drama connected by narrative. In some reports, narrative will predominate, and in others, scenes will predominate. Scenes tend to prevent a report from being boring. (Caulley, 2008, pp. 428–429)

Caulley is definitely a proponent of the "show" part of "show and tell." Here is a specific example to help you understand what he means.

Show, Don't Tell

"Show, don't tell" is standard advice given to writers. However, it is not always clear what this means. One way of showing is to give realistic details as discussed above. Burroway (2003) gives three writings on the same topic to illustrate what is meant by show rather than tell. I will give the first and third versions. The first version is like academic writing that one might find in a typical qualitative research report:

Debbie was a very stubborn and completely independent person and was always doing things her way despite her parents' efforts to get her to conform. Her father was an executive in a dress manufacturing company and was able to afford his family all the luxuries and comforts of life. But Debbie was completely indifferent to her family's affluence. (p. 76)

This version contains abstract concepts (not images as was discussed earlier) such as stubbornness, independence, and indifference without concrete details from the research data to illustrate them. What things was she always doing? What efforts did her parents make to get her to conform? What level of executive? What dress manufacturing company? What luxuries and comforts?

Burroway (2003) rewrites the first version to counter the telling rather than the showing:

One day Debbie brought home a copy of *Ulysses*. Mrs. Strum called it "filth" and threw it across the sun porch. Debbie knelt on the parquet and retrieved her bookmark, which she replaced. "No, it's not," she said.

"You're not so old I can take a strap to you!" Mr. Strum reminded her.

Mr. Strum was controlling stockbroker of Readywear Conglomerates and was proud of treating his family, not only on his salary, but also on his expense account. The summer before, he had justified their company on a trip to Belgium, where they toured the American Cemetery and the torture chambers of Ghent Castle. Entirely ungrateful, Debbie has spent the rest of the trip curled up in the hotel with a shabby copy of some poet. (p. 77)

Now we know a lot more about Debbie and her parents as well as about Debbie's stubbornness, independence, and indifference. Burroway has used conversation and used realistic details. She has shown rather than told. In addition, the above version has been rewritten in the active voice. In the generalized original version, there are passive verbs: *was stubborn, was doing things, was executive, was able, was indifferent*. In the rewrite, the characters *brought, called, threw, knelt, retrieved, replaced, said, reminded, justified, toured, spent*, and *curled up*, which are all active verbs. (Caulley, 2008, pp. 433–434)

Jennifer Nicol (2008) helps us see how vocative texts can be used to understand the idea of "show" more completely. She offers many interesting examples in her article on the experience and meaning of listening to music for the chronically ill. She gives a clear description of the five elements of vocative text originally presented by van Manen (1997).

Here are the five elements:

concreteness—use of specific and particular descriptions;

evocation—using words that evoke and vividly reveal, that is, an experience and its meaning is called forth;

intensification—selecting words that show full poetic value;

tone—the way in which readers are addressed; and

epiphany—the way in which the readers feel changed.

Nicol (2008) offers some examples of vocative writing. Here is one you might like:

I was the shortest kid in my class during most of elementary school. What began to bother me as I approached puberty was not my height per se, but the fact that I couldn't fit into the grown up clothes and shoes like many of my classmates. I felt stuck in my childishness. At some point, I began to be woken at night with sharp pains in my legs. Neither aspirin nor comfort from my parents helped. A trip to the doctor confirmed that these were growing pains and nothing to be concerned about. My leg pains represented the beginning of a growth spurt: a critical period that was both confusing and exhilarating. While physical growth spurts are now behind me, I wonder whether psychological growth proceeds in the same stop-and-start fashion. There are certainly times when I experience stuckness and others when I can barely keep up with the changes. As I embark on my career in counselling, I am conscious not only of my clients' needs for development, but also my own. What needs to happen for me to grow and develop as a professional and as a person? How will I overcome stuckness in this career? When can I expect to be an expert at what I do? These are the kinds of questions that led me to this research project. ([Woodcock, 2005] p. 1) (Nicol, 2008, pp. 324–325)

One other idea Caulley (2008) discusses that has particular appeal to me is the use of first person. Here is what he has to say about using first person.

One answer is to say that the researcher should use the voice and style that best and most comfortably tell the story. The use of *I* has the immediacy of an eyewitness account. If the researcher has been a participant observer, then the use of the first person could be appropriate. If the researcher has done short interviews of a number of people, then the third person is probably appropriate. The methodology section could be written in the first person, for example, how the research participants were selected to interview and why. Gutkind (1997) gives some useful advice:
How essential are you (the "I") to the successful dramatization of the story you are telling? If your presence is integral—if the story is enhanced by the writer becoming part of it—then obviously, write in the first person. If, on the other hand, the writer's presence interrupts the flow of the narrative, then obviously the third person is the preferable point of view. Some of the most highly respected creative nonfiction writers consider the third person the more challenging point of view to master. (p. 72)

Gerard (2001) warns against entering the story as the upright pronoun "I" as it distracts and annoys the reader, diverting attention from the real "star" of the piece. To the reader, it seems as if the author is clamoring for attention.

Cheney (2001) likens the first person to a close-up shot with a camera and the third person to a wide-angle distance shot. The close-up shot is more intimate, more immediate, and more involving. On the other hand, the third person can deal with more people, more descriptions of people, and more settings. Gerard (2001) talks about psychic distance as "how near or far the writer, and thus the reader, remains from the people and events in the story" (p. 53) (Caulley, 2008, p. 441–442).

I encourage you to read Caulley's complete article to learn other ideas of how to make your writing more engaging and stimulating.

"GRAB" AND GOOD SCIENCE: TECHNIQUES TO AVOID THE SILENCING OF INFORMANTS AND RESEARCHERS

Other authors warn of the boring nature of qualitative research reports. However, in this case, Gilgun suggests that one reason an article is boring is because "I knew the voices of informants were swirling below the surface"(Gilgun, 2005, p. 256). She lays the blame squarely on graduate school professors, "who mute the voices of informants and their own, and who encourage their students to do the same" (Gilgun, 2005, p. 257). She admonishes them to rethink their own distanced, third-person styles. Tierney suggests that many texts are stuck in the past and that "a preponderance of texts that either employ old-style narrative voices or flawed experimental voices, . . . [results in] individuals . . . not . . . [getting] much help in figuring out how to construct their own voice" (Tierney, 2002, p. 395).

I was reminded by Gilgun that it was almost 100 years ago that the chair of the Department of Sociology at the University of Chicago (A. W. Small) wrote a first-person account of 50 years of sociology in the United States. While Small's influence was substantial, his views about writing apparently were not widely known.

Here are Gilgun's (2005) words related to the idea of "Grab":

> Qualitative researchers have a marvelous range of choices in how they convey their findings. Yet, so many continue to write as if they are unaware of this amazingly creative work that engages their colleagues. For the sake of consistency, why not write up qualitative research in ways that show that the medium is the message, that is, to ensure that the forms we choose are consistent with researchers' philosophies of science? I do not think all researchers should blur genres and use literary forms to convey their research, but I do think many researchers could loosen up. After all, we as researchers want others to read and remember what we write.

> Years ago, Glaser and Strauss (1967) stated that the credibility of qualitative research rests on several strategies. Some of them are specific to particular types of qualitative research, such using "abstract social science terminology" (p. 228) when researchers' goals are theory development. By using terms that are familiar, other researchers will readily understand the ideas.

> Another strategy, however, is relevant to many forms of qualitative research. Glaser and Strauss (1967) suggested that researchers present findings so that readers are "sufficiently caught up in the description so that he [sic] feels vicariously that he [sic] was also in the field" (p. 230). Glaser (1978) later called for "grab" in writing up research, a term he did not define, but he noted that readers should find the material interesting and memorable. (Gilgun, 2005, p. 261)

SELF-EVIDENT IT WOULD SEEM: WHY DO WE WRITE?

I was not really sure I wanted to include this topic in a chapter on writing. After all, don't we know we have to write to communicate? At least, writing is expected of us. While you might want to make a video and post it on YouTube, I do not think your institution will accept it as the only source of your report of research. Colyar (2009) asks us to consider not just the product of writing. She wants us to examine the process. "In many ways, *process* is not a term in qualitative researchers' and scholars' vocabularies" (Colyar, 2009, p. 424; emphasis in original).

I am most taken with her argument that writing is a reflection of the rhetorical self. She suggests it is a way of connecting with the self, of looking inward. Consider her assertion that writing is "an act of self-witnessing and self-knowledge." She continues, and is "proof of who and what we are" (Colyar, 2009, p. 429). This may be a little too heady for you to accept. You might be more prone to accept the idea that writing is sense making or that writing is methodology.

Some final ideas to take away from Colyar are given below:

> I end these pages wondering, still, about the connection between thinking and writing. But rather than wondering about the specific cognitive steps, I wonder about our (my) resistance to including writing more explicitly in our courses, our papers, and our methodologies. Perhaps doing so points too forcefully at the unfinishedness of our work, the ways in which what we know as we write is constantly reshaping itself. Derrida (1997) might call this an anxiety of "undecidability," the fact that despite all the writing, a text cannot have a stable meaning. Meanings and memory unfold over time and change shape in different contexts; though text presents a permanent trace of ideas and signs, our interpretations of that trace are inexhaustibly complex.

> Perhaps this reluctance to engaging the writing process is also a reflection of the invisible pull of positivism, which asks that we know, not that we are in the process of knowing. Perhaps we are reluctant to express our own uncertainty that what we know *now* is not what we may know *later*, in another version or text. Perhaps we are reluctant to admit that the first draft of our papers are messy, more incomplete than substantive, full of blank spaces and filler phrases that will be carefully edited out. Perhaps that writer, the one with the blank spaces, is the writer I don't want others to see. That writer expresses uncertainty in too many ways. (Colyar, 2009, pp. 434–435).

The Whole Is Greater Than Its Parts: Collaborating With Others

So often writing is a solitary activity. I get up each morning, turn to my computer, and let my fingers fly. I sit in my home office and think about what I want to say and how I want to say it. But writing can be a process of collaboration. Here are some new ideas.

In 2005, Ken Gale and Jonathan Wyatt became involved in an interactive interview via e-mail while both were pursuing their doctoral studies. Their account captures the style that Caulley urges. Here is the beginning of their article (Gale & Wyatt, 2006):

Prologue: Morning, May 3, 2005

Heathrow Airport, London

We wait in the departure lounge ready to board our plane to Chicago. (Don't you think that purgatory—a liminal space? an inter/view?—must resemble an airport lounge? A mass of people in transit, trapped until given direction to leave. So much movement, enforced lingering, uncertainty.)

As we wait, we begin to relax. Anxiety—about leaving home, tasks unfinished and what might delay our respective journeys from Oxford and Plymouth—has been with each of us. Checking in was straightforward; seeing our luggage disappear was disconcerting. No turning back.

Now, we feel anticipation. We begin to talk about the conference in Illinois where we are each presenting papers. We exchange conversation describing our hopes for the next few days. And we realize we have the opportunity to discuss, for the first time since completing it, our shared writing project: our interview.

We clear the table of cups and other debris, take out a copy of our manuscript, and begin to read.

Introduction

We—Ken and Jonathan—enjoy discussing and sharing work and have noticed during our doctoral studies the contrast between how each writes. Ken's writing is more consistent with traditional academic writing, whereas Jonathan's transgressive "I" is prominent. If these writings were landscape, Ken's would be a rich, verdant forest reached only via a long, satisfying trek over mountains, and Jonathan's a beach in the Costa del Sol with easy access via Ryanair. (Gale & Wyatt, 2006, pp. 1117–1118)

You might quibble whether this is about collaboration or interaction. Whichever way you see it, there are several points to be taken from their joint and parallel writings. First, I want you to read a bit of their initial discussion.

Ken reflects on how Jonathan has influenced him in his final comments:

He not only writes himself but also writes to me, about me. His writing has allowed me to begin to say the unsayable and to write in ways that have surprised me. In response to him, I have begun to find a different voice.

And I mean this in not only the therapeutic but also the political sense. I think again of stammering: Our writing together, as Jonathan says, had its own dynamic, signifiers—like "stammering"—leading us in an endless play as our reflexive engagements placed meanings sous rature (Derrida, 1978). We began to nurture an alertness, immanently enriching our positions within each moment of communication, a kind of empowerment I think. Writing together had political energy. (Gale & Wyatt, 2006, p. 1132)

More cautiously, Jonathan speaks of Ken's behaviors:

The picture of his putting himself on the line at the doctoral unit is vivid. My experience of him at these events is that I enjoy the way he engages with material so openly and value how much he has read. I had not registered how much of a risk it is to speak and therefore how much courage he demonstrates. There is the risk he takes too in the writing; he makes himself vulnerable again. (Gale & Wyatt, 2006, p. 1130)

That these two men so strongly influenced each other is patent throughout the article. At times, I confess I am a little uncomfortable. Sometimes they tell me more than I want to know. But the central point is clear: talking and writing about ideas and engaging in a typically solitary activity in an interactive manner can profoundly influence what one thinks and how one expresses oneself.

Here is another collaborative account driven by students. Artemi Sakellariadis and her colleagues (2008) describe how a group of people who describe themselves as academic nomads collaborated and reflected on their work. All were based in the United Kingdom. Technology linked these people, even though they faced unexpected problems setting up a jiscmail account (a type of e-mail list for academic communities) in the United Kingdom.

Our first real difficulty with technology was when we tried to set up a jiscmai13 list with an archive. A ring-fenced academic networked community sounded ideal: no spam, easy, secure, closed access. In the event, it proved a disaster. For some mysterious reason, the service would not recognize half our e-mail addresses, every time we tried to log them on people fell off, communication broke down, and the creative period of the project ground to a halt.

We are simply waiting for an electronic system to link us all together, but there seem to be problems. This feels almost embarrassing, as if technology itself is deciding which one of us to keep in and who to spit out.

I felt terribly frustrated when we couldn't get jiscmail to work for us. Nobody could trust the process or knew if anybody else could hear them. This was a low point in the project; in fact the whole thing was nearly destroyed by technology. The process we had set up in the face-to-face workshops was now being undermined by technology's failure. (Sakellariadis et al., 2008, p. 1207)

Much of the text is written in this manner. Several voices are heard simultaneously. While this group did come together, they sometimes despaired:

So it seems technology has been somewhat divisive for us, at times leaving some feeling apprehensive or excluded. Much electronic technology seems to come from a different world, and perhaps it cannot be tamed or harnessed for our meanderings. It seems to have threatened to impose its own values of speed, competence, structure, and anonymity, within the goal-focused climate of an academic context. Instead, we have thrived on collaboratively setting our own pace and boundaries and on our joint sense of connectedness; not to mention the commitment to a journey where both route and destination seemed unclear. (Sakellariadis et al., 2008, p. 1218).

POEMS, STORIES, PLAYS, AND THE LIKE: TELLING IT ANOTHER WAY

Let's learn from those who have actually demonstrated what we have talked about. Stephen Banks (2000) offers us "Five Holiday Letters: A Fiction." Keep your mind open as you read a portion of his account:

The Balfour Family News—Yuletide 1992

Dear friends and family,

Here it is holiday season once again, and it seems like just yesterday that the Balfour clan were all together at Grammy and Grandpa Balfour's for last year's New Years Eve celebration. A lot has happened to the five of us since that gathering, and here are some of the highlights.

Ted started the year with A PROMOTION!!! He's now managing director of the Easton plant, and IREX has been sending him for executive training seminars at a famous university in Cambridge, Massachusetts (being a true Blue Devil, Ted is reluctant to say the "H word" in public). He has been kept so busy with the new job that his fly-tying bench in the basement is covered with cobwebs, and Ginny had to do all the snow shoveling through both the infamous "Big Beast" storm in February and the freak snow we had in late March (a foot of snow on downtown Reston in March??!!).

Good guy that he is, though, Ted took the whole family (including Scooter) with him on an IREX trip to Utah in May. While he was busy managing his boring meetings at the Lago Seco Conference Center, Ginny, Rick, Molly, and Beth spent the days mountain biking (yes, even Beth, who gleefully rode behind Mom or Rick up and down the most treacherous slopes!), rock hounding (Rick found an authentic thunder egg the size of a football), and shopping at Sundance. Scooter enjoyed the pedigreed company at the resort's canine compound!

As if that wasn't enough adventure, Ted and Ginny stole a week in June by themselves in the French Pyrenees (Thanks, Mopsie and Dad, for entertaining the kids!).

. . .

Beth came through her first term away from Mom with flying colors and dozens of new friends after a few bumpy days of adjustment (now Mom has another set of delivery and pickup routes to drive).

. . .

Do let us hear from you and come by for a visit if you can.

Love,

Ted, Ginny, and the kids—Rick, Molly, and Beth (and Scooter the wonder hound) (Banks, 2000, pp. 392–394)

Moved by a desire to evoke in readers some possibilities for subjective meaning and emotional experiences available in reading personal correspondence, the author offers a set of five fictional holiday letters. The decision to use fiction is justified by recourse to current scholarship on nontraditional narratives in qualitative research. The author further discusses the grounds for this fictional presentation of research results by explaining his ambition to share his understanding of the structural properties of the holiday letters epistolary genre and its situated writers, which he acquired in earlier, more traditional qualitative studies, without minimizing the gains of fiction writing. More central to the purposes of this effort is his desire to create a unique character who gives voice to particular human struggles and values at the juncture of the modern and postmodern experience: Ginny Balfour is inspired by specific women letter writers but is a construction of his imagination. (Banks, 2000, p. 392)

This explanation actually precedes the first letter in Banks's article. What are you to make of this letter and those that follow? I want you to read portions of his account that appear at the conclusion of the letters:

This set of holiday letters is a fictional creation. Although, as far as I know, there is no actual family comprising Ted and Ginny Balfour and their children and although the events and characters who enter their lives also spring from my imagination, all are inspired by actual persons and stories contained in holiday letters my colleagues and I have collected and studied for nearly 5 years.

In the past, we have used more traditional qualitative methods to conduct a grounded theory (Strauss & Corbin, 1990) study and analysis of narratives (Polkinghorne, 1995) of the majority of our nearly 200 letters. Those investigations have yielded descriptive categories of the content that identifies holiday letters as a genre of writing, and we have set forth a principled argument to explain how that epistolary genre helps persons manage multiple dialectical tensions in contemporary social life by creating self-identities (see Banks, Louie, & Einerson, in press). Our finding is that holiday letters, like personal home pages on the World Wide Web, are a creative mechanism by which persons engage the multiple dialectical tensions between modern and postmodern influences in contemporary society, between the public and private realms of experience, and between the perceived real and desired ideal within individuals' lives.

In our earlier work on holiday letters, however, we were unable to convey the emotional tenor of the letters or what had powerfully struck us as the poignancy of lived experience evident in the narratives. Like Diversi (1998), we wanted also to "connect, at least initially, in an emotional realm, human beings living in extremely different social contexts" (p. 133). Moreover, we were unable to give readers our own subjective responses to those emotional and existential properties of individual letters. In other words, although we had established an interpretation of the holiday letters genre and had reported on that interpretation, we failed to evoke in our reports our understanding of the subjectivity that resides within and can be read off from each letter in our collection, as well as our own felt experience of reading holiday letters (Banks, 2000, pp. 399–400).

Banks concludes his explanation:

The wish to experiment with fiction underlies desire. By this term, I mean to convey the notion that writers have affections for genres of writing and are drawn to produce in their work texts that affirm those affections. This idea poaches Krieger's (1991) comment about theory: "Rather than asserting that one was choosing mode X because of its superior power to explain the world, it might be more honest to admit that you were fond of it" (p. 21). I have chosen fiction because I desire the challenges, freedom, immediacy, and palpability of creative writing. I have chosen fiction because I am attracted to the charm of the single case that evokes the universal. I have chosen fiction because I enjoy affiliating with the tradition that values truth over facticity. Finally, I sometimes also choose fiction because I am not compelled to choose it; the rigidities of the tradition's prescribed genres of research writing have always felt confining to me, as dictatorial and self-protective. Risking the choice to write fiction seems like choosing emancipation. At the same time, it holds me accountable not for my facts but for communication of my interpretations and vision, my experiences, my emotions and values, and indeed, my craft. (Banks, 2000, pp. 403–404)

Juanne Clarke and her colleagues (2005) offer stories of formerly homeless mentally ill patients through the use of poetry. Here is one of the poems.

Poem 1

> I was born in
> Poland.
> My real mother died in a car accident
> When I was nine years old.
>
> And so I was sent to Canada
> When I was ten on a plane
> Because my father was here.
>
> My father remarried.
> I have a stepmother and I have a brother.
> They had a baby.
> I have a stepbrother from that other lady
> Not my real mom.
>
> I had a special English class.
> But I got in trouble with the law.
> Because my father and stepmother had separated.
> So I tried to put them back together
> I punched an old lady in a store.
> I was charged with an assault.
>
> I was all over treatment.
> Maplegrove, Half- way- there Homes,
> Stepsvilles Assessment, Breentown,
> Then a boarding home.

They trained me to live on my own.
I moved out when I was twenty-one.
I went into convulsions in my apartment
So I ended up in the hospital.

I liked the Psychiatric Hospital
I didn't want to leave.
In the hospital my room had pictures

The doctor took me off
The Zephrix
I started hallucinating
Again
I am anti-psychotic
And she took me off the psychotic drug

I ended up in seclusion

I like it here because you get
Your own bathroom
And you get support care workers.

We have coffee and tea
I crochet and knit
I like needlepoint
I make pillows

I wanted to be a nurse.

                                                    (Clarke et al., 2005, pp. 918–919)

As pointed out by Laurel Richardson (2002) poetic representation can both cohere and conflict with normative writing. In other words, the poetic and the normative need not be mutually exclusive but may be complementary. Poetic representation offers opportunities for alternative expressions of people's lives as well as opportunities for critical attention to knowledge claims about them (Richardson, 2002, p. 881). Furthermore, poetic representation honors the arts as a legitimate path to knowing and expressing truths about lived experience (Richardson, 2002, p. 887). Paraphrasing Richardson (p. 888), we view poetic representation as a powerful tool for understanding the social, for altering the self, and for breathing new life into the research community that claims knowledge of our lives. (Clarke et al., 2005, p. 929)

Melisa Cahnmann (2003), in writing about poetry in educational research, concludes as follows:

Arts-based approaches are not an either-or proposition to traditional research paradigms. We do no service to ourselves as arts-based researchers to define ourselves in opposition to traditional practices. Rather, the literary and visual arts offer ways to stretch our capacities for creativity and knowing, creating a healthy synthesis of approaches to write in ways that paint a full picture of a heterogeneous movement to improve education. In educational research and practice we are working with human beings in all their ever-changing complexity. Incorporating the craft, practice, and possibility of poetry in our research enhances our ability to understand classroom life and support students' potential to add their voices to a more socially just and democratic society. Thus, I do not suggest a poetic approach replace qualitative or quantitative study, merely that poetry enhance and add to our research.

Likewise, the work of ethnographers in education can enhance the direction of contemporary poetry. Social scientists often work from the presupposition of social responsibility. This is especially true of ethnographers of education, aiming to inform and improve education for all youth. Poetry has a lot to learn from disciplines that take on social and cultural themes, political activism, and social change. Our audiences should help dictate the kinds of genres we use but should not eliminate the possibility for mergers between the work of artists and social scientists, adding dimensionality and empowerment to both. (Cahnmann, 2003, p. 34)

Last, my answer to the "so what test" is to answer, "why not?" The available traditions for analysis and write up of research are not fixed entities, but a dynamic enterprise that changes within and among generations of scholars and from audience to audience (Gioia, 1999, p. 32). We cannot lose by acquiring techniques employed by arts-based researchers. We must assume an audience for our work, an audience that longs for fresh language to describe the indescribable emotional and intellectual experiences in and beyond classrooms. We may not all write great popular or literary poems, but we can all draw on the craft and practice of poetry to realize its potential, challenging the academic marginality of our work. We might decide to read more poetry, take a creative writing class, and take more risks in our field notes and articles. My hope is for educational researchers to explore poetic techniques and strategies beyond those mentioned here to communicate findings in multidimensional, penetrating, and more accessible ways. (Cahnmann, 2003, p. 35)

Yen Yen Woo (2008) describes how she translated a narrative of members of the Loh family into film. She uses stories that she developed into vignettes. Here is a description:

Collective Stories

To structure the research data as a film, I needed stories, connections, characters, and textures beyond the narrow focus of the original research study. My partner and I began writing the screenplay by compiling vignettes related to the widely accepted touchstones of personal success in Singapore, the so-called 5C's: cash, car, credit card, condominium, and country club membership (Chua, 2003; Goh & Woo, 2001; Koh, 2006). Our first step was to review the research data for mentions of any of these touchstones of success. We then started gathering anecdotes from personal memories and experience, as well as news stories and e-mails we had received from readers of a book chapter that we had written earlier, which explored the same themes (Goh & Woo, 2001).

This method of data collection, which I used in the original research study and expanded across various texts in crafting the screenplay, is adapted from Frigga Haug's work (1987/1992) on collective memory. In her research, Haug gathered groups of individuals who would share and then "redraft" their stories of female socialization. By hearing each other's stories, the individuals in Haug's sessions found points of commonality and difference; they then explored the contextual conditions that made their experiences similar or different. The collective stories became cultural stories that resonated beyond the individuals in the group, and also beyond the group to other readers, as they continued to evoke comparisons and reassessments of one another's experiences. (Woo, 2008, pp. 322–323)

She continues:

Can Art Be Research?

The first question inevitably is whether the film can be considered a product of research. I believe the answer to this is an unequivocal yes. If, according to Mayer (2000), research is the use of data to support arguments, then clearly I engaged in data collection and analysis in the making of the film. Whether or not I conducted a formal research study that first appeared in academic research reports, there was clearly a theoretical framework underlying my various translation, scripting, and directorial decisions, including production design in the preproduction phase, the direction of the actors and shot setups in the shooting phase, editing choices, and the multitude of enhancements to sound and color, and so forth, during the various stages of postproduction. During the postproduction phase, I also conducted screenings with test audiences and fielded surveys to determine whether the film was successful in conveying the plot points and character arcs that we intended and whether the themes resonated with viewers. (Woo, 2008, p. 325)

WHAT REMAINS TO BE DONE?

I have offered you a variety of ways to write about your research. Each way is designed in some way to convey research results. Some researchers rely on collaboration. Some choose poetry or holiday letters. Others provide very specific writing techniques.

We can touch only so many people as we travel through life. Although our culture has become increasingly visual, we still rely on the written word for much communication. I am somewhat encouraged that there are voices out there that take this topic seriously. I ask that you move yourself beyond your own comfort zone. Try writing one paper using a technique or style or device you have never used before.

A number of years ago when I was teaching a course in qualitative research, I asked students to write about a parent using metaphors. Two papers come vividly to mind: one described her father as Santa Claus and the other described her father as Hitler. I can see both of these students in front of me. The class told me they had never done anything like that before. I hope some of them tried again.

REFERENCES

Banks, S. (2000) Five holiday letters: A fiction. *Qualitative Inquiry, 6*(3), 392–405.

Cahnmann, M. (2003). The craft, practice, and possibility of poetry in educational research. *Educational Researcher, 32*(3), 29–36.

Caulley, D. (2008). Making qualitative research less boring: The techniques of writing creative nonfiction. *Qualitative Inquiry, 14*(3), 424–449.

Clarke, J., Febbraro, A., Hatzipantelis, M., & Nelson, G. (2005). Poetry and prost: Telling the stories of formerly homeless mentally ill people. *Qualitative Inquiry, 11*(6), 913–932.

Colyar, J. (2009). Becoming writing, becoming writers. *Qualitative Inquiry, 15*(2), 421–436.

Denzin, N. & Lincoln, Y. (2005). *The SAGE Handbook of Qualitative Research.* Thousand Oaks, CA: Sage.

Gale, K., & Wyatt, J. (2006). Inquiring into writing: An interactive interview. *Qualitative Inquiry, 12*(6), 1117–1134.

Gilgun, J. (2005). "Grab" and good science: Writing up the results of qualitative research. *Qualitative Health Research, 15*(2), 256–262.

Lapadat, J. (2009). Writing our way into shared understanding: Collaborative autobiographical writing in the qualitative methods class. *Qualitative Inquiry, 15*(6), 955–979.

Nicol, J. (2008). Creating vocative texts. *The Qualitative Report, 13*(3), 316–333.

Richardson, L., & St. Pierre, E. A. (2005). Writing: A method of inquiry. In N. K. Denzin & Y. S. Lincoln (Eds.), *The SAGE Handbook of Qualitative Research* (3rd ed., pp. 959–978). Thousand Oaks, CA: Sage.

Sakellariadis, A., Chromy, S., Martin, V., Speedy, J., Trahar, S., Williams, S., et al. (2008): Friend and foe: Technology in a collaborative writing group. *Qualitative Inquiry, 14*(7), 1205–1222.

Tierney, W. (2002). Get real: representing reality. *The International Journal of Qualitative Studies in Education, 15*(4), 385–398.

van Manen, M. (1997). From meaning to method. *Qualitative Health Research, 7*(3), 345-369.

Woo, Y. (2008). Engaging new audiences: Translating research into popular media. *Educational Researcher, 37*(6), 321–329.

Source: All extracts in this chapter are reprinted with permission.

Chapter 13

REFLEXIVITY

Reflexivity in qualitative research is acknowledged as a very important topic. *The Forum: Qualitative Social Research* (*FQS*) devoted a full issue (volume 3, number 3) in 2002 to the topic. The issue contains more than a dozen articles. A second issue appeared one year later. In the second issue, the editors decided to concentrate on three main topics: foundations and theoretical frameworks; the meaning of subjectivity; and reflections on the subjective nature of scientific knowledge.

Franz Breuer, Katja Mruck, and Woff-Michael Roth (2002) lay out the argument regarding subjectivity and reflexivity. Let me paraphrase their explanation. A traditional view of research adopts the position that in order for results of research studies to be accepted by the community of scholars or policy makers, the data and results should be independent of the person conducting the research. In other words, all aspects of the research should be objective. One way to demonstrate objectivity is to write in a remote manner, avoiding the use of the first person. This posture of objectivity is the hallmark of "good science." Furthermore, in spite of evidence generated from many fields that personal and social factors influence the process and results in any kind of research, the fiction of objectivity (their words) has continued by using standardized methods to avoid subjectivity.

Now here is the problem. Typically, qualitative research approaches do not use standardized methods. So how have qualitative researchers behaved? They tend to deal with the issue in a reflective manner. In fact, they are encouraged to reflect.

So the question is: how are subjectivity and objectivity connected? It seems as though there are two opposing viewpoints. On the one hand, objectivity is said to negate subjectivity: "The investigator's values are said to define the world that is studied. One never really sees or talks about the world, per se. One only sees and talks about what one's values dictate. A world may exist beyond values, but it can never be known as it is, only as values shape our knowledge of it" (Ratner, 2002, p. 2).

Postmodernists assert that subjective processes interfere with objectivity. A seemingly opposite contention is that subjective processes enable researchers to objectively comprehend psychological phenomena (Ratner, 2002).

It has been seven years since those ideas were articulated in *FQS*, although the topic of reflexivity has been addressed during that time.

In this chapter, I focus on two central ideas: One idea is concerned with the general topic of reflexive analysis in qualitative research. A second idea relates to questions of ethics and reflexivity.

It might help you to think about reflexivity in this way: it is concerned with identifying the interconnections among a researcher, the text, the participants being studied, and the larger world.

REFLEXIVE ANALYSIS IN QUALITATIVE RESEARCH

Douglas Macbeth (2001) asserts that in the past 15 years:

> . . . few topics have developed as broad a consensus as the relevance of analytic "reflexivity." By most accounts, reflexivity is a deconstructive exercise for locating the intersections of author, other, text, and world, and for penetrating the representational exercise itself. As with deconstruction more generally, reflexivity has become an identifying move within a recognizable program of premillennial social science. The program's consensus is not easily described, and the play of reflexivity in the literature is far more diverse than a single, or several, positions can account for. And although this diversity assures us that any account of it can only be tendentious, it may still be useful to try to build one. The "reflexive thesis" (Ashmore, 1989) has become so well established—and nearly obliged—as to be worthy of a critical review. (Macbeth, 2001, p. 35)

Reflexivity Can Be Multidimensional

While initially reflexivity was thought of in general terms, some writers have discussed different kinds of reflexivity. Macbeth suggests three. One type is positional reflexivity. In this type, a researcher looks at place, biography, self and other as they influence the analysis. A second type is textual reflexivity. In this case, the research analyst looks at how textual representation is disrupted by an analysis. Macbeth focuses on a third type: constitutive reflexivity, which is related to ethnomethodology. Here are Macbeth's (2001) words:

> I mean by positional reflexivity those formulations of the reflexive exercise that treat it as a self-referential analytic exercise. . . . [P]ositional reflexivity takes up the analysts' (uncertain) position and positioning in the world he or she studies and is often expressed with a vigilance for unseen, privileged, or, worse, exploitative relationships between analyst and the world (cf. Anderson, 1989; Denzin, 1994; Lather, 1986; Lincoln & Guba, 1990). (Macbeth, 2001, p. 38)

> A positionally reflexive view of the field thus implicates a disciplined view and articulation of one's analytically situated self, and for some researchers (cf. Ellington, 1998; Richardson, 1998; Ronai, 1998), positional reflexivity has directly autobiographical and sometimes nearly clinical attachments. Reflexivity leads the analyst to take up the knots of place and biography and to deconstruct the dualities of power and antipower, hegemony and resistance, and insider and outsider to reveal and describe how our representations of the world and those who live there are indeed positionally organized (see also Frieden, 1989; Haraway, 1988; Heron & Reason, 1997; Lather & Ellsworth, 1996). By interrogating the borders of the hermeneutic circle in this way and recognizing those orders of analysis and interpretation that fail to transform, positional reflexivity often intends to leverage emancipatory possibilities from the unnoticed commitments and adhesions of nonreflexive agency and worlds.

> Especially in educational studies, positional reflexivity has become insinuated into the very methods of qualitative methodology. It is recommended as of a piece with methodological discipline, informing the very possibility of postpositivist and/or poststructural analytic rigor (Ball, 1990; Hertz, 1996; Lather, 1994). (Macbeth, 2001, p. 38)

Then he discusses textual reflexivity. Textual reflexivity is concerned with how the analyst examines and disrupts textual representation:

> In American social science, the reflexivities of the text first came to attention in anthropology. The textually reflexive move arrives on the deconstruction and seeming collapse of the respectability of representational language games, although still and again, insofar as doubt requires a first certainty, arguments for textual reflexivity routinely deploy and, in this sense preserve, the certainties they deconstruct. (Macbeth, 2001, p. 41)

Macbeth (2001) goes on to describe a very interesting writing by Lather and Smithies in 1997 that he calls a "carefully crafted exemplar":

> Their interview study of a support-group community of women living with HIV/AIDS writes a graphic organization of the page across the women's voices, their own, and still other intertextual discourses and registers. They do so to resist, if not defeat, the normal complicities and expectations of a text that is available for realist readings, and it yields a distinctive textual array. Graphically, the book is organized along a hemispheric divide: In the northern space of the page and across the binding, we hear the words of the women, collected in group settings and on those special occasions of birthdays and mournings that are part of the life of the support groups. Edited for purposes of "theme development [and] dramatic flow" (p. xvii), the text of the women's voices is presented plainly and in their own voices. The authors' purposes were, in part, to produce "a 'K-Mart book,' a book that is widely accessible to HIV-positive women like themselves, their families, and those with whom they work" (Lather, 1996, p. 530).
>
> In the southern space of the page, we hear the authors' voices remarking on and considering the project itself; taking the measure of their own positions in the world, their relationships to the women and to each other, their divisions of labor and not always congruent interests; and otherwise reporting on the work of relationship and reporting. Crafted to do the work of a reflexive text, I want to consider further the spatial and discursive organization of their pages as reflexive, articulating, and disrupting intertextual arrays.

The North

> The divide between the north and the south is striking, both graphically and narratively. The north, the women's edited voices, is organized within a thoroughly realist caption. Not only is what these women are saying engaging, revealing, compelling, and sometimes arresting, but their interview fragments are (re)presented as transparent documents of lives lived. These are native, first-person accounts, realist fragments of a language game wherein what is said is a faithful narrative of what is lived and known. By implication, these accounts are not, for example, local productions fitted to the occasions of the interviews and group meetings that produced them, but are rather more like vivid frames lifted from larger fields of lived experience, whose faithfulness and correspondence to those larger fields premise their textual powers rather than problematize them. (Macbeth, 2001, p. 44)

The South

> Bordering the north is the southern textual space. The divide inverts our familiar geopolitical sense for the possessions and dispossessions of north and south. Here are the voices of the authors, and as reflexivity requires its objects and attachments—the intelligibilities to be disrupted—the south works as a meta-discourse, operating on a first naive field (including the lives of the women and their support

groups and the practical life of the study itself) and laying out still others—for example, boxed inserts from the popular press, fragments of medical and governmental reports on the experience of HIV/AIDS in society, and poems and letters from the women. As the authors intend it,

> We wanted a book that used a "flood" of too much too fast, data flows of trauma, shock and every-dayness juxtaposed with asides of angel breathers to break down the usual codes we bring to reading. Hence the book "works" by not working the way we expect a book to work. (Lather & Smithies, 1997, p. 48) (Macbeth, 2001, p. 45)

Unfortunately, much of Macbeth's writing is quite dense and you have to unpack it to make sense of it. I think position reflexivity is concerned with the position of the researcher (what he calls "analyst") in the world he studies. This is what many people speak of when they talk about reflexivity. He also introduces the term "textual reflexivity." Here we think about the relationship of the analyst to the text. What interests Macbeth most is something he calls the "constitutive reflexivity" (related to ethnomethodology) of everyday life. This relates to how order, fact, and meaning in everyday life are produced as practical objectivities. He offers the example from the Lather and Smithies work to illustrate this point.

Linda Finlay (2002) offers us some guidance about the process of engaging in reflexivity. For her this is not an easy task—she talks about muddy ambiguity and multiple trails as researchers negotiate through the swamp. Her metaphors seem a little dire to me.

She talks about reflexivity from five dimensions: introspection, intersubjective reflection, mutual collaboration, social critique, and discursive deconstruction. In this brief history Finlay helps you see the twists and turns taken.

> Although not always referred to explicitly as reflexivity, the project of examining how the researcher and intersubjective elements impinge on, and even transform, research, has been an important part of the evolution of qualitative research. Critical self-reflexive methodologies have evolved across different qualitative research fields in a story of turns and shifts. (Finlay, 2002, p. 210)

> Early anthropological "realist tales," where researchers conscientiously recorded observations in an effort to prove their scientific credentials, have gradually given way to more personal "confessional tales" where researchers describe decisions and dilemmas of their fieldwork experience. With this movement, most evident from the 1970s, comes a growing "methodological self-consciousness." The ethnographic critique of ethnography (led by writers such as Clifford and Marcus, 1986) pushed qualitative researchers into a "new paradigm, placing discovery of reflexivity at the centre of methodological thinking" (Seale, 1999: 160).

> The concern of ethnographers and anthropologists (among other qualitative researchers) to unravel how their biographies intersect with their interpretation of field experiences led, initially, to highly subjectivist accounts of fieldwork. In such research, fieldworkers portrayed themselves as infiltrating a group and then reporting on their experiences as an "insider." Other researchers, on a more objective mission, sought to increase the integrity and trustworthiness of their findings. Through critical reflection, they used reflexivity to continually monitor, or even audit, the research process. As the research process is made transparent, they argued, personal experience is transformed into public, accountable knowledge. (Finlay, 2002, p. 210)

> But these uses of reflexivity, to offer better, more committed (thus "truer"?) accounts as part of trying to affirm the validity of the research, were quickly challenged as regretful backward glances at positivist ideals. Post-modern researchers began to seek a more radical relativism as they embraced the negotiated and socially constructed nature of the research experience. Attempts were made to erode the

researcher's privileged position—an explicit and particular critique of earlier imperialist and colonialist anthropologies (for example, Clifford and Marcus, 1986). Greater attention was placed on how ethnographers, for instance, stood at the margins between two cultures (Barthes, 1972), decoding and reinterpreting the host culture for the home culture.

Concerns about the unexamined power of the researcher led to an emergence of feminist versions of reflexivity—for example, Wilkinson (1988) and Reinharz (1992). These aimed to reframe power balances between participants and researchers. (Finlay, 2002, pp. 210–211)

Today, "narratives of the self" have proliferated. . . ."Self-reflexivity unmasks complex political/ideological agendas hidden in our writing" (Richardson, 1994: 523). The researcher "appears not as an individual creative scholar, a knowing subject who discovers, but more as a material body through whom a narrative structure unfolds" (Bruner, 1986: 150).

The last couple of decades has also seen a surge of interest in ethnographic and sociological writing itself. (Finlay, 2002, p. 211)

In terms of current practice, it could be argued that reflexivity, in its myriad forms, is now the defining feature of qualitative research (Banister et al., 1994). Most qualitative researchers will attempt to be aware of their role in the (co)-construction of knowledge. They will try to make explicit how intersubjective elements impact on data collection and analysis in an effort to enhance the trustworthiness, transparency and accountability of their research. The debate resides largely between qualitative researchers of different theoretical persuasions who lay claim to competing accounts of the rationale and practices of reflexivity. (Finlay, 2002, pp. 211–212)

You can tell from the historical explanation above that qualitative researchers view reflexivity somewhat differently depending on their philosophical bent. Some, like Macbeth, are interested in nuances and subcategories of reflexivity. Finlay speaks of the co-construction of knowledge. It is interesting that qualitative researchers draw different interpretations of the role and meaning of reflexivity. The debate is not only between quantitative and qualitative researchers, but also between qualitative researchers who come from different traditions. You can conclude that reflexivity has many meanings, perhaps like qualitative research itself.

Reflexivity Has Many Uses

Jane Agee (2009) writes about how reflexivity influences various stages of the research process. For example, she describes how the reflective process can be used to develop effective research questions. She observes that good qualitative questions are "developed or refined in *all* stages of a reflexive and interactive inquiry journey" (p. 432; emphasis added). What is critical for Agee is the refinement of questions throughout a study, rather than thinking about research questions fixed and immutable.

The use of a reflexive journal is important for many researchers. Diane Watt (2007) suggests that by using reflection researchers can learn what lets them see as well as what inhibits their seeing. She discusses using a research journal to assist with reflections:

My research journal contains a permanent record of the pilot study, and served as a memory prompt for this second level of reflection. Drawing on excerpts from the journal, I made links between the literature on methodology, decisions taken during the project, the process of reflexivity, and my evolving understanding of the complexities of qualitative research. I analyzed journal entries for what they revealed about the management of each phase of the study, the issues and tensions which arose, and the ways I dealt with these as a new researcher. A retrospective examination of my own research permitted me to make meaningful connections between theory and practice. This inquiry thus provoked a depth of learning which may not have been possible through any other methodological means. By reconsidering my pilot study in this way, I experienced the extent to which reflection is an essential mediator in the research process. Reflective writing allowed me to meaningfully construct my own sense of what it means to become a qualitative researcher. (Watt, 2007, p. 83)

Watt reviews her own experience with using a reflective model. She concludes that writing the narrative was critical as she went through the process.

Although I learned a great deal about qualitative inquiry and reflexivity while engaged in my original pilot study, writing this narrative consolidated and extended that learning. If I had not kept a journal much would have been lost, both during and now after the project. Having access to journal entries permitted me to consider my research holistically. This secondary level of reflection led to an increased recognition of the central role the journal played in the initial study. Through using writing as a method of inquiry I was able to make links between how I carried out my study, reflective journal entries, and the literature on qualitative methodology. This process enabled me to connect theory and practice, thereby gaining new insights into the complexity of qualitative inquiry and what it means to be a qualitative researcher. My own fledgling practice thus served as the foundation for what turned out to be a very personal and powerful learning experience. Looking back on my struggles at each stage of my study led to a deeper understanding of the nature of the qualitative research process, and a fuller appreciation of the vital role of reflexivity both in accomplishing a project, and in my ongoing development as a researcher. Perhaps most significantly, writing this account has altered my sense of identity (Richardson, 2000). Revisiting my study has strengthened my confidence in my ability to negotiate the complex process of qualitative inquiry, and I now *see myself as a researcher*. The multiple layers of reflection drawn upon in writing and revising this paper have made me more cognizant of how far I have come, and have taken me further along the path to becoming a qualitative researcher. At the same time, I know there can be no final destination, for each time I return to the original journal entries and my reflections on them, something new emerges. As I discover more about theory, the topic of study, the research process, and myself, my perspective shifts. Becoming a qualitative researcher is, indeed, a never-ending process. (Watt, 2007, p. 98; emphasis in original)

Cynthia Gerstl-Pepin and Kami Patrizio (2009) also describe how to use a reflexive journal for memories and reflections. They suggest that such a journal provides for reflection on the research process. Finlay accepts the practice, but questions how to go about doing it. Here is her statement about the current state of affairs:

From this brief—and all too neatly constructed—history, it is clear that reflexivity, in its multiple guises, has a firm place within the qualitative research agenda. As qualitative researchers engaged in contemporary practice, we accept that the researcher is a central figure who influences, if not actively constructs, the collection, selection and interpretation of data. We recognize that research is co-constituted, a joint product of the participants, researcher and their relationship. We understand that meanings are negotiated within particular social contexts so that another researcher will unfold a different story. We no longer seek to eradicate the researcher's presence—instead subjectivity in research is transformed from a problem to an opportunity. In short, researchers no longer question the need for reflexivity: the question is how to do it.

When it comes to practice, the process of engaging in reflexivity is perilous, full of muddy ambiguity and multiple trails. To what extent should researchers give a methodological account of their experience?

How much personal detail can be disclosed and what forms can it take? How are researchers to represent a multiplicity of voices while not hiding themselves? In some ways, embarking on reflexivity is akin to entering uncertain terrain where solid ground can all too easily give way to swamp and mire. The challenge is to negotiate a path through this complicated landscape—one that exposes the traveller to interesting discoveries while ensuring a route out the other side. Researchers have to negotiate the "swamp" of interminable self analysis and self disclosure. On their journey, they can all too easily fall into the mire of the infinite regress of excessive self analysis and deconstructions at the expense of focusing on the research participants and developing understanding. Reflexive analysis is always problematic. Assuming it is even possible to pin down something of our intersubjective understandings, these are invariably difficult to unfold, while confessing to methodological inadequacies can be uncomfortable. (Finlay, 2002, p. 212)

ETHICAL RESEARCH IN REFLEXIVE RELATIONSHIPS

One issue that concerns those writing about reflexivity is the power discrepancy between those who do the research and those who are studied. Some are troubled particularly because often those who are studied live marginal lives—they may be drug addicts, young pregnant teens, or minority students.

Jane Agee (2009) contends that part of the process of question development is to reflect on two issues related to participants: how the questions will affect the lives of the participants and how those questions will position the researcher in relation to those participating. Agee is especially concerned when those being studied are marginalized. I draw your attention to the quote Agee offers from Said's work *Orientalism*:

Modern thought and experience have taught us to be sensitive to what is involved in representation, in studying the Other, in racial thinking, in unthinking and uncritical acceptance of authority and authoritative ideas, in the socio-political role of intellectuals, in the great value of a skeptical critical consciousness. Perhaps if we remember that the study of human experience usually has an ethical, to say nothing of a political, consequence in either the best or the worst sense, we will not be indifferent to what we do as scholars. (Said, 1979, p. 327) (Agee, 2009, p. 439)

I think you will gain an understanding of this issue by reading some of Kim Etherington (2007):

I have also been strongly influenced by feminist principles relating to equality and power that challenge researchers to make transparent the values and beliefs that lie behind their interpretations and to let slip the cloak of authority, lower the barrier between researcher and researched, and allow both sides to be seen and understood for who they are (Etherington, 2004). Those challenges have helped legitimize the reflexive use of "self" in research: reflexivity being at the heart of feminist methodologies and increasingly other methodologies too. "It [reflexivity] permeates every aspect of the research process, challenging us to be more fully conscious of the ideology, culture, and politics of those we study and those we select as our audience" (Hertz, 1997, p. viii). (Etherington, 2007, p. 600)

For years, qualitative researchers have interpreted and brought meaning to what they study. Etherington (2007) wants researchers to lower barriers and let both sides be seen as who and what they are. This seems to change the power relationship. So now we talk about the reflexive use of self. By doing this she tries to achieve what she calls ethical research in a reflexive relationship:

Traditionally, as ethical researchers have been expected to think about informed consent, the right to information concerning the purposes, processes, and outcomes of the study (related to fairness), the right to withdraw at any stage (related to autonomy), and confidentiality (to protect the right to privacy and do no harm), these ideas are usually held within guidelines or codes of ethical practice. However, many researchers are now asking if "dutiful ethics" are sufficient to the cause of research that upholds the values of human worth and dignity, when "it may not be possible to satisfy both the demands of the ethical guidelines and those maintaining standards for conducting research" (Helgeland, 2005, p. 553), if we do not also take into account the demands of the context (Denzin, 1997; Villa-Vicencio, 1994).

For instance, participants cannot be expected to give informed consent prior to knowing what they are agreeing to: The researcher can usually provide information about the purposes and practices of research in advance but may not be able to provide information about processes that have yet to unfold, in particular when using heuristic or narrative inquiry (Etherington, 2004). Ethical conduct in these instances relies on our awareness of the need to recognize and talk about the potential dilemmas raised by the research and our openness to engage in "the ebb and flow of dialogue" (Helgeland, 2005, p. 554). Ethical considerations for reflexive researchers will also include the need to remain aware of, and sensitive to, cultural difference and gender (Cloke, Cooke, Cursons, Milbourne, & Widdowfield, 2000; Denzin, 1997). This would mean being sensitive to the rights, beliefs, and cultural contexts of the participants, as well as their position within patriarchal or hierarchical power relations, in society and in our research relationship. This notion has often been addressed within the body of feminist literature on ethical research, in terms of power relationships when researching with counseling clients or ex-clients, but it may also be true of other research relationships where power imbalance is a feature. (Etherington, 2007, pp. 601–602)

Have you thought about the idea that consent (the consent to allow oneself to be studied, for example) is a process rather than an event? You can see how troubled Etherington is in this next brief section. It is almost as though she is creating a problem when one isn't really there. Etherington reports her discussion with a student:

Our conversation began with me outlining the importance of consent as a process rather than an event:

Kim: . . . and then . . . for us to . . . to make sure—all the way through—that you . . . are aware . . . that you can withdraw. That is really important . . . for you and me—*really* important, . . . because . . . um . . . because of my other roles with you.

Joe: [quietly] Right, I'm with you.

Kim: . . . you know . . . at any point . . . you must never think that . . . that [withdrawal] would upset me or . . .

Joe: . . . or that I've *got* to do this.

Kim: No. Because you're a student . . . you know, . . . the fact that I'm your supervisor . . . this is going to affect . . .

Joe: I feel comfortable with that but uh . . .

As I speak, I am aware of my own discomfort: wondering what colleagues might say if they knew I was engaging with a student in this way, while also weighing up the potential benefits for both of us and remembering that his involvement in the study was something he had asked from me.

I notice how I reemphasize his right to withdraw, and how in my anxiety, I might come across as not listening or respecting his ability to say "no":

Kim: It's really important for you to know that it'll be fine to say "no" at any stage, and that I mean that.

Joe: Yeah. I hear you, and I'm aware of that.

Kim: . . . and to me, you know, it's much more important to be respectful and honoring of the person's rights in this . . . to. . . . I'm not *relying* on your story. I've got other stories.

Joe: And . . . I hear that but uh . . . I . . . I don't perceive any trouble . . . but if there was . . . at any point, I would let you know.

In my effort to relieve him of any undue responsibility toward me—telling him that I'm not relying on his story—I fear I may have implied that his story was not unique and valuable in itself. I press the point again, needing to convince myself that he is aware that it might not be so easy to say no to me, because of his perception of the power held within my role:

Kim: Yeah. But I am also aware that you kind of view me as a bit of an authority figure.

Joe: Right. I know.

Kim: But . . . you know—that's the way it is.

Joe: And . . . a . . . [sighs] . . . when I say I view you as an authority figure . . . that's just your position—being a lecturer at the university. Actually, I don't see you . . . I mean obviously you're in charge of the course, so yeah, you're in a position of authority, but I see you as someone I can approach, and disagree with or whatever. And so I'm not, I don't have that kind of . . ."you're the boss, I better comply" feeling with you.

Kim: So . . . if you wanted to withdraw, if you didn't like the way I had construed your story . . .

Joe: I . . . I would inform you.

Listening to the tape of this conversation and reading back over it, he seems more confident than I do. My thinking was that his relative naivety about the dynamics that can build up in research relationships, and my own awareness of how this can happen, might be a problem, even though he repeatedly reassures me. Joe told me later that our conversation had made him think about the dual relationships he held within his own research context and how important it had felt to name that as a potential ethical problem. From examining this transcript and writing about it, I have learned that, even in my efforts to hold to the feminist ethic of care, anxiety to get it right can cause me to lose sight of a participant as an independent actor who possesses the power to say what he feels (Helgeland, 2005). (Etherington, 2007, pp. 603–604)

Here are Etherington's (2007) thoughts about reflexivity as ethical practice:

Although reflexivity is sometimes recognized as a useful tool for ensuring rigor, improving the quality and validity of research, and recognizing the limitations of the knowledge that is produced, it is not usually considered as a tool for ensuring ethical research processes and practices (Guillemin & Gillam, 2004). The *link between reflexivity and ethical research seems to rest on transparency*. When the reader is shown the interactions between researchers and participants (as above), we can observe the behaviors involved in respecting the autonomy, dignity, and privacy of participants (or not!); the risks of failing to do so; the "ethically important moments" that might have occurred; and the means by which they are ethically negotiated (Guillemin & Gillam, 2004). (Etherington, 2007, p. 604; emphasis added)

Here is the guidance Etherington (2007) offers:

In summary, therefore, I offer suggested guidelines for ethical research in reflexive relationships:

- To remain aware of the potential power imbalance between researcher and participants, especially where there are current or previous boundary issues created by dual relationships, and where there are issues of race, gender, age, etc.;

- To negotiate research decisions transparently with participants, and to balance our own needs with those of participants and agencies involved;

- To provide ongoing information as it becomes available, even when that requires the use of appropriate and judicious researcher self-disclosure;

- To include in our writing and representations information about research dilemmas that may occur, and the means by which they have been resolved. (Etherington, 2007, p. 614)

We have much to learn from Etherington. We cannot treat informed consent as a hurdle through which we must jump or as some perfunctory rule that we just need to follow to get by. We must be cognizant of our explicit or implicit relationship with our participants. We also must be aware of the power dynamics operating between those being studied and those doing the research. Her admonition of transparency is one that will be helpful as we consider ethical issues and reflexivity.

Marilys Guillemin and Lynn Gillam (2004) describe a situation they have encountered:

Picture this scene. You are a researcher working on a study examining women's experiences of heart disease. You are interviewing Sonia, a woman in her late 40s with diagnosed heart disease. Sonia lives on a remote farming property in a rural region. She is married and has one teenage daughter living at home with herself and her husband. The interview is progressing well. Over a cup of tea in Sonia's kitchen, you inquire about the impact of heart disease on her life. Sonia stops and closes her eyes. After a few moments' silence, you notice tears welling up in Sonia's eyes. Sonia tells you that she is not coping—not because of her heart disease, but because she has just found out that her husband has been sexually abusing her daughter since she was a child.

This kind of scenario is not unusual when conducting qualitative research. Most qualitative researchers can describe similar experiences they have encountered, usually with considerable emotion and crystal-clear recall. The issues raised in this scenario have ethical and legal implications. How as researchers do we respond to such disclosures when they occur, and are there existing conceptual frameworks and principles that we can draw on to assist us? Our focus in this article is on what we refer to as the "ethically important moments" in doing research—the difficult, often subtle, and usually unpredictable situations that arise in the practice of doing research. We are interested in the ethical practice of research and how this is achieved. We examine existing ethical principles and frameworks for both their limitations and what they offer researchers and then turn to reflexivity as a potential tool for ethical research practice. (Guillemin & Gillam, 2004, pp. 261–262)

Although reflexivity is a familiar concept in the qualitative tradition, we suggest that it has not previously been seen as an *ethical* notion. We propose that reflexivity is a helpful conceptual tool for understanding both the nature of ethics in qualitative research and how ethical practice in research can be achieved. (Guillemin & Gillam, 2004, pp. 262–263; emphasis in original)

Consider the issue of what they call ethically important moments. They suggest that what is important is to connect these moments with reflexivity. They see the construction of knowledge as a reflexive process consisting of the kind of knowledge that is produced and how it is generated:

Rather, reflexivity in qualitative research is usually perceived as a way of ensuring rigor (Finlay, 1998; Koch & Harrington, 1998; Rice & Ezzy, 1999). Reflexivity involves critical reflection of how the researcher constructs knowledge from the research process—what sorts of factors influence the researcher's construction of knowledge and how these influences are revealed in the planning, conduct, and writing up of the research. A reflexive researcher is one who is aware of all these potential influences and is able to step back and take a critical look at his or her own role in the research process. The goal of being reflexive in this sense has to do with improving the quality and validity of the research and recognizing the limitations of the knowledge that is produced, thus leading to more rigorous research. It does not have an overtly ethical purpose or underpinning.

To see how a useful connection can be made between reflexivity and ethics, consider again the accounts of reflexivity that we offered. These accounts suggest that reflexivity is not necessarily focused only on the production of knowledge in research (what might be called the epistemological aspect of research practice) but also on the research process as a whole. Adopting a reflexive research process means a continuous process of critical scrutiny and interpretation, not just in relation to the research methods and the data but also to the researcher, participants, and the research context.

This would include issues about the ultimate purpose of the research. (Guillemin & Gillam, 2004, p. 275)

The concept of microethics is a valuable discursive tool to allow us to talk about, validate, and better understand the ethically important moments in research practice. It is limited, however, when it comes to offering guidance in how to deal with these ethical events. We have argued that this is where the notion of reflexivity is most useful. Reflexivity is something that most qualitative researchers are aware of and incorporate into their research practice; it is not a new concept. However, what we suggest is that its meaning be expanded so that reflexivity be considered and enacted as a way of ensuring not just rigorous research practice but also ethical research practice. Being reflexive in an ethical sense means acknowledging and being sensitized to the microethical dimensions of research practice and in doing so, being alert to and prepared for ways of dealing with the ethical tensions that arise. As we have stated, reflexivity does not prescribe specific types of responses to research situations; rather, it is a sensitizing notion that can enable ethical practice to occur in the complexity and richness of social research. (Guillemin & Gillam, 2004, pp. 277–278)

I have touched on several topics in this chapter. First, I considered the general notion of reflexivity in qualitative research. Many writers acknowledge its increasing importance, especially since 2000. Although we often think of reflexivity as a single dimension, Macbeth and Finlay provide their detailed analyses of how reflexivity consists of a number of dimensions. According to many writers, reflexivity pervades all aspects of the qualitative research process. Some writers have offered suggestions on how to learn about and practice reflexivity. The chapter ends with considerations of reflexivity and ethical issues.

My purpose in introducing you to this topic is to help you see that reflexivity and qualitative research go together. Rather than striving for objectivity—a component of traditional quantitative research—qualitative researchers acknowledge the role of the self in all aspects of research. They embrace its use rather than make apologies for the involvement of the researcher.

REFERENCES

Agee, J. (2009). Developing qualitative research questions: A reflective process. *International Journal of Qualitative Studies in Education, 22*(4), 431–447.

Breuer, F., Mruck, K., & Roth, W-M. (2002). Subjectivity and Reflexivity: An Introduction [10 paragraphs]. *Forum Qualitative Sozialforschung / Forum: Qualitative Social Research, 3*(3), Art. 9, http://nbn-resolving.de/urn:nbn:de:0114-fqs020393. © 2002. Retrieved July 28, 2009, at http://www.qualitative-research.net/index.php/fqs/article/view/822/1785

Ellis, C. (2007). Telling secrets, revealing lives: Relational ethics in research with intimate others. *Qualitative Inquiry, 13*(1), 3–29.

Etherington, K. (2007). Ethical research in reflexive relationships. *Qualitative Inquiry, 13*(5), 599–616.

Finlay, F. L. (2002). Negotiating the swamp: The opportunity and challenge of reflexivity in research practice. *Qualitative Research, 2*(2), 209–230.

Gerstl-Pepin, C., & Patrizio, K. (2009). Learning from Dumbledore's pensieve: Metaphor as an aid in teaching reflexivity in qualitative research. *Qualitative Research, 9*(3), 299–308.

Guillemin, M., & Gilliam, L. (2004). Ethics, reflexivity, and "ethically important moments" in research. *Qualitative Inquiry, 10*(2), 261–280.

Macbeth, D. (2001). On "reflexivity" in qualitative research: Two readings, and a third. *Qualitative Inquiry, 7*(1), 35–68.

Ratner, C. (2002). Subjectivity and objectivity in qualitative methodology [29 paragraphs]. *Forum Qualitative Sozialforschung / Forum: Qualitative Social Research, 3*(3), Art. 16, http://nbnresolving.de/urn:nbn:de:0114-fqs0203160. Revised 2/2007. Retrieved July 28, 2009, at http://www.qualitative-research.net/index.php/fqs/article/view/829/1801

Said, E. (1979). *Orientalism.* New York: Vintage.

Watt, D., (2007). On becoming a qualitative researcher: The value of reflexivity. *The Qualitative Report, 12*(1), 82–101.

Source: All extracts in this chapter are reprinted with permission.

Chapter 14

Negotiating Through Graduate School

The challenge of completing a graduate degree is not new. I suspect that when you decided to continue with your education, you knew there would be obstacles to overcome. In this chapter, I offer you some reflections on being a student.

Outside the Mainstream

The feelings of alienation in graduate school are much more prevalent than I could have imagined. What follows are several accounts by people who write about issues not related to learning methods or negotiating course work or even balancing work and home and school. These authors search for a place of their own. They write about their feelings, using a variety of formats.

Leigh Hall and Leslie Burns (2009) explore mentoring of students by faculty among students who are preparing to be educational researchers. Hall and Burns are especially interested in how students negotiate new identities. In particular, they suggest that students enact identities valued by their mentors. They offer several suggestions for mentoring—reconceptualizing the researcher identity, making formation of identity explicit, incorporating culturally responsible teaching practices, and offering training and support for faculty.

One way of presenting what it feels like for students is to use an approach that builds on ethnography. In this case, the mode is called performance autoethnography. Although I have not discussed this type of research specifically, by now you should be able to determine that it will be a nontraditional presentation. You can think of autoethnography as an intense and close look at the self. Claudio Moreira wrote these autoethnographies while he was a graduate student in communication research. He struggles as an outsider: he is a student in a U.S. university but his country of origin is Brazil. He wants to find his place and voice in academia. In this piece, he acknowledges the influence of Holman Jones's account that appears in the 2005 third edition of *The SAGE Handbook of Qualitative Research*. Moreira's work is part poetry, part prose. It is self-revealing, and almost cathartic in nature. It is in your face, confronting, and poignant. It is definitely not academic writing. I offer you a brief sense from this man's perspective:

A Paper Inside a Paper or Some Crazy Poetry

Because
I am a
Smart ass PhD student
Streetwise lost in a doctoral program
In a fight with my trained mind and in love with my body
I am
Full of hope and shit
And I care and believe
Life is unfair in an unphilosophical sense
Andrezinho was raped
And so was Celita2
And Knowledge is power
And Knowledge is legit, and experience is not
After working all day long, Domício Diniz, age 55, fainted when he tried to
get on the buss. He died before help arrived. It seems that the cause was
excessive work. It may have been. Domicio cut an average of 12 tons of cane
per day. (*Folha de Sao Paulo,* October 4, 2005)
I am trapped in a Foulcaltian power system
That disciplines and punishes
Whose name is Higher Education.
Every time I understand hook's words better: Do not forget the pain

(Moreira, 2008b, pp. 663–664)

Here is an excerpt from another piece he published one month earlier:

Act 9
Life 9
Living in Threat

Many voices
I like your work, but I never meet a junior faculty doing this.
People might be moved by your prose, but they will not hire you.
You have to be flexible as scholar.
Don't let the anger get the best of you.
It's nice, but why do it here in academia?
A Brazilian with a chip on his shoulder.
There are more,
voices
but I am too tired.
What is this? Am I not able to land a job because I do not behave, do and
think, do not ask/answers, and do not write/research/perform the same
questions like the others?
SILENCE
A different voice
Claudio, go home and tell Dani that you will find a job. You will find a
job because of what you do.
BREAK

Norman's [Denzin] office is a good place. I feel safe here. He is working with
Giardina. I interrupt them.
"Hi, Norm, do you have a minute?"
"Sure."
"I got the idea for this new performance and I want to you look at it. I
got the title, and the first act and the last. Can you look at it now?"
After some time . . .
"Am I going too far? I mean, I wanna make sure . . ."
"Never," says Norman.
"Never in this office," says Giardina.
We all smile.
BREAK
The theoretical being.
The doctoral student.
The human being.
The thug

(Moreira, 2008a, p. 599)

You might ask yourself: Why am I so moved by his words and feelings? Very rarely do you find a place in academia that will accept a student for what he or she is. Apparently, Moreira has found such a spot. I hope you have as well. If you deconstruct some of his words, you begin to see the interweaving of personal, professional, and academic challenges.

Moreira is not the only student to feel like an outsider. Elizabeth Murakami-Ramalho and her colleagues (2008) look for their identity as researchers from the perspective of students of color. In their article, they use personal narratives and collaborative portraits to describe their experiences. Emphasis is on voice, reflexivity, and context in the stories they tell. I am struck with the idea of a temporary loss of identity. In this narrative, they make extensive use of metaphors: the wanderer, the chameleon, and the warrior. The article begins in a traditional manner—with a literature review on the experiences of doctoral students of color. I was not familiar with research regarding Latinos and Chicanos but was not surprised that the academic setting is restrictive and that students experienced self-doubt and invisibility. More research on African American doctoral students revealed that the students experienced isolation. With a type of narrative research, Murakami-Ramalho and her colleagues used reflection, dialogue, and authenticity to present personal narratives or autoethnographies making use of metaphors. They each write about their journey from a personal perspective.

We learn from Dalia Rodriguez (2006) what she refers to as the hidden truth—"racism in the White academy" (p. 1067). Through the use of narrative, this article takes a strong position based on critical race theory.

Using race-based theories such as CRT, Black feminist thought, and Chicana feminist epistemology, I aim not only to unmask the reality of racism but also to reveal the process of achieving critical consciousness for women of color. I write these stories in an effort to give voice to the experiences of women of color who continue to struggle with the historical legacy of colonization and current mechanisms that continue to haunt us daily. (Rodriguez, 2006, pp. 1072–1073)

Rodriguez intersperses personal narratives with reflections on critical race theory in her account. Somewhat later, she continues with this story:

We're in my driveway and, as usual, we can't seem to stop talking. Lashawna's upset because she has been dealing not only with school officials at her daughter's school but also with one of her committee members with regard to her qualifying exams. As we sit in my driveway, I can see the frustration on Lashawna's face. "Now what happened with your damn committee members?!?!" I yell, as I've heard numerous stories about the difficulty Lashawna has had in her graduate program. Her committee members repeatedly give her a hard time about everything she writes. "Ya wanna know what my damn advisor said to me? I turned in this assignment and I get my paper back and in the margins she wrote, 'What do you mean by white supremacy? Isn't that a little harsh? You have to have citations. . . . '" Waving around her paper, marked up in red ink, she points to several of the comments, "How is slavery related to where African Americans are today? . . . Don't you think saying white supremacy is a bit of an exaggeration?" Repeatedly being told that her work was "not quite there," Lashawna has been dealing with racism in graduate school at every stage of her dissertation. While in the special education department, she was consistently questioned about her work. "I guess I'm nothin' but a dumb nigga!" Hearing her say that hurts and I just want to yell at her to not say that and that the more we verbalize these negative images Whites have about us, the more we contribute to our own oppression. If she truly believes that then, well, THEY would have won.

Hearing her talk, I begin to wonder how many times we have questioned our own abilities. As Tijerina (1989) argues, "We take from the oppressor the instruments of hatred and sharpen them on our bodies and our souls." Once, while at a departmental colloqium, a professor asked me, in front of other faculty and graduate students, "Oh, hey Dalia, what are you doing here?" Confused as to what he was getting at, I naïvely asked, "What do you mean?" He smiled and said, "Well, I'm just surprised you came back, I mean, I just didn't expect to see you again this semester." (Rodriguez, 2006, p. 1079)

I can't say it any better than she does.

Balancing Demands of a Complicated Life

Using what they call cogenerative ethnography, Robin Grenier and Morag Burke (2008) explore the lived experiences of graduate students balancing school and motherhood. They explain that they did not use phenomenology or ethnography since it did not quite fit what they were going to do. Like the other writers above, they selected an autoethnographic modified approach when they brought their stories together jointly. Their detailed accounts of other parts of their lives tell the story so well:

Robin too, found support from other graduate students, especially when her husband, Robert was unexpectedly hospitalized on their daughter's first birthday.

I have met a few women who have had babies while getting their Ph.D.s but it's tough to talk with them because our schedules are so full. Where I have really found support academically is with my dissertation support group. Although I am the only mom, they have helped me with everything, from comps to babysitting when Robert was in the hospital . . .

Another source of power that we found reoccurring throughout our narratives was the support we have from our spouses. While we both admitted that there were occasions our husbands added to our load, they overwhelmingly fell on the side of power. In Robin's case, her husband moved with her to Georgia so she could attend graduate school. He negotiated with his employer to telecommute from his office in Tampa, Florida, and left behind a well-established network of colleagues, friends, and family. In a narrative, Robin describes how Robert was instrumental in her academic success.

I joke that it's Robert's fault I am here. When I was finishing my masters he asked me one day why I wasn't getting my Ph.D. Well, I didn't have a good answer, and here I am! Robert is my rock. Where I can doubt my abilities and why I am in this program, he has never questioned my work. He's my cheerleader, spiritual counselor, comic relief, and press secretary. He pushes me to succeed and helps to make it happen. For example, I have dreaded taking statistics since I enrolled, and finally I could no longer avoid it. Robert's the math geek, he can do anything with numbers, so he has tutored me. He walks me through all the examples and sample tests. He explains, re-explains, and explains once more, and makes sure that I am prepared for those tests. He could tell me it's my problem, but he doesn't. I always joke that he should have some graduate credits by the time I'm done.

Mo's narratives also identify her husband, Peter, as a source of power throughout her doctoral studies.

Peter is my single greatest source of support and strength. He is my cheering section and makes it possible for me to be in graduate school. Everything from talking to me about my hopes and fears, to basic logistical support like sharing childcare and making it possible for me to attend night classes which entails a three hour commute. Me being in graduate school is a major part of his load!

The examples from the data exemplify the impact of power in our lives as we work to find a way to manage our roles as graduate students and responsibilities as wives and future mothers. The influence of faculty was significant and the support of fellow students and our spouses was critical to our ability to manage the stress related to pregnancy and motherhood. (Grenier & Burke, 2008, pp. 592–593)

Karen Lee (2005) also writes about her doctoral journeys. Through an autobiographical account, she describes the process of becoming. Here is how she begins the account:

Last Friday I struggled to write, but my neck was too twisted. My lower lip quivered and my right hand trembled. There was numbness. My arm was separate from my body. Briefly, I wondered if I had suffered clinical death. I had to bear my decision to write for twelve hours a day, the last four days. A huge price for a few hundred words. A cascade of thoughts. I had erupted with lava. It wore me down. I lay on my heating pad and checked the time.

Continue to write. I was in a groove. More beginnings about the end. A dissertation to finish. I gripped the heating pad but was not in charge. I felt nauseous. An uncomfortable void in my stomach. I dragged myself to the kitchen and boiled water for instant noodles. Noodles have a way of calming me down. An Asian addiction I have had for years. Sometimes, I add an egg for flavor. When the water boiled, I ate immediately. Systematically, and rather absently, I finished my noodles. But my stomach rose, and vomit spewed onto the table and floor. I could not breathe. I ran to the bathroom and threw up more. (Lee, 2005, p. 933)

Some pages later she talks again about doing the dissertation.

It has taken six years to understand what a dissertation can do. Others have seen me grow and change. For some, it has been overwhelming. There is fear on their faces watching my life unroll with intense periods of both joy and anguish. Broken images and shattered dreams. If there was a way to ensure that a doctoral dissertation would keep the world the same, research would not progress. My obsessive-compulsive disorder of a dissertation must make a difference. A tremendous amount of satisfaction came from being a writer. Truth is, I am saddened by the end.

The unspoken postulate of a doctoral program is that one will change both emotionally and intellectually. Life will be sliced differently after a magnum opus. It challenges and delights, but also brings agony and pain. In this society, writing gives me the pleasure of birds who build a nest and gloat. After floating for years, I embrace wounds and resolutions.

Being a writer is like being a musician. It takes you to a secret place of honor. I realize how tempestuous my life will be as a writer. (Lee, 2005, p. 937)

Grenier and Burke (2008) explain their complex method:

Drawing from autoethnography served our need to be evocative, self-reflective, and authentic in our narratives (Ellis & Bochner, 2000), while using cogenerative dialogues (Roth, Lawless, & Tobin, 2000) incorporated two voices and gave room for us to build off each other's contributions. Drawing from ethnographic work in education, we incorporated the use of data collection techniques such as concept maps that provided a unique source of visual data derived from reflective processes that occurred over time.

When combined with our on-going dialogues, written text, and artifacts, the concept maps offered a way for us to visually represent the interconnectiveness of our experiences and have potential heuristic value for other researchers using a method of inquiry similar to our cogenerative ethnography. Analytic autoethnography guided our application of theory to self-reflective narratives, and validated our use of more traditional analysis methods, such as taxonomies. (Grenier & Burke, 2008, p. 600)

ROLE IDENTITY

Some move from professional working positions to the role of students. They begin to wonder who they really are. Lesley Atkinson-Baldwyn (2009) writes about her contrasting lives between her role as a worker and her role as a student. Using a novel presentation style, she writes about another identity from two perspectives. Using a regular font and straightforward narrative in the left-hand column and an italicized font and reflexive narrative in the right-hand column, she presents contrasting viewpoints. One is factual, and the other about feelings. I encourage you to look up the article. You will enjoy reading it.

FINAL THOUGHTS

Navigation through graduate school has always been associated with many obstacles. In this chapter, I have introduced three main ideas with regard to graduate school: Some students feel alienated because they are outside the middle class White mainstream. Others speak about difficulties juggling demands of complicated lives. Still others explore inner feelings about their own conflict and understanding roles of professional or graduate student.

As you embark on your own journey, these student comments might be challenging and inspiring. At least you will know others have traversed the same waters.

REFERENCES

Atkinson-Baldwyn, L. (2009). An Other identity: A view of myself. *Qualitative Inquiry, 15*(5), 806–819.

Grenier, R., & Burke, M. (2008). No margin for error: A study of two women balancing motherhood and Ph.D. studies. *The Qualitative Report, 13*(4), 581–604.

Hall, L., & Burns, L. (2009). Identity development and mentoring in doctoral education. *Harvard Educational Review, 79*(1), retrieved July 21, 2009, at http://www.edreview.org.ezproxy.lib.vt.edu:8080/harvard09/2009/sp09/p09hall.htm

Lee, K. (2005). Neuroticism: End of a doctoral dissertation. *Qualitative Inquiry, 11*(6), 933–938.

Moreira, C. (2008a). Life in so many acts. *Qualitative Inquiry, 14*(4), 590–612.

Moreira, C. (2008b). Fragments. *Qualitative Inquiry, 14*(5), 663–683.

Murakami-Ramalho, E., Piert, J., & Mittello, M. (2008). The wanderer, the chameleon, and the warrior: Experiences of doctoral students of color developing a research identify in educational administration. *Qualitative Inquiry, 14*(5), 806–834.

Rodriguez, D. (2006). Un/masking identity. *Qualitative Inquiry 12*(6), 1067–1090.

EPILOGUE

Reading, Writing, and Thinking
About Qualitative Research

I had two primary objectives in preparing this book of readings. First, I wanted to expose readers to published research studies that illustrate various qualitative research approaches. In order to accomplish that, I had to decide what research approaches I wanted to use. This was fairly easy to accomplish. Of course, I didn't include all the qualitative research approaches that are out there. Due to space limitations, I chose to omit autoethnography, biography, and feminist philosophy, among others. However, I believe I selected those approaches most commonly used in education.

What proved much more daunting was the other component to accomplishing this objective: What research studies should I choose? How was I to decide? I had some general guidelines in mind. For instance, I wanted fairly recent studies to illustrate current practices. I also wanted a blend of those studies written by established scholars in the field and those written by scholars just entering the field. I decided to select articles from journals that I knew to be amenable to publishing qualitative research studies.

Next, I was faced with this dilemma: how to locate studies in which the topic was primarily related to education. I broadly defined this by also including studies about students or parents.

I encountered another problem: there was obviously no way to read all the studies published that illustrate a particular research approach. In fact, I read many, and I read the abstracts of many more. At some point, though, I knew I needed to just make a decision. I made a number of false starts. I began with an article and prepared comments, but found that the article was too long, or too cumbersome, or too difficult to understand, so I would abandon it and look for another. Due to space limitations, I decided I would include two examples for each research approach.

What you have just completed reading, then, represents my best efforts to expose you to qualitative research that represents a variety of research approaches, a variety of journals, and a mix of new and established scholars.

I do not want you to come away with the notion that these represent the best of what is out there. Rather, I want you to know these studies illustrate a range of what is available. I believe my comments about each study will help you to see its strengths and shortcomings.

My second objective was to present current issues about qualitative research. Even though you have gained knowledge about qualitative research, you will find that reading about some of the issues and controversies in the field should help you to position your knowledge in a broader context.

In writing the second part, I needed to decide what the issues were. Were some more important than others? I actually began to develop a list of issues and corresponding writing as I pursued my first objective. Once I had identified an issue, I needed to broaden my search. I knew I did not want to write literature reviews related to these issues. Rather, I wanted to expose you to writing by scholars in the field. I reviewed many articles covering a broad range of disciplines.

By no means can I say these are the only issues swirling in the qualitative research waters today, nor do I claim to have done a complete review of all that is written. I do believe that some issues are very important, though. That there is a movement to return to more foundationalist and conservative forms of research is clear. What fueled that movement remains somewhat fuzzy in my mind—politics, conservatism, or perhaps just those who are well intentioned but poorly informed. But if qualitative research is to survive—and I know it will—those in the field have a responsibility to make their voices heard.

A second issue is important to me personally—and to the profession: remove boredom from our writing. I have tried to avoid the use of jargon and obtuse language in my own writing. I have also tried to bring the personal into what I write. For me, at least, this helps overcome boredom. But I want you to take a lesson from Cauley and others and use techniques and language to engage your audience.

This book is about reading, writing, and thinking about qualitative research.

- Reading: This book of readings introduces you to published works related to qualitative research. Some of the readings I have included are meant to be exciting, interesting, and meaningful and others less so. It is also my intention for you to learn about new things and about new ways to conduct research.

- Writing: This book of readings introduces you to various means and manner of writing. Some of the writing is quite academic and detached. I believe that is true for some of the more traditional qualitative research approaches, especially grounded theory. Some of the writing is very personal and reflective. That is true for writing by authors who have a feminist background. Although I did not specifically include an article with a feminist perspective, you will see it permeates some of the writing. Some of the writing uses alternative presentation forms. I have offered you poems and a play.

- Thinking: This book of readings is designed to challenge your own thinking about research in general and qualitative research in particular. I ask you to consider these questions as you move ahead in the field:
  - Who sets the rules and criteria for what is the "right" kind of research?
  - Who should be in charge of this task?
  - How can we ensure that all voices are heard?
  - What role can you play as newcomers to the field?
  - What responsibilities do others already in the field have to the field and to you?

FINAL THOUGHTS

In writing this book, I have relied on published articles. However, we all know that there is a lag time between conception and writing of an article and publication. With new technology, we see almost immediate transmission of information via the Internet. One way to communicate "instantaneously" is through blogging. I suspect some new ideas can emerge through this technique.

As I sit at my computer preparing to submit this manuscript to my editor, I decided to do one final Google search on qualitative research. It is now the middle of August 2009. During my final edit in December 2009 I rechecked the URLs. I added two additional ones. I have been searching this topic for many months. Below are the links that surface today. Some I have already included in other parts of this book. Others are new, and I do not know whether they still will be available online when this book comes out in print.

I searched on the terms "qualitative research blogs, qualitative research syllabus, or qualitative research 2009." I read through 10 screens for each of the three terms. Here is a smattering of what I found. (You can also go to www.sagepub.com/lichtmanreadings and access the sites from the Web).

- http://blogs.ubc.ca/qualresearch

  Qualitative research cafe by Sandra Mathison. August 8, 2009, link to an article from the *New York Times* on conservatism of research boards. You have read my comments earlier on this topic. She includes wonderful illustrations and challenging topics. This blog is important for you to follow.

- http://www.personal.psu.edu/eft111/blogs/edtec_567/2009/07/qualitative-research-data-collection-and-analysis.html

  Qualitative research, data collection, and analysis by Elisha Pospisil. July 21, 2009, and many recent postings.

- http://www.pluggedinco.com/blog/bid/17462/Twitter-as-an-online-qualitative-research-methodology

  Twitter as an online qualitative research method by Matt Foley and Ben Werziner. March 3, 2009, entry. It was only a matter of time before we figured out how to use Twitter.

- http://www.aqr.org.uk/inbrief/document.shtml?doc=james.bance.14–03–2007.blogging

  Blogging as a qualitative method posted by James Bance in 2007.

- http://methodologyblog.imaginativespaces.net/blog

  Qualitative Research Blog: A blog by John Schostak, posting July 26, 2008. I really like this first sentence: "The issue with 'data' is whether we all see the *same thing*."

- http://dinamehta.com/blog/2008/11/03/youtube-qualitative-research-ethnography/

  Conversations with Dina Mehta, posting November 3, 2008. This topic is YouTube, Qualitative Research & Ethnography.

- http://www.pallimed.org/2008/08/bmj-series-on-qualitative-research.html

  A blog in the palliative medical field. The blog on August 15, 2008, provides many links to qualitative research articles.

- http://silenceandvoice.com/archives/2009/05/22/qualitative-research-and-the-internet/

  Silence and Voice: Research and Practice in Postmodern Learning by Jeffrey Keefer. Entry to May 22, 2009, is about qualitative research and the Internet.

- http://researchosu.blogspot.com/

  Digital tools for qualitative research blog for a class at Ohio State University. Lots of interaction on this blog.

- http://www.nova.edu/ssss/QR/syllabi.html

  As its name implies, this is a list of links to qualitative research online syllabi.

- http://www.coe.uga.edu/syllabus/qual/index.html

  An extensive listing of qualitative research courses offered by the University of Georgia. Last updated 2008.

- I found the link to Jo Shaw's personal story about being a qualitative researcher very interesting. You can read it at http://www.aqr.org.uk/inbrief/document.shtml?doc=jo.shaw.25–05–2009.metamorphosis

- http://onqualitativeresearch.blogspot.com/

  A blog with stories about qual research. Aimed at marketing rather than academic audiences.

- http://yellowsubmarinequal.wordpress.com/

  Also in the marketing arena, but emphasizes the use of pictures in qualitative research.

Qualitative research—a dynamic, evolving field designed to study humans in their natural settings. This book adds a small piece to the enormous puzzle.

INDEX

ABOUT THE AUTHOR

Marilyn Lichtman in front of destroyer in St. Petersburg, Russia (2009)

Marilyn Lichtman is a retired professor of educational research and evaluation. After receiving her doctorate in educational research and statistics from The George Washington University, she taught at The Catholic University of America. She then relocated to Virginia Tech (Northern Virginia and Blacksburg) where she taught quantitative and qualitative research courses and directed many students as they completed their dissertations. Lichtman was an early user of the Internet for teaching, having put many of her qualitative courses and syllabi online. She has conducted numerous research studies for school systems and the Department of Defense Schools worldwide; she has served on review panels for the Department of Education; and she has consulted for local and state systems in Maryland and Virginia. Lichtman serves on the boards of *Forum: Qualitative Social Research (FQS)* and *The Qualitative Report* (both online journals). In 2006 (revised 2009) Lichtman published *Qualitative Research in Education* for SAGE.

In addition to her professional work in education, she has taken a strong interest in art. Having served as a docent at the Corcoran Gallery of Art in Washington, DC for more than 15 years and most recently chairman of the Docent Council, she has integrated thoughts about art and qualitative research. She recently completed two courses in writing art criticism and issues in contemporary art in the joint program of The University of Illinois and the Phillips Gallery of Art in Washington, DC. Culminating her interest in art, she took the Grand Tour of art venues in 2007, traveling with her daughter and son-in-law (both artists) to Art Basel (in Basel, Switzerland), Documenta 12 (in Kassel, Germany), and the Venice Biennale (Italy). You can read her blog at http://thegrandtour07.blogspot.com.

Lichtman can be contacted at MarilynLichtman09@gmail.com or mlichtma@vt.edu.